The Political Economy of
Development in Kenya

The Political Economy of Development in Kenya

Kempe Ronald Hope, Sr.

BLOOMSBURY

NEW YORK · LONDON · NEW DELHI · SYDNEY

Bloomsbury Academic
An imprint of Bloomsbury Publishing Plc

1385 Broadway	50 Bedford Square
New York	London
NY 10018	WC1B 3DP
USA	UK

www.bloomsbury.com

First published by Continuum International Publishing Group 2012
Paperback edition first published 2013

Library of Congress Cataloging-in-Publication Data
Sr. Hope, Kempe R.
The political economy of development in Kenya/Kempe Ronald Hope, Sr.
p. cm.
Includes bibliographical references and index.
ISBN-13: 978-1-4411-9121-2 (hardback: alk. paper)
ISBN-10: 1-4411-9121-6 (hardback: alk. paper) 1. Kenya—Economic conditions—1963–
2. Kenya—Economic policy. 3. Kenya—Politics and government—2002– I. Title.
HC865.H67 2011
338.96762–dc23

2011027920

ISBN: HB: 978-1-4411-9121-2
PB: 978-1-6235-6534-3

Typeset by Newgen Imaging Systems Pvt Ltd, Chennai, India
Printed and bound in Great Britain

To the Kenyan People, who hold the balance

Contents

List of Figures and Tables

Figures

Tables

Preface

Kenya is the most important country in the East African subregion both in terms of its geopolitical and economic significance. It borders on, and is a primary gateway to, failed, fragile, and/or terrorist states such as Somalia and Sudan, for example, and is the regional hub for trade, finance, communication, and transportation linkages in East Africa. The country has had a relatively prosperous economy and a stable government since independence in 1963, and it performs better in almost all socioeconomic indicators compared to its other East African neighbors. However, Kenya is still a poor country, one of the most unequal in the world, and one of the most corrupt in the world also.

Political stability in the country was severely tested following the contested general election in December 2007. The violence that erupted in 2008 resulted from pent up resentment and frustration of the increasingly centralized and corrupt behavior of the government. The attempts of the sitting government to manipulate the results of the December 2007 elections became the final straw in the frustration of much of the populace which then led to violent ethnic/tribal clashes. Peace was eventually restored through the brokering of a government of national unity, also known as the "grand coalition cabinet," that, among other power sharing agreements, established the Office of the Prime Minister which was assumed by the political leader who many thought was the winner of the Presidency. In August 2010, a new constitution was approved by Kenyans by more than a two-thirds majority. The preparation and ratification of a new constitution was a key element of the agreement establishing the government of national unity and that constitution provides very clear instruments for the devolution of executive power; for the protection of the weak and vulnerable; and for securing the social, economic, political, and civil rights of all members of society.

Kenya has demonstrated its resilience over the years. However, the country still needs to confront a number of risks and challenges as it transitions from centralized state power to devolved government, and a clear separation of powers as the 2010 constitution demands. Some of those risks and challenges are weighted on the downside and, hence, the fate of the country hangs in the balance. This book provides a critical analysis, from a political economy perspective, of post-independence socioeconomic development in Kenya. Following from that analysis, it also offers a policy framework for sustaining development in the country and within the context of the opportunities and environment provided by the 2010 constitution. That 2010 constitution can be regarded as Kenya's emancipation proclamation to the extent that it offers and provides the freedom of use of legal policy frameworks that open the political space, entrench rights, and empower key institutions, such as the judiciary and parliament, for example, to act independently of the executive branch to enforce the rule of law equitably, fairly, and without fear of intimidation or worse.

In preparing the book I benefited from the assistance and generosity of a number of colleagues. Some of them I engaged in interviews, discussions, or debates, the outcomes of which crystallized my thinking and analytical approaches. Some steered me in the right direction to access and/or obtain key documents. Others read drafts of the manuscript and offered excellent suggestions for improvement. Four of them deserve particular mention here for going beyond the call of duty and once again demonstrating their consummate professionalism in promptly responding to my questions and/or providing their comments on various parts of the draft manuscript—Professor Bornwell Chikulo of North West University, South Africa; Dr Asfaw Kumssa, UNCRD, Africa Office, Nairobi; Professor John Mukum Mbaku of Weber State University; and Mr Stephen Wainaina, Ministry of Planning and Vision 2030, Office of the Prime Minister, Nairobi. I am grateful to all of these colleagues. However, as is customary, any errors or omissions are mine solely.

Kempe Ronald Hope, Sr.

Abbreviations and Acronyms

AAGR	Average annual growth rate
AARCPU	Average annual rate of change of the proportion urban
ACBF	African Capacity Building Foundation
ACEC	Anti-Corruption and Economic Crimes
ACPU	Anti-Corruption Police Unit
ADF	African Development Forum
AERC	African Economic Research Consortium
AETF(s)	Assessment and Evaluation Task Force(s)
AFC	Agricultural Finance Corporation
AfDB	African Development Bank
AGF	Africa Governance Forum
AGOA	African Growth and Opportunity Act
AHTF(s)	Ad Hoc Task Force(s)
AICD	Africa Infrastructure Country Diagnostic
AIDS	Acquired Immune-Deficiency Syndrome
AMLAB	Anti-Money Laundering Advisory Board
ANU	Africa Nazarene University
APRM	African Peer Review Mechanism
ARA	Assets Recovery Agency
ASCA(s)	Accumulating Savings and Credit Association(s)
ASDS	Agricultural Sector Development Strategy
ATMs	Automatic Teller Machines
AU	African Union
AWSB	Athi Water Services Board
BOM	Build-Own-Maintain
BOO	Build-Own-Operate
BOOT	Build-Own-Operate-Transfer
BOT	Build-Operate-Transfer
BPO	Business process outsourcing
CARF	Criminal Assets Recovery Fund
CART	Continental Advisory Research Team
CBD	Central business district
CBK	Central Bank of Kenya

CCAC	Cabinet Committee on Anti-Corruption
CDF	Constituency Development Fund
CET	Common external tariff
CIA	Central Intelligence Agency
CIDA	Canadian International Development Agency
CKRC	Constitution of Kenya Review Commission
COMESA	Common Market of Eastern and Southern Africa
CPI	Corruption Perceptions Index
CSDC(s)	Citizen Service Delivery Charter(s)
CSRP	Civil Service Reform Program
C-YES	Constituency Youth Enterprise Scheme
DB	Design Build
DBFO	Design-Build-Finance-Operate
DBFOM	Design-Build-Finance-Operate-Maintain
DBFOMT	Design-Build-Finance-Operate-Maintain-Transfer
DBM	Design-Build-Maintain
DBO	Design-Build-Operate
DBOM	Design-Build-Operate-Maintain
DfID	Department for International Development
DFRD	District funds for rural development
DGE	Department of Governance and Ethics
DPM	Directorate of Personnel Management
DPP	Director of Public Prosecutions
DWT	Deadweight tonnage
EAAACA	East African Association of Anti-Corruption Authorities
EABI	East African Bribery Index
EAC	East African Community
EACC	Ethics and Anti-Corruption Commission
EACS	East African Community Secretariat
EMB(s)	Electoral Management Body (ies)
EPC	Export Promotion Council
ERS	Economic Recovery Strategy for Wealth and Employment Creation
ESAAMLG	Eastern and Southern African Anti-Money Laundering Group
ESMF	Environmental and Social Management Framework
EU	European Union
E-YES	Easy Youth Enterprise Scheme
FBI	Federal Bureau of Investigation
FDI	Foreign direct investment
FEWS NET	Famine Early Warning Systems Network

FfP	The Fund for Peace
FRC	Financial Reporting Center
FSD	Financial sector deepening
FY	Fiscal year
GDP	Gross domestic product
GFM	Government Financial Management
GJLOS	Governance, Justice, Law and Order Sector
GSM	Global System for Mobile Communications
HDI	Human Development Index
HIV	Human Immunodeficiency Virus
HPI	Human Poverty Index
HRW	Human Rights Watch
IAEA	International Atomic Energy Agency
IAFFE	International Association for Feminist Economics
ICC	International Criminal Court
ICG	International Crisis Group
ICJ	The International Commission of Jurists
ICLS	International Conference of Labor Statisticians
ICT	Information and communication technology
ICTJ	International Center for Transitional Justice
IDEA	Institute for Democracy and Electoral Assistance
IDLO	International Development Law Organization
IDP(s)	Internally displaced person(s)
IEA	Institute of Economic Affairs
IEBC	Independent Electoral and Boundaries Commission
IFES	International Foundation for Electoral Studies
ILO	International Labor Office/Organization
IMF	International Monetary Fund
IPAR	Institute of Policy Analysis and Research
IPPD	Integrated Payroll and Personnel Database
ISS	Institute for Security Studies
ISWM	Integrated sustainable waste management
KACA	Kenya Anti-Corruption Authority
KACAB	Kenya Anti-Corruption Advisory Board
KACC	Kenya Anti-Corruption Commission
KANU	Kenya African National Union
KCAU	Kenya College of Accountancy University
KCSE	Kenya Certificate of Secondary Education
KenGen	Kenya Electricity Generating Company Limited
KEPSA	Kenya Private Sector Alliance
KESSP	Kenya Education Sector Support Program

KETRACO	Kenya Electricity Transmission Company Limited
KIA	Kenya Institute of Administration
KIE	Kenya Institute of Education
KIHBS	Kenya Integrated Household Budget Survey
KIPPRA	Kenya Institute for Public Policy Research and Analysis
KKK	Kikuyu, Kalenjin, and Kamba
KNAC	Kenya National Audit Commission
KNAO	Kenya National Audit Office
KNBS	Kenya National Bureau of Statistics
KNCHR	Kenya National Commission on Human Rights
KNHDR	Kenya National Human Development Report
KNYP	Kenya National Youth Policy
KPA	Kenya Ports Authority
KPLC	Kenya Power and Lighting Company Limited
KRA	Kenya Revenue Authority
KYEEI	Kenya Youth Empowerment and Employment Initiative
KYEP	Kenya Youth Empowerment Project
LATF	Local Authorities Transfer Fund
LDO	Lease-Develop-Operate
MAPSKID	Master Plan Study for Kenya's Industrial Development
MDGs	Millennium Development Goals
MOYA	Ministry of State for Youth Affairs
MOYAS	Ministry of Youth Affairs and Sports
MP	Member of Parliament
MPI	Multidimensional Poverty Index
MPs	Members of Parliament
MSMEs	Micro, small and medium enterprises
MTEF	Medium-Term Expenditure Framework
MTP	Medium Term Plan
NACC	National AIDS Control Council
NACCSC	National Anti-Corruption Campaign Steering Committee
NACP	National Anti-Corruption Plan
NARA	National Accord and Reconciliation Agreement
NARC	National Rainbow Coalition
NCPPP	National Council for Public-Private Partnerships
NCWSC	Nairobi City Water and Sewerage Company
ND	No date
NEPAD	New Partnership for Africa's Development
NGOs	Nongovernmental organizations
NICHE	Netherlands Initiative for Capacity Development in Higher Education

NIMES	National Integrated Monitoring and Evaluation System
NMR	Nairobi Metropolitan Region
NPI	Nairobi Peace Initiative
NPM	New Public Management
NSE	Nairobi Stock Exchange
NTA	National Taxpayers Association
NYC	National Youth Council
OCHA	United Nations Office for the Coordination of Humanitarian Affairs
ODI	Overseas Development Institute
ODM	Orange Democratic Movement
OECD	Organization for Economic Cooperation and Development
OJT	On-the-job training
O&M	Operations and Maintenance Contract
OMM	Operations-Maintenance-Management
OP	Office of the President
OPHI	Oxford Poverty and Human Development Initiative
OPM	Office of the Prime Minister
PCAML	Proceeds of Crime and Anti-Money Laundering
PCD	Performance Contracting Department
PC(s)	Performance Contract(s)
PCSC	Public Complaints Standing Committee
PCsSC	Performance Contracts Steering Committee
PI(s)	Performance indicator(s)
PMPS	Prime Minister Press Service
PNU	Party of National Unity
POE	Public Officer Ethics
PPARB	Public Procurement Administrative Review Board
PPD	Public Procurement and Disposal
PPI	Private participation in infrastructure
PPIAF	Public-Private Infrastructure Advisory Facility
PPOA	Public Procurement Oversight Authority
PPOAB	Public Procurement Oversight Advisory Board
PPP(s)	Public-private-partnership(s)
PPSRRB	Permanent Public Service Remuneration Review Board
PRIC	Police Reform Implementation Committee
PRSP(s)	Poverty Reduction Strategy Paper(s)
PS	Permanent Secretary
PSDS	Private Sector Development Strategy
PSP	Parliamentary Strengthening Program

PSRDS	Public Service Reform and Development Secretariat
PSRPC	Public Sector Reforms and Performance Contracting
PSTD	Public Sector Transformation Department
PSTS	Public Sector Transformation Strategy
PTA	Preferential Trade Area for Eastern and Southern African States
PU	Proportion urban
RBM	Results-based management
RCK	Refugee Consortium of Kenya
RECs	Regional economic communities
RETs	Renewable energy technologies
RMLF	Road Maintenance Levy Fund
ROSCA(s)	Rotating Savings and Credit Association(s)
RRI	Rapid results initiative
SACCO(s)	Savings and Credit Cooperative(s)
SAP(s)	Structural adjustment program(s)
SDR(s)	Special Drawing Right(s)
SEAPREN	Southern and Eastern Africa Policy Research Network
SEWA	Self-Employed Women's Association
SEWU	Self-Employed Women's Union
SOE(s)	State-owned enterprise(s)
TEU(s)	Twenty Foot Equivalent Unit(s)
TI	Transparency International
TIVET	Technical, Industrial, Vocational, and Entrepreneurship Training
TVET	Technical and Vocational Education and Training
UAE	United Arab Emirates
UK	United Kingdom
UNAIDS	Joint United Nations Programme on HIV/AIDS
UNCAC	United Nations Convention against Corruption
UNCRD	United Nations Center for Regional Development
UNCTAD	United Nations Conference on Trade and Development
UNDP	United Nations Development Programme
UNDESA	United Nations Department of Economic and Social Affairs
UNECA	United Nations Economic Commission for Africa
UNEP	United Nations Environment Programme
UNESCO	United Nations Educational, Scientific and Cultural Organization
UN-HABITAT	United Nations Human Settlements Programme
UNHCR	United Nations High Commission for Refugees

UNICEF	United Nations Children's Fund
UNIDO	United Nations Industrial Development Organization
UNODC	United Nations Office on Drugs and Crime
UNRISD	United Nations Research Institute for Social Development
UNSC	United Nations Security Council
USAID	United States Agency for International Development
VERS	Voluntary Early Retirement Scheme
WHO	World Health Organization
WTTC	World Travel and Tourism Council
YEDF	Youth Enterprise Development Fund
YES	Youth Entrepreneurship and Sustainability

1

Economic Performance and Socioeconomic Trends

Kenya's economy has emerged as a market-based one, within a liberalized trade structure, and is now the regional hub for trade, finance, communication, and transportation linkages in East Africa. The country has a vision to become a middle-income economy by the year 2030. In fact, the *Kenya Vision 2030* (the long-term development blueprint for the country, motivated by a collective aspiration for a better society by the year 2030) proposes to create a "globally competitive and prosperous country with a high quality of life by 2030. It aims to transform Kenya into a newly-industrializing, middle-income country providing a high quality of life to all citizens in a clean and secure environment" (Republic of Kenya, 2007: vii). During the past several decades, Kenya's economy has undergone many changes and economic performance has been characterized by periods of stability, decline, or unevenness. As will be shown in this book growth and development in the country have been significantly influenced, in varying ways and at various periods, by some combination of endogenous and exogenous factors that include, but are not limited to, severe droughts, erratic rains, reliance on several primary goods, persistent corruption, weak commodity prices, low investor confidence, meager donor support, political violence, global financial and oil crises, and bad policy choices.

During the 1960s, the growth rate of Kenya's gross domestic product (GDP) was positive except for 1961 when it declined to -8.0 percent. The average annual growth of GDP from 1961 to 1969 was 5.7 percent as shown in Figure 1.1. However, although positive rates of growth were recorded, there were several years of decline from previous years, but with 1966 recording the highest rate of growth in the period at 15 percent (World Bank, nd). After independence in 1963, Kenya pursued economic growth through public investment, encouragement of smallholder agricultural production, and incentives for private investment (US Department of State, 2010). Economic growth during the 1960s was stimulated primarily through agricultural production whose increase was the result of the redistribution of estates, the diffusion of new crop strains, and the opening of new areas

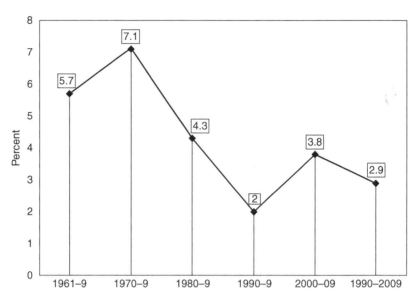

FIGURE 1.1 Annual average GDP growth rates, 1961–2009
Source: Author, based on data from World Bank (nd).

to cultivation (US Department of State, 2010). During this period the GDP at current prices averaged US$1.1 billion (World Bank, nd).

In the 1970s, economic growth expanded moving from the annual average of 5.7 percent in the 1960s to an annual average rate of 7.1 percent, with nominal GDP averaging US$3.4 billion, and 1970 being the only year of negative growth at -5.0 percent, while 1971 recorded the highest rate of growth in the country's history to date at 22 percent (World Bank, nd). This commendable rate of growth was made possible, in addition to increased agricultural production, by increased productivity and favorable terms of trade (Republic of Kenya, 2000a). After experiencing moderately high growth rates in the 1960s and 1970s, Kenya's economic performance during the 1980s and 1990s was less impressive and far below its potential. In the 1980s, the economy grew by an annual average rate of only 4.3 percent and by less than half of that, at 2 percent, in the 1990s. The average annual GDP at current prices was US$7.1 billion and US$9.9 billion in the 1980s and 1990s, respectively (World Bank, nd). The 1990s can be regarded as Kenya's "lost decade" in terms of development performance with negative growth (-1.0 percent) in 1992 and zero growth in 1993 and 1997.

The decline in Kenya's economic performance in the 1980s and 1990s has been attributed to a number of factors. The US Department of State (2010), for example, noted that this decline was largely due to inappropriate policies related to agriculture, land, and industrial development which were compounded by poor international terms of trade and weaknesses in governance. Moreover, the "increased government intrusion into the private sector and import substitution policies made the manufacturing sector uncompetitive. The policy environment, along with tight import controls and foreign exchange controls, made the domestic environment unattractive for both foreign and domestic investors" (US Department of State, 2010: 7). One of the government's own assessments also observed that, in addition to exogenous factors, the erosion of growth was compounded by inadequate macroeconomic policy responses resulting in structural dislocations that acted as major constraints to economic growth (Republic of Kenya, 2000a).

This state of affairs led the government to engage the World Bank and the International Monetary Fund (IMF) in the introduction of structural adjustment programs (SAPs). The use of SAPs in Africa and elsewhere in the 1980s and 1990s proved very controversial and much has been written about their origins and impact (see, e.g., Hope, 1997a; Naiman and Watkins, 1999). SAPs were eventually scrapped amid mounting evidence that they were causing more harm than good, by lowering instead of raising living standards, for the most part, and the World Bank and IMF subsequently admitted that was indeed the case. SAPs were replaced in 1999 by poverty reduction strategies which were designed to enhance country ownership of the development policy process. Poverty Reduction Strategy Papers (PRSPs) are prepared by governments with the active participation of civil society and other development partners. The PRSPs are then considered by the Executive Boards of the IMF and World Bank as the basis for concessional lending and debt relief from the two institutions (IMF, 2009a).

Very good accounts and analyses of Kenya's experience with SAPs in the 1980s and 1990s, and their impact on growth, development, poverty, and other socioeconomic indices, can be found in several publications (see, e.g., Kabubo-Mariara and Kiriti, 2002; Rono, 2002; and Swamy, 1994). Structural adjustment loans to Kenya supported, among other things, trade liberalization; exchange rate depreciation; export development; and agricultural, industrial, and financial sector development. The design of these loans was found to be faulty as being too general in nature, based on outdated information, and having too many conditions (Swamy, 1994). Moreover, the SAPs, as a whole, "failed to create the conditions for sustainable recovery of gross domestic product (GDP) growth to levels attained in the 1960s and 1970s" (Kabubo-Mariara and Kiriti, 2002: 2). The result was an increase in poverty.

In the first decade of the twenty-first century Kenya's economic growth began to recover and posted an annual average rate of 3.8 percent. However, as discussed below, this growth rate was disappointing and was again influenced by several exogenous and endogenous factors. Annual average GDP at current prices for the period 2000–09 was US$19.9 billion. The IMF, which had resumed loans in 2000 to help Kenya through the severe drought of 1999 to 2000, again halted lending to the country in 2001 when the government failed to institute several governance measures. With the elections of December 2002, a new government came to power in 2003 and began an ambitious economic reform program in conjunction with resumed cooperation with the World Bank and the IMF. One of the notable reform measures instituted was the *Kenya: Economic Recovery Strategy for Wealth and Employment Creation 2003-2007* (*ERS 2003-2007*).

The *ERS 2003-2007* was published in 2003. It identified key policy actions necessary to spur the recovery of the Kenyan economy and was based on four pillars as well as crosscutting themes reflecting the overall goals of society (Republic of Kenya, 2003). The first pillar was improved economic growth which was to be achieved in an environment of macroeconomic stability underpinned by four policy reforms related to increased revenues as a proportion of GDP: restructuring of expenditures toward a pro-growth and pro-poor orientation; deficit financing through nondomestic sources to allow private sector credit to grow; a low inflation monetary policy. The second pillar was the strengthening of the institutions of governance based on the fundamental premise that good governance underpins sustainable development. The third pillar was the rehabilitation and expansion of physical infrastructure to modernize and uplift key economic infrastructure to first world standards and improve the efficiency and reduce the cost of production. The final pillar was investment in the human capital of the poor based on the premise that a well-educated and healthy population is an important factor in enhancing productivity and the overall performance of the economy (Republic of Kenya, 2003).

Under the *ERS 2003-2007*, investor confidence was somewhat restored, farm prices improved, and rural electrification proceeded in many parts of the country. In addition, access to clean water and affordable health care services also improved, and school enrolments increased (AfDB et al., 2008). In fact, between 2003 and 2007, economic growth rebounded increasing from 3 percent in 2003 to 7 percent in 2007. The *ERS 2003-2007* was replaced by the *Kenya Vision 2030*, referred to earlier on, and is the country's new development blueprint covering the period 2008–30. The Vision was developed through an all-inclusive and participatory stakeholder consultative process and also benefited from the lessons of experience of the newly industrializing countries around the world that leaped from poverty to widely shared prosperity and equity among their populace. The Vision is based on three pillars: the economic, the social, and the political (Republic of Kenya, 2007).

The economic pillar aims to improve the prosperity of all Kenyans through an economic development program covering all the regions of the country and with the intent of achieving an average GDP growth rate of 10 percent per annum as of 2012. The social pillar seeks to build a just and cohesive society with social equity in a clean and secure environment. The political pillar strives to realize a democratic political system founded on issue-based politics that respects the rule of law, and protects the rights and freedoms of every individual in Kenyan society (Republic of Kenya, 2007). The *Kenya Vision 2030* is being implemented through successive five-year medium-term plans, with the first such plan covering the period 2008–12. The *Kenya Vision 2030: First Medium Term Plan (MTP) 2008-2012* represents the primary document which outlines the Kenya consensus on policies, reform measures, projects, and programs that the government has committed to implement during 2008–12, and delineates the first phase in the implementation of the *Kenya Vision 2030* (Republic of Kenya, 2008). The policies and reforms contained in the Plan aim at achieving faster and significant structural changes in Kenya's economy. The *MTP 2008-2012* also incorporates measures intended to mitigate the effects of the December 2007 postelection violence. One other commendable feature of the Plan is that it is to be evaluated through annual progress reports under the National Integrated Monitoring and Evaluation System (NIMES) to gauge its implementation success (Republic of Kenya, 2008).

The first such evaluation report was published in 2010. It showed that there were some notable achievements under the social pillar, appreciable progress under the political pillar, but below average performance under the economic pillar with the exception of the increase of the average annual income per person which exceeded the target set for 2008–09 (Republic of Kenya, 2010a). Economic performance under the first year of the *MTP 2008-2012* was affected primarily by: (1) a downturn in the tourism sector, which had one of its worst performances in recent years as the volume of tourist arrivals declined from 1.8 million in 2007 to 1.2 million in 2008 due to perceived instability and rising levels of insecurity as well as negative travel advisories issued against Kenya by countries which represent the key tourist source markets; (2) marginal increase in the manufacturing sector's contribution to GDP from 10.4 percent in 2007 to 10.6 percent in 2008 with a growth rate of 3.8 percent compared to 6.5 percent in 2007; (3) a declining trend in the wholesale and retail trade sector from a growth of 11.5 percent in 2007 to 5.1 percent in 2008; (4) dismal growth of zero percent in 2007–08 (Republic of Kenya, 2010a).

In fact, in 2008, Kenya's GDP grew at a paltry 2 percent (rounded up from the actual 1.7%). This poor performance was due to a reduction in private consumption, reflecting the adverse effects occasioned by drought, the high cost of food and fuel, the global financial crisis, a dysfunctional coalition government, and the violence that broke out after the December 2007 elections (Republic of Kenya, 2009a; US Department of State, 2010). In 2009, GDP grew marginally by 3 percent. This was occasioned, to a major extent, by the measures undertaken by the government that included an economic stimulus package and austerity measures which had a moderate impact on economic growth (PriceWaterhouseCoopers, 2010). The pace of economic expansion was sustained in 2010 with a real growth rate averaging 6 percent. The economic stimulus package was maintained in the fiscal year (FY) 2010–11 budget with a projected real GDP growth rate of between 3.5 and 5.7 percent for 2011 with this growth expected to be driven primarily by increased investments in key sectors, including agriculture, services, infrastructure, health, and education as well as through targeted strategic development interventions (KNBS, 2011; Republic of Kenya, 2010b).

Looking at Figure 1.2, we can gauge the relative importance of per capita GDP by comparing real rates of growth with population growth. By doing

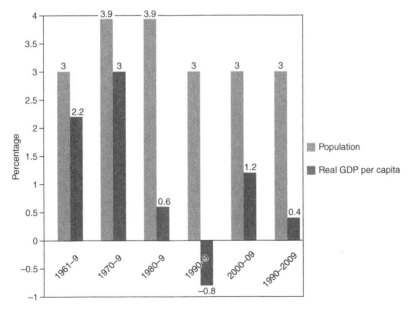

FIGURE 1.2 Average annual growth rates of population and real GDP per capita, 1961–2009
Source: Author, based on data from World Bank (nd).

this we are able to arrive at conclusions pertaining to changes in standard of living. That is, we are able to say something about whether the population may be better off, or not, due to growth in per capita GDP. During the period 1961–2009, average annual population growth not only exceeded the annual average rate of growth of real per capita GDP in each of the decades but also annual average per capita GDP growth was negative in the 1990s—"the lost decade"—when the standard of living of Kenyans plummeted significantly. Of course, in some individual years, real per capita GDP growth exceeded population growth. This occurred primarily in the 1960s (4 years) and the 1970s (3 years) and in 2006 and 2007. At no time in the 1980s and 1990s did real per capita GDP growth exceed population growth (World Bank, nd). Between 2004 and 2009, real per capita GDP increased from US\$424 to 485 (IMF, 2010).

Another factor influencing the standard of living, relative to disposable income, is inflation. Figure 1.3 depicts the annual average inflation rate. In each ten-year period, from the 1960s through to the end of the 1990s, the annual average rate of inflation has been increasing before decreasing significantly in the first decade of the twenty-first century. Analyses of the components of inflation in the overall household consumption pattern reveal that high food prices is the major direct contributor to the overall cost of

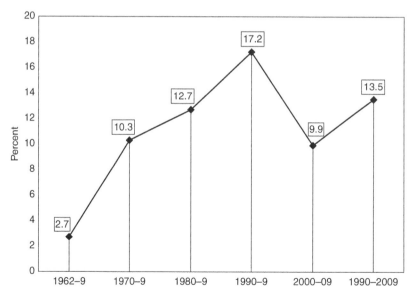

FIGURE 1.3 Average annual inflation rate, 1962–2009
Source: Author, based on data from KNBS (nda).

living as measured by changes in the consumer price index. This is partly due to the large share of the item in the overall household consumption basket (KIPPRA, 2009). Over the years, high fuel prices have also combined with high food prices to spur inflation.

However, given that the poorest segment of the population spends a significantly higher share of income on food, clearly then food price inflation affects the poorest more than the rest of society (KIPPRA, 2009). In 2009, the government adopted a new methodology for measuring inflation (from the arithmetic to the geometric mean method) consistent with international best practice. Moreover, in 2010, the government also revised the consumer price index, reducing the weight for food. Consequently, future inflation rates are expected to be within the Central Bank of Kenya (CBK) policy targets (Republic of Kenya, 2010c). By June 2010, the average annual inflation rate, continuing its downward trend, reached 5.4 percent compared to 15.1 percent in June 2009 (CBK, 2010). The overall annual inflation rate in 2010 was 4.1 percent compared to 10.5 percent in 2009 (KNBS, 2011).

Sector Performance

Figures 1.4 and 1.5 show the sectoral performance of the Kenyan economy from 1960 to 2009. During the 1960s, agriculture contributed a little more than one-third of the GDP, services a little more than two-fifths, and industry more than one-tenth. However, by the first decade of the twenty-first century, the services sector was contributing more than one-half of the GDP while agriculture's share declined to one-quarter and the share of industry held steady.

Agriculture

Despite services being the major sectoral contributor to GDP, Kenya's economy relies primarily on the performance of agriculture particularly in terms of export earnings and employment. The agricultural sector's value added to GDP averaged 38 percent in the 2000–09 period. By 2009, agriculture contributed 24 percent to GDP, while services and industry contributed 59 percent and 17 percent, respectively (Republic of Kenya, 2010a; World Bank, nd). Agriculture, while accounting for about one-quarter of Kenya's GDP, employs more than 50 percent of the labor force (AfDB et al., 2010). Other publications indicate that almost 75 percent of working Kenyans are currently making their living on the land with about one-half of total agricultural output being nonmarketed subsistence production (Wikipedia, 2010).

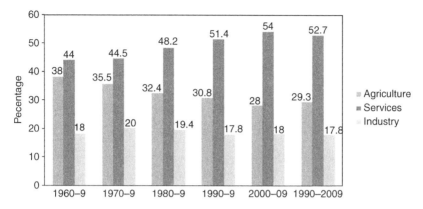

FIGURE 1.4 Sector value added to GDP, 1960–2009
Source: Author, based on data from World Bank (nd).

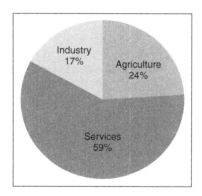

FIGURE 1.5 Sectoral composition of GDP, 2009
Source: Author, based on data from World Bank (nd).

KIPPRA (2009) has also estimated that the agricultural sector contributes about 19 percent of the formal wage employment, 60 percent of all households and 75 percent of the work force are engaged in farming activities, and 84 percent of rural households keep livestock.

Through linkages with agro-based sectors and associated industries, agriculture also indirectly contributes a further 27 percent to Kenya's GDP (Republic of Kenya, 2010a). The government of Kenya has also noted that:

> Agriculture accounts for 65 percent of Kenya's total exports, 18 percent and 60 percent of the formal and total employment, respectively [and] remains the main source of livelihood for the poor and is also one of the

sectors identified to deliver the 10 percent economic growth rate under Vision 2030. (Republic of Kenya, 2010c: 129)

By the first half of 2010, as economic performance improved, the increase in output was attributed, to some extent, to agricultural growth due to good rains in the latter part of 2009 and in early 2010. The average agricultural growth through to June 2010 was 6.1 percent with a rate of growth of 6.5 percent and 5.8 percent, respectively, for the first and second quarter (CBK, 2010).

Undoubtedly, the performance of Kenya's economy is therefore dependent to a large extent on the agricultural sector. The country's main agricultural products include cereals (maize and wheat), horticulture, industrial crops (sugar cane and pyrethrum), permanent crops (coffee and tea), and livestock. The shares of crops and livestock have remained almost constant over the past decade. For the period 2004–08, it was estimated that crops comprised 70 percent of agricultural GDP, livestock 25 percent, and the rest 5 percent. What happens with crops therefore has a major influence on the performance of the agricultural sector as a whole (Republic of Kenya, 2010c). The government's strategy for the development and transformation of the agricultural sector is outlined in the *Agricultural Sector Development Strategy (ASDS), 2009-2020* and the *MTP 2008-2012*. The key policy goals, among other things, include: raising agricultural productivity through increased resource allocations; exploiting irrigation potential; increased commercialization of agriculture; undertaking a comprehensive review of the legal and policy framework for agriculture; improving governance of agricultural institutions and land development (Republic of Kenya, 2010c). The overriding outcome of the strategy is to achieve a progressive reduction in unemployment and poverty by transforming the agricultural sector into a profitable economic activity capable of also attracting private investment.

However, there are several challenges to transforming the sector from one that is predominantly based on subsistence to one of commercial farming. Commercialization is constrained by insufficient access to credit, other input and output markets for small-scale producers, and opportunities for value addition (Republic of Kenya, 2010c). The lack of access to agricultural credit is a fundamental problem affecting agricultural activity in Kenya. Agricultural credit plays an important role in development of the agricultural sector. A primary issue seems to be unequal access with the major constraint in the use of credit coming from inadequate supply particularly for the small-scale farmers despite the fact that smallholders continue to play a crucial role in the cultivation of the food crops for the domestic market and are also responsible for the production of the great majority of the export cash crops of rice, cotton, sugar cane, coffee, and fruits and vegetables.

Recently, some steps have been taken to attempt to alleviate this credit access problem. The Agricultural Finance Corporation (AFC), the government's main effort at addressing agricultural needs, has developed strategies to deepen and broaden their client base particularly with respect to small-scale entrepreneurs (Mwangi, 2008). The strategy paper first recognizes that Kenyan small-scale entrepreneurs in agribusiness face limitations to fully participate in commodity markets due to problems related to: (1) the small size of the businesses coupled with low productivity in agriculture; (2) risks related to input sourcing due to irregular input supply; (3) lack of transport/poor infrastructure leading to high freight costs when shipping products to the market; (4) competition from other countries due to high cost of production; (5) lack of transparency in the supply chain; (6) lack of communication and coordination between the trading partners; (7) the disconnect between the farmer and the market (Mwangi, 2008). Those limitations are noted to have the binding factor of the lack of capital and access to finance by the small-scale entrepreneurs.

Among the steps being taken by the AFC for improving access to credit is the development of strategic partnerships through which credit can be channeled. These include: (1) partnering with the Sugar Board of Kenya to lend to sugar cane farmers including loans to meet personal needs such as school fees and medical bills; (2) partnering with the Coffee Board of Kenya to lend to coffee growers as an intermediary for the purpose of disbursement and recovery of loans and advances made by the coffee development fund; (3) partnering with selected enterprises and agencies to provide affordable credit to farmers to finance the production of garden peas, snow peas, and sugar snaps; (4) partnering with the Kenya Dairy Board to finance the dairy production value chain; (5) partnering on insurance to provide AFC-financed clients with insurance cover to guarantee that their outstanding loan balances are repaid in case of death or permanent disability; (6) partnering with the cell phone service provider, Safaricom and the Western Union money transfer agency to allow small-scale farmers to access money transfer facilities to enable them to repay loans without incurring the high transaction costs experienced through commercial banks (Mwangi, 2008).

Debates over development strategy have often swirled around the relative importance to be assigned to agriculture versus other sectors such as industry. Historical evidence suggests that this dichotomy is frequently overstated. Specifically, the notion that pursuing industrialization entails a total neglect of agriculture is erroneous for it underestimates the importance of the mutually beneficial links between agricultural development and development of other sectors. Indeed, in most developing countries successful development of other sectors, especially industry, has been supported by sustained and broadly based agricultural growth. Given the importance of agriculture in the Kenyan economy—looming large, despite growing urbanization as discussed in Chapter 2, as the sector which provides employment for the bulk of Kenyans, contains the majority of poor people, and is the birthplace of many of the urban poor—it would seem, therefore, that the major issues in agricultural development in the country are how to sustain a rate of growth that allows for a balanced expansion of all parts of the economy, and how to ensure that the pattern of agricultural growth is such as to make a strong and direct impact on rural poverty and, indirectly, on the reduction of migration of the poor to urban areas. As also noted by KIPPRA (2009), improved agricultural productivity is critical for Kenya to achieve accelerated growth, sustainable development, and poverty and inequality reduction.

Manufacturing Industry

The industrial sector has been contributing an annual average of 18 percent to GDP since the 1960s with the exception of the 1970s and 1980s when its contribution was slightly higher at 19–20 percent. Although Kenya is the most industrially developed country in East Africa, the manufacturing industry still accounts for only about 10 percent of GDP and also contributes 14 percent to wage employment (KIPPRA, 2009). Analyses of the quarterly GDP indicate a 6.8 percent growth in total manufacturing in the second quarter of 2010 compared to a decline of 0.4 percent for the second quarter of 2009 (CBK, 2010). Manufacturing in Kenya is dominated by food processing and processing of consumer goods. The country also refines crude petroleum into petroleum products which are mainly consumed locally. Industrial activity is concentrated around the three largest urban centers of Nairobi, Mombasa, and Kisumu. About one-half of the total investment in the industrial sector is foreign, with the United Kingdom (UK) providing one-half of that. Although the manufacturing sector in Kenya is diversified in terms of activities, agro-processing of food commodities and refining of petroleum products are the main industries in terms of value added. The country has therefore not substantially transformed its manufacturing sector from traditional industries (KIPPRA, 2009).

The Kenyan manufacturing industry has been supported primarily by a vibrant domestic demand and regional market. Most of Kenya's manufactured goods go to the regional Common Market for Eastern and Southern Africa (COMESA) discussed below. However, manufacturing industry has not reached its full potential in the country. At various periods since the 1960s, the sector has experienced a number of challenges, in various combinations, that include: (1) depressed demand for manufactured exports in the COMESA market; (2) competition from cheaper imports, particularly from China, due to higher unit labor cost; (3) inadequate, costly, and unstable supply of energy; (4) low levels of penetration and high cost of information and communication technology (ICT); (5) underdeveloped and/or dilapidated transport network and other key infrastructure; (6) weak legal, regulatory and institutional frameworks, for example, registration/incorporation of businesses and lack of judicial capacity to handle e-trade-related litigations; (7) the influx of sub-standard, counterfeit and contraband goods into the local market; (8) inadequate capacity of manufacturers to meet rapidly changing consumer needs and local and international quality requirements and standards; (9) limited access to formal financial services such as credit products and trade guarantees, especially for the micro, small, and medium enterprises (MSMEs); (10) lack of development of strategic management and technical skills (Republic of Kenya, 2008). In addition, the growth of the manufacturing industry has also been affected by corruption (as discussed in Chapter 4) which has influenced the levels and flows of private investment.

To deal with these challenges the government of Kenya has, over the years, developed and attempted to implement several industrial development strategies or policies. These include the *Sessional Paper Number 2 of 1996 on Industrial Transformation to the Year 2020* whose objective was to achieve the transformation of the Kenyan economy to a newly industrializing country by the year 2020—a similar objective to the now *Kenya Vision 2030*. The goal of the *Sessional Paper* was to provide a framework of government policies to stimulate economic growth and employment through the expansion of the industrial sector (Republic of Kenya, 1996). The foundations or prerequisites for industrial transformation were recognized as: (1) good governance encompassing political, social, and economic stability; (2) the creation and maintenance of microeconomic stability; (3) increased primary production and value adding; (4) human resource development. The industrial strategy was then based around the need to develop core industrial sectors to promote backward and forward linkages with other industrial sectors and implementation was based on a two-phase approach.

The first phase entailed the promotion of MSMEs, utilizing and adding value to local raw materials, and requiring relatively modest capital investment. Examples were agro-processing, building and construction materials, and the tourism industries. Phase II was concerned with the promotion of capital-intensive manufacturing that required heavy capital investment, good infrastructure, and well developed technologies and human resource skills. Examples were petrochemical, metallurgical, pharmaceutical, machinery and capital goods, and telecommunication and information processing (Republic of Kenya, 1996). The strategy framework, therefore, sought to provide incentives, improve technological capabilities, and provide an appropriate institutional framework to ensure a private sector-led industrialization process (Republic of Kenya, 1996; Ronge and Nyangito, 2000). In that regard, foreign direct investment (FDI) was expected to play an important role utilizing increased capital investment and technology transfer through formulation of linkages in the manufacturing industry (Gachino, 2009).

In 2006, a *Private sector Development Strategy (PSDS)* was formulated covering the five-year period 2006–10. It was intended to enhance private-sector growth and competitiveness which was to contribute, in turn, to the country's medium-term objectives as outlined in the *ERS 2003-2007* and thereby catalyze the provision of an enabling environment to enhance private sector growth and competitiveness. The main approach advocated in the PSDS was the fast tracking of existing and new government initiatives by: (1) addressing constraints to public service delivery through catalytic activities; (2) supporting faster implementation of macroeconomic reforms in key areas such as trade, deregulation, and access to finance; (3) funding specific initiatives to fast-track growth and competitiveness of MSMEs. In addition, five key goals were developed to achieve the overall objectives of the PSDS as follows (Republic of Kenya, 2006):

- Improve Kenya's business environment by providing adequate and good quality infrastructure; designing additional measures to combat crime and insecurity; enforcing anti-corruption measures; catalyzing public-private sector dialogue; reducing legal, regulatory, and administrative barriers.
- Accelerate industrial transformation by promoting a culture of change in the public and private sectors, and through reform of public institutions for better service delivery to the private sector.
- Facilitate economic growth through trade expansion by finalizing the trade and industrial development policy; revitalizing trade facilitation; increasing access to trade finance.
- Improve productivity by enhancing labor productivity; improving the productivity of capital; stimulating research and development activities; promoting adoption of modern, appropriate technology.
- Support entrepreneurship and indigenous enterprise development by facilitating the development of new enterprises; improving access to capital; facilitating the graduation and evolution of enterprises; promoting firm-to-firm linkages; promoting broader MSME representation in business associations.

In 2008, the final report of a Master Plan Study for Kenya's Industrial Development (MAPSKID) was also completed. Its intent is to provide the roadmap for development of the industrial sector with an emphasis on targeted subsectors identified as agro-processing; agro-machinery; and electrics, electronics/information, communication and technology (Republic of Kenya, 2008). However, the MAPSKID referred to one of its purposes as being "to have the Master Plan adopted as a component of the ERS [2003-2007]" (JICA and Republic of Kenya, 2008: 2) despite the fact that the *ERS 2003-2007* was replaced by the *Kenya Vision 2030* in 2008. Notwithstanding this oversight, the MAPSKID still represents an excellent analysis and action plan for the promotion of industrial development in Kenya as a complementary framework to the *MTP 2008-2012* of the *Kenya Vision 2030*.

Services

Undoubtedly, Kenya is becoming a service-driven economy. The services sector improved its annual average percentage contribution to GDP from 45 percent in the 1960s to 54 percent by the first decade of the twenty-first century (World Bank, nd). During the past two decades services contributed an annual average of 53 percent to GDP. However, some publications indicate that the sector may be contributing as much as 60 percent of GDP with a corresponding 68 percent of employment creation (see, e.g., World Bank and EPC, 2010). Two areas that have emerged as strong growth subsectors of Kenya's services sector are business process outsourcing (BPO) and financial services. BPO essentially is the process of a company hiring another company to handle some of its business activities. It is the practice of using a third party, contracted to perform specific, specialized processes on a company's behalf with at least a guaranteed equal service level. It encompasses a number of functions that are considered noncore to the primary business of the hiring company. These outsourcing deals frequently involve multi-year contracts and include, but are not limited to, such areas as customer relationship management, call centers and telemarketing, tele-servicing and product support, payroll maintenance, finance/accounting/billing, logistics management, and insurance claims processing. The global BPO industry has flourished at a frantic pace in the past few years and companies have ended up with huge savings by participating in the industry. By outsourcing some of their business processes to cheaper nations like Kenya, companies can cut costs, better concentrate on their core business and areas of comparative advantage, and realize better customer satisfaction.

The BPO subsector is a key component of Kenya's economic development blueprint. The *Kenya Vision 2030* and the *MTP 2008-2012* have recognized BPO as an emerging and growing sector expected to become the sector of choice for employment among the youth and young professionals (Republic of Kenya, 2010a). According to the *Kenya Vision 2030*, the BPO subsector was to create 7,500 direct jobs with an additional GDP contribution of the equivalent of US$125 million by 2012 (Republic of Kenya, 2007). The government has also created the right environment for the BPO sector to take off, particularly through investing in undersea-fiber cables and completion of, or steady progress toward, the implementation of other projects such as: (1) the establishment of a BPO/ICT park with 3,500 dedicated BPO seats; (2) marketing Kenya as a BPO destination in the United Kingdom, United States, and Canada; (3) skills development training programs in entrepreneurship for youths; (4) the provision of incentives such as bandwidth support to BPO operators; (5) the development of a BPO and contract center policy (Republic of Kenya, 2010a).

However, in 2009 McKinsey and Company completed a report, which was commissioned by the Kenya ICT Board, which sought to develop Kenya's go-to-market strategy for the BPO subsector. Among other things, the report found that the BPO subsector has huge potential in Kenya despite the fact that the country does not have the scale to become a global player like India or the Philippines and would therefore need to focus on becoming a niche player (McKinsey and Company, 2009). It was recommended that Kenya should initially concentrate on basic Voice, specifically sales and customer care, and should start with targeting African opportunities and Africa-friendly clients in the United States and the United Kingdom. By pursuing such a strategy, accompanied by an estimated investment of US$100 million (60% of which is open to funding from nongovernmental sources and distributed as US$76 million for skills development, US$12 million for incentives, US$10 million for markets, and US$3 million for a one-stop shop and policy development), Kenya can reap an internal rate of return exceeding 110 percent resulting in a BPO subsector that moves from its current worth of US$2.1 million to US$540 million by 2015 while creating 20,000 new direct jobs as well as 60,000 new indirect jobs during the same period (McKinsey and Company, 2009). In addition, revenue streams will be created from corporate and income taxes leading to additional net revenues for the government of US$88 million by 2015 with the cumulative net revenue between 2009 and 2015 being US$237 million, and an estimated contribution to GDP of US$862 million resulting in a GDP growth-rate increase of between 7 and 17 percent between 2011 and 2015 (McKinsey and Company, 2009).

With respect to financial services, this subsector plays a critical role in the development of the country by providing intermediation between savings and investments. It contributes about 4 percent to GDP and provides assets equivalent to about 40 percent of the GDP (Republic of Kenya, 2010a). Kenya's financial services subsector can be categorized as banking, capital markets, informal financial services, and non-bank financial intermediaries such as insurance and pension schemes. The regulator is the CBK. The country has now emerged as the hub for financial services in East Africa as previously mentioned with a highly ranked Nairobi Stock Exchange (NSE) within the African continent, in terms of market capitalization. The key objective for the financial services subsector as laid out in the *MTP 2008-2012* is to mobilize domestic savings in order to realize a savings to GDP ratio of 25–29 percent as envisaged in the macroeconomic framework underpinning the *Kenya Vision 2030* (Republic of Kenya, 2010a).

Several surveys and analyses of Kenya's financial services subsector have been spearheaded by the Financial Sector Deepening Trust of Kenya (FSD Kenya). FSD Kenya was established in early 2005 to support the development of financial markets in the country as a means to stimulate wealth creation and reduce poverty. It operates as an independent trust under the supervision of professional trustees with the goal of expanding access to services among lower income households and smaller scale enterprises (FSD Kenya, nd). In a most recent survey on financial services access (FinAccess Secretariat, 2009), FSD Kenya and its partners determined that, during the period 2006–09:

- Usage of non-bank financial institutions more than doubled from 7.5 to 18 percent;
- Dependence on only informal financial services declined from 33 to 27 percent;
- Access to financial services improved in both rural and urban areas with access to the formal strand (use of banks, postal bank, or insurance products) increasing in urban areas from 32 to 41 percent;
- Usage of formal financial services increases significantly with level of education rising from 5 percent for those with no education to 70 percent for those with tertiary education;
- Exclusion decreases as level of education increases, from 56 percent for those with no education to 8 percent for those with tertiary education;
- The proportion of the population excluded from access to financial services shrank from 38 to 33 percent;
- Fifty-two percent of the population are currently using a savings product;
- Usage of credit products has increased from 31 to 38 percent with a higher proportion of people in urban areas (41%) having credit compared to those in rural areas (37%);

- The incidence of in-country remittances received increased from 17 to 52 percent while for international remittances received it increased from 2.8 to 4.3 percent;
- Current usage of insurance increased slightly from 5.9 to 6.8 percent with higher usage among males and in urban areas.

What these survey data indicate is that although the situation has improved markedly in recent years, and despite the fact that Kenya is a financial services hub in East Africa, there is still limited access to financial services for the majority of Kenyans leaving room for considerable market penetration and the development of appropriate financial products in that regard. This implies the tackling of supply side barriers to access. By reducing barriers to financial services, such policies could stimulate household investment, thereby contributing to growth and poverty reduction. However, it must be acknowledged here that one approach to fill the void, and an interesting development in the supply of financial services, has been the manner in which mobile phone operators have encroached on the space of the financial institutions through the launch of the innovative and hugely popular and successful mobile money products such as "M-Pesa" from Safaricom, "yuCash" from Essar Telecom Kenya, "Airtel Money" from Airtel Kenya (formerly Zain Kenya), and "Orange Money" ("Iko Pesa") from Orange (Telekom) Kenya. These products have made electronic transactions easily accessible to those without a bank account primarily the poor. Getting cash into the hands of those who need it and can use it most is limited on the supply side rather than the demand side. There is no shortage of funds, but it is the ability to move money from the sender to the receiver (velocity of money) that is the stumbling block (Hughes and Lonie, 2007).

Perhaps the most well-known of these products—and on which several case studies have been written—is M-Pesa which was launched in March 2007 (see, e.g., Agrawal, 2010a, 2010b; Arthur D Little, 2010; Hughes and Lonie, 2007; Mas and Radcliffe, 2010; Mbogo, 2010; Morawczynski, 2007). M-Pesa is derived from the Swahili word "pesa" meaning cash and the "M" is for mobile. The product concept is very simple. An M-Pesa customer can use his or her mobile phone to move money quickly, securely, and across great distances, directly to another mobile phone through which the user can conduct other financial transactions. Neither customer needs to have a bank account. They register instead with Safaricom for an M-Pesa account. Customers turn cash essentially into e-money at Safaricom dealers, and then follow simple instructions on their phones to make payments through their M-Pesa accounts. The accounts are very secure, protected by personal identification numbers, and supported by a 24-hour service provided by Safaricom

(Hughes and Lonie, 2007). The system provides money transfers as banks do in the developed world. In fact, M-Pesa allows users to make four basic types of transaction: (1) transfers from person to person; (2) transfers from individuals to businesses; (3) cash withdrawals and deposits at designated outlets; (4) loan receipt or repayment (Agrawal, 2010a). It is a secure, convenient, low cost system of financial inclusion where all transactions are authorized and recorded in real time. Individual customer accounts are maintained by Safaricom but the company deposits the full value of its customers' balances on the system in pooled accounts in regulated banks. Thus, Safaricom issues and manages the M-Pesa accounts, but the value in the accounts is fully backed by highly liquid deposits at commercial banks (Mas and Radcliffe, 2010).

The success and popularity of M-Pesa can be gleaned from the following information and statistics (Arthur D Little, 2010; Lime, 2010; Safaricom, 2011; Zimmerman and Holmes, 2010):

- As of December 2010, there were 13.3 million subscribers to the service which is more than one-third of Kenya's population.
- By the end of December 2010, there were close to 24,000 agents/outlets nationwide which are more than 13 times the number of automatic teller machines (ATMs) and more than 20 times the number of bank branches in the country.
- Before the launch of M-Pesa, 43 percent of people sent money by hand, 20 percent by bus, 18 percent by post office money order, 8 percent by direct deposit, and 12 percent by other means. After the launch of M-Pesa and by 2009, 47 percent of people were sending money by M-Pesa, 32 percent by hand, 9 percent by bus, 6 percent by direct deposit, and another 6 percent by other means.
- Transactions exceed US$10 million per day.
- In 2009, revenue from M-Pesa represented 2.1 percent of Safaricom's total revenue for that financial year.
- Banks, such as Equity Bank, have engaged in partnership with Safaricom to offer M-Pesa-type products, such as the M-Kesho savings account, to grow their customer base while at the same time providing an interest-earning savings account for the poor and under-served. Kesho is Kiswahili for "tomorrow" or "future."
- The M-Pesa platform was replicated, rolled out, and launched in Tanzania in 2008 and in South Africa in 2010.

Undoubtedly, M-Pesa has met a need in Kenya and now elsewhere also. The service is scoring very high on financials as well as in customer satisfaction and confidence. It has also been expanded to capture international remittances (although currently in a limited scale). More innovative supply side products of this nature are needed. The commercial banks, in particular, need to develop more customer-friendly products to enhance financial inclusion in the country. As observed by Mas and Radcliffe (2010), M-Pesa has certainly provided one glimpse of a commercially sound, affordable, and effective way to offer financial services to all. M-Pesa, as well as the other mobile money systems, has transitioned recently from a pure money transfer system into a payment platform that allows institutions and businesses to send and receive payments. According to UN-HABITAT (2011: 36), "it is rumored that even Kenya Police now routinely collect [some of their bribes, as discussed in Chapter 4] using M-Pesa."

Travel and Tourism

In addition to agriculture, wholesale and retail trade, manufacturing, business process outsourcing, and financial services, tourism is also identified in the *MTP 2008-2012* as one of the six priority sectors targeted by the government to spur economic growth by increasing the national GDP growth rate to 10 percent by 2012 (Republic of Kenya, 2010a). Tourism currently contributes about 5 percent of GDP and 4 percent of total employment in Kenya. However, through backward and forward linkages, the general tourism economy, as a whole, contributes about 12 percent to GDP and almost 23 percent of foreign exchange earnings (KIPPRA, 2009). In terms of world ranking, by 2010 Kenya's travel and tourism industry was ranked (out of 181 countries) 84 in absolute size, 85 in relative contribution to national economy, and 34 in terms of real growth (WTTC, 2010). The ranking in sub-Saharan Africa (out of 42 countries) in 2010 placed Kenya at 5 in absolute size, and 9 in relative contribution to the economy (WTTC, 2010). The real growth forecast rankings by 2020 (annualized real growth adjusted for inflation for the period 2011–20) is 88 globally and 24 in sub-Saharan Africa (WTTC, 2010).

Kenya is therefore one of the leading tourist destinations in sub-Saharan Africa and there is tremendous potential for the tourism sector to play the role envisaged for it in the *MTP 2008-2012*. Over the years, and through to 2007, tourist arrivals and tourism earnings have been steadily increasing. From 1990 to 2007, tourist arrivals increased from 814,000 to 1.8 million resulting in tourism earnings of approximately US$939 million in 2007 (Honey and Gilpin, 2009; Republic of Kenya, 2010a). However, the 2008 postelection violence took a heavy toll on the tourism sector as tourist arrivals contracted to 1.2 million during that year while earnings from the sector declined by 19 percent to approximately US$761 million (Republic of Kenya,

2010a). Partly due to the impact of the global economic downturn and the residual effects of the 2008 postelection violence, the expected recovery and growth of the tourism sector in Kenya did not materialize in 2009. Tourist arrivals in 2009 numbered 1.5 million representing a 25 percent increase over the 2008 arrivals but this was 17 percent less than the volume of arrivals in 2007 prior to the postelection violence. Similarly, tourism earnings rose to approximately US$803 million which was 5.5 percent higher than for 2008 but 14 percent less than for 2007 (KNBS, 2010). However, the data for 2010 point toward continued improving fortunes for the recovering travel and tourism industry. Tourist arrivals in 2010 were 1.6 million. Compared to 2009, this represented a 7 percent growth in tourism arrivals with earnings of approximately US$930 million (KNBS, 2011). These 2010 earnings were 16 percent higher compared to earnings in 2009.

Population, Labor, and Employment

As can be seen in Figure 1.6, the total population of Kenya has almost quadrupled between 1969 and 2009 from 10.9 million to 38.6 million. Figure 1.7 depicts the intercensal population growth rates which had an annual average range of 2.9–3.4 percent. Kenya's population characteristics, based on the 2009 census data, include the following (Republic of Kenya, 2010d, 2010e):

- An almost even gender distribution of 49.7 percent males and 50.3 percent females.

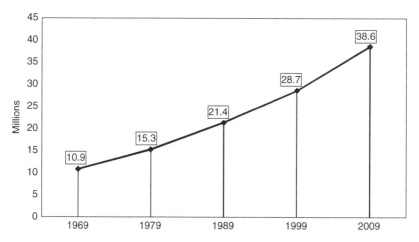

FIGURE 1.6 Population distribution, 1969–2009
Source: Author, based on data from Republic of Kenya (2010d).

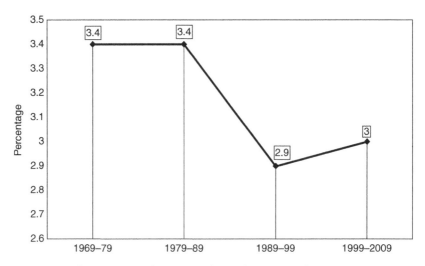

FIGURE 1.7 Average annual intercensal population growth rates, 1969–2009
Source: Author, based on data from Republic of Kenya (2010d).

- A total (national) density of 66 people per square kilometer increasing from 49 in the 1999 census.
- Total households of 8.8 million (a household is defined as a person or group of persons who reside in the same homestead/compound but not necessarily in the same dwelling unit, have the same cooking arrangements, and are answerable to the same household head).
- A rural population of 26.1 million (comprising 67.7% of the total population) with 5.4 million households and a density of 46 people per square kilometer.
- An urban population of 12.5 million (comprising 32.3% of the total population) with 3.4 million households and a density of 730 people per square kilometer.
- A total population age group distribution of 43 percent for 0–14 years old; 54 percent for 15–64 years old; and 3 percent for 65 years and older. This implies that 46 percent of the population depends on 54 percent of the population who are of the productive age group of 15–64 years. The resulting dependency ratio is 85.2.
- A youthful population (15–24 years old) totaling 7.9 million, comprising a little more than one-fifth of the country's total population with a distribution of 51.2 percent female and 48.8 percent male.
- A capital city/county, Nairobi, with a population of 3.1 million (8 percent of total population) with 985,016 households and a density of 4,515 people per square kilometer. The second largest city/county, Mombasa, has

a population of 523,183 (1.3% of total population) with 140,535 house-holds and a density of 4,144 people per square kilometer.

Over the past several decades, as shown in Figure 1.8, Kenya's labor force has increased from 6.7 million to 19.2 million in 2010 with a projection estimate to reach 25.5 million by 2020. Currently, the labor force of Kenya is estimated at approximately 50 percent of the total population. The num-ber of workers in the labor force is dependent on both the pool of existing

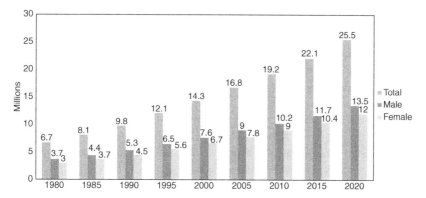

FIGURE 1.8 Economically active population by sex: estimates and projections, 1980–2020
Source: Author, based on data from ILO (nda).

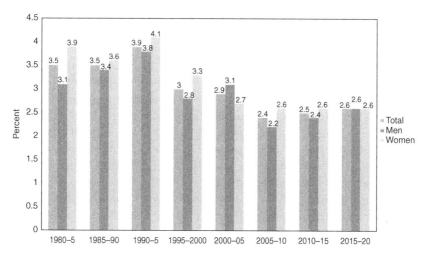

FIGURE 1.9 Average annual rates of growth of labor force by sex, 1980–2020
Source: Author, based on data from ILO (nda).

workers and those entering the labor force. In fact, the labor force which is synonymous with the economically active population comprises all persons of either sex, and above a certain age, who furnish the supply of labor for the productive activities during a specified time-reference period. It includes all persons who are willing and able to work and therefore they fulfill the requirements for inclusion among the employed (employees or self-employed) or the unemployed. The growth rate is contingent upon population increase, net migration, and social and economic factors such as education and socialization.

Figure 1.9 contains the growth rates of the total labor force as well as its male and female components. From the data several conclusions can be drawn. First, the growth of the total labor force, having reached almost 4 percent during 1990–95, declined to less than 2.5 percent by 2005–10. Second, with the exception of the 2000–05 period, the rate of growth of the female sex in the labor force was greater than that of the male sex. This reflects a trend that is becoming more pronounced, namely, the increase of women in the labor force as more women seize the opportunities available to them to pursue formal education. Even though the ratio of male to female distribution in the labor force has hovered around 1:1, the increase has been enough to influence the average growth of the labor force as a whole. Undoubtedly, participation rates tend to rise with the level of formal education. The higher the level of education the higher the level of labor force participation rates.

This brings us, therefore, to the labor force participation rates. As can be seen in Figure 1.10, the labor force participation rates for women have been increasing while, for men, it has been basically decreasing. Kenya's labor force participation rates have been consistently higher than for sub-Saharan Africa by 15 points or more. Undoubtedly, opportunities are now much more available for women to hold good jobs in Kenya. The education system, especially in the urban areas, prepares women as fully as it prepares men. The labor force participation rate is a measure of the proportion of a country's working-age population that actively engages in the labor market, either by working or looking for work. It provides an indication of the relative size of the supply of labor available to engage in the production of goods and services. The working-age population is the population above a certain age, prescribed for the measurement of economic characteristics. The labor force participation rate is calculated by expressing the number of persons in the labor force as a percentage of the working-age population. In Kenya, the working age is 15–64 years.

However, despite increasing labor force participation rates and increasing access to the labor market by Kenyan women, a number of studies point

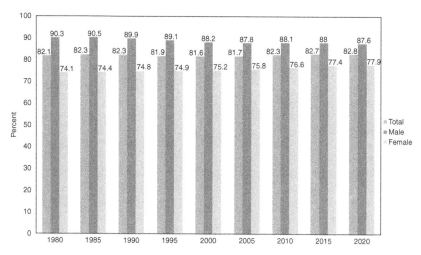

FIGURE 1.10 Labor force participation rates by sex, 1980–2020
Source: Author, based on data from ILO (nda).

to gender disparities in Kenya's labor market and, in fact, the *MTP 2008-2012* articulates the government's commitment to continued mainstreaming of gender into government policies, plans, budgets and programs as an approach geared toward achieving gender equity in all aspects of society and as a means of realizing the aspirations of the *Kenya Vision 2030* goals (Republic of Kenya, 2010a). The labor market gender disparities that have been identified in Kenya include: (1) women accounting for about 30 percent of total formal sector wage employment despite constituting a little more than 50 percent of the total population; (2) higher rates of unemployment for women compared to men; (3) lower earnings for women, even after adjusting for the type of employment, occupation, and hours of work; (4) less time engaged in wage employment and more time devoted to household production by women than men (Atieno, 2009; Ellis et al., 2007; IEA-Kenya, 2008, 2010; Kabubo-Mariara, 2003; Odhiambo, 2004; Wanjala and Were, 2009).

The sectoral distribution of wage employment is shown in Table 1.1. As can be seen, the services sector employs the largest number of wage earners. The four sectors in descending order of magnitude of wage employment have consistently been: services; agriculture; manufacturing; and trade, restaurants and hotels. The latter also contains elements of services. However, the transport and communications sector has been consistently expanding and has almost doubled its share of wage employment between 2000 and 2009. It is also clear that the shift taking place in wage employment is away

TABLE 1.1 Wage employment by sector, 2000–09 (thousands)

Sector	2000	2003	2004	2005	2006	2007	2008	2009
Agriculture	311	316	320	327	335	340	341	340
Mining & Quarrying	5	5	6	6	6	6	7	6
Manufacturing	218	239	242	248	259	264	264	267
Electricity & Water	22	21	21	20	20	19	19	20
Building and Construction	78	77	77	78	80	81	85	93
Trade, Restaurants and Hotels	155	163	168	175	186	196	202	215
Transport and Communications	83	87	101	114	131	149	157	144
Finance, Insurance, Real Estate and Business Services	85	84	84	89	92	95	94	97
Community, Social and Personal Services	719	735	745	751	749	760	774	818
TOTAL	**1,676**	**1,727**	**1,764**	**1,808**	**1,858**	**1,910**	**1,943**	**2,000**

Sources: KNBS (ndb, 2010, 2011) and ILO (ndb).

from agriculture and into services. Undoubtedly, this is being driven by the greater opportunities for employment in that latter modern sector as a result of the growth there as previously discussed.

An important aspect of labor force participation is looking for work. This is usually a good barometer of the unemployment situation in an economy. Official unemployment data for Kenya is either scarce or obsolete. However, the economic problem that seems to be the most prevalent in the country is that of the high level of unemployment that exists. Based on a thorough search, Table 1.2 represents the most credible data found on estimates of national unemployment rates in Kenya. Nonetheless, as also noted by others (see, e.g., Wambugu et al., 2009), some of these unemployment rates derived from government sources may be perceived as too low due to a much narrower definition of unemployment used by the Kenya National Bureau of Statistics (KNBS) which excludes some categories of the labor force.

However, the current international standards for labor force statistics are the responsibility of the International Labor Organization (ILO). These standards are set by the International Conference of Labor Statisticians (ICLS) which is convened by the ILO. The international standard definition of unemployment was adopted by the 13th ICLS in 1982 and is based on three criteria which have to be met simultaneously (ILO, 1982). Accordingly, the unemployed comprise all persons above the age specified for measuring the economically active population who during the reference period were:

(1) "without work," that is, they were not in paid employment or self-employment as per the international definition of employment;
(2) "currently available for work," that is, they were available for paid employment or self-employment during the reference period;
(3) "seeking work," that is, they had taken specific steps in a specified recent period to seek paid employment or self-employment.

The international definition of unemployment is intended to refer exclusively to a person's particular activities during a specified reference period. Consequently, unemployment statistics based on the international definition may differ from statistics on narrow surveys that do not incorporate the three criteria above which seems to be the case in Kenya. The overall unemployment rate for a country is a widely used measure of its unutilized labor supply. The unemployment rates by specific groups, defined by age, sex, occupation, or industry, are also useful in identifying groups of workers and sectors most vulnerable to joblessness. The usual policy goal of governments, employers, and trade unions is, therefore, to have a rate that is as low as possible yet also consistent with other economic and policy objectives such as low inflation and a rising standard of living.

The fundamental characteristics of unemployment and underemployment in Kenya that have emerged from the limited official national statistics and the most recent literature (ILO, 2010; KIPPRA, 2009; KNBS, ndc, 2008; Wambugu et al., 2009) suggest the following:

(1) An increasing trend of higher urban unemployment rates which, however, may seem consistent with higher labor force participation rates in urban areas. The urban and rural unemployment rates were

TABLE 1.2 Unemployment rate, 1999–2008 (%)

Year	Rate
1999	14.6[a]
2001	40.0[b]
2006	12.7[c]
2008	40.0[b]

Sources: [a] KNBS (ndc), [b] CIA (2010), and [c] KNBS (2008).

25.1 percent and 9.4 percent, respectively, in 1999 and 19.9 percent and 9.8 percent, respectively, in 2006.

(2) Higher rates of unemployment for women compared to men, although the gap seemed to have narrowed considerably in recent years as more qualified women enter the job market. In 1999, the female unemployment rate at 19.3 percent was almost twice that of males—which was 9.8 percent—compared to 11.2 percent and 14.3 percent for males and females, respectively, in 2006.

(3) The highest rates of unemployment by age distribution can be found among the youth aged 15–24. In 1999, this age group had a 25.7 percent unemployment rate which ticked up slightly to 25.8 percent in 2006 and was double that of the total unemployment rate in that year.

(4) Much higher unemployment rates than the sub-Saharan Africa average. In 1999, the sub-Saharan Africa unemployment rate was 8.2 percent while for Kenya it was 14.6 percent and in 2006 the comparable rates were 8.2 percent for sub-Saharan Africa and 12.7 percent for Kenya.

(5) The underemployed amounted to 3.5 percent of the labor force in 1999 and was more than five times that at 18.7 percent of the labor force in 2006.

Unemployment may be one of the best indicators a country has about the state of its economy. In Kenya, unemployment and underemployment means a loss of income, less food, poorer shelter, less of all the basic elements needed to satisfy human needs, and a general perpetuation of the state of poverty of those who are the victims of such deprivation. Thus, the problem of unemployment is on the one hand a sterile statistic used by economists and policy makers as an indicator of economic performance, but on the other hand, to millions of Kenyans it signifies anxiety, helplessness, hunger, poor health, frustration, idleness, and poverty. The latter is discussed next.

Poverty/Inequality and HIV/AIDS

Two critical factors related to, and even influencing, the magnitude of population, labor, employment, and economic progress are the poverty–inequality nexus and HIV/AIDS (human immunodeficiency virus/acquired immune deficiency syndrome). Both of these factors have exhibited signs of reduced incidence in recent years. Nonetheless, they remain very influential in terms of their impact on socioeconomic development and progress in Kenya, and therefore major challenges for policy-makers.

Poverty and Inequality

Poverty in Kenya, like it is throughout Africa, is multifaceted. Although the incidence of poverty has fallen in Africa, including in Kenya, in recent years, poverty continues to be a significant and deepening socioeconomic problem in both locations. Poverty in Kenya is characterized by, among other things, a lack of purchasing power, rural and female predominance, exposure to environmental and other risks, insufficient access to social and economic services, and few opportunities for formal sector income generation. In addition, there are other influential dimensions such as poor health, malnutrition, and lack of shelter, for example.

There are essentially three perspectives on poverty (Hope, 2004a, 2008). First, the income perspective designates a person as poor if, and only if, their income level is below the defined poverty line. The poverty line is usually demarcated in terms of having sufficient income for a specified amount of food. Second, the basic-needs perspective regards poverty as deprivation of material requirements for minimally acceptable fulfillment of human needs, including food. This notion of deprivation goes well beyond the lack of private income. It also includes the need for basic health, education, employment, and services that have to be provided by States or communities to prevent people from becoming poor. The third, the capacity perspective pertains to the absence of some basic capabilities to function. These capabilities vary from such physical ones as being well nourished, being adequately clothed and sheltered, and avoiding preventable morbidity, to more complex social achievements such as participating in the life of the community. The capability approach is regarded as reconciling the notions of absolute and relative poverty, since relative deprivations in incomes and commodities can lead to an absolute deprivation in minimum capabilities.

The various poverty perspectives allow for the measurement and profiling of poverty that, in turn, allow analysts to identify groups of poor people, to assess the size of those groups and the severity of their poverty and, therefore, to track and model how changes in the socioeconomy influence poverty. This further enables policy-makers to see how their choices, by inducing such changes, are likely to affect poverty, and—if they wish—to change the choices accordingly (Lipton and van der Gaag, 1993). However, despite the emergence of various measurements of poverty, the income–poverty index is the one most used to identify the poor and determine the intensity of their poverty. Usually, three indicators of income poverty are used. These are the percentage of poor, the aggregate poverty gap, and the distribution of income among the poor.

Based on the available official statistics, poverty rates in Kenya are on the decline. As can be seen in Table 1.3, national absolute income poverty

TABLE 1.3 Absolute poverty rates, 1994–2006 (%)

Poverty variable	1994	1997	2006
Total	43.7	52.3	45.9
Overall rural	46.7	52.9	49.1
Overall urban	28.9	49.2	33.7
Proportion of urban male-headed households	21.2	45.9	30.0
Proportion of urban female-headed households	27.1	63.0	46.2
Proportion of rural male-headed households	39.4	52.5	48.8
Proportion of rural female-headed households	39.6	54.1	50.0

Sources: Republic of Kenya (1998, 2006) and KNBS (2007).

fell from 52 percent in 1997 to 46 percent in 2006 after it had increased between 1994 and 1997. Significant declines in urban poverty were also recorded from 49 percent in 1997 to 34 percent in 2006 which not only widened the gap between the distribution of the urban and rural poor population but also reinforced the rural predominance of poverty in the country. The data indicate that by 2006, 49 percent (down from 53% in 1997) of rural Kenyans had levels of expenditure (income) that were insufficient to meet basic food and nonfood needs. In terms of gender distribution, urban households showed the most dramatic changes. Poverty among male-headed and female-headed urban households declined by 16 and 17 percent, respectively, between 1997 and 2006. The changes were considerably less dramatic for rural households with declines of approximately 4 percent for each gender.

What also emerges is the fact that female-headed households are still the majority poor households despite comprising a significantly smaller share of the total households. For example, by 2006, 72.5 percent of rural households and 77 percent of urban households were male-headed but 49 and 30 percent, respectively, of these fell below the absolute poverty line. On the other hand, although female-headed households constituted 27.5 and 23 percent, respectively, of rural and urban households, they represented 50 percent of poor rural households and 46 percent of poor urban households, respectively. The difference in head count, poverty gap, and severity of poverty is, therefore, much more significant between male and female-headed households in the urban areas than in the rural areas. Generally, rural poverty is marked by its common connection to agriculture and land with low agricultural productivity, inadequate nonfarm employment opportunities, and low access to health care and schooling, whereas urban poverty can be mostly explained by labor market distortions (Wambugu et al., 2010).

Another popular and often-cited measure of poverty is the poverty headcount rates based on an international poverty line. This international poverty line is a consumption poverty line that was developed by the World Bank to enable consistent comparisons of the incidence of poverty across borders. It takes into account purchasing power differences that are not captured by official nominal currency and exchange rates and it sets a common poverty threshold. The current estimation is US$1.25 a day based on "Cost of Basic Needs," which estimates the cost of securing basic food and nonfood needs for poor households (World Bank, 2010a). Based on the World Bank calculations, Table 1.4 shows Kenya's headcount poverty ratio and poverty gap at poverty lines of US$1.25 and US$2 per day from 1993 to 2006. The poverty gap is a measure of the depth of poverty. It is based on both the percentage of the population below the poverty line and the average income of the poor relative to the poverty line. It ranges between zero and 100 percent. The larger it is, the deeper the poverty. At the US$2 per day poverty line there is a consistent decline in the percentage of the population below the poverty line since 1993 whereas at the US$1.25 poverty line the decrease in poverty is less consistent. However, at the US$2 per day and higher poverty lines, poverty rates are much higher than at the US$1.25 poverty line, reflecting the magnitude of, and access to, income of the poor. Nonetheless, these international poverty line comparisons do not reveal anything particularly different from the trends depicted in Table 1.3 which is based on official national statistics.

TABLE 1.4 Headcount and poverty gap indices for international poverty lines of US$1.25–2.00, 1993–2006 (% living below)

Year	US$1.25 Poverty line		US$2 Poverty line	
	Headcount ratio	Poverty gap	Headcount ratio	Poverty gap
1993	38.4	15.3	59.3	28.2
1994	28.5	9.3	53.7	21.5
1997	19.6	4.6	42.7	14.7
2006	19.7	6.1	39.9	15.1

Source: World Bank (2010a).

Also used as a poverty measure that deserves some attention here is the Human Poverty Index (HPI) which was developed by the United Nations Development Programme (UNDP) as a composite index measure of the different features of deprivation in the quality of life to arrive at an aggregate judgment on the extent of poverty in a community. For developing countries, the HPI focuses on the proportion of people below certain threshold levels in each of the dimensions of the Human Development Index (HDI) that was also developed by UNDP. Rather than measure poverty by income, the HPI therefore uses indicators of the most basic dimensions of depriva- tion. The three indicators or deprivations are: (1) survival or longevity—liv- ing a long and healthy life—which is measured by the proportion of people not expected to survive to age 40; (2) knowledge or education—exclusion from the world of reading and communication—which is measured by the percentage of adults who are illiterate; (3) a decent standard of living— particularly overall economic provisioning—which is measured by the un- weighted average of people not using an improved source of water and the proportion of children under age 5 who are underweight for their age. Table 1.5 depicts the HPI for Kenya for the period 2000–08. It shows that human poverty (severe deprivations) is slowly declining. The proportion of Kenyans experiencing severe deprivations has gone down from a high of 37.8 percent in 2001 to 29.5 percent by 2007.

TABLE 1.5 Human Poverty Index, 2000–08 (%)

Year	Human Poverty Index
2000	31.9
2001	37.8
2002	37.5
2003	35.4
2004	35.5
2005/06	30.8
2007	29.5

Source: UNDP (nd).

One other poverty measure, that was developed by the Oxford Poverty and Human Development Initiative (OPHI) and UNDP and introduced by the latter in its *Human Development Report 2010,* is the Multidimensional Poverty Index (MPI). The MPI replaces the HPI. According to UNDP (2010: 95), the HPI suffered from the shortcoming that "it could not identify specific individuals, households or larger groups of people as jointly deprived." On the other hand, as noted by UNDP (2010: 95):

the MPI addresses this shortcoming by capturing how many people expe- rience overlapping deprivations and how many deprivations they face on average. It can be broken down by dimension to show how the composition of multidimensional poverty changes in incidence and intensity for differ- ent regions, ethnic groups and so on—with useful implications for policy.

The MPI is the outcome of the multidimensional poverty headcount (the share of people who are multidimensionally poor) and the average number of deprivations each multidimensionally poor household experiences (the intensity of poverty). It identifies people who contend with multiple deprivations across the same three dimensions of the HDI—education, health, and standard of living—and uses ten indicators which largely reflect the Millennium Development Goals (MDGs) and thus international standards of poverty. Each of the three dimensions is equally weighted. The MPI shows (1) incidence of poverty—the proportion of multidimensionally poor people; (2) intensity of poverty—the average number of deprivations poor people face at the same time; (3) composition of poverty and differences—across states, ethnic groups, rural/urban areas. A household is multidimensionally poor if it is deprived in at least two of ten indicators (OPHI, 2010a; UNDP, 2010).

Based on data from Kenya's demographic and household survey of 2003, the incidence of poverty (proportion of population in multidimensional poverty) was determined to be 60.4 percent and the population at risk of multidimensional poverty was 23.2 percent (UNDP, 2010). Kenya's headcount of the multidimensionally poor was slightly lower than for the sub-Saharan Africa region whose proportion was 64.5 percent (Alkire and Santos, 2010). The top two indicators with the highest proportion of the population that are poor and deprived in Kenya are electricity (59.1%) and sanitation (58.8%) (OPHI, 2010b). The proportion of the population with at least one severe deprivation in living standards was 86.2 percent, in health (41.4%), and in education (21.9%) (UNDP, 2010). The MPI reveals great variation in poverty within countries and the composition of poverty also differs among ethnic groups. However, much more important for this book is the contribution of the three dimensions and their indicators to multidimensional poverty in Kenya. These disaggregations show that the percent contribution of deprivations in education, health, and standard of living were 14.5, 26.2, and 59.3 percent, respectively (Alkire and Santos, 2010). Consequently, standard of living dimension issues are dominant with the proportion of people who are poor and deprived being almost 60 percent in its indicators of electricity, sanitation, and cooking oil; exceeding 50 percent for floor (households deprived of it have a dirt/sand floor or palm bamboo and wood planks); and at, or exceeding, 45 percent for assets and drinking water (Alkire and Santos, 2010).

High income poverty is usually associated with high human poverty, and low income poverty with low human poverty. However, the two forms of poverty can move in different directions. High income poverty can coexist with lower human poverty as was found to be the case in Kenya in the 1990s (Hope, 2004a), and is still the case today, and low income poverty can coexist with higher human poverty as is the case in some other African countries.

This is so because progress in reducing poverty in income and progress in reducing poverty in human choices do not always move together. Some countries have done better in reducing income poverty than human poverty and others, such as Kenya, have done better in reducing human poverty than income poverty.

Income poverty is, inevitably, a state of lack of the requisite income to acquire specified amounts of food and other nonfood items. In many African countries, like Kenya, the inequality in income is quite significant. The ratio of the income or expenditure of the richest 10 percent of the population in Kenya to that of the poorest 10 percent was 21 by 2007. The most frequently used measure of income inequality is the Gini index or coefficient. It ranges from zero (complete equality) to 100 (complete inequality). In Figure 1.11 the income inequality as measured by the Gini index is shown for the period 1994–2006. High income inequality levels persist in Kenya increasing from a Gini index of 42.5 percent in 1997 to 47.7 percent in 2006.

Apart from income and human poverty, which has resulted in large numbers of Kenyans being socially disadvantaged and leading most of them into severe poverty or being vulnerable to poverty, some other factors have also influenced the magnitude and nature of poverty in Kenya. These are primarily, but not limited to, rising youth unemployment because of inadequate

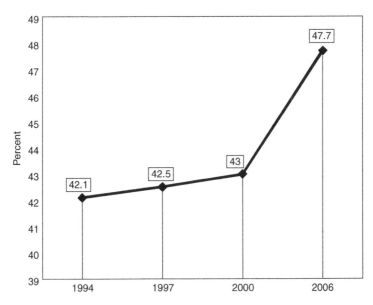

FIGURE 1.11 Gini Index, 1994–2006
Source: Author, based on data from World Bank (2010a) and KIPPRA (2009).

access to formal sector employment opportunities; inadequate access to credit and to markets for the sale of goods and services, particularly for the rural poor; inadequate access to basic social assistance; and the HIV/AIDS disease that is a continent-wide problem. With the exception of the HIV/AIDS situation, which is examined below, all of the other afore-mentioned factors are discussed in appropriate chapters of this book.

HIV/AIDS

HIV/AIDS has had a devastating impact on African countries and continues to be a major challenge for almost all countries on the continent including Kenya. AIDS kills adults in their prime, robbing schools of teachers, leaving children as orphans, pushes back hard-won gains in health and education, and slows the development trajectory (Hope, 2001, 2008). HIV/AIDS in African countries also contributes to poverty through its incapacitating or killing of heads of households (the primary breadwinners) which, in turn, considerably constrains family income and thereby intensifies the deprivation already being experienced by many Africans including Kenyans. As HIV prevalence rises, poverty generally deepens as the near poor get poor and the poor get poorer. However, it has been reported in one study by Mishra et al. (2007) that Kenya is among a few countries where HIV prevalence has been found to be higher among adults in the wealthiest quintile than among those in the poorest quintile.

Kenya's first HIV case was diagnosed in 1984. HIV prevalence peaked in the late 1990s followed by more or less steady declines as shown in Figure 1.12.

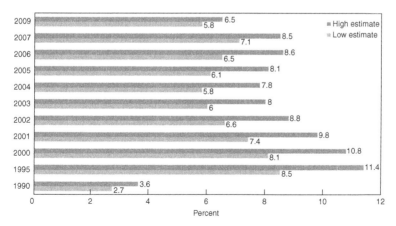

FIGURE 1.12 HIV prevalence rates, 1990–2009
Source: Author, based on data from UNAIDS (2008, 2010).

The more internationally comparative data compiled by UNAIDS (Joint United Nations Programme on HIV/AIDS) used in Figure 1.12 gives an estimate of current prevalence rates of between 5.8 and 6.5 percent. However, two recent Government of Kenya surveys have provided different estimates. The Kenya AIDS Indicators Survey (2007) estimated the average HIV prevalence among the general population aged 15–49 at 7.4 percent while the Kenya Demographic and Health Survey (2008–09) estimated prevalence for the same population at 6.3 percent (NACC, 2010). However, the difference between the HIV prevalence estimates of the two surveys is not statistically significant and all sources of data point to a stabilization of adult HIV prevalence in the past few years.

Women have a higher prevalence rate than men, with younger women being three to four times more likely to be infected than boys of the same age group. The overall female prevalence stands at 8.0–8.4 percent compared to 4.3–5.4 percent for men (NACC, 2010). Prevalence among uncircumcised men is four times higher than for the circumcised. In the rural areas, current prevalence among adults aged 15–64 years is estimated at 6.7 percent compared to 8.4 percent among adults living in urban areas. Over time, prevalence among urban Kenyans has decreased among women from an estimated 12.3 percent in 2003 to 10.4 percent in 2008 and from 7.5 percent in 2003 to 7.2 percent in 2008 for men. Women in urban areas have a higher HIV prevalence than those in rural areas (10.4% and 7.2%, respectively), while among men, the current HIV prevalence rate in urban areas is marginally lower than in rural areas (3.7% and 4.5%, respectively). However, given that the vast majority of Kenya's population (68%) reside in rural areas, the absolute number of HIV infections is higher in rural than in urban areas. An estimated 1 million adults in rural areas are infected with HIV, compared to an estimated 0.4 million adults in urban areas (NACC, 2010). After peaking in the early years of the twenty-first century, AIDS deaths in adults and children have been declining and by 2009 were estimated at 61,000–99,000 compared to 120,000–170,000 in 2003 (UNAIDS, 2008, 2010). The number of orphans due to death of one or both of their parents from AIDS is estimated at 980,000–1,400,000 (NACC, 2010; UNAIDS, 2010).

External Trade

Trade is a key element in the trajectory toward achieving and sustaining development. In fact, international trade, comprising both imports and exports of goods and services, is a critical instrument for economic growth. The *MTP 2008-2012* has also identified the trade sector to play a significant role toward the attainment of national development objectives including the MDGs and particularly the first goal on Eradicating Extreme Poverty and Hunger, and goal number 8 on Developing Global Partnerships for Development (Republic of Kenya, 2008).

Kenya's external trade patterns are heavily influenced by both global market conditions and the country's vigorous pursuit of regional integration despite that, in the latter case, there is a growing body of literature that points to the costly and unrewarding proliferation of cross-memberships in Africa's regional integration bodies (see, e.g., Hope 2004b; UNECA, 2006). Kenya is a member of both the East African Community (EAC) and COMESA. In 1996, Kenya, Uganda, and Tanzania reestablished the EAC which was originally established in 1967 and then dissolved in 1977. The objectives of the EAC include harmonizing tariffs and customs regimes, free movement of people, and improving regional infrastructures. In July 2000, the Treaty on the Establishment of the EAC entered into force. The Treaty envisages integration among the East African countries from a Custom Union to a Common Market, then a Monetary Union and ultimately a Political Federation (EACS, 2010a). In 2004, Kenya, Uganda, and Tanzania signed a Customs Union Agreement paving the way for a common market. The Customs Union and a Common External Tariff (CET) were established on January 01, 2005. Rwanda and Burundi joined the EAC as full members in July 2007. In July 2010, the EAC Common Market Protocol came into force and a Monetary Union is planned for 2012 (EACS, 2010a).

COMESA was established in 1994 after the Treaty (which was signed in November 1993) creating it came into force. It replaced the Preferential Trade Area for Eastern and Southern Africa States (PTA) which had been in existence since 1981 when the Treaty establishing the PTA was signed. The PTA Treaty came into force in September 1982. Currently, COMESA has a membership of 19 countries—Burundi, Comoros, Democratic Republic of Congo, Djibouti, Egypt, Eritrea, Ethiopia, Kenya, Libya, Madagascar, Malawi, Mauritius, Rwanda, Seychelles, Sudan, Swaziland, Uganda, Zambia, and Zimbabwe. From 1997 to present, and for varying political and economic considerations, several member states—Angola, Lesotho, Mozambique, Namibia, and Tanzania (all members of the Southern African Development Community (SADC) also)—opted to withdraw from COMESA. With a total population exceeding 425 million covering a geographical area exceeding 11.6 million square kilometers and a GDP exceeding US$470 billion, COMESA is a major marketplace for both external and internal trading and therefore one of the most significant regional economic communities (RECs) in Africa. In October 2000, COMESA launched a free trade area and in June 2009 launched its customs union. By 2025, COMESA expects to remove all tariff barriers (UNECA, 2010).

Informal and formal trade in Kenya account for approximately 10 percent of GDP and 10 percent of formal employment, and most of the employment is in the informal sector (KIPPRA, 2009). The main sectors in Kenya's external trade are in services, agriculture and manufacturing and the country's overall trade partners are Africa, the European Union (EU), the United Arab Emirates (UAE), India, China, Japan, the United States, the EAC, and COMESA. The African continent accounts for about 24 percent of Kenya's total trade, the EU accounts for about 20 percent, and the share with the EAC partner states is about 9 percent while for COMESA it is about 12 percent (KNBS, 2010). Over the period 1990–2009, the value of total exports of goods and services increased more than threefold. Exports totaled US$2.21 billion in 1990 compared to US$7.65 billion in 2009. However, aggregate (volume or total) trade was heavily impacted by the growth in imports also. The value of imports increased more rapidly (fourfold) than the value of exports from US$2.69 billion in 1990 to US$11 billion in 2009. The result has been a widening deficit in the trade balance from US$0.48 billion in 1990 to US$3.36 billion in 2009 as shown in Figure 1.13. Exports as a percentage of GDP declined from 27 percent in 2006 to 25 percent in 2009 while imports increased from 39 percent of GDP in 2006 to 41 percent in 2009 (Republic of Kenya, 2010c). In 2010, through to July, the value of goods and services increased to US$9.54 billion while imports were US$11.3 billion leading to

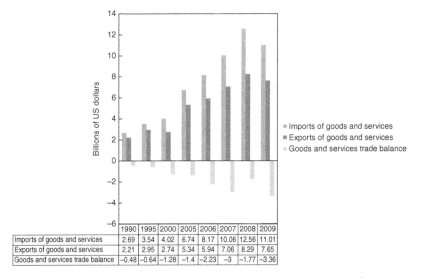

FIGURE 1.13 Imports, exports, and trade balance of goods and services, 1990–2009
Source: Author, based on data from World Bank (nd).

a trade balance deficit of US$1.76 billion (CBK, 2010), which was about one-half of what it was for all of 2009.

Kenya's aggregate composition of exports has remained basically the same over the years. In terms of broad economic categories, food and beverages lead the way accounting for a little more than two-fifths of total exports by 2009; followed by industrial supplies at 27 percent; consumer goods at 25 percent; and the remaining just more than 5 percent comprises fuels and lubricants, machinery and other capital equipment, and transport equipment (KNBS, 2010, 2011). Looked at by principal commodity reveals that Kenya's exports are highly concentrated in a few products. Tea, horticulture, coffee, and articles of apparel and clothing accessories are the leading exports, collectively accounting for a little more than one-half of the total exports (KNBS, 2010, 2011). This suggests that Kenya's product export base is not sufficiently diversified which, in turn, makes the country vulnerable to external shocks which can, and have had, the effect of reducing demand for imports (exports from Kenya as well as from elsewhere). The direction of trade data indicate that the top four destinations for the country's exports are Africa, the EU, Asia, and the Americas accounting for approximately 46, 24, 17, and 5 percent, respectively (KNBS, 2010, 2011). Exports to the Americas are primarily to the United States which gets 92 percent of Kenya's exports to that region. Kenya does benefit significantly from the African Growth and Opportunity Act (AGOA) of the United States in the export of apparels but the country's industry faces stiff competition from Asia.

The broad economic categories for imports show industrial supplies, fuel and lubricants, machinery and other equipment, transport equipment, food and beverages, and consumer goods in descending order of importance. They comprise 32, 22, 19, 12, 7, and 7 percent, respectively, of total imports (KNBS, 2010, 2011). By principal commodity, there are about 13 products that account for two-thirds of Kenya's total imports. The top five imports are industrial machinery (18%), petroleum products (13%), crude petroleum (8%), road motor vehicles (6%), and iron and steel (4%) (KNBS, 2010, 2011). Imports originate primarily from Asia (60%) with the UAE, India, China, and Japan the main exporters; the EU (18%) with the UK the lead exporter; Africa (12%) with South Africa the dominant exporter; and the Americas (6%) with the United States being the principal exporter. Although Kenya's trade preferences are primarily with the EU, the United States, and Africa, the bulk of the country's imports originate from Asia, specifically from the Middle and Far East. This, in all likelihood, reflects easier sourcing and much greater price competitiveness for goods and products from those subregions.

With respect to regional integration trade, two trading blocs—the EAC member states and COMESA—provide the largest market for Kenyan products with COMESA being the leading export destination. In 1997, Kenya's intra-EAC trade showed a positive balance of US$498 million with the value of exports exceeding the value of imports by more than 24-fold. By 2010, that trade balance was approximately US$1 billion with the value of exports exceeding the value of imports by more than seven-fold (EACS, 2010b; KNBS, 2010, 2011). Kenya dominates the EAC regional trade, accounting for more than 45 percent of the total value of trade by 2010. The country's major EAC export markets continue to be Uganda and Tanzania accounting for 51 and 33 percent, respectively, of its total EAC trade (KNBS, 2010, 2011). Intra-COMESA trade for Kenya had a positive balance of approximately the equivalent of US$1.24 billion in 2008 compared to a positive balance of US$499 million in 1997. The country's intra-COMESA imports were valued at one-fourth of the value of its intra-COMESA exports in 2008. As with intra-EAC trade, Kenya dominates the export market share for intra-COMESA trade with 24 percent in 2008 compared to an import market share of 5.6 percent. Its major non-EAC member intra-COMESA export destinations are currently Sudan, Egypt, and the Democratic Republic of Congo which account for a combined 73 percent of the country's non-EAC member intra-COMESA exports in 2010 (KNBS, 2011).

Kenya's external trade patterns suggest significant economic and trade liberalization, and particularly so given its membership in multiple and overlapping RECs. Trade liberalization can be defined as a removal or reduction in those trade practices that thwart the free flow of goods and services from one nation to another. It includes the dismantling of tariffs (such as duties, export subsidies, and surcharges), which raise the price of imports, and as well as nontariff barriers such as quotas (which place a physical limit on the quantity of goods that can be brought into a country), arbitrary standards, and licensing regulations and legislation (that make it very difficult for foreign competitors to sell goods in another country). One measure of the impact of trade liberalization in Kenya is the degree of openness of the economy. The index of openness is calculated as the sum of exports and imports of goods and services as a share of GDP. By 2009, Kenya's index of openness was 0.61. The country has, therefore, made significant progress in opening its economy to trade and particularly imports.

As noted by the World Bank (2006), Kenya is among the few developing countries that have experienced some shrinkage in its external sector over the past five decades. The country's exports as a share of GDP have declined from 40 percent in 1960 to 25 percent in 2009 primarily due to some stagnation in its traditional agricultural exports, mainly tea and coffee, as a result of weak governance in marketing institutions (World Bank, 2010b). However, Kenya also developed its horticulture products and exports (flowers, vegetables) and there has been an increase in its service exports such as tourism and BPO as previously discussed. Nonetheless, these emerging growth areas were not sufficient to offset the downward trend in exports as a percent of GDP (World Bank, 2010b). Consequently, with the rapid increase in imports to support its domestic economy, the country's trade deficit has been widening in the past few years. This state of affairs has led the World Bank (2010b) to conclude that the drivers of Kenya's economy are not in balance which, in turn, may preclude the country from achieving high growth over an extended period of time as it is running on one engine. Kenya's strong engine runs on domestic consumption, which accounts for 75 percent of GDP, and its weak engine remains its exports that have been declining significantly in relative importance (World Bank, 2010b).

Despite Kenya's negative trade balances, coupled with current account deficits, during the period 2000–09 and the first half of 2010, its overall balance of payments was only negative in 2005 and 2008. This is so due to the fact that the current account deficit is being financed by increasing capital flows, which reached a record 9.5 percent of GDP by 2009 and resulted in an overall balance of payments (including grants) surplus of approximately US$966 million compared to a deficit of US$479 million in 2008 (KNBS, 2010). In the first half of 2010, the balance of payments surplus was US$665 million (CBK, 2010). The total capital and financial account improved from a surplus of US$1.2 billion in 2008 to a surplus of US$2.8 billion (more than double) in 2009 and US$2.4 billion in the first half of 2010 as a result of relatively improved inflows of capital to the private sector and government. The latter benefited from additional allocations of special drawing rights (SDRs) from the IMF to mitigate the adverse effects of the global recession (CBK, 2010; KNBS, 2010). These inflows drive investments in the construction and services sector and have helped to keep the exchange rate relatively stable (World Bank, 2010b). The surplus in the balance of payments also indicates improvement in Kenya's accumulation of international reserves. The country's official foreign exchange reserves have increased from approximately US$1.7 billion in 2005 to approximately US$3.3 billion in 2009 and approximately US$3.8 billion by June 2010 (CBK, 2010; KNBS, 2010), covering about 4 months of imports of goods and services.

One major element of capital flows into Kenya is international remittances which have become Kenya's largest source of foreign exchange as well as a key social safety net. According to the CBK, international remittances were estimated to be US$609 million by 2009 with the source markets maintaining the same share on average with North America contributing 53 percent and Europe contributing 27 percent of the total (CBK, nd), and representing an increase of about 80 percent between 2004 and 2009. However, a more recent survey report, compiled by Bendixen and Amandi International, under commission from the World Bank, indicates that Kenyan remittances were at least US$1.9 billion in 2009 (World Bank, 2010c), triple the amount previously estimated by the CBK and equivalent to about 5 percent of the country's GDP. The CBK's estimates are based on information collected from formal channels only that include commercial banks and other permitted international remittances service providers in Kenya (CBK, nd). This significantly underestimates these flows since, according to World Bank (2010c), informal channels also contribute between 5 and 14 percent of the means used to remit money to loved ones, relatives, and others in Kenya.

Moreover, the CBK estimates were also considerably lower than other estimates previously compiled by the World Bank as well and available from the latter's "Migration and Remittances Data" website. In fact, a recent World Bank publication confirms that remittance flows to Kenya averaged US$1.7 billion during 2009–10 (Ratha et al., 2011). Other interesting findings of the World Bank (2010c) survey are: (1) 59 percent of remittance recipients are male and 41 percent are, therefore, female; (2) 14 percent of Kenyan adults regularly receive remittances on an average of 7 times per year, 66 percent receive them 4–12 times per year, 23 percent 2–3 times per year, and 11 percent 24 times per year; (3) the average remittance each time is US$105; (4) 69 percent of the recipients use about one-half to all of their money on daily expenses such as food, clothing, utilities, and medicine while 35 percent also use part of those remittances to invest in small business; (5) 15 percent are dissatisfied with the services of their bank or remittance company.

Remittances to Kenya, and other developing countries as well—given their magnitude, being in foreign currency, and going directly to households—can, therefore, have a significant impact on poverty reduction, funding for housing and education, basic essential needs, and even business investments. It's a critical lifeline for families particularly with respect to poverty reduction. Remittances directly affect poverty by increasing income (purchasing power) of the recipients. They also impact national poverty through their effects on growth, inflation, exchange rates, and access to capital. There is now also a growing body of empirical evidence that shows that remittances, in fact, do reduce poverty. In Kenya's case, based on poverty headcount rates for 1997, it was determined that when remittances are removed, the poverty headcount rate increases by at least 2 percent (World Bank, 2006).

Public Finance

A good fiscal outcome can be a major influence on economic performance. In that regard, the pursuit of rapid, sustainable, and shared growth requires effective and strategic public financial management (Hope, 2008; KIPPRA, 2009). The fiscal performance of Kenya, as it is elsewhere, is integrally related to the economy of the country. Since 2001, Kenya's fiscal performance, on the revenue side, has been steadily improving. Total revenue (including grants) increased from the approximate equivalent of US$2.8 billion in 2000–01 to the approximate equivalent of US$7.2 billion in 2008–09 (IMF, 2009b; KNBS, 2010). This improved performance was due primarily to reforms in revenue administration, including automation and the introduction of electronic tax registers (KIPPRA, 2009). In terms of fiscal ratios, total revenue and grants as a proportion of GDP have moved unevenly from 25.8 percent in 2000–01 to 26.2 percent in 2008–09 (IMF, 2009b; Republic of Kenya, 2010c). This represents one of the highest revenue mobilizations in sub-Saharan Africa. In the first quarter of the FY 2010–11 (July–September), total revenue, including grants, was the approximate equivalent of US$1.7 billion, which was roughly the same equivalent amount for the corresponding period in FY 2009–10, but representing 4.9 percent of GDP compared to 5.4 percent of GDP for FY 2009–10 (Republic of Kenya, 2010g).

Tax revenue, not surprisingly, is the major source of central government revenue in Kenya. Tax revenues are still of major importance in the development process as well as an important fiscal tool. This is so primarily because the nature and rate of taxation are internally controlled and, as such, not subject to developments in the international money markets, for example, which are difficult to foresee. Taxation, therefore, remains the major fiscal tool on the revenue side. It is that fact that rationally dictates that borrowing should only occur when government expenditures exceed revenues and tax revenue cannot be beneficially increased. Moreover, both lessons of experience and the empirical evidence show that true development is only sustainable when it is dependent on a nation's own resources. As also observed by Waris et al. (2009: 10), "while aid might, in the short term, contribute to solving some of the challenges facing Kenya, the country will only join the league of developed nations if it manages to free itself from dependence on external resources."

Tax revenue in Kenya increased from the approximate equivalent of US$2.2 billion in 2000–01 to the approximate equivalent of US$6.2 billion in 2008–09 representing an increase from approximately 79 percent of total revenue in 2000–01 to approximately 86 percent in 2008–09 (IMF, 2009b; KNBS, 2010). As a proportion of GDP, tax revenue increased from approximately 20 percent in 2000–01 to approximately 23.3 percent in 2008–09 (IMF, 2009b; Republic of Kenya, 2010c). The principal components of tax revenue in Kenya are the indirect taxes (on goods and services and trade) which comprised approximately 67 percent of the total tax revenue in 2000–01 and approximately 60 percent in 2008–09. As a proportion of GDP, the indirect taxes were 13 percent in 2000–01 and 13.8 percent in 2008–09. Direct taxes (on income and profits) were, therefore, 33 percent of total tax revenue in

2000–01 and 40 percent in 2008–09, while as a proportion of GDP they were 7 percent and 9.3 percent in 2000–01 and 2008–09, respectively (IMF, 2009b; KNBS, 2010; Republic of Kenya, 2010c).

On the other side of the public finance equation, we find central government total expenditure and net lending increasing from the approximate equivalent of US$3 billion in 2000–01 to the approximate equivalent of US$9.1 billion in 2008–09. As a proportion of GDP, total expenditure and net lending was 27.8 percent in 2000–01 and 31.4 percent in 2008–09. As one would expect, recurrent expenditure grabs the largest share of total expenditure at 85.4 percent in 2000–01 and 23 percent in 2008–09 as the government has been attempting to increase its outlays on development projects. In relationship to GDP, recurrent expenditure was 23.7 percent in 2000–01 and 23 percent in 2008–09 (IMF, 2009b; KNBS, 2010; Republic of Kenya, 2010c). In the first quarter of FY 2010–11 total expenditure and net lending amounted to approximately US$1.9 billion, roughly equivalent to the same amount for the corresponding period in FY 2009–10 (Republic of Kenya, 2010g). As can be gleaned from the foregoing, the relationship between government expenditure and net lending, on the one hand, and revenue and grants on the other hand, point to negative overall balances (fiscal deficits). In 2001–02 this deficit was equivalent to 1.9 percent of GDP and in 2008–09 it was 8.5 percent of GDP (IMF, 2009b; KNBS, 2010; Republic of Kenya, 2010c). In the first quarter of FY 2010–11 the overall fiscal deficit was equivalent to 0.8 percent of GDP compared to 2.2 percent of GDP for the same period in FY 2009–10 (Republic of Kenya, 2010g).

Deficits lead to borrowing to meet the difference (shortfalls in revenue or excessive spending depending on one's point of view). Kenya's total public debt increased from the approximate equivalent of US$7.2 billion in 2002 to the approximate equivalent of US$15 billion in 2009 and moving downward from 54 percent of GDP in 2002 to 44 percent of GDP in 2009 (IMF, 2009b; KNBS, 2010; Republic of Kenya, 2010c, 2010f). With public debt as the fiscal policy anchor, the country's fiscal policy has targeted low and falling domestic public debt in proportion to GDP. During the recent past, the net debt stock in proportion to GDP has been reduced as a result of privatization receipts, some bilateral debt relief, and some growth in GDP. In particular,

> since the fiscal situation was close to balanced from 2003-04 to 2006-07, the government used the fiscal space to pay-down principal debt payments, and used available privatization receipts to lower the debt stock. So while the fiscal performance has resulted in a widening fiscal deficit, so far, there has been the room to accommodate this by raising the public debt to GDP ratio within debt sustainability parameters. (Republic of Kenya, 2010c: 22–3)

By June 2010, the total debt to GDP percent had climbed slightly to 48 percent (CBK, 2010).

This prudent debt management by the government has allowed for fiscal retrenchment, as it were, over the last decade. The debt retirement policy, as part of a broader debt management strategy, has resulted in a reduction in total debt, as a share of GDP, from 60 percent in 2000 to 44 percent by 2009 before climbing to 48 percent by June 2010 and a consequent decline in debt service payments thereby creating space for funding core priorities (CBK, 2010; Republic of Kenya, 2010c). Also to be noted here, is the changing composition of total debt and domestic debt. There has been a significant increase in the proportion of domestic debt over the years reflecting the desire of the government to reduce its reliance on external sources. By 2009, the distribution of total debt had reached a 51 to 49 percent share of domestic to external debt, respectively, and by June 2010 the corresponding composition was 54 percent domestic and 46 percent external (CBK, 2010; Republic of Kenya, 2010f). The composition of domestic debt has also been changed from short maturity to longer-term profile with domestic (treasury/sovereign) bonds now constituting more than 70 percent of total domestic debt. This prudent management of Kenya's public debt is being carried forward also in the country's publicly available Medium Term Debt Management Strategy which provides a systematic approach for decision-making on the appropriate composition of external and domestic borrowing to finance the budget, taking into account both cost and risk (Republic of Kenya, 2009b).

Savings and Investment

Increasing rates of savings and investment contribute to increasing rates of economic growth. Countries with positive per capita real growth are characterized by positive government savings, increases in government investment, and strong increases in private savings and investment. On the other hand, countries with negative per capita real growth tend to be characterized by declines in savings and investment. For Africa, it has also been determined that those countries that improved their macroeconomic policies achieved higher rates of growth, domestic savings, and private investment (Hope, 1996, 1997).

Savings

In the literature on savings, the accumulation of savings is usually identified as one of the most important prerequisites for economic development and savings mobilization has become a peripatetic recommendation for development strategies. This is particularly so for those developing countries, such as Kenya, where domestic borrowing is financing an increasing share of public sector expenditures. A macroeconomic approach is usually used to indicate the magnitude of domestic savings needed to complement whatever sources of funds may be available. The rate of savings has, therefore, been historically regarded as a key performance indicator in the development process, and developing countries have always been encouraged to increase their savings ratio as a necessary step for achieving economic growth. Increases in the savings ratio were, naturally, expected to lead to a reduction in dependence on foreign financing by these developing countries. Domestic savings can be divided into (1) public sector savings (government savings plus retained profits of public enterprises); and (2) private sector savings (savings by households and businesses). The magnitude of savings in each category is directly affected by government policies.

For the Kenyan authorities, one of the primary objectives of fiscal policy is to see to it that the country does not become overly dependent on foreign financing for its future development (Republic of Kenya, 2007). Consequently, it is imperative to ensure that the bulk of the investment effort is domestically funded and the country has been moving in that direction as previously discussed. To fund its development expenditures and investment programs, the government had estimated that it needed to increase gross national savings from its 15.6 percent of GDP in 2006–07 to approximately 26 percent by 2012–13 and to 29 percent of GDP by 2030 (Republic of Kenya, 2007). Public savings was expected to rise from 1.6 percent of GDP in 2006–07 to approximately 3 percent by 2012–13 and to 3.8 percent of GDP by 2030 (Republic of Kenya, 2007). This means that the bulk of the

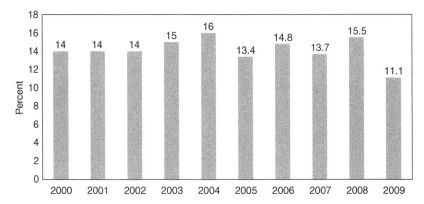

FIGURE 1.14 Gross national savings, 2000–09 (% of GDP)
Source: Author, based on data from KNBS (2010) and World Bank (nd).

increased savings will be coming from the private sector. In that regard, private savings have been targeted to rise from 14 percent of GDP in 2007–08 to 23 percent in 2012–13 and to 25.5 percent of GDP in 2030 (Republic of Kenya, 2007). However, as seen in Figure 1.14, these targets for gross savings were not even close to being achieved. Consequently, greater policy efforts need to be made to encourage national savings.

Based on lessons of experience, as well as the empirical evidence, some broad observations can be made with respect to national savings in the development process that can be useful to the Kenyan authorities. One general conclusion that emerges is that aggregate savings is a function of a number of interdependent variables that, together with savings propensities, determine the course of economic development. Second, the national savings rate is positively related to the level of income and its growth rate. Finally, the mobilization of savings is an important role of government in the process of development and increasing domestic savings through all available means that do not hamper productive activity must continue to be vigorously pursued. Despite the emphasis on private savings over public savings in Kenya, public savings have a dual role to play. On the one hand, they constitute a convenient source of finance for public investment, and on the other hand, they may serve to raise the rate of savings in the economy.

Investment

To achieve the *Kenya Vision 2030* growth objectives, the government has targeted an increase in the level of investment to 32.6 percent of GDP by 2012–13, which is by approximately 10 percentage points, and then remain above 32 percent for the 2014–30 period (Republic of Kenya, 2007, 2008). However, by 2007–08, the investment/GDP ratio was estimated at 19.4 percent compared to a target of 22.9 percent for that period (Republic of Kenya, 2010a). Foreign direct investment (FDI), in particular, has underperformed. Kenya has dramatically been unable to attract major and sustained flows of FDI over at least the past two decades. This is a consequence of a number of factors that include increasing corruption, deteriorating infrastructure, and insecurity, rather than of formal restrictions on FDI entry (UNCTAD, 2005). As shown in Figure 1.15, FDI net inflows declined from US$79 million in 1980 to US$57 million in 1990 and to US$42 million in 1995, then rebounded to US$111 million in 2000, declined to US$21 million in 2005, increased significantly to US$729 million in 2007, declined to US$96 million in 2008 due mostly to the postelection violence, and climbed back up to US$ 141 million in 2009 (UNCTAD, 2005, 2010; World Bank, nd).

FDI net inflows are the inflows of investment to acquire a lasting management interest (10% or more of voting stock) in an enterprise operating in

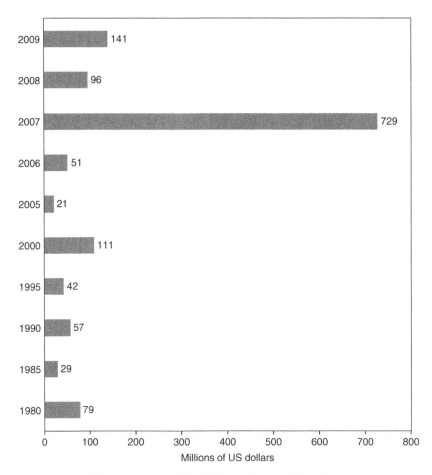

FIGURE 1.15 FDI net inflows, 1980–2009 (millions of US dollars)
Source: Author, based on data from World Bank (nd) and UNCTAD (2010).

an economy other than that of the investor. It is the sum of equity capital, reinvestment of earnings, other long-term capital, and short-term capital. It is, therefore, new investment inflows from foreign investors less divestment (World Bank, nd). In 2009, Kenya's share of FDI inflows to all of Africa was 0.24 percent and for East Africa it was 4.8 percent (UNCTAD, 2010). As a proportion of GDP, Kenya's FDI inflows declined from 2.6 percent in 2007 to 0.5 percent in 2009. As a percentage of gross fixed capital formation the decline was from 14 percent in 2007 to 0.5 percent in 2009 (UNCTAD, 2010).

Despite the poor performance of FDI in the past two decades, Kenya still remains a natural destination for investment flows into the region. The country possesses regional advantages such as its air transportation network and the quality of its workforce. One avenue that Kenya can vigorously pursue in the quest to attract higher levels of FDI flows is that of investment from developing and transition economies. Investors from these economies have been found to be less apprehensive about the deterioration of locational factors in Africa than investors in developed countries (UNIDO, 2007). Moreover, these new sources of FDI can provide a buffer against the impacts of global crises by offering more resilient flows and a broader base of financial resources (UNCTAD, 2010). Among the key investment sources in this regard is China. Chinese FDI stock in Africa had reached US$7.8 billion by 2008 but accounting for only 4 percent of China's total outward FDI stock (UNCTAD, 2010). Based on the available data, Kenya's share of China's outward FDI stock in Africa was pegged at 4 percent in 2005 (Kaplinsky and Morris, 2009). However, looking at other evidence, this is surely underestimated. In particular, Kenya should vigorously attempt to position itself to benefit from the China-Africa Development Fund which is an equity investment fund of China that focuses on investments in Africa.

Conclusions

Kenya's economic performance and socioeconomic trends over the past several decades have been influenced by a number of factors that include political instability, poor governance, corruption, inadequate infrastructure, insecurity, bad policy choices, unfavorable weather patterns, low investor confidence, and external shocks such as rising energy prices and global financial crises. Nonetheless, Kenya remains the most resilient and important economy in Eastern Africa. It is still the most industrialized country in East Africa and a country with tremendous economic potential and development promise. Within the EAC, Kenya has the strongest economy contributing 40 percent to the EAC's total GDP (World Bank, 2010d). It is a country, whose recent development policies have also been lauded by its development partners. It has a well-educated workforce but poverty rates, although declining, are still too high.

Nonetheless, Kenya is on the move again but, to be sure, there are still many obstacles in the way as this book shows. Maintaining a steady course forward will therefore meet with some challenges but there are many frameworks in place to counteract them. Principal among these are the *Kenya Vision 2030* and its accompanying medium-term plans, the first of the latter being the *MTP 2008-2012*. As noted by Njuguna Ndung'u (Governor of the CBK) (2010), the five common characteristics of sustained growth—good leadership and governance; openness, imports of knowledge and exports to the world markets; market allocation; macro stability, including sustainable finances; and future orientation of the government to long-term development—are achievable under the new constitutional dispensation and the *Kenya Vision 2030*. Trade, savings, and investment loom large in Kenya's growth and development strategy which, in turn, will have a major influence on the improvement of the country's socioeconomic indicators such as productive employment and inequality. These three factors of trade, savings, and investment will need to demonstrate better performance not only to meet the objectives of the *Kenya Vision 2030* but also for sustainable development beyond that. Among other policy initiatives are: (1) for trade, full advantage must be taken of all preferential trade arrangements and new markets sought for expanding and diversifying exports; (2) for savings, more attractive savings products are needed with higher (real) interest rates to induce private financial savings; and (3) for investment, public-private-partnerships (PPPs) must be pursued and promoted particularly with respect to infrastructure development as discussed in Chapter 7.

As also previously mentioned, some of Kenya's recent economic policies and strategies have been lauded by its development partners. Among these policies is the country's approach to reduce its reliance on external borrowing through prudent debt management and fiscal policy, for example. This is further laudable, from this author's point of view, because dependence on external sources of finance is not sustainable. Such dependence leads to exposure and vulnerability to global shocks, among other things, as we have seen in the past. For Kenya, and the rest of Africa for that matter, trade, savings, and investment are the engines of growth and development.

References

AfDB (African Development Bank), OECD (Organization for Economic Cooperation and Development), and UNECA (United Nations Economic Commission for Africa) (2008), *African Economic Outlook 2008*. Paris: AfDB/OECD.

— (2010), *African Economic Outlook 2010*. Paris: AfDB/OECD.

Agrawal, M. (2010a), "M-Pesa Transforming Millions of Lives." Available at: http://www.telecomcircle.com/2010/01/m-pesa/ [Accessed October 12, 2010].

— (2010b), "Socio-Economic Benefits of Mobile Money Transfer." Available at: http://www.telecomcircle.com/2010/01/benefits-of-mobile-money-transfer/ [Accessed October 12, 2010].

Alkire, S. and Santos, M. E. (2010), "Acute Multidimensional Poverty: A New Index for Developing Countries", *OPHI Working Paper No. 38*. Available at: http://www.ophi.org.uk/wp-content/uploads/ophi-wp38.pdf [Accessed November 2, 2010].

Arthur D Little (2010), "Case Study on M-Pesa, Kenya." Available at: http://www.aicto.org/fileadmin/medias/Seminars/M_payment/presentations/MP_AICTO_Mr_Morsi_Berguiga.pdf [Accessed October 12, 2010].

Atieno, R. (2009), "Government Policy and Female Labor Market Participation in Kenya: Implications for Poverty Reduction." Paper Submitted to the Annual IAFFE (International Association for Feminist Economics) Conference, Boston, June 26–28, Available at: https://editorialexpress.com/cgibin/conference/download.cgi?db_name=IAFFE2009&paper_id=35 [Accessed October 12, 2010].

CBK (Central Bank of Kenya) (nd), "Remittances from Diaspora." Available at: http://www.centralbank.go.ke/forex/Diaspora_Remit.aspx [Accessed November 5, 2010].

— (2010), *Monthly Economic Review: August 2010*. Nairobi: CBK.

CIA (Central Intelligence Agency) (2010), "Kenya," *World Fact Book*. Available at: https://www.cia.gov/library/publications/the-world-factbook/geos/ke.html [Accessed October 12, 2010].

EACS (East African Community Secretariat) (2010a), *Trade Report 2008*. Arusha: EACS.

— (2010b), *East African Community Facts and Figures—2009*. Arusha: EACS.

Ellis, A., Cutura, J., Dione, N., Gilson, I., Manuel, C., and Thongori, J. (2007), *Gender and Economic Growth in Kenya: Unleashing the Power of Women*. Washington, DC: World Bank.

FinAccess Secretariat (2009), *FinAcess National Survey 2009: Dynamics of Kenya's Changing Financial Landscape*. Nairobi: FSD Kenya and Central Bank of Kenya.

FSD Kenya (Financial Sector Deepening Trust of Kenya) (nd), "Who we Are." Available at: http://www.fsdkenya.org [Accessed September 25, 2010].

Gachino, G. (2009), "Industrial Policy, Institutions and Foreign Direct Investment: The Kenyan Context," *African Journal of Marketing and Management*, 1(6), 140–60.

Honey, M. and Gilpin, R. (2009), "Tourism in the Developing World: Promoting Peace and Reducing Poverty," *Special Report 233*. Washington, DC: United States Institute of Peace.

Hope, K. R. (1996), *Development in the Third World: From Policy Failure to Policy Reform*. Armonk, NY: M.E. Sharpe.

— (ed.) (1997a), *Structural Adjustment, Reconstruction and Development in Africa*. Aldershot: Ashgate Publishers.

— (1997b), "Growth, Savings and Investment in Botswana," *Savings and Development*, 21(2), 195–210.

— (2001), "Africa's HIV/AIDS Crisis in a Development Context," *International Relations*, 15(6), 15–36.

— (2004a), "The Poverty Dilemma in Africa: Toward Policies for Including the Poor," *Progress in Development Studies*, 4(2), 127–44.

— (2004b), "Economic Performance, Trade, and the Exchange Rate in Ethiopia, 1990-2002," *African and Asian Studies*, 3(1), 61–76.

— (2008), *Poverty, Livelihoods, and Governance in Africa: Fulfilling the Development Promise*. New York: Palgrave Macmillan.

Hughes, N. and Lonie, S. (2007), "M-Pesa: Mobile Money for the 'Unbanked': Turning Cellphones into 24-Hour Tellers in Kenya," *Innovations* (Winter & Spring). Available at: http://www.policyinnovations.org/ideas/policy_library/data/m_pesa/_res/id=sa_File1/INNOV0201_pp-63-81_hughes-lonie_1.pdf [Accessed October 12, 2010].

IEA (Institute of Economic Affairs)—Kenya (2008), *Profile of Women's Socio-Economic Status in Kenya.* Nairobi: IEA-Kenya.

— (2010), *The Dynamics and Trends of Employment in Kenya.* Nairobi: IEA-Kenya.

ILO (International Labor Organization) (nda), "Economically Active Population." Available at: http://laborsta.ilo.org/STP/guest [Accessed October 10, 2010].

— (ndb), "Paid Employment by Economic Activity." Available at: http://laborsta.ilo.org/STP/guest [Accessed October 10, 2010].

— (1982), "Resolution Concerning Statistics of the Economically Active Population, Employment, Unemployment, and Underemployment, Adopted by the Thirteenth International Conference of Labor Statisticians (October 1982)." Available at: http://www.ilo.org/public/english/bureau/stat/download/res/ecacpop.pdf [Accessed October 13, 2010].

— (2010), *Global Employment Trends.* Geneva: ILO.

IMF (International Monetary Fund) (2009a), *The Poverty Reduction and Growth Facility (PRGF).* Washington, DC: IMF.

— (2009b), *Kenya: Selected Issues and Statistical Appendix.* Washington, DC: IMF.

— (2010), *Regional Economic Outlook: Sub-Saharan Africa: Resilience and Risks.* Washington, DC: IMF.

JICA (Japan International Cooperation Agency) and Republic of Kenya (2008), *The Master Plan Study for Kenyan Industrial Development (MAPSKID) in the Republic of Kenya: Final Report.* Available at: http://www.industrialization.go.ke/index.php?option=com_rokdownloads&view=folder&Itemid=83 [Accessed September 8, 2010].

Kabubo-Mariara, J. (2003), "Wage Determination and the Gender Wage Gap in Kenya: Any Evidence of Gender Discrimination?" *AERC Research Paper 132.* Nairobi: African Economic Research Consortium.

Kabubo-Mariara, J. and Kiriti, T. W. (2002), "Structural Adjustment, Poverty and Economic Growth: An Analysis for Kenya," *AERC Research Paper 124.* Nairobi: African Economic Research Consortium.

Kaplinsky, R. and Morris, M. (2009), "Chinese FDI in Sub-Saharan Africa: Engaging with Large Dragons," *European Journal of Development Research*, 21(4), 551–69.

KIPPRA (The Kenyan Institute for Public Policy Research and Analysis) (2009), *Kenya Economic Report 2009: Building a Globally Competitive Economy.* Nairobi: KIPPRA.

KNBS (Kenya National Bureau of Statistics) (nda), "Inflation Trends 1961-2007"; and "Monthly Inflation Rates for 2004-2009." Available at: http://www.knbs.or.ke [Accessed September 2, 2010].

— (ndb), "Total Recorded Employment: June, 2003-2007." Available at: http://www.knbs.or.ke [Accessed October 12, 2010].

— (ndc), "Labour Force 1998/9 Summary." Available at: http://www.knbs.or.ke [Accessed October 12, 2010].

— (2007), *Basic Report on Well-Being in Kenya*. Nairobi: KNBS.

— (2008), *Labour Force Analytical Report*. Nairobi: KNBS.

— (2010), *Economic Survey 2010*. Nairobi: KNBS.

— (2011), *Economic Survey 2011*. Nairobi: KNBS.

Lime, A. (2010), "Upgrade to Shut M-Pesa for Weekend," *Daily Nation*, November 11, 1–2.

Lipton, M., and van der Gaag, J. (1993), "Poverty: A Research and Policy Framework." In M. Lipton and J. van der Gaag (eds), *Including the Poor*. Washington, DC: World Bank, pp. 1-40.

Mas, I. and Radcliffe, D. (2010), "Mobile Payments go Viral: M-Pesa in Kenya," *Working Paper No. 54338*. Available at: http://www.wds.worldbank.org/external/default/WDSContentServer/WDSP/IB/2010/05/03/000334955_20100 503043912/Rendered/PDF/543380WP0M1PES1BOX0349405B01PUBLIC1. pdf [Accessed October 12, 2010].

Mbogo, M. (2010), "The Impact of Mobile Payments on the Success and Growth of Micro-Business: The Case of M-Pesa in Kenya," *The Journal of Language, Technology & Entrepreneurship in Africa*, 2(1), 182–203.

McKinsey and Company (2009), *Seizing the Power—Driving BPO Sector Growth in Kenya*. Nairobi: Kenya ICT Board. Available at: http://www.doitinkenya.com/images/docs/Seizing.pdf [Accessed September 21, 2010].

Mishra, V., Bignami-Van Assche, S., Greener, R., Vaessen, M., Hong, R., Ghys, P. D., Boerma, J. T., Van Assche, A., Khan, S., and Rutstein, S. (2007), "HIV Infection does not Disproportionately Affect the Poorer in sub-Saharan Africa," *AIDS*, 21(Supp. 7), S17–S28.

Morawczynski, O. (2007), "Innovations in Mobile Banking: The Case of M-Pesa." Paper Presented at the First National Consultative Forum on Microfinance, November 12–14, Khartoum. Available at: http://www.mfu-cbos.gov.sd/html/res/File/Olga%20Morawczynski-M-PESA-Final.pdf [Accessed October 9, 2010].

Mwangi, H. (2008), "Strategies of Deepening and Broadening Client Base." Nairobi: Agricultural Finance Corporation.

NACC (National AIDS Control Council) (2010), *UNGASS 2010: United Nations General Assembly Special Session on HIV and AIDS: Country Report—Kenya*. Nairobi: NACC, Office of the President.

Naiman, R. and Watkins, N. (1999), *A Survey of the Impacts of IMF Structural Adjustment in Africa: Growth, Social Spending and Debt Relief*. Washington, DC: Centre for Economic Policy Research.

Ndung'u, N. (2010), "Kenya's Development Paradigm and Cooperation with Emerging Economies." Presentation to UNCTAD on: South-South Cooperation and the New Forms of Development Partnerships, Geneva, September17. Available at: .http://www.centralbank.go.ke/downloads/Presentations/UNCTAD-%20 SEPT%202010%20-final%203.ppt [Accessed November 19, 2010].

Odhiambo, W. (2004), *Pulling Apart: Facts and Figures on Inequality in Kenya*. Nairobi: Society for International Development.

OPHI (Oxford Poverty and Human Development Initiative) (2010a), "Multidimensional Poverty Index." Available at: http://www.ophi.org.uk/wp-content/uploads/MPI-One-Page-final.pdf [Accessed November 3, 2010].

— (2010b), "Country Briefing: Kenya: Multidimensional Poverty Index at a Glance." Available at: http://www.ophi.org.uk/wp-content/uploads/Kenya. pdf [Accessed November 3, 2010].

PriceWaterhouseCoopers (2010), *Crossroads of Change: Budget 2010/2011: Kenya Budget Review*. Available at: http://www.pwc.com/en_KE/ke/pdf/kenya-budget-bulletin.pdf [Accessed August 2, 2010].

Ratha, D., Mohapatra, S., Özden, C., Plaza, S., Shaw, W., and Shimeles, A. (2011), *Leveraging Migration for Africa: Remittances, Skills, and Investments*. Washington, DC: World Bank.

Republic of Kenya (1996), *Sessional Paper No. 2 of 1996 on Industrial Transformation to the Year 2020*. Nairobi: Republic of Kenya.

— (1998), *First Report on Poverty in Kenya: Volume II: Poverty and Social Indicators*. Nairobi: Ministry of Planning and National Development.

— (2000a), *Sessional Paper No.1 of 2000 on National Population Policy for Sustainable Development*. Nairobi: National Council for Population and Development, Ministry of Finance and Planning.

— (2000b), *Second Report on Poverty in Kenya: Volume I: Incidence and Depth of Poverty*. Nairobi: Ministry of Finance and Planning.

— (2003), *Kenya: Economic Recovery Strategy for Wealth and Employment Creation 2003-2007*. Nairobi: Ministry of Planning and National Development.

— (2006), *Private Sector Development Strategy 2006-2010*. Nairobi: Ministry of Trade and Industry.

— (2007), *Kenya Vision 2030: A Globally Competitive and Prosperous Kenya*. Nairobi: Republic of Kenya.

— (2008), *Kenya Vision 2030: First Medium Term Plan (2008-2012)*. Nairobi: Republic of Kenya.

— (2009a), *Quarterly Economic and Budgetary Review: Third Quarter 2008/2009*. Nairobi: Office of the Deputy Prime Minister and Ministry of Finance.

— (2009b), *Medium Term Debt Management Strategy: 2009/10—2011/12*. Nairobi: Office of the Deputy Prime Minister and Ministry of Finance.

— (2010a), *First Annual Progress Report on the Implementation of the First Medium Term Plan (2008-2012) of Kenya Vision 2030*. Nairobi: Republic of Kenya.

— (2010b), *Budget Speech for the Fiscal Year 2010/2011*. Nairobi: Republic of Kenya.

— (2010c), *Public Expenditure Review: Policy for Prosperity 2010*. Nairobi: Ministry of State for Planning, National Development and Vision 2030.

— (2010d), *The 2009 Kenya Population and Housing Census: Volume 1A: Population Distribution by Administrative Units*. Nairobi: Kenya National Bureau of Statistics.

— (2010e), *Kenya: 2009 Population and Housing Census Highlights*. Nairobi: Kenya National Bureau of Statistics.

— (2010f), *Quarterly Economic and Budgetary Review: Third Quarter 2009/2010*. Nairobi: Office of the Deputy Prime Minister and Ministry of Finance.

— (2010g), *Quarterly Economic and Budgetary Review: First Quarter 2010/2011*. Nairobi: Office of the Deputy Prime Minister and Ministry of Finance.

Ronge, E. E. and Nyangito, H. O. (2000), "A Review of Kenya's Current Industrialization Policy," *KIPPRA Discussion Paper No. 3*. Nairobi: KIPPRA.

Rono, J. K. (2002), "The Impact of Structural Adjustment Programmes on Kenyan Society," *Journal of Social Development in Africa*, 17(1), 81–98.

Safaricom (2011), "M-Pesa Key Performance Statistics." Available at: http://www. safaricom.co.ke/index.php?id=1073 [Accessed March 22, 2011].

Swamy, G. (1994), "Kenya: Structural Adjustment in the 1980s," *Policy Research Working Paper 1238*. Washington, DC: World Bank.

UNAIDS (Joint United Nations Programme on HIV/AIDS) (2008), *2008 Report on the Global AIDS Epidemic*. Geneva: UNAIDS.

— (2010), *Global Report: UNAIDS Report on the Global AIDS Epidemic2010*. Geneva: UNAIDS.

UNCTAD (United Nations Conference on Trade and Development) (2005), *Investment Policy Review: Kenya*. Geneva: United Nations.

— (2010), *World Investment Report 2010*. Geneva: United Nations.

UNDP (United Nations Development Programme) (nd), "Human Development Reports." Available at: http://hdr.undp.org/en/reports/ [Accessed October 20, 2010].

— (2010), *Human Development Report 2010: The Real Wealth of Nations: Pathways to Human Development*. New York: Palgrave Macmillan.

UNECA (United Nations Economic Commission for Africa) (2006), *Assessing Regional Integration in Africa II: Rationalizing Regional Economic Communities*. Addis Ababa: UNECA.

— (2010), *Assessing Regional Integration in Africa IV: Enhancing Intra-African Trade*. Addis Ababa: UNECA.

UN-HABITAT (United Nations Human Settlements Programme) (2011), *Infrastructure for Economic Development and Poverty Reduction in Africa*. Nairobi: UN-HABITAT.

UNIDO (United Nations Industrial Development Organization) (2007), *Africa Foreign Investor Survey 2005*. Vienna: UNIDO.

US Department of State (2010), "Background Note: Kenya." Available at: http:// www.state.gov/r/pa/ei/bgn/2962.htm [Accessed August 25, 2010].

Wambugu, A., Munga, B., and Onsomu, E. (2009), *Unemployment in Kenya: The Situational Analysis*. Nairobi: KIPPRA.

— (2010), *Growth, Poverty and Income Inequality in Kenya: Suggested Policy Options*. Nairobi: National Economic and Social Council, Office of the President.

Wanjala, B. M. and Were, M. (2009), "Gender Disparities and Economic Growth in Kenya: A Social Accounting Matrix Approach," *Feminist Economics*, 15(3), 227–51.

Waris, A., Kohonen, M., Ranguma, J., and Mosioma, A. (2009), "Taxation and State Building in Kenya: Enhancing Revenue Capacity to Advance Human Welfare." Available at: http://www.taxjustice.net/cms/upload/pdf/ Kenya_1004_TJN_Spreads.pdf [Accessed October 10, 2010].

Wikipedia (2010), "Economy of Kenya." Available at: http://en.wikipedia.org/ wiki/Economy_of_Kenya [Accessed August 2, 2010].

World Bank (nd), "World Development Indicators Database." Available at: http://search.worldbank.org/data?qterm=KENYA&language=EN&format=h tml&_databaseexact=WDI [Accessed August 25, 2010].

— (2010a), "Poverty Headcount Rates Based on an International Poverty Line." Available at: http://web.worldbank.org/WBSITE/EXTERNAL/TOPICS/EX TPOVERTY/0,,contentMDK:22567983~pagePK:210058~piPK:210062~theSit ePK:336992,00.html [Accessed October 19, 2010].

— (2010b), *Kenya Economic Update: Running on One Engine: Kenya's Uneven Economic Performance with a Special Focus on the Port of Mombasa*. Nairobi: World Bank.

— (2010c), "Remittances to Kenya." Available at: http://www.slideshare.net/ africaremittances/remittances-to-kenya-world-bank-survey-results [Accessed November 6, 2010].

— (2010d), *Kenya Economic Update: Kenya at the Tipping Point*. Nairobi: World Bank.

World Bank and EPC (Export Promotion Council (2010), *Assessment of Kenya's Export Potential and Supply Capacities in Selected Professional Service Sectors: Final Report*. Nairobi: World Bank/EPC.

WTTC (World Travel and Tourism Council) (nd), "Economic Data Research Tool: Results for Kenya." Available at: http://www.wttc.org/eng/Tourism_ Research/Economic_Data_Search_Tool [Accessed October 4, 2010].

— (2010), *Travel and Tourism Economic Impact: Kenya*. London: WTTC.

Zimmerman, J. and Holmes, J. (2010), "The M-Banking Revolution: Why Cell Phones Will do More for the Developing World than Laptops Ever Could," *Foreign Policy*, August 27. Available at: http://www.foreignpolicy. com/articles/2010/08/27/the_m_banking_revolution?page=full [Accessed October 12, 2010].

2

Urbanization and Urban Growth

One of the most significant changes in Africa of recent times, and one that seems to be of even greater importance in the future, is the rapid growth of the urban population. And, like most of Africa, Kenya is also characterized by rapid urbanization and urban growth. Urbanization is conventionally defined as the process of growth in the urban proportion of a country's entire population, rather than merely in the urban population per se. So defined, then the appropriate measure of the rate of urbanization is the difference between the growth rates of the urban population and the national population. At high levels of urbanization the task of socioeconomic development can become complicated and appropriate national urbanization policies need to be implemented.

Urban growth is the rate of growth of an urban population. In fact, more specifically, it is growth and decline of urban areas or urban agglomerations. It is, therefore, different to urbanization but, as an economic phenomenon, it is inextricably linked with the process of urbanization. As also noted by Ioannides and Rossi-Hansberg (nd), the pattern of concentration of economic activity and its evolution have been found to be an important determinant, and in some cases the result, of urbanization, the structure of cities, the organization of economic activity, and national economic growth. The size distribution of cities, for example, is the result of the patterns of urbanization, which result in city and urban growth and city/urban area creation.

Urbanization Trends

Over the past four decades, between 1970 and 2010, the urban population of Eastern Africa soared from 11.2 to 77.2 million with the urban proportion increasing from 10 to 24 percent during the same period (UN-HABITAT and UNEP, 2010). For Kenya, its total population increased from 10.9 million in 1969 to 38.6 million in 2009 at an annual average intercensal growth rate ranging from 2.9 to 3.4 percent as shown in the previous chapter. As depicted in Figure 2.1, the urban population as a proportion of the

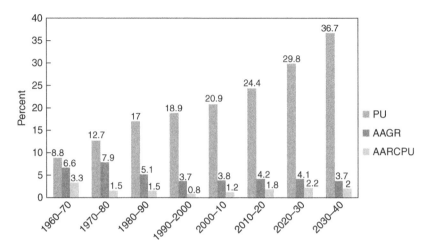

FIGURE 2.1 Urban population trends and projections: proportion urban, average annual growth rate, and average annual rate of change of the percentage urban, 1960–2030
Source: Author, based on data from UNDESA (2010).
Notes: PU=Proportion urban; AAGR=Average annual growth rate;
AARCPU=Average annual rate of change of proportion urban.

total population increased from 8.8 percent in 1960–70 to 20.9 percent in 2000–10 and is projected to exceed 36 percent by 2030–40; the urban population has been growing at an annual average rate exceeding 7.9 percent in 1970–80 and is projected to average about 4 percent beyond 2010 through to 2040; and the average annual rate of change of the urban percentage was 3.3 percent in 1960–70 and was estimated to average 2 percent by 2040. The average annual rate of change of the percentage urban is the average exponential rate of change of the percentage urban in a given period (UNDESA, 2010). These data indicate that one out of every five Kenyans currently live in urban areas compared to one out of twelve in the 1960s.

To the analyst or keen observer it may be readily apparent that the data portrayed in Figure 2.1 would seem inconsistent with official government statistics and that is indeed the case. The data from the UN's *World Urban Population* database reflect much lower urban population distribution as well as growth rates. For example, the 2009 Kenya population census puts the proportion of the total population that is urban at 32.3 percent (as reported in Chapter 1), while the UN data for that year pegs the proportion at 21.9 percent (Republic of Kenya, 2010a; UNDESA, 2010). This discrepancy may have something to do with definitions pertaining to urban classification especially as they relate to cities and towns. Although the UN relies on country national census data for its calculations, it only considers the population for the "urban core" to ensure consistency with previous censuses (UNDESA, 2010). Nonetheless, the UN population data are the most comprehensive and are, therefore, widely used throughout the UN and by many other international organizations as well, such as the World Bank. However, whatever the source of the urbanization and urban growth data, whether from official government statistics directly or compiled using such statistics, the trends are the same. Urbanization and urban growth in Kenya have been proceeding at a rapid pace over the past almost five decades since independence.

Drivers of Urbanization

The rapid growth of the urban population in Kenya is the direct result of a shift in the balance between the urban and rural economies. This shift is closely linked to economic growth and to the changing patterns of demand for, and supply of, employment; in other words, to the urban bias or urban primacy in the country, as it is in much of Africa (Hope, 1997). This urban bias/primacy remains very strong in Eastern Africa and its roots can be traced to the subregion's colonial past (Hope, 1997; UN-HABITAT and UNEP, 2010). The colonizers established centers of life (manifested by administrative, cultural, economic, and recreational activities) in those areas that gave them easy access to ports and roads for the movement of goods. Consequently, the spatial structures of most African economies, including Kenya's, became strongly focused on a small number of economic geographic areas (cities). It was on these cities that the newly established transport systems concentrated and it was toward these cities that the population drifted.

Within these cities, or in their immediate surroundings, there were usually extensive open spaces for the exclusive use of the Europeans. These polo fields, parks, cricket fields, golf courses, rugby fields, and so on also served as *cordon sanitaires* separating the colonizers (and later the privileged non-Africans) from the colonized. Remarkably, such areas still exist in some African cities, including in Kenya, where they still strive to retain some or all of their degree of exclusiveness. This is particularly true of the privately owned or leased spaces such as school playing fields or golf courses. Following on from independence, Kenya, and other African countries as well, sustained this urban bias as the local elite began to gain entry into these formerly exclusive European settlements. The consequence was the continued development of commerce and industry; and the growth of transportation, communication, education, and other types of infrastructure in the urban areas (Hope, 2009).

That historical evolution led to the urban areas (and cities in particular, especially capital cities) becoming dominant in Africa. Cities in Kenya therefore remain the focal point of both public and private sector activities and, as such, they have become the rational settling place for the population. In that regard, the country's urbanization process has been dominated by the capital city—Nairobi—which, based on 2009 census data, has 25 percent of the total Kenyan urban population compared to 21 percent in 1999, and is now six times larger than the next largest urban center—Mombasa—compared to three times bigger in 1999. Since 1969 through to 1999, Nairobi's intercensal growth rates have held steady at approximately 5 percent but declined to approximately 4 percent in the 1999–2009 intercensal period. However, the growth rate of households has been declining steadily during the 1979–89 to 1999–2009 intercensal periods from 6.5 percent in 1979–89 to 5.3 percent in 1989–99 and to 4.2 percent in 1999–2009 (Republic of Kenya, 2001a, 2010b), but the city's population is on course to nearly double to almost 6 million by 2025 (UN-HABITAT and UNEP, 2010). However, today's urban challenges in Kenya, and the rest of Africa for that matter, are increasingly from the outcomes of post-independence political, economic, and social policy choices, albeit built on top of the model established under colonial rule. The primary variables driving rapid urbanization and urban growth in Kenya can be categorized as: (1) natural population increase; (2) rural–urban migration; and (3) other factors.

Natural Population Increase

A natural population increase occurs when birth rates exceed mortality rates. Africa remains the continent with the highest fertility rates in the world (although declining in recent years) and the lowest life expectancy. In Kenya, national birth rates currently exceed mortality rates by 27.3 per 1,000 population. In the urban areas, rising fertility rates and natural growth of the urban population are estimated to account for approximately 55 percent of Kenya's urban growth (Oxfam International, 2009). Like the rest of Africa, in Kenya childbearing is influenced by such factors as marriage and reproductive and contraceptive behavior patterns. For example, childbearing tends to be encouraged, irrespective of economic circumstances, as a matter of cultural norms. Consequently, women in Kenya, both the educated and uneducated, want and have more children than their counterparts in the rest of the world although educated Kenyan women want fewer children than do the uneducated ones. In general, the average number of children per woman should decline as the woman's level of education increases. It has long since been determined that female education bears one of the strongest negative relationships to fertility. In other words, education has a depressant effect on fertility (Hope, 1998, 2009). Kenya's total fertility rate (number of children born per woman) has been declining each decade since the 1960s from 8 to 5.0 currently with a projected rate of 2.7 by 2040 (KNBS, 2008a; UNDESA, 2009).

Kenyan women with secondary education or higher continue to experience declines in their fertility while the fertility of women with no formal education has been observed to increase by about one child on average from the late 1990s (Askew et al., 2009). Further empirical evidence on the relationship between education and fertility in Kenya is provided by Duflo et al. (2010). They have shown that there is both a strong positive correlation between education and delay in the onset of fertility, and a strong negative correlation between education and the number of children. Education can increase the opportunity cost of women's time leading them to have fewer and, generally, more highly educated children. This prominent role played by education in fertility behavior can be decomposed into two components. The first is the effect of individual educational attainment on individual-level fertility, and the second is the iconic value of education in the sense that some individuals may aspire to the attributes of other higher educated groups in a population (Iyer and Weeks, 2009).

Undoubtedly, women with secondary or higher education have, on average, lower fertility than women with no education. A study of 30 sub-Saharan African countries, including Kenya, found that the corresponding average fertility rates were 3.4 births per woman with secondary or higher education compared to 6.3 births (almost double) for women with no education (Bongaarts, 2010). The same study confirmed that the averages of contraceptive use and demand for contraception are positively associated with level of education. Differences by level of education within countries are also generally consistent with the conventional wisdom that education levels are positively associated with demand for and use of contraception and negatively associated with fertility and desired family size. Better-educated women have greater knowledge of contraception, higher autonomy to make decisions regarding their reproductive lives, better access to services, and greater motivation to implement demand (Bongaarts, 2010; Iyer and Weeks, 2009).

The foregoing studies have essentially provided results that are more or less consistent with the results of the most recent Kenya Integrated Household Budget Survey (KIHBS) conducted in 2005/06 as reported in KNBS (2008a). Overall, the total national fertility rate recorded by the KIHBS 2005/06 is 5 children while for urban women it is 3.2 children compared to 5.5 children for their rural counterparts. Urban women from poor households have slightly more than one-child than those from nonpoor households

(4.1 compared to 2.9). Women in Nairobi had a fertility rate of 2.8 children. Comparing by education, at the national level, women with no education had a total fertility rate of 6.3 children, women with primary education had a fertility rate of 4.6, while for women with secondary education and above the total fertility rate was 2.8 children. Urban women with no education had a total fertility rate of 4 children, those with primary education also had a fertility rate of 4 children, while those urban women with secondary education and above had a fertility rate of 2.3 children. In general, urban women have lower fertility levels compared to rural women. This is not surprising since urban women usually have better access to education, higher social mobility, better access to maternal health, marry later, and generally face higher costs of raising children (KNBS, 2008a).

Despite declining fertility rates, the crude birth rate per 1,000 population in Kenya is more than three times the crude death rate per 1,000 population. Due mainly to the decline in mortality rates, population growth has accelerated in both the urban and rural areas, albeit at a much faster pace in the urban areas. The primary factors in the decline in mortality in Kenya, and around the world, have been well documented and are better understood than the factors in the decline in fertility. These factors are threefold and have to do with their interaction as they affect an individual's physical well-being. They are: (1) public health services, such as immunization, which affect mortality regardless of individual behavior; (2) health and environmental services (e.g., clean water), which reduce the costs of health to individuals but require some individual response; and (3) an array of individual characteristics, including both income, which affects health through food consumption, and housing; and education, which affects the speed and efficiency with which individuals respond to health and environmental services (Birdsall, 1980; Hope, 1998). Of these three sets of factors affecting mortality, the benefits of the first have been more or less fully harvested. Further mortality declines depend therefore on changes in individual behavior that are facilitated by increasing income and education as well as better access to health services.

The primary demographic factors that make for future natural urban population increase in Kenya are: (1) the expected increase in population growth; (2) the very high proportion of children and youth in the general population where 45 percent of the total population is 15 years of age or younger, 27 percent of this total reside in urban areas, and 38 percent of total urban population is 15 years of age or younger (Republic of Kenya, 2010b). Thus, when those in this age group enter their reproductive period of life, their sheer numbers will represent an awesome potential for large population increases, regardless of the fact that the rate of increase is predicted to diminish in the future; and (3) time itself. A lengthy period is needed for a population structure to mature and attain a balance. This occurs when the death rate has passed through its transition period (from high to low levels) and the birth rate has done likewise. In time, the age structure will also evolve so that a large proportion of the population is adult.

Rural–Urban Migration

Rural to urban migration is the next important driver of urbanization and urban population growth. During the period 1975–90, the migrant share of urban growth in Kenya was estimated at 64 percent (Findley, 1993). Between 1989 and 1999, in-migration contributed 17 percent of the Nairobi population and 16 percent of the Mombasa population (Republic of Kenya, 2004; Wainaina, 2008). Currently, rural-migration accounts for an estimated 25 percent of urban growth (Oxfam International, 2009). Because the vast majority of migrants tend to be young adults in the peak reproductive age groups with higher fertility than the urban population as a whole, the long-term contribution of rural–urban migration to urban population growth is actually much greater.

   Rural–urban migration in Kenya, as it is in the rest of Africa, is primarily influenced by the need for economic betterment. People migrate to urban areas primarily in response to the better employment and economic opportunities available there (pull factors). But, they also migrate to escape negative conditions—like drought, flooding, famine, internal conflict such as civil strife, or inequalities in the spatial distribution of social, cultural, and/or political opportunities (push factors) (Hope, 1998). As a way to escape poverty, large numbers of Kenyans look for better opportunities by migrating to cities. In fact, as observed by the World Bank (2009a: 1), "migration to urban areas is unavoidable and even desirable as a way to improve allocation of human resources, especially in land-scarce countries." It also has significant positive impacts on people's livelihoods. The *Report of the 1998/9 Labour Force Survey* showed that the mean monthly earnings from paid employment in the urban areas were twice that of the urban areas (KNBS, 2003). In the absence of more recent credible data on earnings we use, as a proxy, household consumption (expenditure) patterns from the KIHBS 2005/06. It shows that the undeflated (absolute) mean food and nonfood expenditure per adult equivalent in the urban areas was 3 times that of the rural areas with nonfood expenditure being very pronounced in the urban areas at 4.6 times that for the rural areas (KNBS, 2007). This indicates the much higher levels of disposable income in the urban areas. In addition to income and employment opportunities, the expectation of better education facilities for children is also usually cited as a major reason for migration to urban areas (Hope, 1998).

There are also some demographic factors that tend to influence migration selectivity. Young adult men predominate among migrants. Logically, young men are more likely than older men to move from rural to urban areas or even to move across urban areas. They are usually unmarried. However, an increasing number of married men are now migrating from the rural areas in search of the means to take care of their families. Also, in recent times, there has been an increase in the number of unmarried, separated, divorced, and widowed women moving to the cities on their own (Amnesty International, 2010). Many of these women engage themselves in meaningful economic activities primarily in the informal sector. As discussed in Chapter 3, one significant characteristic of the informal sector is that, as it has grown, it has also become an important employer of the female labor force in the country.

Another factor in migration selectivity in Kenya is that of education. A large proportion of the migrants tend to be well educated and highly motivated relative to the population at the point of origin. Individuals with formal education, especially at the secondary level or higher, can obtain good jobs in government or commerce. These jobs are located in major urban centers, especially Nairobi, and hence aspiring employees must migrate to those centers. The cities and urban centers that receive migrants thus are therefore not, on balance, burdened with a flood of uneducated, unskilled, and unmotivated individuals and households. Some empirical evidence on the relationship between education and rural–urban migration is provided by Miguel and Hamory (2009). They determined that high ability young adults are more likely to migrate out of rural Kenya and into cities, and that the magnitude of these efforts is quite large. A two standard deviation increase in academic test score was found to result in a 17 percent increase in the likelihood of rural–urban migration and a 3 year increase in schooling increases the likelihood of migration by more than 5 percentage points or roughly 16 percent.

Migration is also multisectoral in nature and is closely linked to the problems associated with rising population pressure, land tenure uncertainties, poor land use, and environmental stress. The latter, in particular, is a significant contributor to rural–urban migration and urbanization processes throughout Africa (Hope, 2009). Barrios et al. (2006), for example, have provided evidence that climate change has been an important determinant of rural–urban migration in sub-Saharan African countries including Kenya. They showed that rainfall, for instance, has been an important determinant of urbanization growth in sub-Saharan Africa. They further demonstrated that rainfall pushes people out of rural/agricultural areas to urban areas. Kumssa and Jones (2010) have also noted that with erratic rainfall and frequent droughts, rural dwellers find it very difficult to work on their farms and are forced to abandon their rural settlements and migrate to urban areas in search of better livelihoods.

Fundamentally, the negative economic impact of climate change as a push factor in rural–urban migration throughout Africa continues to loom large. For example, by the 2080s, climate change is estimated to place an additional 80–120 million people at risk of hunger and 70–80 percent of these will be in Africa (Hope, 2009). In East Africa, the declining rainfall during 1996–2003 has been observed to result in declining production in several crops (Case, 2006). For Kenya, the analyses have clearly indicated cohesive patterns of observed climate change during the 1960–2009 period in both rainfall and temperature and, when extended to 2025, it is found that large parts of Kenya will experience more than a 100 millimeter decline in long-season rainfall by that date (Funk et al., 2010). In Central Kenya, an area that has already experienced, and will likely continue to experience, substantial and important changes in climate as a result of recent and projected trends in rainfall and temperature, there will be strong negative impacts on agriculture in the eastern and northern flanks of the highlands (Funk et al., 2010). These areas are located around cities and urban areas like Eldoret, Nakuru, Nyeri, and Meru which will likely be the first urban areas to which the residents of the highlands will migrate in search of replacement income-earning opportunities.

Undoubtedly, rural–urban migration will continue in Kenya, and the rest of Africa, in the foreseeable future given rapid population growth, the limited development activities within the vast majority of the rural areas, and the seemingly permanent attraction of Kenya's capital city as it maintains its status as the most economically and politically important city in East Africa. It is the most populous city in East Africa, the twelfth largest urban agglomeration in all of Africa, and is the home to many companies and organizations including being the location of the regional or global headquarters for many UN agencies, bilateral development partners, and nongovernmental organizations.

Other Factors

In Kenya, although natural growth, rural–urban migration and, to some extent *in-situ* urbanization (the absorption of smaller settlements on the growth path of larger cities) are now the major drivers of urbanization and urban growth, there is at least one other factor that is exerting some influence—refugees and asylum seekers. As urbanization proceeds, refugees too have been increasingly moving to cities and towns. Currently, according to the United Nations High Commission for Refugees (UNHCR), more than one-half of the world's 15.2 million refugees reside in urban areas and the number continues to grow (UNHCR, 2010a). In Kenya, the sixth major refugee hosting country in the world, there were 412,193 refugees at the end of September 2010 with an increase of more than 30,000 from the six months prior mainly as a result of new arrivals from Somalia due to persistent conflict and insecurity in that country (OCHA, 2010). Although more than 80 percent of Kenya's refugee population is from Somalia, the country also hosts refugees from countries such as Ethiopia, Sudan, Congo, Rwanda, Eritrea, and Uganda, for example.

Most of the refugees in Kenya live in overcrowded camps in the east of the country. Yet, it is accepted that there is a large and growing number of refugees in the urban areas. In April 2010, the UNHCR (2010b) estimated that there were 45,246 refugees in Nairobi (about 12 percent of the total refugee population in Kenya). By September 2010, OCHA (2010) estimated there were 46,487 refugees residing in Nairobi but the proportion of the total had declined to 11 percent. However, the exact size of the refugee population in Nairobi is not known. Despite what the official figures indicate, unofficial estimates put the figure closer to 100,000 (Dix, 2006; Pavanello et al., 2010; RCK, 2008). Urban refugees tend to be highly mobile and reluctant to come forward due to fears of deportation or being sent to refugee camps. "This makes them a largely 'invisible' population, despite their significant need for protection and other support mechanisms" (Pavanello et al., 2010: 7). These urban refugees live throughout the city with the majority of them located in Eastleigh.

Their reasons for coming to Nairobi vary, but most of them seek to make their way to the urban areas to escape the harsh living conditions in the camps and in search of better opportunities. Overcrowded conditions and inadequate shelter in the camps have contributed to conflicts over scarce resources, especially firewood, between the refugees and the local community and an increase in sexual and gender-based violence, for example, have also pushed many of the refugees to seek out increased security in the urban areas. Many others have also reported the frustration of having to live in camps, where there is virtually no chance of employment, and so they moved to urban areas to seek economic independence and a better life, utilizing their ethnic or clan networks where those exist. Despite the difficult conditions in the refugee camps, which is increasingly influencing the refugees to move to urban areas, with impacts on urban population growth and urbanization, the measure of the relative impact of hosting refugees puts Kenya as the fifth largest in the world. By comparing a refugee population with the average income level of a country (measured by GDP at purchasing power parity per capita), a measure can be obtained of the relative impact of hosting refugees. At the end of 2009, Kenya was hosting 237 refugees per US$1 GDP per capita (UNHCR, 2010a).

Consequences of Rapid Urbanization

Once regarded as being positively associated with higher productivity and industrialization, it has now become increasingly clear that there are negative consequences associated with the concentration of economic activity and population in urban areas. The "overurbanization" that results leads to poverty, income inequality, unemployment, underemployment, inadequate housing and access to public services, traffic congestion, and environmental degradation, for example, and it is these consequences that now need to be addressed—as a key development issue. As discussed below, rather than regard urbanization as something to be resisted, controlled, or curbed, which would represent the old way of thinking or the old paradigm, the new paradigm recognizes that urbanization is not only inevitable but also a powerful force for economic growth.

The principal measurement of how well urban areas have absorbed the rapid population growth is through estimates of urban unemployment. One of the major consequences of the rapid urbanization experienced by Kenya has been the increasing supply of urban job seekers. In Kenya, and all other African countries, the supply of urban job seekers far exceeds demand. Kenya's urban unemployment rate was estimated at 25.1 percent in 1999 and 19.9 percent in 2006 as shown in Chapter 1. The youth unemployment rate tends to average two times or more the national unemployment rate. In 2006, the official national unemployment rate was 12.7 percent and the national youth unemployment rate was averaging 24.5 percent (KNBS, 2008a). While the total urban unemployment rate was 19.9 percent (with 15 percent for males and 25.9 percent for females) in 2006, for the youth the total urban unemployment rate was 40.6 percent with the urban male and urban female unemployment rates being 36.2 and 44.3 percent, respectively (KNBS, 2008b; Njonjo, 2010).

Despite the fact that average household incomes in Kenya tend to be systematically and considerably higher in urban than in rural areas, as previously discussed, in the urban areas, unemployment and underemployment have a negative income impact on the family and often contribute to its instability and poverty. Sub-Saharan African countries have the

TABLE 2.1 Distribution of urban poverty, 2006 (%)

Urban areas	Food poverty	Absolute poverty	Hardcore poverty
Total urban	40.5	33.7	8.3
Nairobi	29.5	21.3	4.2
Mombasa	50.4	37.6	1.7
Kisumu	46.8	43.4	4.3
Nakuru	49.3	50.2	13.0
Other urban	46.8	42.3	14.2

Source: KNBS (2007).

highest levels of urban poverty in the world. In Kenya, urban poverty rates are declining as discussed in Chapter 1. The distribution of urban poverty, based on the most recent official statistics (2006), is depicted in Table 2.1. Absolute urban poverty declined from 49.2 percent in 1997 to 33.7 percent in 2006, urban food poverty increased from 38.3 to 40.5 percent during the same period, and urban hardcore poverty increased from 7.6 to 8.3 percent during the same period also (KNBS, 2007). Among, the five major urban areas shown in Table 2.1, Nairobi had the lowest incidence of both the food poor and the absolute poor and held the next to last place, in terms of lowest incidence, of hardcore poor (KNBS, 2007).

However, while the proportion of Kenya's urban population living in absolute poverty has been on the decline in the past decade and more, according to Oxfam GB (2009), this conceals the fact that the percentage share of the very poorest urban groups—such as the "food poor" and the "hardcore poor"—has been increasing. Oxfam GB (2009) further observed that: (1) there are over 4 million urban food poor in Kenya, with almost one-third of them located in Nairobi; (2) 60 percent of Nairobi's population—about 2 million people—live in slums; (3) urban inequality is rising; (4) the poorest urban residents spend up to 75 percent of their income on staple foods alone; (5) there are insufficient schools in some Nairobi slums; (6) women in the slums are almost 5 times as likely as men to be unemployed. The majority of the urban poor in Kenya work in the informal sector which is discussed in Chapter 3.

Among the characteristics of urban poverty in Kenya is that of income inequality. In many African countries, including Kenya, the Gini coefficient (defined in Chapter 1) within urban areas is substantially higher than in rural areas where standards of living tend to be more homogenous. Inequality also appears to increase with city size, though this has not been tested widely. In urban Kenya, the Gini coefficient is rising while in the rural areas it is declining. In urban areas, the Gini coefficient increased from 0.43 in 1997 to 0.45

in 2006. On the other hand, the rural Gini coefficient fell from 0.42 to 0.38 during the same period. The Gini coefficient for Nairobi, as measured in 2006, is 0.59 (UN-HABITAT and UNEP, 2010). The degree of inequality in both income and consumption is greater in urban than in rural areas in general. According to the distinct groupings used by UN-HABITAT (2008), Gini values ranging from 0.500 to 0.599 fall in the very high inequality bracket, which is the case for Nairobi, which point to institutional and structural failures in income distribution. Gini values ranging from 0.400 to 0.449, as for all urban areas in Kenya, are considered as relatively high inequality.

Urban poverty also manifests itself in inequality in access to adequate housing. For example, the majority of the urban and peri-urban poor tend to live in ecologically fragile zones where they overuse the surrounding lands for, among other things, fuelwood and subsistence and small cash-crop production, further endangering their physical environment, their health, and the lives of their children. One result is that the urban poor are disproportionately threatened by the environmental hazards and other risks posed by such things as climate change effects, for example (Hope, 2009). These patterns of informal settlements by the urban poor have resulted in the emergence and growth of slum communities. The term informal settlements indicates the nonpermanence of such settlements and implicitly justifies, from the point of view of policy makers, the lack of infrastructure and services, including water, electricity, health services, and even law enforcement. In these settlements, living conditions are deplorable, with toilets in short supply, safe water unavailable, and garbage collection virtually nonexistent. They are basically settlements of the urban poor developed through the unauthorized occupation of land. Many of their residents live in one-room shacks made of semipermanent materials such as mud, wooden planks, or metal sheets. These one-room structures are approximately 10 feet by 10 feet, or 100 square feet. They are self-contained, meaning that one room is all rooms: living room, dining room, kitchen, washroom, study, bedroom, and even depending on how safe it is after dark, temporary toilet. Ventilation is through the door and, sometimes, a small window (Neuwirth, 2005). Consequently, they are regarded by many as unhealthy and overcrowded blights on the urban landscape (Erulkar and Matheka, 2007; Huchzermeyer and Karam, 2006).

By 2010, the proportion of the urban population living in slums in sub-Saharan Africa was estimated to be 61.7 percent (UN-HABITAT, 2008). For Kenya, it is estimated that more than 50 percent of the urban population live in slums or other informal settlements (UN-HABITAT and UNEP, 2010), while 60 percent or more of the population of Nairobi live in such settlements (NCWSC and AWSB, 2009; Oxfam GB, 2009). However, data now available and derived from the 2009 census suggest that the Nairobi slum population is about 33.7 percent of the city's total population; with 350,739 households, and a gender distribution of 54 percent male and 46 percent female (Republic of Kenya, 2010a; UN-HABITAT and UNEP, 2010). The accuracy of these census data has been challenged by some NGOs and international organizations (see, e.g., UN-HABITAT and UNEP, 2010). However, others have dismissed these challenges as representing nothing more than attempts at program and funding preservation (see, e.g., Karanja, 2010; Warah, 2010).

Associated with the urban pattern of slum settlements in Kenya is also the inadequate access to basic urban services and infrastructure. Although urban areas overall have much better access to basic services than the rural areas, the slum households tend to lack, among other things, clean water, improved sanitation, and adequate collection and disposal of sewage and solid waste. In all of these slum communities there generally tends to be a frequent problem with foul smells emanating from the decomposition of waste, sewage ponds, informal abattoirs, irregularly emptied pit latrines, and/or industrial wastes (Hope, 2009). Some characteristics and examples of access to services in the urban areas and slum settlements, based on actual survey data as well as other literature, follow below, bearing in mind that there are an estimated 200 informal settlements in Nairobi "where living conditions are among the worst in Africa due to extremely high population densities" (UN-HABITAT and UNEP, 2010: 140).

The key emerging elements and profiles regarding and influencing access to services in the urban areas and slums are the following:

- The total urban population aged 5 years and above is 10.6 million representing 85 percent of the total urban population of Kenya. The total population of Nairobi aged 5 years and above is 2.7 million, comprising 22 percent of the total urban population (Republic of Kenya, 2010b).
- Only 38 percent of the total urban households in Kenya have access to piped water, only 14 percent have access to water piped into their dwelling, and only 24 percent depend on water from spring/well/borehole. In Nairobi approximately 52 percent of households have access to piped water, while only 23 percent have access to water piped into their dwelling, and 7 percent depend on spring/well/borehole water (Republic of Kenya, 2010b).
- Only about 20 percent of the total urban households have access to a main sewer as the primary mode of human waste disposal compared to 68 percent with access to pit latrines, 19 percent with access to a septic tank, and 0.7 percent with cess pool access. For Nairobi, the corresponding

shares are 48 percent of its households with access to a main sewer as the main mode of human waste disposal, 40 percent with access to pit latrines, 10 percent with access to a septic tank, and 1 percent with cess pool access (Republic of Kenya, 2010b).

- Approximately 50 percent of total urban households have electricity as their main type of lighting and fuel, 24 percent depend on lanterns, 22 percent use tin lamps, and 0.8 percent use pressure lamps. In Nairobi, 72 percent of households have access to electricity as their main type of lighting and fuel, 13 percent use lanterns, 12 percent depend on tin lamps, and 1 percent use pressure lamps (Republic of Kenya, 2010b).

- In Nairobi's informal settlements only 22 percent of households were found to have water connections serviced by the Nairobi City Water and Sewerage Company (NCWSC), with the majority (75%) purchasing water from water kiosks or other water delivery services (NCWSC and AWSB, 2009). One other report by the government noted that by 2007 sustainable access to water was as low as 20 percent in the settlements of the urban poor (Republic of Kenya, 2007). The residents of Nairobi's slum settlements also pay significantly higher and for poorer quality water, than those residents with home connections to the municipal water network (UN-HABITAT and UNEP, 2010). This prohibitive cost of water leads, inevitably, to rationing of water use by households in the informal settlements and result in the frequent foregoing of bathing and the occasional washing of clothes, for example (Amnesty International, 2009).

- Access to sanitation is another major challenge for the poor in most East African cities including in Kenya. In Nairobi's slums, the majority of households use shared pit latrines that are overused and inadequately maintained. These communal latrines serve a large number of people from the surrounding area. The official water and sanitation regulator and provider estimated that only 24 percent of residents in Nairobi's informal settlements have access to toilet facilities at a household level, 68 percent rely on shared facilities, while 6 percent have no access to toilets. On average, one pit latrine is shared by 50–150 people (Amnesty International, 2010). As a result of such poor sanitation facilities, many slum dwellers resort to the use of plastic bags as toilets which are then randomly discarded. In some slums, more than 80 percent of excreta is disposed of in this manner. These plastic bags are referred to as "flying toilets" and the practice is that they are flown (thrown) at night, which contributes to the unsanitary conditions in the settlements. Not surprisingly, as noted by UN-HABITAT and UNEP (2010), informal and slum settlements are associated with high incidences of cholera, which is linked directly to the prevailing unsanitary conditions.

- Associated with the inadequate access to toilets/latrines and bathing facilities in the immediate household vicinity is the risk women in the settlements face of sexual and other forms of gender-based violence. Most women have to walk more than 300 meters, at times, from their dwelling to use the available latrines. Getting to these latrines is unsafe for women and especially at night when they are more likely to become the victims of rape and assault (Amnesty International, 2010).
- Access to electricity connection and supply in the slums of Nairobi range from 20 to 22 percent of households while 77–78 percent of the slum households use kerosene/paraffin as an alternative source of home lighting (Gulyani et al., 2010; Oxfam GB, 2009).

Another aspect of urbanization related to urban poverty in Kenya is child labor. In general, in Africa, with persistent poverty, more and more children at younger and younger ages have been engaging in paid economic activities (Hope, 2005). While other regions, such as Asia-Pacific, Latin America, and the Caribbean, continue to reduce child labor, sub-Saharan Africa has witnessed an increase in both relative and absolute terms and has the highest incidence of children working, with one in four children engaged in child labor based on 2008 data (ILO, 2010). In Kenya, in 1999 there were 1.9 million working children aged 5–17 years constituting 17.4 percent of all children of that age range and 14.4 percent of the total working population. The proportion of working children to the total population of children aged 5–17 years was more than double in the rural areas (19.7 percent) compared to urban areas (9 percent). In Nairobi, the proportion of working children to the total population of the city's children aged 5–17 years was 11.4 percent (Republic of Kenya, 2001b). The majority of the working children (43.6 percent) aged 5–17 years in 1999 fell within the 10–14 year age bracket, and 30.1 percent fell within the 15–17 year age bracket (Republic of Kenya, 2001b). Between 1999 and 2006, the number of working children dropped from 1.9 million to 1.3 million, and between 1999 and 2007, 26 percent of children aged 5–14 years were engaged in child labor comprising 25 percent of all girls and 27 percent of all boys (CART, 2010; IDLO, 2010).

Poverty and other socioeconomic circumstances act as major influences on child labor in Kenya and the rest of Africa. There are significantly greater proportions of children involved in child labor activities in the poorest 20 percent of households than in the richest 20 percent of households. Also, there is a greater incidence of child labor among children whose mothers had no education than among children whose mothers had some education (Hope, 2005). The relationship between poverty and child labor seems obvious enough and is borne out by the data for Kenya and the rest of Africa.

Census and other survey data show, for example, that the proportion of working children in Kenya diminishes with improved household expenditure (income). In other words, as household income rises, the lower the proportion of working children coming from such households (Republic of Kenya, 2001b).

Other poverty characteristics also play a role in pushing children into the world of work. In Kibera, for instance, a major slum in Nairobi, one survey found that adolescent children who lived on their own or only with their mother accounted for 49 percent of the girls and 35 percent of the boys and were economically worse off than those children who lived with both parents or their father, and they contributed a much higher proportion of the child labor (Erulkar and Matheka, 2007). Poverty, as the major cause of child labor, then leads to a situation where children may have to engage in hazardous work or other worst forms of child labor to subsist. Moreover, high levels of child labor translate into very low levels of school enrollment, which then affects children's opportunities later in life. Consequently, if a child supplies more labor and gets less education as a child, he or she will grow up to be poorer as an adult. On the other hand, a child who manages to attend school is much more likely to escape child labor and acquire a larger income as an adult (Hope, 2005).

One final consequence of Kenya's rapid urbanization that must, obviously, be considered here is the issue of traffic congestion. It is estimated that traffic congestion is costing Kenya the approximate equivalent of US$434 million a year due to lost productivity, stress, fuel consumption, and environmental degradation (Republic of Kenya, nd). The country's road networks have not grown with the times. With the rapidly increasing population and the crowding of motorized traffic onto a limited street network, traffic congestion in Nairobi has now taken on a legendary status. Nairobi suffers maddening congestion primarily because the authorities had failed to update road networks built decades ago to serve colonial administrations. Recent studies have estimated the traffic situation in Nairobi as comprising 7.5 million person trips per day translating to approximately 2.5 trips per person with a travel mode composition of minibus taxis (known locally as *matatus*) (29%), private car/taxi (15%), school or college bus (3%), motor cycle (2%), and walking (47%) (Irungu, 2007; Kumar and Barrett, 2009). Ninety-three percent of traffic within Nairobi's boundary is assessed to originate from, or arrive at, Nairobi, while the other 7 percent is pass-through traffic and with daily traffic volumes (vehicles per day) on both directions of the eight major roads totaling 518,168 comprising 36 percent passenger cars, 23 percent pick up/4 wheel drives, 3 percent buses, and 27 percent minibus taxis (Irungu, 2007). However, in addition to the poor and inadequate road network, there are also problems with traffic flow and driver behavior.

With respect to traffic flow, the accumulation of vehicles in the limited road network minimizes traffic flow and concentrates the traffic congestion. The primary contributors to this state of affairs are the traffic circles (better known as roundabouts in former British colonies). These traffic circles are abundant in Nairobi, to say the least, and they are used to manage major intersections. However, because of the magnitude of the motorized traffic and driver behavior (discussed next), these traffic circles have become very annoying traffic choke points and the location of most of the accidents in Nairobi. Accidents in these traffic circles have become so predictable that a large number of tow trucks are usually parked in their immediate vicinity waiting like vultures to attack a carcass. Traffic circles are obsolete and totally inconsistent with modern-day traffic movement and management. Yet, in order to drive into or out of the city center, vehicles must pass through one of six gateway traffic circles on the edge of the central business district (Gonzales et al., 2009).

The current experience with traffic circles in Nairobi is simply a negative one, characterized by high accident rates and congestion problems. For low traffic demands, traffic circles may be useful. However, in high traffic demand situations, like Nairobi, traffic circles are totally ineffective. As Gonzales et al. (2009) noted, the principal problem with traffic circles is that they are susceptible to jamming in all directions from queue spillbacks when the road network becomes congested. This undesirable effect occurs because the traffic circle serves all directions simultaneously on the same circular section of road and thereby resulting in gridlock. This is in contrast to a signal-controlled cross intersection where only the approach upstream of the intersection is blocked, and traffic headed in the crossing direction is not impeded. Due to the many traffic circles in Nairobi (with several along some of the major and more popular roads) the gridlock at one leads to traffic jamming at others as entry and exit from each become impeded. Uhuru Highway, for example, which runs right through the city, is punctuated by a string of traffic circles acting as anarchic traffic traps (Mood, 2007).

In terms of driver behavior, Kenya has a culture of bad driving. In Nairobi, bad driving is an art form and it flourishes due to lax surveillance and enforcement of the road rules and traffic laws by the police along with the latter's penchant for accepting bribes, as discussed in Chapter 4, rather than proceed with enforcement. Consequently, these bad drivers, and especially those driving the minibus taxis operate with impunity. These minibus taxis have become Nairobi's main form of public transport and their kamikaze driving habits are now emulated by most other drivers. They turn two-lane roads into four lanes, they careen down the wrong side of the street to beat traffic jams, they run red lights, and, screech to a halt to allow passengers to enter and exit—often in the middle of the road (Muhumed, 2008). These driving habits, that would cost a driver his/her license in most countries, are ignored by the police who seek and accept bribes to do so. These bribes are referred to as *kitu kidogo* (something small). Not surprisingly, the minibus taxis are the principal mode of transportation of the urban poor throughout Kenya.

Managing Rapid Urbanization

The new paradigm on urbanization regards function, rather than size, as the rationale for measuring performance in cities and other urban areas. Indeed, it is becoming increasingly recognized by many policy-makers, as mentioned before, that urbanization is not only inevitable but that it is also a powerful force for economic growth and poverty reduction (World Bank, 2009b). Consequently, the question that emanates from the new paradigm is how can urbanization be managed to harness its potential for economic development?; in other words, developing and implementing policy to mitigate the consequences emanating from rapid urbanization as opposed to attempting to curb urbanization.

Urban centers, and in particular capital cities like Nairobi, will continue to offer important opportunities for economic and social development (Cohen, 2006). As previously noted, cities have always been focal points for economic growth and employment given their historical development and natural advantage in transport routes. Moreover, cities like Nairobi are also centers of modern living, where female labor force participation is greatest and where indicators of general health and well-being, literacy, women's status, and social mobility are higher. Nairobi is also an important social and cultural center in Kenya—housing museums, theaters, recording studios, and other important cultural centers.

As discussed above, urbanization and city growth in Kenya are caused by a number of different factors including natural population increase and rural–urban migration. Although much of the popular rhetoric on urbanization has left the impression that Kenya's urban areas are currently growing too fast and that growth should be limited or somehow diverted, it is important not to disregard the fact that, for the most part, there is an economic logic to the pattern of that urbanization. High urban growth rates are therefore a reflective indicator of success rather than failure. The challenge of managing Kenya's urbanization in the twenty-first century is, therefore, about finding policy solutions to the consequences of rapid urbanization. Such policy should also focus on increasing the efficiency of the benefits of urban growth to the national economy.

Employment Generation

The most effective way to combat urban poverty, or poverty in general, is through employment generation. The poor, and society in general, would benefit most from growth activities that allow the former to work their way out of poverty (Hope, 2004). The basic issue to be dealt with, therefore, is how the urban labor supply can be absorbed at decent wages without further increasing the rural–urban wage differential and retarding economic activity by increasing production costs. Perhaps the most powerful stimulus to employment generation, and hence labor demand, is economic growth. Economic growth leads to rapid labor absorption throughout an entire economy in both urban and rural areas. Policies aimed at improving the economic growth of Kenya are, therefore, very important elements of any employment strategy. Such policies must always be outward-looking. Among other things, they must promote trade and private investment and result in the growth of the manufacturing and service activities sectors.

Since independence, the Kenyan authorities have progressively moved toward the recognition of the employment imperative for poverty reduction and improving human well-being in the country. Omolo (2010), for instance, provides an excellent summary and analysis of the past and current employment creation policies and programs pursued in Kenya. These policies and programs have been seen as part and parcel of the basic framework for economic growth and development. The underlying premise has been that faster economic growth would lead to employment creation and that income generation through employment would, in turn, lead to improvement in the standards of living and eradication of poverty. The focus has been, and continues to be, on the slow growth of formal sector employment. However, an important element of employment generation for African countries, such as Kenya, is that related to the role of the informal sector. As discussed in Chapter 3, the informal sector is a dynamic and growing one which is expected to continue to absorb the majority of new labor force entrants into the foreseeable future.

One of the distinguishing features of the informal sector is that its economic activities are concentrated on services and small- and medium-scale enterprises. The sector, therefore, has a major role to play in alleviating the urban poverty and urban unemployment problem in Kenya and, as such, must be allowed to flourish through a committed means of recognition of its positive role in the development process and the implementation of policies to promote it. Kenya and other African governments can promote the informal sector by removing regulatory constraints, by simplifying bureaucratic procedures, by eliminating harassment of those engaged in non-illegal activities in the sector, and also by providing tangible supports, such as technical assistance and low-interest credits.

Improving Access to Urban Infrastructure and Services

Undoubtedly, access to urban infrastructure and services in Kenya needs to be substantially improved and particularly so for those urban residents in the informal settlements. Moreover, the problems of accessing infrastructure and services are particularly acute for the urban poor. While access is typically higher in urban areas than rural, it can still be extremely low for the urban poor, of inadequate quality, and unaffordable as discussed above. There must, therefore, be deliberate and significant attempts to scale up the provision of urban infrastructure and services. However, bearing in mind that infrastructure and services requirements that go along with urbanization can be enormous in terms of investments in housing, water and sanitation, waste disposal, power, and transportation, for example, Kenya faces daunting challenges for the future projected increases in urbanization.

Consequently, and essentially, the government of Kenya needs to provide an encouraging and enabling environment for the private provision (through public–private partnerships primarily) of urban infrastructure and services. This approach would be especially useful and helpful to low-income urban households. It has been shown, for example, that incrementally built housing is a more effective means to increase the volume and improve the quality of shelter than public housing (Brennan, 1993; Hope, 1999). Given the resource constraints in Kenya, incremental building emerges as the appropriate framework for solving the country's housing problem. A considerably larger number of households would, therefore, be able to acquire basic structures that can then be extended room by room as their economic and family circumstances permit. In addition, such an approach would certainly encourage the principles of self-help and self-reliance, both at the household and wider community levels, and thereby lead to greater efforts and outcomes from slum upgrading. Programs improving living conditions in slums through extending affordable services to slum dwellers and investing in upgrading can also have enormous benefits in health outcomes, reduce environmental and social costs, as well as generate new employment opportunities (World Bank, 2009b).

One other critical area in the requirement to improve access to urban infrastructure and services is that of solid waste management. Globally, the thinking on solid waste management is shifting from merely removing waste before it becomes a health hazard to creatively minimizing its environmental impact (UN-HABITAT, 2010). Although waste reduction is desirable, rapid urban growth has resulted in increases in the volume of solid waste. However, solid waste data in many urban areas, including those in Kenya, are considerably unreliable and seldom capture informal activities or system losses. According to data published by UN-HABITAT, the volume of municipal solid waste currently generated in Nairobi is 219 kg per capita per year (0.6 kg per capita per day) equivalent to 1,314 kg per household per year (3.6 kg per household per day) (UN-HABITAT, 2010). Managing this waste requires a committed implementation to an integrated sustainable (solid) waste management (ISWM) program.

ISWM is designed to improve the performance of the solid waste system and to support sound decision-making. It is composed of three elements: (1) waste collecting; (2) waste treatment and disposal; and (3) waste prevention. Waste collection coverage in Kenya's urban areas was estimated to average 29 percent while for Nairobi the average collection coverage is 65 percent (UN-HABITAT, 2010). Waste disposal in Nairobi is estimated at 23,000 tons per year at simple controlled landfills, 370,000 tons per year at dumped disposal sites, while 263,000 tons per year are lost or dumped illegally (UN-HABITAT, 2010). With the exception of the illegally dumped waste elements, all other waste collection and disposal averages need to be significantly increased in Nairobi and other urban areas utilizing the ISWM framework.

Traffic Decongestion and Management

In Kenya, and in Nairobi particularly, traffic congestion inevitably occurs as urban growth proceeds while mass transport facilities have not been expanded and modernized to meet demand. The explosive increase in automobiles in Nairobi, for example, exerts tremendous demand on the existing road network. Moreover, the nature of the road network, with its extensive traffic circles, which act as inhibitors to a smooth and disciplined flow of traffic, has been a major contributor to the traffic congestion and chaos that currently exists in Nairobi and other urban areas in Kenya. Although traffic congestion can be seen as a sign of a vibrant city, as traffic demand grows in the future, the streets will become even more congested, so measures must be taken to improve the system. Traffic decongestion and management is, therefore, an important aspect of policy for managing rapid urbanization in the country.

Three areas of policy recommendation, among others, should be considered by the Kenyan authorities. The first two are: (a) control the accumulation of vehicles in the road network so that traffic flow is maximized; and (b) increase the capacity of the streets in the network (Gonzales et al.,

2009). Indeed, some steps are being taken in this regard by the government. A Nairobi Metropolitan Region (NMR) traffic decongestion program has been developed as part of the *Nairobi Metro 2030 Strategy*. The NMR traffic decongestion program contains short, medium, and long-term measures that include interventions for: (1) one-way (uni-direction) traffic movement; (2) dedicated bus routes in the central business district (CBD); (3) relegating of the minibus taxis to outside the CBD and re-instatement of the bigger capacity buses inside the CDB; (4) creating of park and ride facilities along the key approaches to the CBD; (5) construction of bypass and ring roads; (6) expansion of the CBD; (7) effective enforcement (Republic of Kenya, nd). These measures must be vigorously pursued.

The third area is the removal of traffic circles. All traffic circles, and particularly those in the CBD, should be converted to standard signal-controlled intersections. Traffic circles tend to spread congestion faster than if intersections were signal-controlled. A standard signal-controlled (electronic or traffic police) intersection allows opposing directions of traffic to flow simultaneously. When electronic signals are used there is the added advantage of synchronizing or varying them depending on time-of-day traffic flow. Traffic signals are an invaluable tool for the safe and efficient movement of vehicles and pedestrians. They assist in controlling traffic in a safe, orderly, and efficient manner. They benefit the public by providing orderly movement of vehicles, improved safety, reduced travel times, and by increasing the amount of traffic that an intersection can handle.

Conclusions

Rapid urbanization can be a function of urban and national economic progress given the role of cities as engines of growth and development. However, there are consequences from that urbanization, as this chapter has demonstrated, and that suggests some priority should be given to implementing policies to manage the situation and derive the necessary efficiencies emanating from urban growth. Cities provide large efficiency benefits and there is no evidence that they systematically hurt particular groups. Furthermore, existing urban inefficiencies do not imply that cities are less efficient than their rural alternatives. In fact, the very success of cities in developing countries points to the opposite. However suboptimal cities may turn out to be, they typically offer higher returns and better long-term opportunities (Duranton, 2009). Urbanization is, therefore, inevitable and attempts to resist, control, or curb it would be futile. It therefore needs to be embraced.

In that regard, the national government, through its Ministry of Nairobi Metropolitan Development, has put forward the previously mentioned

Nairobi Metro 2030 Strategy (Republic of Kenya, 2008). The vision of that strategy is to create a world class African metropolis that will serve as a regional and global services hub by the year 2030. That world class metropolis is also to have world class governance-dedicated, innovative, creative, and integrity institutions with a personnel-performance orientation. Among the initiatives covered in the strategy are: (1) deploying world class infrastructure and utilities; (2) optimizing mobility and accessibility through effective transportation; and (3) enhancing the quality of life including access to medical services, access to education, access to housing, elimination of slums, and environmental management. Implementation is now an imperative.

References

Amnesty International (2009), *Kenya: The Unseen Majority: Nairobi's Two Million Slum-Dwellers*. London: Amnesty International.

— (2010), *Insecurity and Indignity: Women's Experiences in the Slums of Nairobi, Kenya*. London: Amnesty International.

Askew, I., Ezeh, A., Bongaarts, J., and Towsend, J. (2009), *Kenya's Fertility Transition: Trends, Determinants and Implications for Policy and Programmes*. Nairobi: Population Council.

Barrios, S., Bertinelli, L., and Strobl, E. (2006), "Climatic Change and Rural-Urban Migration: The Case of Sub-Saharan Africa," *Journal of Urban Economics*, 60(3), 357–71.

Birdsall, N. (1980), "Population and Poverty in the Developing World," *Staff Working Paper No. 404*. Washington, DC: World Bank.

Bongaarts, J. (2010), "The Causes of Educational Differences in Fertility in sub-Saharan Africa," *Working Paper No. 20*. New York: Population Council.

Brennan, E. M. (1993), "Urban Land and Housing Issues Facing the Third World." In J. D. Kasarda and A. M. Parnell (eds), *Third World Cities: Problems, Policies, and Prospects*. London: Sage, pp. 74–91.

CART (Continental Advisory Research Team) (2010), *State of the Union Kenya Report 2010*. Available at: http://www.stateoftheunionafrica.org/documents/State_of_the_Union_Kenya_Report_2010.pdf [Accessed October 10, 2010].

Case, M. (2006), *Climate Change Impacts on East Africa: A Review of the Scientific Literature*. Gland, Switzerland: World Wide Fund for Nature.

Cohen, B. (2006), "Urbanization in Developing Countries: Current Trends, Future Projections, and Key Challenges for Sustainability," *Technology in Society*, 28(1–2), 63–80.

Dix, S. (2006), "Urbanization and the Social Protection of Refugees in Nairobi," *Humanitarian Exchange Magazine*, Issue 35. Available at: http://www.odihpn.org/report.asp?id=2841 [Accessed November 10, 2010].

Duflo, E., Dupas, P., and Kremer, M. (2010), "Education and Fertility: Experimental Evidence from Kenya." Available at: http://econ.duke.edu/uploads/assets/Workshop%20Papers/Education&Fertility_feb2010.pdf [Accessed November 2, 2010].

Duranton, G. (2009), "Are Cities Engines of Growth and Prosperity for Developing Countries?" In M. Spence, P. C. Annez, and R. M. Buckley (eds), *Urbanization and Growth*. Washington, DC: World Bank, pp. 67–114.

Erulkar, A. S. and Matheka, J. K. (2007), *Adolescence in the Kibera Slums of Nairobi, Kenya*. Nairobi: Population Council.

Findley, S. E. (1993), "The Third World City: Development Policy and Issues." In J. D. Kasarda and A. M. Parnell (eds.), *Third World Cities: Problems, Policies, and Prospects*. London: Sage, pp. 1–31.

Funk, C., Eilerts, G., Davenport, F., and Michaelsen, J. (2010), "A Climate Trend Analysis of Kenya—August 2010." FEWS NET (Famine Early Warning Systems Network) Fact Sheet 2010-3074. Available at: http://pubs.usgs.gov/fs/2010/3074/pdf/fs2010-3074.pdf [Accessed October 10, 2010].

Gonzales, E. J., Chavis, C., Li, Y., and Daganzo, C. F. (2009), "Multimodal Transport Modeling for Nairobi, Kenya: Insights and Recommendations with an Evidence-Based Model," *Working Paper UCB-ITS-VWP-2009-5*. Available at http://escholarship.org/uc/item/6dv195p7 [Accessed September 8, 2010].

Gulyani, S., Talukdar, D., and Jack, D. (2010), "Poverty, Living Conditions, and Infrastructure Access: A Comparison of Slums in Dakar, Johannesburg, and Nairobi," *Policy Research Working Paper 5388*. Washington, DC: World Bank.

Hope, K. R. (1997), *African Political Economy: Contemporary Issues in Development*. Armonk, NY: M.E. Sharpe.

— (1998), "Urbanization and Urban Growth in Africa," *Journal of Asian and African Studies*, 33(4), 345–58.

— (1999), "Managing Rapid Urbanization in Africa: Some Aspects of Policy," *Journal of Third World Studies*, 16(2), 47–59.

— (2004), "The Poverty Dilemma in Africa: Toward Policies for Including the Poor," *Progress in Development Studies*, 4(2), 127–41.

— (2005), "Child Survival, Poverty, and Labor in Africa," *Journal of Children and Poverty*, 11(1), 19–42.

— (2009), "Climate Change and Urban Development in Africa," *International Journal of Environmental Studies*, 66(5), 643–58.

Huchzermeyer, M. and Karam, A. (eds) (2006), *Informal Settlements: A Perpetual Challenge?* Cape Town, South Africa: UCT Press.

IDLO (International Development Law Organization) (2010), *Kenya Country Report: Strengthening the Legal Protection Framework for Girls in India, Bangladesh, Kenya and Liberia*. Rome: IDLO.

ILO (International Labor Office) (2010), *Accelerating Action against Child Labor: Global Report under the Follow-up to the ILO Declaration on Fundamental Principles and Rights at Work*. Geneva: ILO.

Ioannides, Y. and Rossi-Hansberg, E. (nd), "Abstract: Urban Growth". Available at: http://www.princeton.edu/~erossi/UG.pdf [Accessed November 29, 2010].

Irungu, K. Z. (2007), "Decongesting Nairobi—Urban Transportation Challenges." Available at: http://www.scribd.com/doc/2382775/Decongesting-Nairobi-City-Kenya [Accessed November 10, 2010].

Iyer, S. and Weeks, M. (2009), "Social Interactions, Ethnicity and Fertility in Kenya." Available at: http://www.econ.cam.ac.uk/dae/repec/cam/pdf/cwpe0903.pdf [Accessed November 2, 2010].

Karanja, M. (2010), "Myth Shattered: Kibera Numbers Fail to Add Up." Available at: http://www.nation.co.ke/News/Kibera%20numbers%20fail%20to%20 add%20up/-/1056/1003404/-/13ga38xz/-/index.html [Accessed November 15, 2010].

KNBS (Kenya National Bureau of Statistics) (2003), *Report of the 1998/9 Labor Force Survey*. Nairobi: KNBS.

— (Kenya National Bureau of Statistics) (2007), *Basic Report on Well-Being in Kenya*. Nairobi: KNBS.

— (Kenya National Bureau of Statistics) (2008a), *Well-Being in Kenya: A Socio-Economic Profile*. Nairobi: KNBS.

— (Kenya National Bureau of Statistics) (2008b), *Labor Force Analytical Report*. Nairobi: KNBS.

Kumar, A. and Barrett, F. (2009), "Stuck in Traffic: Urban Transport in Africa," *Africa Infrastructure Country Diagnostic Background Paper 1*. Washington, DC: World Bank.

Kumssa, A. and Jones, J. F. (2010), "Climate Change and Human Security in Africa," *International Journal of Sustainable Development and World Ecology*, 17(6), 453–61.

Miguel, E. and Hamory, J. (2009), "Individual Ability and Selection into Migration in Kenya," *Human Development Research Paper 2009/5*. New York: UNDP.

Mood, B. (2007), "Kenya's 'City in the Sun' Chokes with Traffic." Available at: http://www.mg.co.za/article/2007-09-24-kenyas-city-in-the-sun-chokes-with-traffic [Accessed December 8, 2010].

Muhumed, M. M. (2008), "Swarms of Cars, Trucks Plague Kenyan Capital." Available at: http://www.usatoday.com/news/world/2008-08-03-3906294309_x.htm [Accessed December 11, 2010].

NCWSC (Nairobi City Water and Sewerage Company) and AWSB (Athi Water Services Board) (2009), *Strategic Guidelines for Improving Water and Sanitation Services in Nairobi's Informal Settlements*. Nairobi: NCWSC and AWSB.

Neuwirth, R. (2005), *Shadow Cities: A Billion Squatters, a New Urban World*. New York: Routledge.

Njonjo, K. S. (2010), *Youth Fact Book: Infinite Possibility or Definite Disaster?* Nairobi: IEA-Kenya.

OCHA (United Nations Office for the Coordination of Humanitarian Affairs) (2010), "Displaced Populations Report," *September Issue 8*. Nairobi: OCHA Sub Regional Office for Eastern Africa.

Omolo, J. (2010), *The Dynamics and Trends of Employment in Kenya*. Nairobi: IEA-Kenya.

Oxfam GB (2009), "Urban Poverty and Vulnerability in Kenya." Available at: http://www.irinnews.org/pdf/Urban_Poverty_and_Vulnerability_in_Kenya. pdf [Accessed October 20, 2010].

Oxfam International (2009), "Kenya Threatened by New Urban Disaster." Available at: http://www.oxfam.org/en/pressroom/pressrelease/2009-09-10/kenya-threatened-new-urban-disaster [Accessed October 1, 2010].

Pavanello, S., Elhawary, S., and Pantuliano, S. (2010), "Hidden and Exposed: Urban Refugees in Nairobi, Kenya," *Humanitarian Policy Group Working Paper*. London: Overseas Development Institute.

RCK (Refugee Consortium of Kenya) (2008), *Enhancing the Protection of Refugee Women in Nairobi: A Survey on Risks, Protection Gaps and Coping Mechanisms of Refugee Women in Urban Areas*. Available at: http://www.rckkenya.org/www.rck-kenya.org/docs/Enhancing%20Protection%20of%20Refugee%20Women.pdf [Accessed December 8, 2010].

Republic of Kenya (nd), *The Nairobi Metropolitan Region (NMR) Traffic Decongestion Program*. Nairobi: Ministry of Nairobi Metropolitan Development.

— (2001a), *1999 Population and Housing Census: Volume 1: Population Distribution by Administrative Areas and Urban Centers*. Nairobi: Central Bureau of Statistics, Ministry of Finance and Planning.

— (2001b), *The 1998/99 Child Labor Report*. Nairobi: Central Bureau of Statistics, Ministry of Finance and Planning.

— (2004), *Kenya 1999 Population and Housing Census: Analytical Report on Migration and Urbanization: Volume VI*. Nairobi: Central Bureau of Statistics, Ministry of Planning and National Development.

— (2007), *Summary of the National Water Services Strategy 2007-2015*. Nairobi: Ministry of Water and Irrigation.

— (2008), *Nairobi Metro 2030: A World Class African Metropolis*. Nairobi: Ministry of Nairobi Metropolitan Development.

— (2010a), *The 2009 Kenya Population and Housing Census: Volume 1C: Population Distribution by Age, Sex, and Administrative Units*. Nairobi: KNBS.

— (2010b), *The 2009 Kenya Population and Housing Census: Volume 1I: Population and Household Distribution by Socio-Economic Characteristics*. Nairobi: KNBS.

UNDESA (United Nations Department of Economic and Social Affairs) (2009), *World Population Prospects: The 2008 Revision*. New York: United Nations.

— (2010), *World Urbanization Prospects: The 2009 Revision*. New York: United Nations.

UN-HABITAT (United Nations Human Settlements Programme) (2008), *State of the World's Cities 2010/11: Bridging the Urban Divide*. London: Earthscan.

— (2010), *Solid Waste Management in the World's Cities: Water and Sanitation in the World's Cities 2010*. London: Earthscan.

UN-HABITAT (United Nations Human Settlements Programme) and UNEP (United Nations Environment Programme) (2010), *The State of African Cities 2010: Governance, Inequality and Urban Land Markets*. Nairobi: UN-HABITAT.

UNHCR (United Nations High Commission for Refugees) (2010a), *2009 Global Trends: Refugees, Asylum-Seekers, Returnees, Internally Displaced and Stateless Persons*. Geneva: UNHCR.

— (2010b), "UNHCR Urban Refugee Policy—Nairobi." Available at: http://ochagwapps1.unog.ch/C12573DB0034913E/FB9A3459E0C5A152C1257205004F1C3E/CBA3CA51D73CCEA7C125771D007240B7/$FILE/Full_Report.pdf [Accessed November 8, 2010].

Wainaina, S. (2008), "Statement on Population Monitoring with a Focus on its Distribution, Urbanization, Internal Migration and Development," presented at the 41st Session of the UN Commission on Population and Development, April 7–11, New York. Available at: http://www.kenyaun.org/CountryPaperonPopulationDevelopment.html [Accessed November 12, 2010].

Warah, R. (2010), "How Numbers Game Turned Kibera into 'The Biggest Slum in Africa.'" Available at: http://www.nation.co.ke/oped/Opinion/-/440808/1009446/-/nyf5o7z/-/index.html [Accessed November 15, 2010].

World Bank (2009a), *Africa Development Indicators 2008/09: Youth and Employment in Africa*. Washington, DC: World Bank.

— (2009b), *Systems of Cities: Harnessing Urbanization for Growth and Poverty Alleviation*. Washington, DC: World Bank.

3

The Informal Economy

The informal economy in Kenya, and the rest of Africa also, emerged originally as small enterprise activities in response to the problems of survival associated with rapid urbanization and urban poverty. However, it is no longer a set of survival activities performed by people on the margins of society. It is, instead, a vibrant example of indigenous small enterprise activities leading to its successful growth and development and, as this chapter shows, is now widely recognized to have become a relatively important, autonomous, and self-propelling, representing the beneficial outcome of indigenous small enterprise development (Hope, 2001). In Kenya, the informal economy is also well known as the *jua kali* sector. *Jua Kali* is Swahili for "hot sun" or "fierce sun." It stems from the fact that the workers in the informal economy work under the hot sun beating down on their heads and backs. Gradually, the term was extended to refer to anyone in self-employment or small-scale industry, whether in the open air or in permanent premises. Some of the more recent official government publications, including the *Kenya Vision 2030* and the *MTP 2008-2012*, also use the term *jua kali* to refer to the informal economy.

Undoubtedly, the informal economy—sometimes alternatively referred to in the literature as the subterranean, hidden, underground, shadow, black, invisible, unofficial, second, cash, or parallel economy (Hope, 2001)—now constitutes an important component in the economic activities and process of development in Kenya. Although its relative importance was minimized in the past, the informal economy continues to thrive in Kenya and the rest of Africa. In this work, the informal economy is defined as consisting of those economic units and workers (both professionals and nonprofessionals), who engage in commercial activities outside of the realm of the *formally* established mechanisms for the conduct of such activities. It includes all forms of unregistered or unincorporated small-scale productive, vending, and service activities, and also comprises all forms of employment without secure contracts, worker benefits, or social protection both inside and outside informal enterprises. That is, the informal economy is characterized by: (1) informal employment in informal enterprises including employers, employees, own account operators, and unpaid contributing family workers; and (2) informal employment outside informal enterprises including domestic workers, casual or day laborers, temporary or part-time workers, industrial outworkers, and unregistered or undeclared workers (Hope, 2001; ILO, 2002).

Whereas the old definition of the informal economy included all those who work in informal enterprises, the new expanded concept includes all remunerative work—both self-employment and wage employment—that is not recognized, regulated, or protected by existing legal or regulatory frameworks, as well as nonremunerative work undertaken in an income-producing enterprise (ILO, 2002). This new definition embodies a major conceptual shift. It provides a new approach in defining informality in terms of employment status rather than, as in the earlier conceptualization, to enterprise characteristics. The old thinking on the informal economy defined employment as the self-employed in informal enterprises and their hired employees and assumed that informal entrepreneurs, not informal workers, were avoiding informality. The new thinking underscores the fact that many informal workers do not choose to be informal and would welcome becoming formalized if they were guaranteed secure contracts, worker benefits, social protection, and the right to be organized and represented (Chen, 2005). Consequently, it is now recognized that the informal economy consists of a wide range of informal enterprises and informal jobs.

The Nature of Kenya's Informal Economy

The activities of the informal economy do not show up in official statistics. However, although its exact quantitative magnitude defies any precise estimation, the informal economy, by all accounts, operates so "openly" and on such a vast scale in Kenya that any development policy thrust will be senseless unless it (the informal economy) is recognized and figured into such policy actions, particularly as a measure to cushion the impacts of urbanization and urban poverty, as observed in Chapter 2.

Originally, the activities of the informal economy were conducted primarily by self-employed and urban-based workers, most of whom were rural migrants and were engaged primarily in marginal production, service activities, and the importation of consumer goods which were in heavy demand in the urban areas of Kenya. In their original form, the informal economy activities constituted a manner in which those individuals and households at the bottom of the socioeconomic system were able to command and accumulate resources. It provides for those without the requisite educational credentials and/or skills to participate in the national economy and earn a livelihood. It also provided the wherewithal for those at the bottom of the economic ladder to exploit inefficiencies in the distribution of goods in the formal sector (Hope, 1993). According to Karl (1999–2000: 53), the informal economy is:

> ruled by resourcefulness and imagination. Reflecting the energy of people at the base of the social pyramid, it provides almost the only possibility of escape, and is frequently a source of hope, for those who work in it, either because they have to or out of convenience, with the common objective of improving their living conditions or simply surviving.

However, as far back as the 1970s, an ILO Kenya employment mission, through its fieldwork and its official report, recognized that the traditional sector had not only persisted but expanded also to include profitable and efficient enterprises as well as marginal activities (ILO, 1972). To highlight this view, the Kenya mission chose to use the term "informal" rather than "traditional" sector (Chen, 2005). Reflecting this evolution of the informal economy has been the fact that the Kenyan economy has failed to formally make the kind of sustained economic progress that would have allowed for, among other benefits, low urban unemployment and national poverty rates, and wages and salaries that kept pace with inflation. Despite that, for some time, it was basically accepted that the informal economy was somewhat of a transient phenomenon which would gradually disappear as the process of modernization took place and the formal economy thrived and absorbed more labor. However, such a notion was not only inconsistent with the facts and the emerging trends in Kenya, and other African countries, but was based essentially on the view (a negative one) that deemed such an economy as basically dysfunctional.

More recent analyses, however, including those contained in this book, provide evidence that the informal economy has not disappeared but, in fact, has grown substantially in Kenya and most other African countries also. Viewed from an historical perspective, the informal economy in Kenya today is considerably different to what it was a few decades ago and, now, its sheer size makes it a fundamental development issue in Kenya (Bigsten et al., 2004). Among the characteristics of this informal economy is the increasing rate of participation of women. The currently available evidence indicates that women are overrepresented in the informal economy. In the 1994/2000 period, women's wage employment as a proportion of total non-agricultural informal employment was 67 percent compared to 44 percent for men, and women's informal employment as a percentage of women's non-agricultural employment was 83 percent for the same period compared to 59 percent for men in the same indicator (ILO, 2002). In 2003, the percent of female youth (aged 15–24 years) in informal employment in urban areas was 64 percent and 73 percent in rural areas compared to 5.3 percent and 11.7 percent for males in urban and rural areas, respectively (UN-HABITAT and UNEP, 2010).

Also of significance here in terms of the characteristics of the informal economy is the fact that the activities have shifted outward from their original urban base and have now become more national in scope encompassing almost all areas of economic activity in both the urban and rural sectors. For example, the failure of the formal economy to continue to provide, maintain, and monitor a proper transportation network in Kenya has led to the emergence of *ad hoc*, but vital, transport systems which link up poor rural neighborhoods with the capital city and other urban areas, usually in the form of music-filled minibus taxis (*matatus*) as discussed in Chapter 2. Banio (1994) reported that, in 1989, the informal economy commanded a 51 percent market share of the transportation sector. However, during the past two decades, with the inefficiency and decline of the government-owned Kenya Bus Service, the informal economy's market share of the transportation sector now exceeds 80 percent.

The informal economy has also been differentiated from the formal one with respect to characteristics that include ease of entry, reliance on indigenous resources, family ownership of enterprises, small-scale operation, labor-intensive and adapted technology, skills acquisition outside the formal school sector, unregulated and competitive markets, and low productivity and income. Although those working in the informal economy work in an environment of uncertainty, unlike the formal economy, the informal economy is highly flexible, and entrepreneurs can rapidly change their activities to respond to the changing economic environment and market structures. In that regard, many publications have profiled several individuals and informal associations and organizations that have quickly and successfully adapted to changing market conditions (see, e.g., King, 1996; Kinyanjui, 2008, 2010; Macaria, 2007; Neuwirth, 2005).

Benefits of the Informal Economy

One immediate and obvious benefit derived through the existence and growth of the informal economy is the employment it creates. Jobs are created cheaply and large numbers of individuals, who would otherwise be unemployed and a burden to society, become gainfully employed. Kenya's dynamic informal economy remains the country's major employer and is estimated to currently account for almost 81 percent of the total employment progressively increasing from 23 percent in 1990 as seen in Figure 3.1. It is obvious therefore that the informal economy continues to absorb a large number of new labor force entrants as well as those who cannot find jobs in the formal sector. The creation of jobs in the informal economy is a conclusive demonstration that, given the appropriate environment, large numbers of individuals who are able and willing to work would be in a position to do so. The informal economy in Kenya is dominated by small-scale economic activities largely of self-employed individuals. Most enterprises are owned and run by individuals but some also employ a few people. Not surprisingly, therefore, the informal economy has been targeted by the government of Kenya to create productive and sustainable employment opportunities particularly for women and the youth (Republic of Kenya, 2008).

By 2010, the majority of the informal sector employment (61 percent) was located in the rural areas which means that the other 39 percent was in the urban areas. Not surprisingly, the capital city, Nairobi, had the largest number of informal sector workers in the urban areas at 63 percent and 25 percent of the national total (KNBS, 2011). In terms of employment by economic activity, 60 percent of informal sector workers were engaged in the wholesale and retail trade, hotels and restaurants industry; 20 percent in manufacturing; 10 percent in community, social, and personal services;

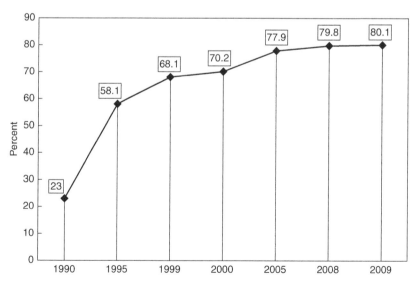

FIGURE 3.1 Informal sector employment as a proportion of total employment, 1990–2009
Source: Author, based on data from KNBS (1993, 1999, 2002, 2010).

3 percent in transport and communications; 2 percent in building and construction; and the remaining 5 percent were in other miscellaneous activities (KNBS, 2011).

Another benefit of the informal economy is its contribution to gross domestic and national product. The fact that the informal economy now permeates so much of economic life in Kenya then one would expect it to contribute an increasing share to national income in the country. Overall, the informal economy in Kenya was estimated to contribute 35 percent of GNP in the 1980s (Main, 1989). The ILO estimated that the informal economy contributed 25 percent to non-agricultural GDP in 1999 (ILO, 2002). Charmes (2006) estimated that the informal economy's contribution to total GDP was 18.5 percent in 1999. Ouma et al. (2007) derived estimates that showed the informal economy accounted for an average of 12 percent of GDP between 1975 and 1980, 19 percent during the period 1980–90, 26 percent during the period 1990–2000, and 20 percent during the period 2000–05. But, perhaps the most currently comprehensive estimates of the size of the informal economy in Kenya and other countries are provided by Schneider et al. (2010) covering the period 1999–2007 and replicated in Figure 3.2 for Kenya. Those estimates indicate that the informal economy averages 35.5 percent of GDP in Kenya. Irrespective of the source of the estimates, it is clear that the informal economy in Kenya is remarkably large and continues to grow. This size and growth

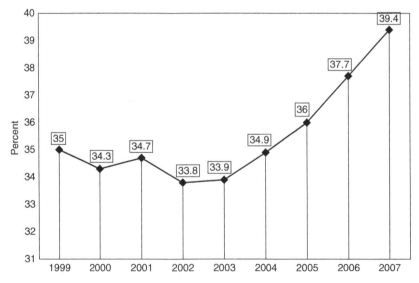

FIGURE 3.2 Size of Kenya's informal economy, 1999–2007 (% of GDP)
Source: Author, based on data from Schneider et al.(2010).

of the country's informal economy correlates with its absorption capacity of the labor force as previously discussed.

One other benefit of the informal economy in Kenya is that it constitutes an important component in the microfinance markets. It is a dominant source of credit particularly in the rural sector in Kenya where the institutional lenders are absent or ineffective and, the access to formal credit is extremely poor. The numerous types of moneylenders and credit suppliers in the informal economy include friends, relatives, landlords, commission agents, storekeepers, agricultural produce dealers, traders, employers of agricultural labor, and semi-informal financial services such as Savings and Credit Cooperatives (SACCOs), Rotating Savings and Credit Associations (ROSCAs), and Accumulating Savings and Credit Associations (ASCAs). Although the proportion of adult Kenyans that depend primarily on informal financial service providers has declined from 35 percent in 2006 to 27 percent in 2009 (FSD Kenya, 2010), the demand for microfinance services in Kenya remains large.

At the national level, the informal economy accounts for most of the financial services provided to small-scale producers and enterprises. Informal deposit services are provided through group savings associations and temporary loans can be arranged. It is estimated that there are more than 10,800 registered SACCOs serving more than 6.2 million members (FSD Kenya, 2010). Kenya also has many ROSCAs and ASCAs that are a source of savings and credit services. Approximately 29 percent of the country's adult population use ROSCAs, while some 5 percent use ASCAs (FSD Kenya, 2010). These associations operate either as registered (semi-informal) social welfare groups or as unregistered groups of friends and family members. These informal providers mobilize savings and offer credit while at the same time providing important social networks and forms of support in times of difficulty and crisis (FSD Kenya, 2010).

Undoubtedly, the most popular form of informal finance in Kenya is that of the ROSCAs where all members are both savers and borrowers. In ROSCAs, which are referred to as *mabati* or "merry-go-rounds" in Kenya, members pool their money into a common rotating fund. The fund is held by a group leader, informally selected from among the members of the group, who is responsible for periodically collecting a fixed share from each member. In some groups, no leader is chosen and funds are collected when the members gather for regularly scheduled meetings. Each member contributes a predetermined and agreed to amount into the common fund. The money collected is then given in a rotation as a lump-sum payment to each member of the group. The process repeats itself until each member has received the fund. The basic principle by which the fund is shared is balance reciprocity.

Each ROSCA member draws out of the fund or pot as much as he or she puts into it and it allows most of these members to finance some expenditures much sooner than if they had relied on their own other savings efforts.

ROSCAs are said to have existed on the African continent since the mid-nineteenth century with an origin traceable to the Yoruba tribe (Bouman, 1995; Hope, 2008). However, they have now evolved from their use for financing consumption goods, school fees, and the like to become a major source of finance for small enterprises in both the urban and rural areas. In their current structure, there is substantial variation among these ROSCAs with respect to the frequency of contributions to the fund, the amount of the contribution, the number of members, and the manner the order of the receipt of the fund is determined. In some cases, the order of the fund distribution is randomly determined by drawing lots, in others it is done by consensus, and in some it is agreed through a bidding process in which the fund goes to the member bidding the highest minus the bid amount and other members pay their contribution minus their share of the bid amount (Anderson and Baland, 2002; de Aghion and Morduch, 2005; Mersland and Eggen, 2008). Participation in a bidding ROSCA, also known as an auction ROSCA, is comparable to an insurance mechanism. By paying a fee (the highest bid for the pool or pot) the member can access money when needed.

Although ROSCAs are national in scope in Kenya, in the rural areas they are widespread among all segments of the rural population, while in the urban areas they are more prevalent among the low- and middle-income groups. ROSCAs are widespread and popular in Kenya and other African countries for two reasons primarily. First is the very high responsiveness of ROSCAs to the economic and social requirements of their members. For example, limited number of participants; specific duration of the savings/credit cycle; the amount of individual participation; the order of rotation and receipt of funds; absolute freedom of joining; easily understandable rules and procedures; consistency of rules and procedures with sociocultural norms of the environment; very good accessibility and so on. ROSCAs are therefore simpler to understand and run compared to credit cooperatives and associations, for example, because they (ROSCAs) are built on informal understandings among friends and acquaintances, while cooperatives and associations typically have a formal constitution and a degree of legal status (de Aghion and Morduch, 2005). This simplicity has advantages. "The life of a ROSCA has a clear beginning and an end, accounting is straightforward (one only has to keep track of who has received the pot already and who is in line to do so), and storage of funds is not required since money goes straight from one person's pocket into another's" (de Aghion and Morduch, 2005: 59).

The second reason has to do with the very high economic efficiency of the ROSCAs. Transaction costs are low or nonexistent since there are no expenses for office space or personnel, nor for assessing creditworthiness; and repayment rates are high since there are usually no defaults due to strong cultural norms and social pressures and cohesion. ROSCAs not only facilitate savings but they also allow members to finance investment activities, goods, and services much earlier than through individual savings (de Aghion and Morduch, 2005). They, therefore, represent a creative small-scale solution to the problem of access to credit for small-scale entrepreneurs and the poor. Moreover, in terms of savings, ROSCAs have a significant advantage that is missing from other informal mechanisms. The public aspect and precommitment associated with ROSCA membership also serves as a mechanism to foster discipline and encourage savings in ways that may not otherwise be possible. Evidence from the literature on informal financial institutions in Kenya indicates that ROSCAs have been the bedrock of savings mobilization especially in the rural areas. Most participants report that ROSCAs make them committed to save (to get the strength to save), and, further, in the case of women, ROSCAs allow for the protection of their household savings against claims by their partners for use for other household needs or immediate consumption (Anderson and Baland, 2002; Gugerty, 2007; Mutua and Oyugi, 2007).

The final benefit of the informal economy in Kenya is that it depicts and represents a true spirit of innovation and entrepreneurship. It comprises a mixture of small self-employment efforts and dynamic micro- and small enterprises covering a variety of activities that concentrate mainly in the urban areas but are also very evident in the rural areas as well (Bigsten et al., 2004; King, 1996; Kinyanjui, 2010). The informal economy is also an avenue through which unskilled persons who migrate from rural to urban areas acquire skills that enable them to survive in a more challenging urban environment. Skilled individuals are also attracted to the informal economy when they lose formal sector jobs or are beginners in self-employment, engaging themselves in productive activities and breaking away from the system of wage labor. Rather than succumb to hopelessness and helplessness, the informal economy participants adopt an entrepreneurial path for addressing labor market concerns and social protection issues. The entrepreneurial path entails founding micro- and small business in manufacturing, retail trade, transport, repair services, agriculture, personal services, extractive activities, and building and construction, for instance (Kinyanjui, 2010; Macaria, 2007). Social relations and associations address social finance issues, such as savings and credit (Kinyanjui, 2010).

Some Disbenefits of the Informal Economy

Undoubtedly, the benefits derived from the existence and growth of the informal economy in Kenya outweighs, by far, the disbenefits. The principal disbenefit is that it provides potential cover for tax evasion/avoidance, drug trafficking, and smuggling. However, that state of affairs only exists where tax administration and/or law enforcement are inept and/or influenced by corrupt actions. As discussed in Chapter 4, corruption and lax law enforcement are huge problems in Kenya with serious negative consequences on the country's growth and development trajectory. It is perhaps understandable that entrepreneurs in the informal economy would attempt to evade all the taxes they can, particularly given the consideration that in the formal economy such tax evasion would be more difficult.

However, the problem with such tax evasion/avoidance is that it reduces the national revenues and therefore has the potential to reduce the government's ability to expend on national programs by a similar amount. This can lead to the possibility of additional tax burdens (Hope, 1993). Determination of the amount of evasion is very difficult in any country, and particularly in the African countries. It is often heard in many African countries, including Kenya that tax evasion is on the rise. But, quantification of such evasion is almost impossible. Although the forms of evasion vary widely among countries, the major methods used for evading taxes in the informal economy include failure to report all sales, under-invoicing, overstating nontaxable sales, and the nondeclaration of commissions retained overseas.

Empirical studies of tax evasion in Kenya have been few. But, Levin and Widell (2007), in measuring the general effect of tax rates on tax evasion using data on the trade flow between Kenya and Tanzania, estimated the amount of tax evasion in the trade flows between the two countries and found that there was evidence of under-reporting in unit values for the year 2004 as well as evidence of mislabeling. On the other hand, a more recent output by Bouët and Roy (2009) finds a significant and robust impact of tax evasion via quantities. Iarossi (2009) also noted from survey data that Kenyan informal firms declare only 20 percent of their sales, compared with more than 80 percent declared by formal small firms. Nonetheless, and perhaps because the national tax authority is aware of the tax evasion/avoidance problem by informal firms, microfirms are more easily subjected to harassment by tax officials. In that regard, as Iarossi (2009: 94–5) further observed:

> Although microfirms are visited as frequently as formal firms—close to 80 percent of microfirms report having been visited by tax officials last year [2008]—the difference between visits to formal and informal micros is

striking. Firms that have chosen informality are visited once every three to four days by tax officials, compared with formal microfirms, which are visited once every three to four months. That is much higher than in any comparator country.

Some estimates of the potential tax accruable from the informal economy have been provided by Ouma et al. (2007). They found that this economy could have provided tax revenues averaging about 4 percent of GDP between 1975 and 2005, and therefore implying that the government had the potential to expand the tax base by 4 percent of GDP during that period. This, accordingly, would have increased government tax revenues by the approximate equivalent of US$728 million in 2005. This represents significant potential revenue loss to the Kenya treasury.

With respect to smuggling, from the days of the first customs duties, smuggling in a great variety of forms has been the primary form of escape. There are a number of factors that may encourage smuggling in Kenya. These include (1) vast stretches of almost unguarded borders and very lengthy coastlines that make a complete patrol impossible; (2) the general desire to evade taxes; and (3) a desire to get contraband goods into the country where there is a heavy demand and rich dividend from distribution of such goods. In fact, Kenya has become a major point of transshipment of drugs as noted in several media reports. Allen (2006) reported that the Kenyan sea port of Mombasa, East Africa's busiest, is now seen as a key staging post in the international drugs trail. Drugs are smuggled in from such countries as Pakistan, Afghanistan, and Iran and then moved on to other countries often via transborder movements to Uganda and other countries with Europe as the usual final destination. Drug seizures have been increasing in Kenya in recent years and the very size of these busts suggests that the drugs were not destined for Kenya, but for other, more lucrative, markets overseas. Nonetheless, there is a recognized view that the police have a very poor record of investigation and arrests in this area (Muriuki, 2008).

One fundamental constraint is the fact that Kenya is grappling with two simultaneous challenges—a growing indigenous drug problem (both use and transshipment) and high levels of corruption—making it a convenient transit and storage point for international drug cartels (Allen, 2006). Poverty, geography, and corruption all conspire to make Kenya an attractive storage, distribution, and transit point for drugs such as heroin, cocaine, and cannabis because of its excellent airline connections and busy sea port.

Bribery is also a problem associated with the informal economy in Kenya and it stems from the persistent corruption in the country as discussed in Chapter 4. Bribery is a major cost of functioning in the informal economy and informal economy enterprises have to devote a large part of their income to bribing the authorities including tax officials. One survey indicates that 44 percent of informal businesses report being asked for bribes by tax officials compared to 15 percent of formal microfirms. More generally, informal businesses are much more subject to bribes. They pay 1 percent more of sales in illegal payments to get things done compared with formal microfirms (Iarossi, 2009). Such bribery has the potential of increasing the cost of goods and services. In addition, the payment of such bribes represents the purchasing of security from prosecution. This then can be regarded as a negative externality of informality.

Conclusions

Undoubtedly, the informal economy is destined to be a permanent feature of the Kenyan socioeconomic landscape. As shown above, informal economy activities have been expanding in both scenarios of periods of contracting of the formal economy and periods of expansion of the formal economy. Kenya's informal economy has emerged to the point where it is directly responsible for the improvement in the standard of living of large numbers of people and, despite some of its disbenefits, contributes significantly to the bettering of life in general in the country. The principal beneficiaries are the poor and, particularly, the urban poor. Given this generally positive contribution, then the informal economy must be regarded and treated as an integral aspect of the policy framework for improving livelihoods and reducing poverty in Kenya.

The informal economy has exhibited a vibrancy and resilience that, this book argues, must be enhanced. The entrepreneurial spirit of the *jua kali* must be allowed to continue to flourish. There is no inherent conflict with, or disadvantage to, the formal economy in the existence of the informal economy. In fact, it is more and more being shown that the informal economy is both competitive with and complementary to the level of activity of the formal economy and both types of economy are best understood as such rather than as segmented sectors (Hope, 1993, 2001; Oviedo et al., 2009). Encouraging entrepreneurship through micro- and small enterprise development of the type represented by the informal economy is a positive pro-poor development policy. "Facilitating entrepreneurship is a sound strategy—and arguably the best strategy—for accelerating economic growth" (Baumol et al., 2007: 147). This type of entrepreneurship is now promoted as bottom-of-the pyramid innovations indicating the grassroots and lower income levels from which it tends to be driven. Consequently, the debate over the permanence or nonpermanence of the informal economy is over. The evidence is overwhelming. The informal economy is here to stay. In effect, the informal has become normal.

With respect to informal finance, and as noted in Chapter 1, there remains considerable need for savings and credit products on the supply side of the formal economy to match the demand needs of the poor and micro- and small enterprises especially in the rural areas. Nonetheless, as this work has also pointed out, ROSCAs, for instance, will not disappear. They have an historical and cultural base which meets the ideals of a large chunk of the populace. This is so because they provide a simple and straightforward method and process for savings mobilization and access to credit within a local environment and among groups of people who are known to each other and are pursuing the same objectives in terms of access to financial services. However, in the rural areas, there remains the need for the government to play a more proactive role in advancing both the dialogue and promoting product development in the agricultural credit sector.

Finally, as previously discussed, most informal workers would rather have a formal job with social protection coverage. However, for the reasons also discussed above, there are not enough of those jobs being created in Kenya's formal economy. Moreover, the entrepreneurial spirit of the poor has also been driving the growth of informal economic activities in the country. There, therefore, needs to be a focus on social protection for informal workers. Informal work is, by definition, work without access to work-related measures of social protection. As observed by Lund (2009), informal workers, whether self-employed or wage workers, generally: (1) cannot usually afford to purchase private insurance against risk; (2) live in poor communities which cannot co-insure against risk; and (3) are excluded from contributory schemes, such as unemployment insurance and workers compensation, against accidents at work. By providing access to social protection coverage, African societies and countries, such as Kenya, can be seen as investing in the human potential of poorer workers who operate in the informal economy. Social protection, without a doubt, contributes to people being able to escape poverty.

Two frequently cited examples of good practice of social protection coverage for informal economy workers are those provided by the Self-Employed Women's Association (SEWA) in India and the Self-Employed Women's Union (SEWU) in South Africa (Hope, 2001, 2008). The SEWU was modeled on the SEWA. Like the SEWA, the SEWU is a trade union of women who work in the informal economy. The SEWA was established in 1972 and the SEWU was launched in 1994. Both organizations focus on the empowerment of their membership. They provide various direct services or advice to their members to address health care, child care, asset insurance, life insurance, training, social security, maternity benefits, and disability benefits, for example. These empowerment actions stem from the fundamental premise that investment in social protection is a proactive element of ensuring human development as well as a way of tackling poverty.

References

Allen, K. (2006), "Traffickers' Drugs Haven in Kenya." Available at: http://news. bbc.co.uk/2/hi/africa/4753377.stm [Accessed October 12, 2010].

Anderson, S. and Baland, J-M. (2002), "The Economics of ROSCAs and Intra-household Resource Allocation," *Quarterly Journal of Economics*, 117(3), 963–95.

Banio, G. A. (1994), "Deregulation of Urban Public Transport Services," *Third World Planning Review*, 16(4), 411–28.

Baumol, W. J., Litan, R. E., and Schramm, C. J. (2007), *Good Capitalism, Bad Capitalism and the Economics of Growth and Prosperity*. New Haven, CT: Yale University Press.

Bigsten, A., Kimuyu, P., and Lundvall, K. (2004), "What to do with the Informal Sector?," *Development Policy Review*, 22(6), 701–15.

Bouët, A. and Roy, D. (2009), "Trade Protection and Tax Evasion: Evidence from Kenya, Mauritius and Nigeria." Available at: http://catt.univ-pau.fr/live/ digitalAssets/88/88082_Final_draft_evasion_paper__30_april_2009_.pdf [Accessed September 4, 2010].

Bouman, F. (1995), "ROSCA: On the Origin of the Species," *Savings and Development*, 19(2), 117–48.

Charmes, J. (2006), "Measurement of the Contribution of Informal Sector and Informal Employment to GDP in Developing Countries: Some Conceptual and Methodological Issues." Available at: http://www.unescap.org/stat/isie/ reference-materials/National-Accounts/Measurement-Contribution-GDP-Concept-Delhi-Group.pdf [Accessed October 8, 2010].

Chen, M. (2005), "Rethinking the Informal Economy: From Enterprise Characteristics to Employment Relations." In N. Kudva and L. Benería (eds), *Rethinking Informalization: Poverty, Precarious Jobs and Social Protection*. Ithaca, NY: Cornell University Open Access Repository. Available at: http://ecom-mons.cornell.edu/bitstream/1813/3716/1/Rethinking%20Informalization. pdf [Accessed August 4, 2010].

De Aghion, B. A. and Morduch, J. (2005), *The Economics of Microfinance*. Cambridge, MA: The MIT Press.

FSD (Financial Sector Deepening) Kenya (2010), *FSD Kenya Impact Assessment: Summary Report*. Nairobi: FSD Kenya.

Gugerty, M. K. (2007), "You Can't Save Alone: Commitment in Rotating Savings and Credit Associations in Kenya," *Economic Development and Cultural Change*, 55(2), 251–82.

Hope, K. R. (1993), "Growth and Impact of the Subterranean Economy in the Third World," *Futures: The Journal of Policy, Planning and Futures Studies*, 25(8), 864–76.

— (2001), "Indigenous Small Enterprise Development in Africa: Growth and Impact of the Subterranean Economy," *The European Journal of Development Research*, 13(1), 30–46.

— (2008), *Poverty, Livelihoods, and Governance in Africa: Fulfilling the Development Promise*. New York: Palgrave Macmillan.

Iarossi, G. (2009), *An Assessment of the Investment Climate in Kenya*. Washington, DC: World Bank.

ILO (International Labor Office) (1972), *Employment, Incomes and Equality: A Strategy for Increasing Productive Employment in Kenya*. Geneva: ILO.

— (2002), *Women and Men in the Informal Economy: A Statistical Picture*. Geneva: ILO.

Karl, K. (1999–2000), "The Informal Sector," *The Courier*, No. 178, 53–4.

King, K. (1996), *Jua Kali Kenya: Change and Development in an Informal Economy 1970-95*. London: James Currey.

Kinyanjui, M. N. (2008), "Is Informal Enterprise a Path to Urban Socio-Economic Dynamism in Nairobi?," *Paper No. 4*. Milton Keynes, UK: International Development Centre, Open University.

— (2010), "Social Relations and Associations in the Informal Sector in Kenya," *Social Policy and Development Programme Paper Number 43*. Geneva: United Nations Research Institute for Social Development (UNRISD).

KNBS (Kenya National Bureau of Statistics) (1993), *Economic Survey 1993*. Nairobi: KNBS.

— (1999), *Economic Survey 1999*. Nairobi: KNBS.

— (2002), *Economic Survey 2002*. Nairobi: KNBS.

— (2010), *Economic Survey 2010*. Nairobi: KNBS.

— (2011), *Economic Survey 2011*. Nairobi: KNBS.

Levin, J. and Widell, L. M. (2007), "Tax Evasion in Kenya and Tanzania: Evidence from Missing Imports," *Working Paper No. 8*. Örebro, Sweden: Department of Economics, Örebro University.

Lund, F. (2009), "Social Protection and the Informal Economy: Linkages and Good Practices for Poverty Reduction and Empowerment." In OECD (ed.), *Promoting Pro-Poor Growth: Social Protection*. Paris: OECD, pp. 69–88.

Macaria, D. C. (2007), *The Entrepreneurial Spirit: The Jua Kali Micro and Small Enterprises of Kenya*. Bangor, ME: Booklocker.com Inc.

Main, J. (1989), "How to Make Poor Counties Rich," *Fortune*, January 16, 101–6.

Mersland, R. and Eggen, O. (2008), *"You Cannot Save Alone": Financial and Social Mobilization in Savings and Credit Groups*. Oslo: Norwegian Agency for Development Cooperation.

Muriuki, A. (2008), "Kenya: A Popular Drug Trafficking Hub." Available at: http://www.afrika.no/Detailed/16335.html [Accessed October 12, 2010].

Mutua, J. M. and Oyugi, L. N. (2007), "Poverty Reduction through Enhanced Rural Access to Financial Services in Kenya," *SEAPREN (Southern and Eastern Africa Policy Research Network) Working Paper No. 6*. Windhoek: Namibian Economic Policy Research Unit.

Neuwirth, R. (2005), *Shadow Cities: A Billion Squatters, a New Urban World*. New York: Routledge.

Ouma, S., Njeru, J., Khainga, D., Kiriga, B., and Kamau, A. (2007), "Estimating the Size of the Underground Economy in Kenya," *KIPPRA Discussion Paper No. 82*. Nairobi: KIPPRA.

Oviedo, A. M., Thomas, M. R., and Karakurum-Özdemir, K. (2009), *Economic Informality: Causes, Costs, and Policies—A Literature Survey*. Washington, DC: World Bank.

Republic of Kenya (2008), *Kenya Vision 2030: First Medium Term Plan, (2008-2012)*. Nairobi: Republic of Kenya.

Schneider, F., Buehn, A., and Montenegro, C. F. (2010), "Shadow Economies All Over the World: New Estimates for 162 Countries from 1999 to 2007," *Policy Research Working Paper 5356*. Washington, DC: World Bank.

UN-HABITAT (United Nations Human Settlements Programme) and UNEP (United Nations Environment Programme) (2010), *The State of African Cities 2010: Governance, Inequality and Urban Land Markets*. Nairobi: UN-HABITAT.

4

Corruption and Development

"It can hardly be said that corruption in Kenya is limited to a few rogue officials at the top. The culture of corruption has grown roots in society at large and become endemic" (Mogeni, 2009: 1). This entrenchment of corruption in Kenya points to the fact that something has gone wrong in the governance of the country. Institutions, which were designed for the regulation of the relationships between citizens and the State, are being used instead for the personal enrichment of public officials (politicians and bureaucrats) and other corrupt private agents (individuals, groups, businesses). In particular, opportunistic bureaucrats and politicians have been successfully maximizing their take without regard for such perdition on the size of the overall pie and thereby accounting for the growth of corrupt activities and the particularly adverse impact that corruption has in the country (Hope and Chikulo, 2000; Kaufmann, 1997). As further noted by Zutt (2010: 1), "corruption is clearly happening in Kenya, and it involves not only the public sector, but also the private sector and civil society."

Corruption is a governance ill wherever it occurs. It is a characteristic of bad governance. It persists in Kenya primarily because there are people with power and/or influence who benefit from it, and the existing governance institutions lack both the will and capacity to stop them from doing so. Despite the existence of a Kenya Anti-Corruption Commission (KACC) and several other measures that have been put in place to try to tackle the corruption problem, Kenya is still classified as one of the most corrupt States in the world (TI, 2009, 2010a). This chapter takes a governance and development perspective to examine the causes, consequences, and efforts to control corruption in Kenya. It synthesizes and analyzes available data, indicators, and other information in that regard and then offers a set of recommendations for more effective control in this aspect of governance.

Why Corruption Persists in Kenya: Causes

Where corruption persists, as it does in Kenya, it is an indication of things (such as governance institutions) falling apart. Corruption in Kenya is systemic and goes beyond individuals to the structural and institutional levels. As the US Secretary of State, Hillary Rodham Clinton (2009: 1) noted in a speech in Nairobi, "the absence of strong and effective democratic institutions has permitted on-going corruption, impunity, politically motivated violence and a lack of respect for a rule of law." Secretary Clinton (2009: 5) further said that "true economic progress . . . also depends on responsible governments that reject corruption, enforce the rule of law, and deliver results for their people."

The primary cause of corruption in Kenya is, therefore, related to a societal state of being whereby the basic institutions that underpin and support the rule of law and good governance have been deliberately undermined or neglected to the point where they can no longer uphold the rule of law or act in the best interests of the nation. That undermining and neglect have been systematically applied as Kenya's institutions outside of the executive were weakened in favor of personalized presidential power and a centralized presidency that reached a crescendo under the presidency of Daniel Arap Moi (Mueller, 2008) who ruled the country for 24 years from 1978 to 2002. In fact, according to the National Anti-Corruption Plan (NACP), the "emergence of wanton poor institutional governance, an atmosphere of impunity to the rule of law, low morale and inefficiency—contributed immensely to an environment that enabled corruption to thrive and reach devastating levels" (NACP Secretariat, nd: 3). The resultant cause as well as effect is the fact that ethical leadership and, therefore, public accountability became seriously lacking. Public accountability means holding public officials responsible for their actions. It is also central to good governance. Such a lack of real accountability is a major bane of Kenya which has bred irresponsibility among public officials and has further led to much cynicism among Kenyans.

The centralized and personalized presidential power that emerged under President Moi resulted in what can only be characterized as the total exercise of all power attached to national sovereignty. This exercise of State power led to the supremacy of the State over civil society and, in turn, to the ascendancy of patrimonialism with its stranglehold on the economic and political levers of power, through which corruption thrived for it was through this stranglehold that all decision-making occurred and patronage was dispensed. In fact, one analysis asserts that "controlling the state was the means [used by President Moi] to entrench an ethnically defined class and to ensure its enrichment" (Mueller, 2008: 188). Another noted that, "under Moi, economic mismanagement, corruption, and wanton destruction of national resources became rampant" (Khadiagala, 2009: 128). The "control of state power meant control of public wealth leading to patronage, looting and bribery" (NACP Secretariat, nd: 3). Consequently, no distinction was made between public and private interests and government officials simply plundered the Treasury and appropriated State assets. This behavior turned Kenya into a kleptocratic or "vampire state" where the rulers and their associates engaged in the ruthless looting of the country's wealth as they wished. This further popularized the Kenya vernacular "eating"—which means gorging on State resources. This state of affairs, in turn, has led to a crisis of governance where many leaders, working not for the good of the country as such but for themselves and their political supporters, followed a system where power has been centralized in the hands of a few and personalized around the presidency since independence (Hansen, 2009; Waki Commission, 2008).

Such was the pervasiveness of the kleptocracy in Kenya that the citizenry adapted to it. Individuals, as well as those people in positions of authority and/or influence, tended to shift their loyalties and allegiances to the ruling regime for reasons of both personal survival and economic gain. The system of patronage, therefore, thrived and corrupt behavior cascaded down to the society at large. Being part of, or regarded as belonging to, particular groupings became a more acceptable qualification for a given position or contract, for example, than actual capabilities. The result was that the stage became set for corruption to become rampant. It became truly ubiquitous, reaching into the private sector as well. It also became a way of life, particularly for transactions at a governmental level or with public officials. Those transactions sought to do no more than to secure objectives that were private and personal and not in the interests of the country and thereby corroded popular confidence in Kenya's public institutions. In fact, one publication observed that under President Moi "the impact of State House's system of authorized looting, . . . a Minister later estimated to have cost the taxpayer a total of 635 billion Kenya shillings (roughly $US10 billion) in the space of twenty-four years" (Wrong, 2009: 184–5).

Subsequent governments were also caught up in the now entrenched system of corruption in Kenya (Wrong, 2009). In 2002, promising to form a government that was committed to good governance and the rule of law, Mwai Kibaki campaigned on an anti-corruption platform and was elected President in a landslide victory, with 62 percent of the votes, as the presidential candidate of the National Alliance of Rainbow Coalition (NARC), which was an umbrella group of opposition political parties. This victory represented the first transfer of power through elections since independence in 1963 and marked the beginning of some dramatic anti-corruption reforms. Kenyans had, therefore, hoped that with the departure of former President Moi from Kenya's political scene and the ascension to power of the NARC, the political system that had become almost synonymous with corruption would undergo fundamental redemption (Otieno, 2005).

As noted by the World Bank (2009a: 1):

> the initial reforms—the removal of corrupt judges, the passage of a new procurement law, and the strengthening of the Controller and Auditor General's Office—resulted in a surge in national and international optimism about the direction the country had taken and expectations that improved governance would lead to a more secure and prosperous country.

However, the early governance reforms of 2002 and 2003 soon floundered, undermined by new allegations of corruption and the resurfacing of previous ones. "The administration's reformist credentials were badly eroded following the revelation of a number of high-profile corruption scandals [in 2006] that implicated senior members of [the] government" (World Bank, 2009a: 1). Consequently, and "unfortunately, what began as a promising experiment in governance in the African context increasingly presented itself as an unwieldy and unruly collection of warring factions . . ." (Otieno, 2005: 74). "The jostling for power paralyzed decision-making and reignited the past practices of corruption, impunity, and subversion of formal institutions by informal ones" (Khadiagala, 2009: 129). Examples of the scope and magnitude of public sector initiated, or involvement in, corruption in the country abound and there have been many such lists published. Okanja (2010), Global Integrity (2009), and Wikipedia (2010), for instance, have compiled timeline dossiers which put the value of these corrupt activities as hundreds of billion Kenyan shillings (tens of billion US dollars) between 1990 and 2009. This represented considerable revenue leakage with severe consequences for development and economic progress in the country as will be discussed later in this work.

Apart from personalized presidential power accompanied by the weakened institutions of governance, there are also some secondary factors that have been contributing to corruption in Kenya, having cascaded down to society at large. One of these factors is the high incidence of bribery. Whatever the transaction—getting a driver's licence, getting a national identity card, tax administration decisions, and government contracts for goods and/or services, for example—required the bureaucratic exercise of assumed powers. This, in turn, meant that bribes were demanded and had to be paid for the transactions to be completed. This can be regarded as the systematic exploitation of illegal income-earning schemes by public officials and the enhancement of rent-seeking opportunities. Incentives for corrupt behavior have, therefore, arisen in Kenya, as well as some other African states, because public officials have considerable control over the instruments regulating valuable socioeconomic benefits and private parties are willing to make illegal payments to secure those benefits (Hope, 2000).

Several surveys have been completed and much evidence has been gathered about the extent of bribery in Kenya. Transparency International-Kenya, for example, regularly publishes *The Kenya Bribery Index* which is compiled from a "survey that captures corruption as experienced by ordinary citizens in their interaction with officials of both public and private organizations" (TI-Kenya, 2008: 3). Bribes are analyzed in terms of their various purposes based on five categories: (1) law enforcement (avoiding consequences of wrong doing and/or harassment by the relevant authority); (2) access to services (such as medical treatment, school placement, water, electricity, and so on); (3) business (obtaining contracts, expediting payments, and so on); (4) regulatory compliance (to obtain some licence or permit and thus comply with some law or regulation); and (5) employment matters (securing jobs, promotions, transfers, training, and so on). In addition, the five categories are disaggregated within six indicators that capture different bribery dimensions as follows (TI-Kenya, 2008):

- *Incidence*—The proportion of clients who have interacted with an organization and report encountering bribery situations in their official dealings with that organization. This offers a measure of the opportunity for and propensity of officials in an organization to request and accept bribes.
- *Prevalence*—The proportion of the survey respondents who report paying a bribe or were badly treated or not served for failing to do so. This indicator provides a measure of the impact of bribery in an organization related to the population it serves.
- *Severity*—The frequency of denial of service if bribes are not paid. This is a measure of the negative impact of this form of corruption on the public's ability to access goods and services to which entitled.
- *Frequency*—The average number of bribes paid per respondent. This is a measure of the scale of bribery activity in an organization related to those who interact with it.
- *Cost*—The average expenditure on bribery per person. This is an indicator of the extra "tax burden" that results from such practices.
- *Size*—The average size (magnitude) of bribes paid. This is an indicator of the premium that citizens put on a particular service or the cost/penalty avoided or the value that those demanding/receiving such bribes put on the goods and services they are required to deliver.

The most recent Kenya Bribery Index (2008) indicates that 56 percent of respondents encountered bribery in their interactions with both public and private organizations compared to 34 percent in 2005. The mean size of bribe across the five category purposes is approximately US$48 with bribes for employment leading the way with an average size of approximately US$85. However, the majority of the bribes (45%) were to gain access to services while 6 percent were for employment. The most corrupt Kenyan organization, as it relates to bribery, is the Kenya Police. Some 93 percent of respondents reported a likelihood of a bribe demand by the Police, whereas 59 percent reported that they actually encountered a bribe situation with said Kenya Police, and 52 percent reported that a failure or refusal to comply with such a bribe demand resulted in their failure to access the service or their incurring punishment (TI-Kenya, 2008). Paying these bribes imposes a direct financial cost, an additional tax burden, on Kenyans. Most of the bribes paid (52%) are between the equivalents of US$0.01 and 71 paid very frequently (TI-Kenya, 2008).

In terms of comparison with its subregional neighbors, *The East African Bribery Index [EABI] 2010* indicates that Kenya has relinquished its position to Burundi as the most corrupt country in East Africa. The EABI is a governance tool developed to measure bribery levels and the prevalence of corruption in the private and public sectors in the East African subregion. The corruption (bribery) prevalence rate in, descending order of magnitude, was determined to be 36.7 percent in Burundi, 33 percent in Uganda, 31.9 percent in Kenya (down from 45% in 2009), 28.6 percent in Tanzania, and 6.6 percent in Rwanda (TI-Kenya, 2010a). The EABI 2010 clearly shows that apart from Rwanda, where incidents of bribery were found to be negligible, corruption is still an impediment to responsive public service delivery in the East African subregion. Key governance and enforcement institutions such as the police and judiciary continue to feature prominently in the index. The Kenya Police is the third most corrupt subregional institution behind the Revenue Authority in Burundi (first) and the Police also in Burundi (second) (TI-Kenya, 2010a).

Other surveys on corruption in Kenya's private sector also indicate that bribery remains one of the top bottlenecks for firms in the country. Seventy-five percent of firms in Kenya reported having to make informal/illegal payments to "get things done" (Iarossi, 2009). It is estimated that such corruption costs Kenyan firms approximately 4 percent of their annual sales, which is considered to be very high by international comparison (Iarossi, 2009). Moreover, Kenyan firms are required to pay approximately 12 percent of the value of a public contract in informal/illegal payments (Iarossi, 2009). In addition, bribes to tax inspectors are also fairly common in Kenya with about one-third of sampled firms reporting that tax inspectors have requested informal/illegal payments. Similarly, as well, are the requests for informal/illegal payments for licensing and utility connections (Iarossi, 2009). Then there are 71 percent of firms that indicated that they expected to give gifts (make illegal contributions) to secure a government contract compared to 38 percent across sub-Saharan Africa and 28 percent world-wide (Enterprise Surveys, 2007). There is also the aspect of the common practice of police requesting payments from trucks in transit which is not only regarded as unique to Kenya (Iarossi, 2009), but it also confirms the findings regarding the police in *The Kenya Bribery Index* previously alluded to. One Director of the KACC has stated that the transport sector pays bribery to police officers, and other institutions such as the judiciary, equivalent to US$22.5 million annually (Lumumba, 2011).

Also, the bribery culture in Kenya has seeped into the country's Parliament. And, "accusations of bribery within parliament abound" (Otieno, 2005: 76). According to Rugene (2009: 1) "corrupt dealings involving Members of Parliament [MPs] have taken root inside the House" with money frequently changing hands to influence the outcome of some House business. This is both a classic example of a total disregard for the rule of law and the environment of bad governance that it represents. Bribes are allegedly paid to Kenya's MPs from both internal and external sources. Internally, some of their fellow MPs (regarded as wealthy) pay these bribes, while externally the bribes are paid by businesspersons with the same intended outcome—in the guise of lobbying the targeted MPs to debate or vote in a way that favors the interests of the briber (Mars Group Kenya Media, 2004; Rugene, 2009; TI-Kenya, 2010b). The former MP Joe Khamisi has confirmed that "if one asks whether or not MPs are 'bought' to table questions, support, or oppose motions in that august House, the answer would be a strong 'yes' . . . it is no secret that dirty money in brown envelopes is routinely exchanged within the corridors of Parliament [and] some of it is casually stuffed in pigeon holes for MPs to pick at will. With a fee of only several thousand shillings, an interested party can buy an MP's vote on any issue" (Khamisi, 2011: 246–7).

According to Rugene (2009), the politically vulnerable or debt-ridden MPs are generally regarded as soft targets. One MP in a previous Parliamentary corps was said to have bribed colleagues to the tune of approximately US$1,500 each to be elected the Chairperson of a committee, while another MP admitted that the normal rate of bribe is equivalent to US$750–3,000 depending on the weight of the issue (Rugene, 2009). Other MPs have found amusement in these transactions with one quipping that "some MPs came to Parliament wearing 'twisted shoes' only to become overnight millionaires wearing designer shoes and sharp Italian suits, thanks to questionable deals cut in Parliament" (Rugene, 2009: 3). However, a more mature and sobering thought was offered by a former Minister and a current MP who described Parliament as an "auction house where the highest bidder won crucial battles, even if not in the interest of Kenyans" (Kamau, 2009: 4).

Other cases of blatant bribery have also been reported in the press. Caroline Chebet (2010), for instance, was bold enough to write to *The Standard* newspaper complaining about being requested to pay a bribe of approximately US$3 to be able to collect her national identity card from her area Chief's office. This is just one of several such letters that routinely appear in the press but go unheeded by those in authority with the mandate to take action against those public officers demanding these rent-seeking payments and contributing to the rampant corruption and bad governance in Kenya. The 2010 *Biennial Global Economic Crime Survey* conducted by PricewaterhouseCoopers also noted that the risk of bribery and corruption seems to be more prevalent in transactions involving dealings with government officials (PricewaterhouseCoopers, 2010). A good example is the recently discovered and exposed cartel of rogue officers at the Ministry of Lands who had captured thousands of land files that they had no reason to be holding (Opiyo, 2010). These files related primarily to title deeds and they were found in the possession of public officers who were soliciting kickbacks to produce them and their contents. "Kenyans seeking the all-important papers are usually told their files cannot be traced or are simply lost. But after parting with a bribe—sometimes even shares in the land—the documents quickly resurface" (Opiyo, 2010: 11). Similarly TI (2010b) noted that some 87 percent of surveyed respondents in the capital city, Nairobi, reported witnessing the payment of bribes in order to connect to the city's water network. This state of affairs has led to much frustration among Kenyans who have become saddened with the reputation their once most prosperous economy in East Africa has now achieved as "*nchi ya kitu kidogo*: land of the 'little something,' homeland of the bribe" (Wrong, 2009: 2).

Another secondary factor contributing to the persistence of corruption in Kenya is the expanding size of the public sector bureaucracy which has also provided additional opportunities for unlawful gain and enrichment at the expense of taxpayers. At the City Council of Nairobi, for instance, a recent audit report by PricewaterhouseCoopers that was commissioned by the Council and funded by the World Bank, found, among other things, that (1) there were over 4,000 ghost workers on the payroll—constituting about 35 percent of the 12,000 strong workforce with an estimated monthly wage bill of approximately US$800,000; (2) 46 employees had fake degree certificates; (3) 15 employees on the payroll could not be identified; (4) 145 employees on the payroll do not appear on the human resource records; and (5) 307 other employees were holding suspicious employment letters (Mwanzia and

Gichura, 2010). According to the Town Clerk, there is a cartel running the parallel workers list which has been receiving the money and allowances paid to the ghost workers (Mwanzia and Gichura, 2010). Yet, these findings are quite stunning despite the fact that it has been reported elsewhere that: "On employment, most [local] councils have faulty and sometimes non-existent employment procedures. Chief Officers and Councilors disregard qualifications while recruiting people for employment. The procedures and criteria for promotions are vague and many times disregarded" (TI-Kenya, 2009: 18).

Also, in June 2010 MPs further demonstrated their appetite for "eating" by voting themselves generous increases in their salaries and other allowances. These increases were estimated to result in Kenyan MPs moving from earning 79 times the average income in the country to 113 times compared to UK lawmakers who earn 8 times and US Congressmen who earn 11 times the average income in their respective countries (Leftie and Mwaura, 2010). This blatant raid on the Kenyan treasury by the MPs sparked outrage across the country, and teachers and civil servants, whose own pay increases were not yet honored, threatened to go on strike. Many civil society and lobby groups also engaged in protests, including street demonstrations in front of parliament with chants of *mwizi, mwizi* (thief, thief), against this shameless and corrupt financial grab by the MPs. One television commentator further remarked that the legislative body should not be referred as "the House of Parliament but rather as the House of Pirates." Several MPs, led by Prime Minister Raila Odinga and including the Deputy Prime Minister and Minister of Finance Uhuru Kenyatta, also condemned and rejected the salary package increase. Subsequently, President Kibaki also rejected the increase and it, therefore, never found its way into the pockets of the MPs. In fact, some MPs who had voted for the measure reacted to the public outrage by disowning and/or apologizing for their vote as a mistake. The MPs had been rushing to increase their salaries and benefits ahead of the August 4, 2010 referendum vote on a new constitution which, among other things, removed their power to set their own pay. Nonetheless, press reports suggest that the MPs may have won a victory of sorts after President Kibaki and Finance Minister Kenyatta agreed to continue to exempt them from paying taxes until the expiry of the current parliament in 2012 (Mutua, 2010; Rugene and Shiundu, 2010). However, such exemption from paying taxes is now unconstitutional as per the 2010 constitution and its Article on the *Imposition of Tax* which states, among other things, that "No law may exclude or authorize the exclusion of a State officer from payment of tax by reason of (a) the office held by that State officer; or (b) the nature of the work of the State officer" (Republic of Kenya, 2010a: Article 210, Clause 3). It should also be noted here that some of the country's leaders, such as Prime Minister Odinga and Vice President Musyoka, have paid their tax arrears and agreed to pay taxes on their full earnings as MPs.

One other secondary factor as a contributor to corruption in Kenya is what the World Bank now terms "quiet corruption"—when public servants fail to deliver services or inputs that have been paid for by government. According to the World Bank (2010: 2), the term "quiet corruption" is used:

> to indicate various types of malpractice of frontline providers (teachers, doctors, inspectors, and other government officials at the front lines of service provision) that do not involve monetary exchange. These behaviors include not only potentially observable deviations, such as absenteeism, but also hard to observe deviations from expected conduct, such as lower level effort than expected or the deliberate bending of rules for personal advantage.

This type of corruption does not make headlines the way bribery scandals or political level thefts do. It tends to be less noisy and also attracts less public attention. Nonetheless, it is ubiquitous with very harmful long-term consequences, particularly for the poor who are much more reliant on government services (World Bank, 2010). Within very corrupt environments, such as in Kenya, people adjust their behavior and contribute to the general acceptance of the phenomenon, thus corruption persists and bad governance prevails. The resultant effect is that "the system falls into a vicious cycle in which every misconduct is tolerated and the structure of incentives becomes biased against those who adhere to [professional or ethical] standards" (World Bank, 2010: 5). Quiet corruption occurs across a much wider set of transactions affecting a larger number of people directly than does the more publicized grander administrative, political and other types of corruption that can be found in the public sector.

Based on data from the World Bank (2010), the following are examples of quiet corruption in Kenya in some key sectors:

- *Education*—In rural Western Kenya, 2003 survey data found that 20 percent of teachers in primary schools were absent during school hours. A teacher is reported as being absent if he or she cannot be found at a time that he or she is scheduled to be in school. Moreover, even among those teachers who are found present in school, in-class effort is regarded as low with 12 percent of these teachers being found to be outside the classroom when they were expected to be teaching.
- *Health*—In addition to absenteeism in the Kenya health sector, resource leakage is also a major problem in the country. Measured as the difference

between stipulated resource flows (nonbudgetary resources) and actual amounts received, leakage amounted to 38 percent in 2004.

● *Agriculture*—Among the fertilizer products sold on the market, a 2005 survey found a wide fluctuation in the nitrogen and phosphorous concentration that are often not reported on the labels. Moreover, 3 to 5 percent of these fertilizers were deliberately mislabeled in order to sell inferior quality products.

Finally, in this section, to further demonstrate the persistence of corruption in Kenya it is very useful and informative to look at citizen perceptions of corruption over time as provided in the annual surveys undertaken by Transparency International and the Corruption Perceptions Index (CPI) that they provide, as well as the surveys undertaken by the KACC. In Table 4.1, based on the available data, the CPI score, global rank, and regional rank for Kenya are provided covering the period 2005–10, while Figure 4.1 shows a ten-year trend of the CPI score and global rank in relationship to the corresponding number of rankings. The CPI score relates to perceptions of the degree of public sector corruption in a country and ranges between 10 (highly clean) and zero (highly corrupt). It is an aggregate indicator that combines different sources of information about corruption, making it possible to compare countries. The rank shows how one country compares to others, regionally or globally, that are included in the index. During the period 2005–10, Kenya has consistently had a CPI score between 2.1 and 2.2 with its highest regional rank being 32 in comparison with 47 other African countries. By 2010, the country was globally ranked 154 out of 178 in the company of the 25 lowest-scoring countries that have been widely perceived as endemically corrupt. Kenya is listed behind East African regional neighbors Rwanda (ranked 66), Tanzania (ranked 118), Ethiopia (ranked 116),

TABLE 4.1 Kenya CPI score, regional rank, and global rank, 2005–10

Year	CPI score	Regional rank	Global rank
2005	2.1	N/A	144
2006	2.2	35	142
2007	2.1	40	150
2008	2.1	32	147
2009	2.2	32	146
2010	2.1	35	154

Source: Compiled from Transparency International, Corruption Perceptions Index (2005–10). Available at www.transparency.org [Accessed December 12, 2010].

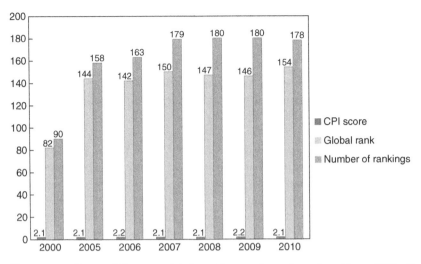

FIGURE 4.1 Kenya CPI score, global ranking, and number of rankings, 2000–10
Source: Author, based on data from Transparency International, Corruption Perceptions Index (2000-10). Available at www.transparency.org [Accessed December 12, 2010].

Eritrea (ranked 123), and Uganda (ranked 127). Both in terms of regional and global rankings, Kenya has therefore consistently been at the bottom one-third of the countries surveyed with the result that it is therefore perceived and regarded as one of the most corrupt countries in the world.

With respect to surveys undertaken by the KACC, their *National Enterprise Survey on Corruption 2009* indicates that greed has been perceived and identified by 50 percent of the respondents as the leading cause of corruption followed by poverty (40%), poor remuneration (20%), unemployment (15%), bad governance (10%), and cultural reasons (10%). These findings compare almost similarly with the results of the 2006 survey that revealed greed (47%), poverty (42%), poor governance (26%), poor remuneration (22%), culture (22 percent), weaknesses in policies, procedures and systems (19%), unemployment (15%), and poor economy (11%) as the leading causes of corruption in Kenya (KACC, 2010). The 2009 survey also revealed that 70 percent of the respondents indicated that bribes are demanded by the service provider compared to 15 percent who indicated that the service seeker offered a payment on his/her own accord; and 29 percent of the respondents indicated that, if corruption in Kenya were to be reduced by one-half, the net income of their business operations will increase by more than 51 percent.

Corruption, Development, and Governance in Kenya: Consequences

The research literature on corruption has begun to affirm the latter's negative impact on governance. By any measure, persistent corruption and bad governance go together. In other words, in those countries where corruption is embedded in their political economy, such as Kenya as this work has shown, there are low governance scores, weak governance institutions, and this translates into sluggish economic performance and lower rates of growth as economic efficiency is impaired. These economic costs of corruption, in turn, fall disproportionately on the poor. Bribes, kickbacks, illegal payments to make things happen are all rent-seeking activities that have the effect of increasing costs directly to the payer or to the public in general as they are simply added to the final costs of the goods and services. Moreover, corruption undermines the delivery of public services such as health care and education on which the poor depend.

As corruption proceeds unchecked it becomes more fundamentally undemocratic as it infringes on the inclusive nature of democracy by, among other things, offering greater access to goods and services to those that are willing to offer bribes or otherwise violate the rules to acquire them. Warren (2004: 329) has observed that "corruption is always a form of duplicitous and harmful exclusion of those who have a claim to inclusion in collective decisions and actions." The privatization of the State by the ruling elite under President Moi, for example, undermined the legitimacy and credibility of the government and of responsible and accountable public servants and institutions. Whether by design or not, corruption also undermines the value system, the norms, and the very cohesion of society (Fraser-Moleketi, 2007). Mueller (2008: 186), for instance, has argued, quite successfully in this author's view, that one of the underlying precipitating factors in Kenya's postelection violence in 2008 was the "deliberately weak institutions, mostly overridden by a highly personalized and centralized presidency that could and did not exercise the autonomy or checks and balances normally associated with democracies." Similar sentiments have been expressed by Githongo (2010). Consequently, democratic values such as trust and tolerance got tossed away and replaced by ethnic violence (Hope, 2010). That violence, in turn, destroyed families, neighborhoods, infrastructure, and scared away investors and tourists—all of which have had a negative impact on economic progress as real growth rates slid from 7.1 percent in 2007 to 1.7 percent in 2008 (Republic of Kenya, 2009a). The government itself has noted that, among other factors, "the poor economic performance reflects the adverse effects of the post-election crisis" (Republic of Kenya, 2009a: 1).

Similarly, theft, embezzlement, and fraud by public officials reduce the availability of funds for development-related activities. For instance, in December 2010, the Permanent Secretary of the Ministry of Finance, in testimony before a parliamentary committee, said that each year corruption and mismanagement of public funds robs Kenya of Ksh 270 billion (approximately a little more than US$3 billion) (Ochami and Njiraini, 2010). To put it in better perspective, this sum was equal to 25–30 percent of the government's budget for FY 2010–11. One Ministry (Ministry of Water and Irrigation) was reported by the said Permanent Secretary to be losing Ksh10 billion (approximately US$123 million), about one-third of its budget, annually through malpractice and mismanagement (Ochami and Njiraini, 2010). Some examples of the development impact of this magnitude of corruption, apart from the obvious leakage of public revenues, are provided below (Ochami and Njiraini, 2010). In other words, alternative uses of and benefits from, these funds, for development activities include:

- Funding of free primary and secondary education for 18 years.
- Meeting the budgets of five critical ministries (Education, Roads, Medical Services, Public Health, and Energy).
- Purchasing of drugs to combat HIV, tuberculosis, and malaria for 10 years and prolong the lives of about half a million Kenyans living with HIV.
- Providing hundreds of thousands of Kenyans with safe drinking water by drilling 135 million boreholes.

Other senior public officials in other branches in government have also voiced their worry about the impact of corruption in Kenya. For instance, the Deputy Speaker of Parliament, during a speech at the opening ceremony of a Parliamentary pre-budget workshop in March 2011, expressed concern over rampant graft in government. As reported by Murage (2011), the Deputy Speaker said that the bulk of the revenue collected by the Kenyan government is lost through corruption and that is why many government-funded projects have stalled. He went on to say that a paltry 30 percent of public cash is spent on projects while the other 70 percent is stolen by bureaucrats, politicians and contractors and, as a result, Kenya loses billions to corruption. This concern by the Deputy Speaker also demonstrates how persistent and entrenched corruption is in Kenya. Each year the National Taxpayers Association (NTA) conducts audits which continue to show an increase in the proportion of public funds for local development projects that has been allocated to ghost projects, embezzled, or outright stolen (see, e.g., NTA, 2011).

Also, in January 2010, the US government announced it was suspending education funding to Kenya following reports that more than US$1 million was missing from the country's primary schooling program (Boswell, 2010; Shiundu, 2010). In a speech to the American Chamber of Commerce in Nairobi, the then US Ambassador Michael Ranneberger (2010: 3) said the planned US$7 million disbursement to the Ministry of Education for a capacity building program will stay suspended "until there is a credible independent audit and full accountability [and] those culpable for the fraud should not merely be sacked, they should be prosecuted and put behind bars." This move followed a British government announcement in December 2009 that it was withholding an approximate US$16 million grant over the disappearance of funds for the free primary education program (Boswell, 2010; Otieno, 2009). The bone of contention for the British was the fact that the Ministries of Finance and Education had failed to account for some US$1.5 million budgeted for constructing new classrooms and buying textbooks for poor students in poverty ravaged districts (Otieno, 2009).

Corruption and bad governance in Kenya therefore not only distort the availability of funds for development activities but also directly affect development assistance partnerships. The United States and the United Kingdom are Kenya's two biggest bilateral donors and they seem to be constantly scolding the Kenyan government and/or withholding/suspending development assistance from it due to persistent corruption. This cannot be good for building and sustaining effective development partnerships where mutual accountability can be assured. Currently, the sheer magnitude of corruption in Kenya, and the culture of impunity that goes along with it, has resulted in a lack of confidence in Kenyan government officials to the extent that alternative methods of funding and implementing development assistance programs are being sought and put in place. According to the British High Commission Nairobi (2009: 2), "only 30 percent of British aid, closely audited, goes through the Government of Kenya because of concerns about financial accountability. British aid to Kenya could be significantly higher each year if corruption and governance concerns were credibly addressed." Similar sentiments have also been echoed by other donors (Moulid, 2010).

One of the alternative approaches to financing and implementing development projects in Kenya is the use of nongovernmental organizations (NGOs). The British government, for example, has signaled its intent to rely more on NGOs, for its development assistance projects in Kenya, than on the country's government by announcing that it will allocate its approximately US$31 million budget for education in Kenya in 2010/11 outside of government systems, until the risks of fraud are substantially reduced (British High Commission Nairobi, 2010). The total estimated loss from the Kenya Education Sector Support Program (KESSP) pool at the time (March

2010) this action was announced was equivalent to US$3 million. In further support of this shift to NGOs, the British High Commissioner said:

> Recently we have witnessed major corruption scandals in the maize, education, oil and local government sectors. All these scandals directly impact on the lives of Kenyan people, stealing funds that were meant for development for all Kenyans and which Kenyan taxpayers largely provide. . . . The government has the opportunity now to show it is serious in tackling corruption, not just in education but across all sectors, and back up its words with action. To stamp out the theft of public money, this action must include ensuring all those who steal are held accountable, including through prosecutions. And not just those with their hands in the till—those who are responsible for preventing such fraud and who fail to act should also be held to account. The wider Kenyan public has a role to play too in continuing to demand greater accountability and rejecting corruption at all levels of society. We will support those within Government and outside of it who are genuinely trying to bring about that change.

While this approach of the British government will bypass the corruption problem within the Kenyan government, it will also result in an increase in the cost of providing development assistance to Kenya since the NGOs have to be compensated for their participation in this new implementation and delivery regime. Of course, one could cynically argue that the compensation to the NGOs would be less, and perhaps considerably so, than the potential embezzlement if such funding were to continue through the government. Nonetheless, the fact that some of the development funding would need to be spent on administrative and other support costs to NGOs will be a welfare loss to Kenyans. Consequently, one net effect of the corruption in the Kenyan government is that it hurts the poorest most and erodes development, adding to the basic daily costs and taking money away from fighting poverty and delivering services. Moreover, bypassing government further undermines and weakens the delivery capacity of State institutions.

> Ceding what should be functions of the state to outside aid agencies, private companies, and NGOs is not sustainable precisely because it undermines the corresponding branches of the state, whose legitimacy is crucial to its functioning . . . Ceding state functions to outside agencies severs the crucial link of accountability between the state and citizens. And once ceded, even if on a temporary basis, entrenched interests develop, which means that the NGO, contractor or agency will lobby for funds to keep performing that function. (Ghani and Lockhart, 2008: 28)

Corruption has also stifled initiative and enterprise in Kenya. Rent-seeking activities tend to have the effect of inflating the cost of doing business and thereby destroying investor confidence and driving them away. According to *The Global Competitiveness Report 2009-2010*, corruption remains the largest obstacle to doing business in Kenya (World Economic Forum, 2009). From a list of 15 factors, respondents were asked to select the five most problematic for doing business in their country/economy and to rank them between 1 (most problematic) and 5 (least problematic). Corruption was ranked number 1 (World Economic Forum, 2009). Other surveys have also corroborated those concerns. The Business Advocacy Fund—which supports business member organizations to engage in private–public dialogue and to advocate an improved business environment in Kenya by providing grant aid, training and mentoring—has conducted surveys of business leader perceptions of the investment climate in Kenya and found in their 2008 report that "corruption is the biggest deterrent to investment, with 65 percent of respondents saying that it would negatively affect their investment decision" (The Business Advocacy Fund, 2008: 9). In addition, "some 40 percent complained that the government is making no effort to tackle corruption" (The Business Advocacy Fund, 2008: 8).

Such rational decision-making by private investors means that corruption has the effect of slowing down investment and economic growth either by crowding out productive investment directly or through the uncertainty created by acts of bribery. Corruption, in this sense, can be regarded as a tax which increases risk and reduces the incentive to invest. Consequently, over the longer term, any economy, such as Kenya's, that is infested with corruption will also suffer from its effects of discouraging potential investors as well as donors as previously discussed. Since private investment, as opposed to public sector spending, spurs growth, generates employment, and can increase tax revenues for public sector expenditures on socioeconomic development programs, and ultimately reduce poverty, the web of corruption in Kenya results in the foiling of efforts to improve infrastructure and educational and health standards (Hope, 2010). For example, a Kenya Judicial Commission of Inquiry estimated that the amount of money lost through one government scandal alone—the Goldenberg Affair—was over the equivalent of US$0.5 billion (Republic of Kenya, 2005a), and had this money been used instead to provide antimalarial bed nets, the entire Kenya population could have been provided with these nets, the entire country could now be almost malaria free, and 34,000 malaria deaths each year could have been prevented (British High Commission Nairobi, 2009). Similar observations have been made about the use of these funds for development projects in Kenya's constituencies (Sichei, 2010). Such "leakage from the economy through [corruption therefore] entails unavailability of financial capital that could have been invested in productive activities within the country" (Sichei, 2010: 147).

Kenya has also found itself on the top 20 list of African countries with outward illicit financial flows. These cumulative flows represent the stock of private assets sent and held abroad by Kenyans. It is illegal capital flight. According to Kar and Cartwright-Smith (2010), an estimated cumulative total of US$5.6 billion flowed illicitly out of Kenya from 1970 to 2008 with trade misinvoicing being a significant part of the problem. In terms of development impact, these cumulative flows represented 18 percent of the country's GDP in 2008, 76 percent of its external debt stock, 329 percent of inward flows of remittances, and 386 percent of the combined total capital flows of foreign direct investment and net official development assistance received.

It is, therefore, obvious from the foregoing that corruption is a direct impediment to Kenya's development and to improving and sustaining good enough governance, while it is also obvious that with good governance corruption can be or is being seriously controlled. Corruption hurts the many and benefits only a few. "It inhibits the ability of government to respond to citizens' needs and to utilize scarce resources in the most efficient and effective manner. It takes away resources from priority areas such as health, social development and education" (Fraser-Moleketi, 2007: 241). It has been demonstrated in this work and elsewhere that it has undermined democracy and good governance in Kenya by subverting the formal processes and rules of conduct to the whims and fancies of a small elite representing "state capture" (the extraction of private benefits by the political and bureaucratic elite) and thereby hindering the capacity of the State to make the right policy choices and to provide overall good governance.

In fact, as Kaufmann (2004: 11) noted: "state capture implies that corruption is not always merely a symptom of more fundamental factors; instead, the very political and economic forces associated with capture play a pivotal role in shaping policies and political economy outcomes." That, in turn has influenced all levels of society with an increasing number of people being virtually forced to adapt to what has become the norm in which corruption of some sort is part of the way of life, whether they like it or not. One negative consequence is that too often, otherwise honest people are forced to resort to corrupt means to carry on with their daily lives. This has, therefore, created the ethical dilemma of a forced coexistence with individuals and groups who operate on the basis of different moral standards and expect all those with whom they interact to behave accordingly (Hassan, 2004).

Consequently, and as evidenced in this work, corrupt activities in Kenya have moved from a passive to an active phase where public servants, in particular, do not wait to be approached and bribed, for example, but actively and boldly solicit individuals to offer bribes or other favors in return for the provision of public services. Such payments are now, unfortunately, regarded as necessary and routine. In other words, they have become the unofficial but operating administrative order. The ultimate consequence is that the integrity, credibility, and professionalism of the public service have been compromised and such governance indicators like government effectiveness (including the quality of public service delivery, the quality of the public service and the degree of its independence from political pressures, the quality of policy formulation and implementation, and the credibility of the government's commitment to such policies) and control of corruption (the extent to which public power is exercised for private gain, including both petty and grand forms of corruption, as well as "state capture" by both elites and private interests) result in very low scores as measured by the World Bank Governance Indicators, for example (Kaufmann et al., 2009).

Some final comments relating to the consequences of "quiet corruption" in Kenya are also in order here. As observed by the World Bank (2010), one direct impact of quiet corruption is the loss of production as a result of the lower quality inputs and efforts. This can have a cumulating effect. When teachers are absent, for instance, learning is hindered, test scores are lower, and that leads to lower levels of learning over the longer term which means appropriate knowledge and skills are not acquired which then leads to low earnings in adult life. On the other hand, in Western Kenya it was found that gains in test scores were in part due to increases in teacher attendance of nearly 6 percentage points (World Bank, 2010). In the health sector, it was determined that by reducing the absenteeism rate for nurses to allow for more systematic pre- and post-HIV test counseling in Kenya's public health facilities could reduce vertical (mother-to-child) transmission of HIV by 0.5–1.5 infections per 1,000 live births (World Bank, 2010). Of course, these negative consequences of quiet corruption not only affect the poor the most but also act as catalysts for driving people into poverty status.

Tackling the Corruption Epidemic in Kenya: Control

As previously indicated, several measures have been put in place over the years to tackle the corruption epidemic in Kenya. Nonetheless, as demonstrated in this work, corruption persists in Kenya for the reasons that this work has also analyzed. This section offers a brief summary and assessment of the key measures that have been put in place to control corruption in the country. Most of these anti-corruption measures were recently put in place—less than a decade ago—and may be categorized as either legal frameworks or as institutional initiatives and other strategies.

Legal Frameworks

The Anti-Corruption and Economic Crimes Act, 2003: In 2003, The Anti-Corruption and Economic Crimes (ACEC) Act was passed by Parliament. It was assented to on April 30, 2003 and commenced on May 02, 2003. The objective of the ACEC Act is to provide for the prevention, investigation, and punishment of corruption, economic crimes and related offences and for matters incidental thereto and connected therewith (Republic of Kenya, 2003a). It employs a very broad definition of corruption to include bribery, fraud, embezzlement or misappropriation of public funds, abuse of office, breach of trust, and any offence involving dishonesty in connection with any tax, rate, or impost levied under any Act. It also goes further to include an offence involving dishonesty under any law relating to the election of persons to public office (Republic of Kenya, 2003a).

Economic crime is defined as an offence involving dishonesty under any written law providing for the maintenance or protection of the public revenue; the fraudulent or otherwise unlawful acquisition of public property, a public service or benefit; mortgaging, charging or disposing of any public property; damaging public property that results in a loss or adversely affects any public revenue or service; or the failure to pay any taxes or any fees, levies or charges payable to any public body or the effecting or obtaining any exemption, remission or abatement from payment of any such taxes, fees, levies, or charges (Republic of Kenya, 2003a). It is also an economic crime for an officer or person whose functions concern the administration, custody, management, receipt, or use of any part of the public revenue or public property to fraudulently make payment or excessive payment from public revenues for substandard or defective goods, goods not supplied or not supplied in full, or services not rendered or not adequately rendered, to willfully or carelessly fail to comply with any law or applicable procedures and guidelines relating to the procurement, allocation, sale, or disposal of property, tendering of contracts, management of funds or incurring of expenditures; or to engage in a project without prior planning (Republic of Kenya, 2003a).

The Act also established the KACC and a Kenya Anti-Corruption Advisory Board (KACAB). The KACC has a long list of functions primarily related to investigation, advising public bodies on anti-corruption practices, educating the public on the dangers of corruption and economic crime (Republic of Kenya, 2003a). The KACAB's principal function is to advise the KACC generally on the exercise of its powers and the performance of its functions under the Act (Republic of Kenya, 2003a). A number of offences were also described in the Act. The KACC has its roots in The Prevention of Corruption Act of 1956, as amended. Due to international pressure, the first comprehensive legislation against corruption was enacted in 1997, when The Prevention of Corruption Act was again amended (ACBF, 2007). This resulted in the creation of the Kenya Anti-Corruption Authority (KACA) which operated until December 2000 when it was declared unconstitutional on the grounds that it may alienate the Attorney-General's power to prosecute cases on behalf of the public. This led to the abolishment of the KACA and the handing over of its case files to the Attorney-General in January 2001. In September 2001, the Anti-Corruption Police Unit (ACPU) was established through a Presidential directive and took over all the cases on file with the disbanded KACA. The ACPU, in turn, was replaced by the KACC in May 2003.

The ACEC Act is seemingly comprehensive, containing some of the key elements of the United Nations Convention against Corruption (UNCAC). However, the fundamental problem is that it is not being used as intended as impunity continues to be the order of the day. Arrests and prosecution of corrupt public officials or private sector individuals are rare despite the rampant corruption in the country. In fact, in 2009 there was an attempt by some MPs to repeal the Act. In addition, others, such as Thiankolu (2006) and Tuta (2005), for instance, have argued that the ACEC Act has many weaknesses including (1) limited scope of the Act; (2) insufficient provision for international cooperation and technical assistance in the prevention of and fight against corruption; (3) inadequate provisions to criminalize corruption in the private sector; (4) limiting the KACC to investigations without prosecutorial powers; and (5) the lack of provisions on freezing, seizure, and confiscation of assets or proceeds of corruption or economic crime.

The Public Officer Ethics Act, 2003: Parliament also passed The Public Officer Ethics (POE) Act in 2003. It was also assented to and commenced on the same dates as the ACEC Act, 2003, respectively, April 30, 2003 and May 02, 2003. The objective of the POE Act is "to advance the ethics of public officers by providing for a Code of Conduct and Ethics for public officers and requiring financial declarations from certain public officers and to provide for connected purposes" (Republic of Kenya, 2003b: 1). Basically, the POE Act provides codes of conduct and ethics for all public officers and is intended to enhance ethics and integrity in the public sector.

Among other things, the POE Act spells out and defines the elements of the code of conduct and ethics as they pertain to performance of duties, professionalism, the rule of law, improper enrichment, conflict of interest, collections and fundraising, acting for foreigners, the care of public property, political neutrality, nepotism, the giving of honest and impartial advice, misleading the public, the conduct of private affairs, sexual harassment, the selection of public officers, the submission of declarations, acting through or influencing others, and the reporting of improper orders. The Act also

provides for the declaration of income, assets, and liabilities by public officers as well as for enforcement of the code of conduct and ethics.

Like the ACEC Act, the POE Act has good intentions but it also has some
shortcomings and it is also not being applied as intended. According to Luh
(2003: 1):

> Kenyan citizens and leaders have long believed that requiring government
> officials to declare their wealth might help stem abuse of power and loot-
> ing of government resources. . . . However, while the Act is a good starting
> point, the scheme it creates has some serious shortcomings that threaten
> its effectiveness as a tool against corruption:
>
> - The Act does not provide for public access to officials' asset
>   declarations.
> - The Act fails to spell out clearly what assets, liabilities, and interests
>   public officers must declare.
> - The Act fails to provide a framework for review or inspection of asset
>   declarations.

Others have voiced their disappointment based on the high expectations of
the Kenyan people with respect to the government of the day—the NARC—
"with many viewing the Act as an indicator of the regime's commitment to
open a new chapter in good governance. But seven years later, the optimism
surrounding the enactment of the Public Officer Ethics Act appears to have
dissipated" (Aluanga, 2010: 1). The many allegations in recent years, ranging
from misappropriation of funds, misleading the public, nepotism, conflict
of interest, and irregular appointment of public officers—all of which are
violations of the POE Act—"have rekindled debate on the effectiveness of the
Public Officer Ethics Act, with calls for 'bigger fish' implicated in corruption
to quit office" (Aluanga, 2010: 1). This further reinforces the reality of the culture of impunity as there is either little or selective action from the Attorney
General's office which is responsible for prosecution under the law.

The Government Financial Management Act, 2004: In 2004, The Government
Financial Management (GFM) Act was enacted by Parliament. It was
assented to on December 31, 2004 and commenced on November 01, 2005.
The objectives of the Act are:

> to provide for the management of government financial affairs, to
> make certain provisions with respect to the exchequer account and the
> Consolidated Fund, to provide for persons to be responsible for govern-
> ment resources and to provide for other related matters. (Republic of
> Kenya, 2004: 4)

The GFM Act consolidated and streamlined government financial processes and put in place procedures and systems for proper and effective management of government money and property. It spells out Ministerial responsibility, treasury duties and powers, expenditure control, specifications for purchase of official government vehicles, required public service offices (such as Accountant General, Director of the National Budget, and Internal Auditor-General), appointment and responsibilities of accounting officers, and appointment and responsibilities of receivers of revenue.

Among all of the legislative frameworks put in place as corruption control measures, the GFM Act seems to be the most effective with the Ministry of Finance/Treasury using the Act to institute ongoing strategic reforms to strengthen public financial management in the country. Among those reforms has been the establishment of independent audit committees in all ministries, departments, and local authorities as part of a wider strategy of risk-based auditing aimed at combating fraud. Consequently, the governance of public finances has been somewhat enhanced.

The Public Procurement and Disposal Act, 2005: In 2005, Parliament enacted The Public Procurement and Disposal (PPD) Act. It was assented to on October 26, 2005 and commenced on January 01, 2007 following the gazetting of the subsidiary legislation entitled *Public Procurement and Disposal Regulations 2006*. The purpose of the PPD Act is to "establish procedures for efficient public procurement and for the disposal of unserviceable, obsolete or surplus stores, assets and equipment by public entities and to provide for other related matters" (Republic of Kenya, 2005b: 52). The objectives of the Act are to (1) maximize economy and efficiency; (2) promote competition and ensure that competitors are treated fairly; (3) promote the integrity and fairness of those procedures; (4) increase transparency and accountability in those procedures; (5) increase public awareness in those procedures; and (6) facilitate the promotion of local industry and economic development.

The PPD Act also established three entities to regulate public sector procurement: (1) the Public Procurement and Oversight Authority (PPOA); (2) The Public Procurement Oversight Advisory Board (PPOAB); and (3) the Public Procurement Administrative Review Board (PPARB). The PPOA is responsible for the oversight, regulation, and policy development of public procurement in Kenya, ensuring that procuring entities adhere to all legal and regulatory requirements. The PPOA operates under the guidance and supervision of the PPOAB while the PPARB is charged with responsibility for handling and reviewing complaints and appeals. In addition, general procurement rules, open tendering requirements, alternative procurement procedures, administrative review of procurement proceedings, PPOA powers to ensure compliance, debarment from participation in procurement proceedings, and disposal of stores and equipment have all been addressed in the Act.

The public procurement system in Kenya has been extremely prone to corrupt practices and has been characterized by decades of wastage of resources through defective and fraudulent public expenditure patterns (IPAR, 2006). It is estimated that public sector expenditure on procurement in the country was US$1.2 billion in 2000/01 (Odhiambo and Kamau, 2003), US$2 billion in 2006 (IPAR, 2006), and US$7.3 billion in 2007/08 (Ogot et al., 2009). Owing to the weak legal and institutional framework, it was estimated that the equivalent of some US$6 billion was lost due to poor public procurement practices for the period 1996–2003 (IPAR, 2006). In fact, it was also estimated that almost 80 percent of real, perceived, and alleged grand corruption in Kenya is procurement related (KACC, 2005). Consequently, a legal and institutional framework, clear tendering processes, and transparent and accountable arbitration systems, for example, as the PPD Act 2005 promises, are all critical elements for arresting corruption in the procurement process.

However, although the PPD Act 2005 promises to dramatically improve the procurement environment in Kenya, and is a good step toward enhancing good governance in the management of public finances, there are a number of shortcomings that have been identified through which some of the problems in the past can sneak back into play. Among them are implementation challenges related to lack of systems or processes to compel timed payment for goods and services and eliminate rent-seeking delays (TI-Kenya, 2009). Also, concerns have been expressed about the exemption of development agreements from the provisions of the procurement regulations which has the potential to dilute the country's lines of accountability (Chêne, 2009). In addition, procurement transparency measures, as part of the implementation compliance with the Act, need to be tightened.

The Proceeds of Crime and Anti-Money Laundering Act, 2009: The Proceeds of Crime and Anti-Money Laundering (PCAML) Act, 2009 was assented to on December 31, 2009 and commenced on June 28, 2010. The objectives of the Act are to provide for the offence of money laundering and to introduce measures for combating the offence; to provide for the identification, tracing, freezing, seizure, and confiscation of the proceeds of crime; and for connected purposes (Republic of Kenya, 2009b). Among other things, the Act established a Financial Reporting Centre (FRC), set out anti-money laundering obligations of a reporting institution, created an Anti-Money Laundering Advisory Board (AMLAB), established an Assets Recovery Agency (ARA) and a Criminal Assets Recovery Fund (CARF), and provided for criminal and civil forfeiture proceedings as well as for the preservation and forfeiture of property (Republic of Kenya, 2009b).

The principal objective of the FRC is to assist in the identification of the proceeds of crime and the combating of money laundering. The AMLAB has been charged with responsibility to advise the Director of the FRC generally on the performance of his/her functions and the exercise of his/her powers under the Act and to perform any other duty as prescribed to be performed by the Board under the Act. The ARA is to be a semi-autonomous body under the Office of the Attorney-General with functions to implement the provisions of the Act pertaining to criminal and civil forfeiture, preservation and forfeiture of property, production orders and other information gathering powers, the CARF, and international assistance in investigations and proceedings. The CARF is to comprise primarily all moneys and property derived from the fulfillment of confiscation and forfeiture orders. The CARF is to be administered by the ARA (Republic of Kenya, 2009b). The PCAML Act commenced in June 2010. Consequently, it is not yet possible to offer any assessment or comments on its application or lack thereof as the case may turn out to be.

Other Legislation: Apart from the afore-mentioned Acts, several other pieces of legislation have also been put in place that can aid in the fight to control corruption and improve the governance environment in the country. Among them are (1) The Privatization Act, 2005 to ensure transparency in the privatization of state-owned enterprises and accountable transfer of public assets in a competitive environment; (2) The Public Audit Act, 2003 which established the Kenya National Audit Office (KNAO) and provided for the audit of government, state corporations, and local authorities as well as for economy, efficiency and effectiveness examinations, and matters relating to the Controller and Auditor-General and the establishment of the Kenya National Audit Commission (KNAC); (3) The Witness Protection (Amendment) Bill, 2010 which is an Act of Parliament that amended the Witness Protection Act, 2006—as the principal Act on protection of witnesses in criminal cases and other proceedings—and provided for the establishment of an independent Witness Protection Agency, an oversight Witness Protection Advisory Board, a Witness Protection Tribunal, and a Victims Compensation Fund; and (4) The Supplies Practitioners Management Act, 2007 which has made provision for the training, registration, and licensing of supplies practitioners and regulation of their practice.

Institutional Initiatives and Other Strategies

In 2003, the Government of Kenya established the Department of Governance and Ethics (DGE) in the Office of the President and headed by a Permanent Secretary (PS). The PS and his Secretariat were intended to advise and assist the President on the development, implementation, monitoring, and strengthening of holistic policies and strategies meant to fight corruption and improve accountability and transparency in the conduct of national affairs (Orowe, 2004). The DGE was also intended to work closely with the Ministry of Justice, National Cohesion and Constitutional Affairs, the KACC, the Director of Public Prosecutions, and the police and intelligence services. The first PS of the DGE was John Githongo who, as the so-called anti-corruption czar and "high priest of good governance," fled Kenya in 2005 in fear for his life, after exposing the ruthless pillaging of public funds by the government. He then resigned from abroad (Otieno, 2005; Wrong, 2009). Since Mr Githongo's resignation no replacement has been appointed. In fact, on the website of the Office of the President, the DGE is not even listed as one of the departments.

In January 2003, through a Presidential circular, the Ministry of Justice and Constitutional Affairs was established with a mandate that included developing anti-corruption strategies and coordinating and facilitating the war against corruption. Now, with an expanded mandate to include national cohesion and renamed accordingly as the Ministry of Justice, National Cohesion and Constitutional Affairs, its core functions currently include (1) setting up structures and institutions for consolidating administration of justice and good governance, transparency, accountability, ethics, integrity, values; (2) review, consolidation, and codification of laws for promotion of democratic governance and rule of law; (3) facilitation of development and institutionalization of anti-corruption strategies and programs; and (4) facilitation and coordination of the Governance, Justice, Law and Order Sector (GJLOS) reforms.

Launched in November 2003, the GJLOS reform program is a sector-wide, cross-institutional development strategy led by the Government of Kenya and supported by more than 15 international development partners. It is coordinated through the Ministry of Justice, National Cohesion and Constitutional Affairs and is based on recognition of the interconnected nature of the justice sector, the "corruption seepage" between its various components, and the need for contemporaneous reforms within the sector as a whole (Republic of Kenya, nda; Orowe, 2004). The vision of the GJLOS reform program is a safe, secure, democratic, just, corruption-free, human rights respecting, and prosperous Kenya for all while its mission is to reform and strengthen sector institutions for enhanced protection of human rights, efficient, accountable, and transparent governance and justice (Republic of Kenya, nda).

In 2003 President Mwai Kibaki established the Cabinet Committee on Anti-Corruption (CCAC). It is chaired by the Minister of Justice, National Cohesion and Constitutional Affairs and its other members are the Minister of State for Provincial Administration and Internal Security, Minister of Finance, Minister of Planning and National Development, Minister of Roads, Minister of Public Works, and the Minister of Local Government. The CCAC's mandate is to oversee the implementation of government policies on corruption and review the progress in the fight against corruption, so as to ensure a sustainable and well-coordinated war against corruption. The Committee advises the President on anti-corruption initiatives and on principles of better governance (Orowe, 2004; TI-Kenya, 2009).

In June 2003, the government released its *Economic Recovery Strategy for Wealth and Employment Creation 2003-2007* (*ERS 2003-2007*) which, among other things, observed that corruption and bad governance had become entrenched in Kenya during the previous two decades (Republic of Kenya, 2003c). The *ERS 2003-2007* (Republic of Kenya, 2003c: 8), before outlining steps the government had already taken or was in the process of implementing to curb corruption, further noted that:

Most of the problems bedeviling Kenya and its people arise from the many years of bad governance and poor economic management. The rapidly growing poverty, food insecurity and economic collapse are largely related to the previous government's inability to manage the country affairs in the best way possible. The poor management, excessive discretion in government, appointments of people of dubious characters and political interference and lack of respect for professionalism led to widespread corruption, gross abuse of public office in many government departments and incorrigible tolerance—if not outright encouragement of mediocrity and lack of standards. For these reasons the solution of the current national crisis is to be found in our ability to reclaim professionalism and confidence in public officers, and guaranteeing efficiency.

In May 2004, the government created the National Anti-Corruption Campaign Steering Committee (NACCSC) through an appointment by the President. It comprises of various stakeholders and representatives from religious organizations, the private sector, senior government officials, statutory commissions, civil society, the media, women's organizations, and universities, for example. The NACCSC is required to work closely with the KACC and its mandate includes: (1) establishing a framework for the nationwide campaign against corruption; (2) mobilizing stakeholders across all sectors and the general public to evolve a strong anti-corruption culture and participate in the fight against corruption; (3) sensitizing the public and encouraging them to participate in the fight against corruption; (4) developing policies for strengthening the campaign against corruption; and (5) developing indices for regular monitoring and evaluation of the anti-corruption campaign and publicly report on the progress made in the fight against corruption (NACCSC, nd; Republic of Kenya, 2009c). The NACCSC Secretariat is housed in the Ministry of Justice, National Cohesion and Constitutional Affairs. In August 2009, the NACCSC mandate was renewed and members appointed for a period of two years.

In its most recent Progress Report released in November 2010 and covering the period July 2008–December 2009, the Chairperson of the NACCSC, Archbishop Eliud Wabukala (2010: ix), noted that "Kenyans have not been spared either [from corruption] and continue to bear the burden of corruption. There are, therefore, very many reasons why Kenyans should continue to fight corruption and all its manifestations." During the report period, the NACCSC undertook several campaign activities (which it deemed as successful) related to communication, research, and advocacy with communication activities (through television, radio, and print) being the central mode of reaching most Kenyans with the anti-corruption messages designed to achieve the required reforms and attitudinal change (NACCSC, 2010).

In May 2006, a National Anti-Corruption Plan was adopted by a National Anti-Corruption Stakeholders' Conference. It was then launched by the government in July 2006. The implementation of the Plan is coordinated by a Secretariat hosted by the KACC. The vision of the NACP is "towards a just, democratic and prosperous Kenya built on good governance, ethics and integrity" (NACP Secretariat, nd: 13). Its scope is to prevent and to fight corruption in all its manifestations in all spheres of social, economic and political affairs of the nation. It "draws from the experiences of Kenyans and recognizes that preventing corruption requires a consistent, coherent, broad-based and collective approach with a long-term perspective" (NACP Secretariat, nd: 5).

The main objective of the NACP is to marshal the efforts and resources of various stakeholders to progressively and systematically reduce—to the extent possible—the causes and the destructive effects of corruption in Kenya. The specific objectives include to: (1) transform the situation where corruption was a low-risk high-gain undertaking to one where it is a high-risk low-gain venture; (2) create public awareness of the causes and terrible effects of corruption and the role of the public in its prevention and eradication; (3) promote good governance in all organizations in every sector in order to prevent and fight corruption; (4) enhance collaboration among Kenyans in ensuring that all corruption cases are reported, investigated, and prosecuted properly; and (5) create an environment where any corrupt activity is seen and expressed as a social aberration. The Plan also provides strategies and actions to be undertaken by the various stakeholders and an implementation approach whose common factor for all stakeholders is the desire to enhance public intolerance toward corruption and harness the capacity of all stakeholders to establish a public–private coalition against corruption (NACP Secretariat, nd).

In 2007, the Public Complaints Standing Committee (PCSC) was established by the President and geared toward enhancing good governance, management, and administration in public institutions. The PCSC is generally mandated to receive, register, sort, classify, and document all complaints against public officers in Ministries, parastatals, statutory bodies, or any other public institution. In addition, the PCSC is also specifically required to enquire into allegations of misuse of office, corruption, unethical conduct, breach of integrity, maladministration, delay, injustice, discourtesy, inattention, incompetence, misbehavior, inefficiency, or ineptitude (Republic of Kenya, ndb). The PCSC is housed in the Ministry of Justice, National Cohesion and Constitutional Affairs and it is to eventually become the Office of the Ombudsman (Republic of Kenya, ndb).

At the regional and international levels, Kenya has also been exhibiting its alacrity for launching anti-corruption initiatives. For instance, it was the first country in the world to sign and ratify the UNCAC which it did in December 2003 (UNODC, 2010). The then Minister of Justice and Constitutional Affairs, Mr Kiraitu Murungi, at the signing ceremony, acknowledged and expressed the country's corruption reputation as follows:

> No other issue has captured more attention in our government's reform agenda . . . than the fight against corruption. This is because Kenya has been one of the most corrupt nations on Earth . . . It is not by accident that Kenya has become the first nation to sign and ratify this Convention. Corruption for us has reached endemic proportions in our society . . . for us in Kenya, the fight against corruption is a matter of life and death. It cannot wait for tomorrow. The time is now. We believe we are doing the right thing by ratifying this Convention today. (Murungi, 2003: 1–3)

In December 2003, Kenya also signed the African Union (AU) Convention on Preventing and Combating Corruption and finally ratified/acceded to it in February 2007 (AU, 2010). In addition, Kenya is also a member of the Eastern and Southern Africa Anti-Money Laundering Group (ESAAMLG) having signed its memorandum of understanding in which member countries agree to, among other things: (1) apply anti-money laundering measures to all serious crimes; (2) implement measures to combat the financing of terrorism; and (3) implement any other measures contained in multilateral agreements and initiatives to which they subscribe for the prevention and control of the laundering of the proceeds of all serious crimes and the financing of terrorist activities (ESAAMLG, 2008).

In the latter part of 2005 and in early 2006 Kenya also subjected itself to a peer review through the African Peer Review Mechanism (APRM) of the New Partnership for Africa's Development (NEPAD). To accomplish the objectives and the outcomes of the NEPAD—an initiative by African leaders to place the African continent on a path of sustainable development encompassing good governance and prosperity—African leaders agreed in 2002, among other things, to subject their countries to peer review through the use of the APRM. The APRM is used to assess the performance of African countries in terms of their compliance with a number of agreed codes, standards, and commitments that underpin the good governance and sustainable development framework (Hope, 2008). Kenya was among the first group of countries to agree to both the NEPAD and to be peer reviewed. The Kenya Peer Review Report dated May 2006 found that "Kenya has had, and continues to have, a significant problem of corruption" (APRM Secretariat, 2006: 25).

In September 2007, Kenya joined other States of the East African Community (EAC) to create the East African Association of Anti-Corruption Authorities (EAAACA). The association, which was launched in November 2007 when the EAAACA constitution was signed, seeks to enhance cooperation in combating corruption among member states (EAAACA, nda). Its objectives include to: (1) promote, facilitate, and regulate cooperation among partner States to ensure the effectiveness of measures and actions to prevent, detect, investigate, punish, and eradicate corruption and other related offences in East Africa; (2) promote and strengthen the development in East Africa by partner States of mechanisms required to prevent, detect, investigate, punish, and eradicate corruption and other related offences in the public and private sectors; (3) accord one another mutual legal assistance regarding detection, investigations, prosecutions, identification, tracing, freezing, seizure, confiscation, and repatriation of property, instruments, or proceeds obtained or derived from corruption; (4) assist in extradition of any person charged with or convicted of offences of corruption and other related offences, carried out in the territory of an EAC partner State and whose extradition is requested by that partner State, in conformity with their domestic laws, any applicable extradition treaties, or extradition agreements or arrangements between or among the partner States, or Memorandum of Understanding and bilateral agreements between the anti-corruption authorities; and (5) facilitate the repatriation of proceeds of corruption or money laundering or ill-gotten wealth and the seizure of any property when requested by any party to the constitution of the EAAACA (EAAACA, ndb).

In February 2010, the government held a Workshop on Strategies to Fight/ Eliminate Corruption in the Public Service for Permanent Secretaries/ Accounting Officers and Chief Executives of State Corporations/Councils/ Boards. The theme of the workshop was "Leadership and Integrity in the Public Service" with an emphasis on the need for the "national leadership to demonstrably implement good governance principles and anti-corruption strategies that enhance national development" (OP, 2010: 1). The objectives of the workshop were to: (1) provide a forum for Permanent Secretaries/ Accounting Officers and Chief Executives of State Corporations/Councils/ Boards to collectively assess the status and challenges facing the fight against corruption in the public service; (2) develop government-wide and institution-specific measures/strategies to fight/eliminate corruption in the public service; (3) evaluate the effectiveness of legislative and administrative frameworks for combating corruption and unethical behavior in the public service; (4) identify specific measures and strategies to combat corruption and unethical conduct in the public service; and (5) enhance synergy in the fight against corruption in the public service (OP, 2010).

The workshop was addressed by President Kibaki as well as Prime Minister Odinga and discussed nine corruption prone thematic areas, identified key challenges, and proposed corruption prevention measures. The thematic areas were (1) financial management; (2) procurement of goods and services; (3) tax administration and immigration; (4) law enforcement; (5) the criminal justice system; (6) public administration and management; (7) land administration and management; (8) implementation of public projects; and (9) information, communication, and technology. An Action Plan was also developed to facilitate implementation of an anti-corruption agenda within the public service. In addition, a communiqué was also issued at the end of the workshop that contained resolutions, undertakings, and a way forward including commitments to implement the directives of President Kibaki and Prime Minister Odinga on the fight against corruption; to mainstream preventive measures to fight corruption; to adopt a holistic approach in the fight against corruption, including development of good governance and anti-corruption curricula for use in education and training programs; to inculcate values of governance and ethical behavior in the daily life of public offices through rigorous application of the POE Act and the Civil Service Code of Conduct; and to respond promptly and decisively to public concerns on incidences of corruption within mandate areas (OP, 2010).

As the foregoing demonstrates, Kenya has put in place several institutional initiatives and other strategies to attempt to control corruption. However, many of these measures exist primarily on paper and are not being used to their full potential. The NACP, as an example, is well thought out, has been embraced by national stakeholders (including the judiciary, the KACC, enforcement agencies, civil society, labor and education sectors, religious organizations, the media, watchdog agencies, and the private sector), and meets many of the requirements of the UNCAC. Yet, its implementation is not demonstrated through the various implementation mechanisms and actions it advocates. The private sector, for instance, whose organizations and members frequently complain about the negative effects of corruption on their investment decisions and bottom line, are still to be fully engaged in the anti-corruption campaign in a meaningful way.

Another example is the PCSC whose performance has been hampered—and rendering it ineffective—by a number of factors including: (1) a lack of cooperation and goodwill from concerned government officers and institutions; (2) the inability to enforce its recommendations and compel public officers to respond to PCSC inquiries and concerns; and (3) manual systems of operation which undermine internal efficiency. In addition, the PCSC lacks the appropriate types and numbers of staff and its corporate governance structure entails multiple sources of authority and unclear administrative reporting lines. More than 80 percent of the complaints received by the PCSC are carried over from one reporting period to the next resulting in a significantly cumbersome backlog of complaints to be processed. On average, only about 6 percent of the complaints received are resolved or channeled elsewhere during a given reporting period (PCSC, nda, ndb).

Towards More Effective Corruption Control: Key Lessons and Recommendations

One of the key lessons from international development research and best practice is that there is strong evidence that the correlation that connects governance to economic development is not a result of higher income leading to improved governance but the other way around. Where there is endemic corruption there is bad governance. Where corruption is controlled, and therefore does not persist, governance is improved and that, in turn, contributes to improved development outcomes. As Kaufmann (2006: 15) has explained:

> Our work finds that there is a very strong and causal link from improved governance to higher incomes, which is summarized by the "300 percent development dividend": a country that improves governance by one standard deviation—which is a realistic improvement where political will exists—can expect to more or less triple its annual per capita income in

the long run. Conversely, we do not find evidence that there is significant causation in the opposite direction, from per capita income to the quality of governance. Merely acquiring higher incomes (say, due to higher oil prices, or infusion of aid), per se will not automatically result in improved governance.

Moreover, better governance diminishes the extent to which resources are siphoned off for corrupt practices or otherwise wasted (de Ferranti et al., 2009). Consequently, more effective control of corruption will improve the governance environment and thereby lead to better development performance, notwithstanding that good governance and anti-corruption are desirable ends on their own. In addition, the policy frameworks used to address corruption have to be consistently implemented to also help improve governance as the ultimate goal, bearing in mind that Kenya already has the gamut of tools required to do the job. Consequently, rather than dreaming up projects and programs to fit the latest development fad, both the government of Kenya and its donors should concentrate more on properly reforming and funding the weakened institutions such as the judiciary, the police, and the public service. With that governance perspective in further focus, below are some recommendations for moving toward more effective control of corruption in the country, drawing on key lessons and best practices in the fight against corruption.

Transformational Leadership

The first recommendation advocated in this work pertains to leadership. There has been much said and written about the lack of political will to tackle the corruption problem in Kenya. Anassi (2004: 109), for instance, correctly remarked that "the political will to fight corruption was absent" because "of the regime's control of all the arms of government, including parliament and the judiciary." Consequently, he noted further:

> Corruption was nurtured and perfected by those in authority. Parliament was impotent, because the party threatened those perceived as against the establishment with expulsions. The judiciary was compromised and it did nothing to improve the situation. As we have seen, the judiciary was also corrupt and that made the bad situation worse (Anassi, 2004: 109).

However, from this author's point of view, there is no universal lack of political will among Kenya's current crop of political leaders. Prime Minister Raila Odinga, for example, has frequently demonstrated the political will to tackle the corruption epidemic in Kenya not only in his speeches and exhortations but also in his actions, including the firing or suspension of government Ministers and other senior public officials for engaging in corrupt and/or unethical behavior. But, political will in isolation has been demonstrated to be impotent (Hope, 1999). What is required also is leadership for change; in other words, transformational leadership. In addition to being publicly perceived as honest, forward-looking, competent, fair, inspiring, and intelligent, such leaders must also be regarded as champions of ideas—good ideas for good governance in this case—who lead and maintain commitment to change ideas and transformation toward a better governance environment, influencing others into accepting the changes, and acting as the "fixer" who coordinates disparate actors to overcome resistance to change and transformation. These leadership actions are intended to ultimately enhance the acceptance and institutionalization of transformational change for the better (Andrews et al., 2010).

Transformation toward good governance is highly desirable in Kenya and that transformation must be significantly geared toward arresting the persistence of corruption in the country. A successful fight against persistent corruption in Kenya must, therefore, involve strong transformational leadership. Transformational leadership leads to positive changes and benefits for those who follow. Through their own credibility and strength of their vision and personality, transformational leaders are able to inspire followers to change motivations, expectations, and perceptions to work toward common goals. Such leaders generally commit to undertake change actions to achieve a set of objectives—in this instance, controlling corruption—and to sustain the costs of those actions over time. This is critically important particularly because transformational leaders, by virtue of their agenda to transform, challenge the *status quo*. This requires, among other things, staying the course and building cross-sectoral coalitions of support that must necessarily go beyond the general public and include public officials, the private sector, and civil society groups, for example.

Where corruption is systemic or persistent, like in Kenya, the institutional culture itself has grown sick. The norm is corruption and penetrating that culture requires building coalitions and mobilizing and coordinating a variety of actors inside and outside of government to transform the environment and sustain the change benefits that will be or have been derived. Unless the war against corruption is led by leaders at the top who embody transformation rather than the *status quo*, it will not be won at the middle or lower levels of the public sector or society in general. As Wamwere (2010) reminds us, the war against corruption has had a positive impact only in countries where the top leaders actually led it but that war failed in all countries where the top leaders themselves were corrupt and fought graft with empty words only.

Punishment as Deterrent

Corruption in Kenya needs to be made a high-risk activity—a high risk that the perpetrators will be caught and severely punished, irrespective of their status or standing in society. In other words, all those who are engaged in corruption activities, in both the public and private sectors, should receive the harshest available punishment and their loot tracked down and confiscated. However, it must also be pointed out here that punitive measures, including adequate capability for enforcement, only work in tandem with preventive measures that reduce opportunities for corrupt practices. Nonetheless, punishment—particularly of prominent, high-level corrupt officials—sends the right signal, throughout a nation, that the country's leadership is indeed very serious about the campaign against corruption. In fact, there should be a zero tolerance policy toward corruption and it should be ensured that offenders do not escape legal punishment. This is the area where Kenya needs to step up and decisively demonstrate visible results in tackling the culture of impunity that has too long been associated with corruption in the country.

To implement a policy of punishment as deterrent also requires the strict enforcement of the various punishment policies both at the administrative and judicial levels. Those involved in corruption must be dealt with severely but transparently. The courts in particular must dispense justice under the rule of law to the fullest extent possible. Those found guilty of corruption, especially grand corruption, must face an appropriate level of punishment to emphasize society's disapproval and abhorrence of their actions and to clearly demonstrate that there is no room for corruption in the country. But, as a first order, investigations and prosecutions of those accused of corruption must be allowed to proceed without interference or undue influence from any quarter, especially the highest levels of the executive branch. In that regard, some critics of the KACC have regarded it as a toothless watchdog institution for lacking prosecutorial powers (Thiankolu, 2006; TI-Kenya, 2009). However, from this author's perspective, KACC's lack of prosecutorial powers is not the issue. It is not the question of which institution is vested with such prosecutorial powers but rather whether the institution with such powers has the necessary capacity, freedom, and independence to use those powers in pursuit of justice, the rule of law, and the good governance agenda generally. In other words, what is required is non-interference in the investigations, recommended prosecutions, and the actual prosecutions of those accused of corruption by the KACC or its successor institution.

Reform Strategies

The reform strategies being recommended here are intended to enhance ethical behavior and improve public accountability. These are strategies to be designed to influence behavior modification and resurrect public confidence in public institutions and officials. Institutions matter for achieving and sustaining good governance. Their integrity, legitimacy, and functioning suffer where corrupt practices occur as this work has shown with respect to Kenya. The country's institutions, therefore, need to be permanently on the guard against corruption. More importantly, institutions are also the means through which anti-corruption—as any other—policies have to be implemented (Hussmann et al., 2009). Institutional strengthening in support of anti-corruption efforts is taken here to mean the improvement of the effectiveness of existing structures, processes, and systems for goods and services delivery in a fair and rent-seeking-free manner. It is the enhancement of governance capacities which may entail reorganization as well as the improvement of the professionalism of the personnel. Before going any further though it must be acknowledged here that it is quite easy and simplistic to advocate for institutional strengthening and other reforms, whether in support of anti-corruption efforts or otherwise, by stating the obvious. However, what follows below is a discussion of the specific areas and mechanisms, which in this author's view, are required as reform strategies for more effective control of corruption in Kenya.

The first of these is related to the police. The post-December 2007 election crisis and violence drove home the point that police reform was necessary and urgent. The police themselves had acknowledged that and various human rights groups and development partners had urged it (World Bank, 2009a). In fact, "the police believe that low morale, lack of professionalism, inadequate resources, political interference, and corruption have all contributed to the weakness of their organization" (World Bank, 2009a:16). International lessons have demonstrated that police reforms are an integral part of the democratization and governance process. Changing the Kenya police culture, particularly as it relates to bribery, is the key to effective reforms. When those sworn to uphold the law engage in corruption themselves, it saps citizen confidence in public institutions and contributes to cynicism toward the notion of democracy itself. Like any type of persistent corruption, police corruption is generally a function of larger systemic problems caused by the lack of overall transparency, the absence of checks and balances, weak rule of law, and fragile institutions (USAID, 2007). Police corruption in Kenya has compromised police service delivery and has saddled the institution with a very bad reputation for bribery. The goal of the reform efforts here must, therefore, not only be an honest police service but to uphold the tenets of democratic policing. The basic tenets of democratic policing require the police to, among other things, uphold the law; be accountable to democratic oversight institutions and the communities they serve; be transparent in their activities; give the highest operational priority to protecting the safety and rights of individuals; and to seek to build professional skills and conditions of service that support efficient and respectful service delivery to the public (Stone and Ward, 2000; USAID, 2007).

One of the key tools required for police reforms in Kenya and to aid in tackling the police bribery problem is to regularly review and improve salaries and benefits. Pay increases should focus, in particular, on the worst paid lower ranks, and try to reduce undue wage differentials between senior and junior police officers. This need for better paid police officers in Kenya has been recognized by the government of Kenya and needs to be given more attention by those currently charged with implementing police reforms in the country. In fact, in July 2010, the government hastily (just prior to the referendum vote in August and undoubtedly to keep the police content and available to maintain law and order during the referendum voting process) arranged salary increases for the police that saw the latter improve their position relative to some of their Eastern African counterparts. Nonetheless, police salaries in Kenya still need to be appropriately set, especially at lower ranks, to take into consideration the public policy imperative to render the police less prone or less amenable to demanding and/or accepting bribes as a standard practice as it is now. Perhaps the Salaries and Remuneration Commission (being established as per the 2010 constitution), whose membership will also include a member of the National Police Service Commission, will fulfill this objective. Moreover, the police reforms also envisaged in the 2010 constitution (discussed below) require the creation and development of a more professionally oriented and disciplined police "service," as opposed to a police "force," not only as part of governance reforms but in the broader context of contributing to the outcomes of the country's Vision 2030 strategy.

Police reform is about change and policing is part of governance at every level. Consequently, the promotion of police reform must be duly regarded as an element of good governance interventions. The police are accountable for producing public safety and for behaving respectfully and within the law. In Kenya, police corruption, especially the bribery aspect, creates a double demand on police by requiring that police adhere to higher standards of conduct while also providing higher standards of service. Addressing police corruption in the country is essential to maintaining public order and the rule of law, to support the legitimacy of the State, and to maintain or restore public trust in democratic processes and institutions. Police reform is also a key component of the GJLOS program—where the police are recognized as a pivotal state institution as well as a key player in the governance and justice system. The foregoing are some of the key issues the Police Reform

Implementation Committee (PRIC)—that was established by the government in January 2010—must keep in mind as it proceeds with reform of the Kenya Police.

Another reform strategy pertains to the entire public service. Currently, the Kenya public service is subjected to performance contracts as discussed in Chapter 6. These performance contracts were piloted in 2004 and rolled out and expanded thereafter such that by 2006 almost the entire Kenyan public service, on the executive side, was participating in performance contracts. It is recommended that performance contracting in Kenya be expanded and refocused. The expansion should be to include all public institutions in all branches and levels of government. The refocusing should occur to use performance contracts—being a tool of performance management—as an anti-corruption measure for strengthening governance.

Although performance contracts have been in use in the Kenya public sector for more than five years now, it was only in 2010 that a standalone corruption eradication target indicator was added with a weight of only 5 percent which seems quite out of proportion with the magnitude and persistence of corruption in the Kenya public sector and its negative impact on the country's governance performance. The weight of the corruption eradication target indicator therefore needs to be substantially increased although there are recommendations in place, made by a Panel of Experts, to reduce the weight instead of increasing it (Republic of Kenya, 2010b). Using performance contracts as an anti-corruption measure can lead to improved governance in Kenya. To the extent it is a measurable indicator of public sector performance, the corruption eradication target indicator can strengthen governance. Performance contracts are tools of performance management that are intended to commit public officials to, and hold them accountable for, specified results, and one of those results in Kenya relates to what each public sector institution is doing to eradicate the corruption within it that stems from the rent-seeking and unethical behavior of its staff. Public sector institutions exist to translate the priorities and directions of the government into tangible benefits and results for Kenyans (Odinga, 2010). Those benefits and results include the creation of corruption-free public institutions and, in turn, society. Well-functioning institutions, led by individuals with high integrity, are fundamental for people's trust in government, for an end to corruption and impunity, and also for good governance.

One other reform strategy advocated here is that the PCSC not only be upgraded, as planned, to an Office of the Ombudsman, but that it should be modeled along the lines of the Office of the Public Protector in the Republic of South Africa with, among other things, (1) a mandate to focus on strengthening democracy by ensuring that all State (national and subnational) organs are accountable, fair, and responsive in the manner they treat all persons and deliver services, including ensuring integrity and general good governance in the management of public resources; (2) the powers to investigate all complaints or allegations of improper conduct by public officials and public office bearers and take remedial action; (3) the requirement that all organs of State, by law, must assist and protect the public and other constitutional institutions to ensure the independence, impartiality, dignity, and effectiveness of these institutions; (4) the powers to treat all information as confidential, including the identity of complainants and their sources of information; and (5) the power to take evidence on oath and to subpoena any material person to appear before it.

Establishing an effective process for handling public complaints requires several preconditions: (1) a sound legislative foundation; (2) the employment of dedicated, competent, and experienced and/or trained personnel to administer it; (3) a reasonable level of commitment and cooperation on the part of the public institutions and personnel to whom the process applies; (4) an adequate degree of knowledge of, confidence in, and willingness to use the process and good faith on the part of potential complainants in particular and the public more generally; and (5) the commitment of adequate resources for full and effective implementation of the process.

A good complaints mechanism should be accessible; fair to complainants and public officers; respectful of rights and dignity; open and accountable; timely; thorough; impartial; independent; and should take account of both the public interest and the interests of the parties involved in the complaint. It should also be appropriately balanced between formal and informal procedures for resolution of complaints. It should provide appropriate systemic information to the government (all branches), and it should avoid unnecessary duplication or overlap with internal disciplinary and grievance processes.

Applying the 2010 Constitution

On August 04, 2010, Kenyans voted overwhelmingly (by a more than two-thirds majority) in a referendum for a new constitution and thereby ushering in the Second Republic. The 2010 constitution contains stronger accountability and transparency safeguards and will serve as the gateway for much needed institutional reforms aimed at curbing corruption in the public sector and it should be used to such full effect. Indeed, the 2010 constitution offers many opportunities for a significant number of general governance reforms, including in the anti-corruption area, to be facilitated and fast tracked. In fact, the 2010 constitution holds enormous appeal and potential for controlling corruption and generally improving governance. For example, it provides the wherewithal for the emergence of a clean judiciary, a more independent Director of Public Prosecutions separated from the Office of the Attorney General, and an improved police service that can assist in the fight against corruption. Judicial authority, judicial independence, judicial offices, and the cadre and appointment of judicial officers are all clearly spelled out and provide hope for the exercise of judicial temperament consistent with the constitution and laws of the land rather than through political influence.

Similarly, the removal of the Director of Public Prosecutions (DPP) from the Attorney General's office and the fact that the former "shall have power to direct the Inspector-General of the National Police Service to investigate any information or allegation of criminal conduct and the Inspector-General shall comply with any such direction," and also "shall not require the consent of any person or authority for the commencement of criminal proceedings and in the exercise of his or her powers or functions, shall not be under the direction or control of any person or authority" (Republic of Kenya, 2010a: Chapter 9, Article 157), augurs well for the strengthening of the fight against corruption. This independence in prosecutorial authority, more so than where such authority resides, is the most significant factor in the decision-making that influences who gets prosecuted and when. Furthermore, the National Police Service, with its framed functions and command structure, as delineated in the constitution, should result in a greater willingness for the police to robustly engage in investigating high crimes and misdemeanors no matter the stature of the accused.

In addition, the 2010 constitution contains key elements related to devolved government and local governance (discussed in Chapter 5) which can have a major impact on the reduction of corruption. Devolved governments tend to improve governance at the local level with positive externalities for national governance. Decentralization/devolution is therefore an unambiguously desirable phenomenon. With respect to controlling corruption, there is a growing body of literature that demonstrates that decentralization/devolution has a deterrent effect on corruption. This link has been shown through the path of the closer proximity of devolved governments to the citizenry which increases transparency in the use of local resources and strengthens downward accountability mechanisms, resulting in a decrease in corrupt practices. Indeed, there is now good empirical evidence that fiscal decentralization is correlated with lower levels of corruption (Devas, 2005). Given all of the evidence and indices that show the epidemic spread of corruption in Kenya and its negative impact on governance, as shown in this work, then controlling corruption has to be a welcome and significantly important potential benefit of the country's efforts to decentralize through devolution.

While decentralization/devolution is used for a variety reasons, especially democratization and improving governance, its emphasis on accountability by bringing participation and decision-making closer to the people provides one of the strongest arguments for anti-corruption efforts (Joaquin, 2004). Decentralization has the effect of reducing central government discretion (derived from the centralization of power) that creates much of the opportunities for corruption. In fact, there is very much a clear relationship between corruption and discretion as well as between corruption and a country's level of centralization as currently exists in Kenya. Politicians and senior bureaucrats, particularly, are able to make use of the bureaucracy/government in illicit ways (Joaquin, 2004). However, this does not suggest that officials at the local levels cannot be corrupted. Rather, decentralization/devolution provides a much more manageable, transparent, and accountable arena to prevent corruption from erupting or to control it if it does. Empowering local governments reduces the frequency of bribery as well as the amount of bribes paid to officials, for example (Ivanyna and Shah, 2010).

Decentralization/devolution can, therefore, be regarded as an important element of combating corruption in countering the lack of transparency and accountability in centralized systems of government such as Kenya's. Moreover, as corruption levels can vary depending on the presence and functioning of democratic institutions, adopting decentralization to institutionalize local democracy offers a tool to fight corruption and thereby disrupt Kenya's current trend toward becoming a predatory State. Decentralization/devolution therefore has the potential to be a very powerful tool with a significant positive good governance effect on corruption (Joaquin, 2004). This point of view has also been confirmed in a post-2010 constitution referendum poll which found that 60 percent of Kenyans believe that devolution, including of state resources, will help reduce corruption, while 46 percent indicated that said devolution will reduce corruption by giving locals more say in resource allocation and utilization (TI-Kenya, 2010c).

One other laudable element of the 2010 constitution that can aid in the fight against corruption is that it specifies that the chief executives of government ministries (to be designated Cabinet Secretaries rather than Ministers as is currently the case) will be appointed from outside parliament and have to be nominated by the President and then confirmed by the National Assembly. MPs that are called upon to take up a Cabinet Secretary appointment will have to resign as legislators. This requirement to appoint Cabinet Secretaries from outside of Parliament does not only ensure separation of powers but allows for the installation of primarily technocrats, as opposed to politicians, as the chief executives of government ministries. This ushers in a new era of technocratic administration that will be less likely to be beholden to special interests and will, therefore, be much more ethical and clean.

Moreover, the 2010 constitution sets out a framework of leadership and integrity as it pertains to officers of the State including clauses on their conduct, financial probity, and restrictions on their activities. It also mandates parliament to enact legislation to establish an independent Ethics and Anti-Corruption Commission (EACC) with the responsibility for ensuring compliance with, and enforcement of, the provisions of its chapter on "Leadership and Integrity." Furthermore, the 2010 constitution sets out values and principles of public service that include, among other things, (1) high standards of professional ethics; (2) efficient, effective, and economic use of resources; (3) responsive, prompt, effective, impartial, and equitable provision of services; (4) accountability for administrative acts; and (5) transparency and provision to the public of timely, accurate information.

In fact, we have already begun to see the impact of the 2010 constitution in terms of its standards with respect to leadership and integrity which demands that public officials charged with corruption must vacate their appointments. In October 2010, for example, in the space of 10 days, two Ministers, a Permanent Secretary, and the Mayor of Nairobi were all forced to leave office upon facing serious allegations of fraud and corruption. Prior to the promulgation of the 2010 constitution there was no real legal instrument to force such individuals from office. These departures can only be described as exceptional events given the past environment of impunity, and this absolutely augurs well going forward in the fight against corruption in the country.

Undoubtedly, for both Kenyans and the international community, there is much riding on the 2010 constitution. The lessons of the 2007 postelection crisis and subsequent violence suggest that a new order governed by a supreme national framework of, among other things, rights, fundamental freedoms, democratic participation, devolved government, and implementation and enforcement authority will go a long way toward eliminating high-level corruption and public financial mismanagement, for instance. Indeed, this is the view of most Kenyans. In a poll conducted by TI-Kenya (2010c), 97 percent of the responding Kenyans reaffirmed that corruption is still a key problem in the country but 75 percent of them also expressed optimism that the 2010 constitution will effectively support anti-corruption efforts.

Conclusions

There is a vocal consensus that combating corruption is one of Kenya's most critical governance and development challenges. Various international assessments continue to rank Kenya as one of the most corrupt countries in the world and Kenyans themselves cite corruption as an issue of major concern for them (World Bank, 2009b). Corruption is embedded in the political economy of Kenya and this work has also demonstrated that corruption in Kenya is a major governance problem with deleterious effects on development (Hope, 2010). The country has come to be regarded as a flourishing swamp of corruption. And, this has damaged its development outcomes and poverty alleviation by limiting economic growth, reducing social cohesion, skewing both public and private investments, and weakening the rule of law. As former Justice and Constitutional Affairs Minister Kiraitu Murungi also acknowledged about the consequences of corruption in Kenya:

> It has ruined our schools and hospitals. It has destroyed our agriculture and industries. It has "eaten up" our roads and jobs. It has robbed, looted and plundered our resources. It has killed our children. It has destroyed our society. Our government has identified corruption as the principal structural bottleneck to all our development efforts. It is the fundamental cause of our high levels of poverty, unemployment and social backwardness. (Murungi, 2003: 2)

The Kenya case is, therefore, a perfect example of the description offered by former United Nations Secretary General, Kofi Annan (2003: 1), when he said, "Corruption hurts the poor disproportionately by diverting funds intended for development, undermining a government's ability to provide basic services, feeding inequality and injustice, and discouraging foreign investment and aid." Wamwere (2010: 1) has also put it much more bluntly, though dramatically, in contextualizing Kenya's corruption consequences as follows:

> In case you don't know, it is because corrupt people steal from us that we are poor, live in slums, our industries are dead, our youths are unemployed, our agriculture is profitless and dying, our roads are a torture, IDPs are languishing in camps, millions are landless and hungry, and our hospitals are frightening death camps.

Corruption is persistent in Kenya primarily because institutions such as the legislature, the judiciary, and many executive entities have been both weakened and become major perpetrators of corruption as well as conduits through which corrupt activities flow. In addition, the rule of law and adherence to formal rules are not rigorously observed, patronage has become standard practice, the independence and professionalism of the public sector has been eroded, and the average Kenyan has come to see corruption as an inevitable facet of life. Moreover, the culture of impunity encouraged, or led to, co-optation of others to participate. This is the main reason, for example, why Cabinet and high-level public service positions have been in such demand. According to Kiai (2010: 214):

> Despite the many official perks that come with these [cabinet and high-level public service] offices, the money one can make from corruption is far greater. It is no accident that the wealthiest Kenyans today have been or still are in some form of "public service," whether as politicians, civil servants, or officials of public companies.

Apart from its negative consequences on various governance indicators, corruption in Kenya has also induced cynicism as people now regard it as the norm. It has undermined social values because many people now find it easier and even more lucrative to engage in corrupt activities than to seek legitimate public service delivery. It has eroded governmental legitimacy by hampering the effective delivery of public goods and services. It has limited economic growth by reducing the amount of public resources available from both domestic and donor sources, by discouraging private investment, and by impeding the efficient use of government revenue and development assistance funds. The so-called eating reduces the resources available to finance public services which, in turn, directly disadvantage the poor. "Eating" is a practice of acquiring ignoble wealth by dishonest means which must be halted. Yet, at the same time, almost all of the necessary tools are in place to combat corruption in the country. Moving toward transformational leadership, using punishment as a deterrent, implementing reform strategies encompassing institutional strengthening, and using the instruments of the 2010 constitution to full effect are recommended for more effective control of corruption and, in fact, to sustain the structures for an effective anti-corruption regime.

References

ACBF (African Capacity Building Foundation) (2007), *Institutional Frameworks for Addressing Public Sector Corruption in Africa: Mandate, Performance, Challenges, and Capacity Needs*. Boulder, CO: Lynne Rienner Publishers.

Aluanga, L. (2010), "Why Ethics Act Is but a Dead Letter," *The Standard*, February 20. Available at: http://www.standardmedia.co.ke/InsidePage.php?id=2000003735&cid=4 [Accessed June 30, 2010].

Anassi, P. (2004), *Corruption in Africa: The Kenyan Experience*. Victoria, BC: Trafford Publishing.

Andrews, M., Mc Connell, J., and Westcott, A. (2010), *Development as Leadership-led Change: A Report for the Global Leadership Initiative*. Washington, DC: World Bank.

Annan, K. (2003), "Statement on the Adoption by the General Assembly of the United Nations Convention against Corruption." Available at: http://www. un.org/webcast/merida/pdfs/03-89343_Update_press.pdf [Accessed May 12, 2010].

APRM (African Peer Review Mechanism) Secretariat (2006), *Country Review Report of the Republic of Kenya.* Midrand, South Africa: APRM Secretariat.

AU (African Union) (2010), "List of Countries which have Signed, Ratified/ Acceded to the African Convention on Preventing and Combating Corruption." Available at: http://www.africaunion.org/root/au/Documents/Treaties/ List/African%20Convention%20on%20Combating%20Corruption.pdf [Accessed July 7, 2010].

Boswell, A. (2010), "Kenya Corruption Scandal Triggers Halt to US Education Funds," January 27. Available at: http://www1.voanews.com/english/news/ africa/Kenya-Corruption-Scandal-Triggers-Halt-to-US-Education-Funds-82802517.html [Accessed June 24, 2010].

British High Commission Nairobi (2009), *Towards a Better Future: Working with Kenya against Corruption.* Nairobi: British High Commission Nairobi.

— (2010), "UK Switches Education Funding Away from Government," March 16. Available at: http://ukinkenya.fco.gov.uk/en/news/?view=News&id =21894965 [Accessed June 17, 2010].

The Business Advocacy Fund (2008), *Business Perceptions of the Investment Climate in Kenya.* Nairobi: The Business Advocacy Fund.

Chebet, C. (2010), "Corrupt Ways of Government Officials," *The Standard,* June 14, p. 13.

Chêne, M. (2009), "The Political Economy of Public Procurement Reform." Available at: http://www.u4.no/helpdesk/helpdesk/query.cfm?id=202 [Accessed July 1, 2010].

Clinton, H. (2009), "Remarks at the 8th Forum of the African Growth and Opportunity Act," August 05. Available at: http://www.state.gov/secretary/ rm/2009a/08/126902.htm [Accessed June 14, 2009].

de Ferranti, D., Jacinto, J., Ody, A., and Ramshaw, G. (2009), *How to Improve Governance: A Framework for Analysis and Action.* Washington, DC: Brookings Institution Press.

Devas, N. (2005), "The Challenges of Decentralization," Paper Presented at the Global Forum on Fighting Corruption, June, Brasilia. Available at: http:// www.cgu.gov.br/ivforumglobal/pdf/nickdevas-2.pdf [Accessed May 4, 2010].

EAAACA (East African Association of Anti-Corruption Authorities) (nda), "About EAAACA." Available at: http://www.eaaaca.org/about.htm [Accessed July 18, 2010].

— (ndb), "Objectives." Available at: http://www.eaaaca.org/objectives.htm [Accessed July 18, 2010].

Enterprise Surveys (2007), "Featured Snapshot Report: Kenya (2007)." Available at: http://enterprisesurveys.org/ExploreEconomies/?economyid=101&year =2007 [Accessed June 21, 2010].

ESAAMLG (Eastern and Southern Africa Anti-Money Laundering Group) (2008), "Memorandum of Understanding of the Eastern and Southern Africa

Anti-Money Laundering Group" (Amended August). Available at: http://www.esaamlg.org/documents_storage/2009-3-3-8-3123_esaamlg_mou_as_amended_by_council_of_ministers_mombasa_kenya_august_2008.pdf [Accessed July 5, 2010].

Fraser-Moleketi, G. (2007), "Towards a Common Understanding of Corruption in Africa," *International Journal of African Renaissance Studies*, 2(2), 239–49.

Ghani, A. and Lockhart, C. (2008), *Fixing Failed States: A Framework for Rebuilding a Fractured World*. New York: Oxford University Press.

Githongo, J. (2010), "Fear and Loathing in Nairobi: The Challenge of Reconciliation in Kenya," *Foreign Affairs*, 89(4), 2–9.

Global Integrity (2009), 'Global Integrity Scorecard: Kenya 2009." Available at: http://report.globalintegrity.org/reportPDFS/2009/Kenya.pdf [Accessed June 17, 2010].

Hansen, T. O. (2009), "Political Violence in Kenya: A Study of Causes, Responses, and a Framework for Discussing Preventive Action," *ISS Paper 205*. Pretoria: Institute for Security Studies.

Hassan, S. (2004), "Corruption and the Development Challenge," *Journal of Development Policy and Practice*, 1(1), 25–41.

Hope, K. R. (1999), "Corruption in Africa: A Crisis in Ethical Leadership," *Public Integrity*, 1(3), 289–308.

— (2000), "Corruption and Development in Africa." In K. R. Hope and B. C. Chikulo (eds), *Corruption and Development in Africa: Lessons from Country Case-Studies*. Houndmills, UK: Palgrave Macmillan, pp. 17–39.

— (2008), *Poverty, Livelihoods, and Governance in Africa: Fulfilling the Development Promise*. New York: Palgrave Macmillan.

— (2010), "Corruption and Development in Kenya." Paper Prepared for Presentation at the African International Business and Management (AIBUMA) Conference, August 25–26, Nairobi.

Hope, K. R. and Chikulo, B. C. (2000), "Introduction." In K. R. Hope and B. C. Chikulo (eds), *Corruption and Development in Africa: Lessons from Country Case-Studies*. Houndmills, UK: Palgrave Macmillan, pp. 1–13.

Hussmann, K., Hechler, H., and Peñailillo, M. (2009), "Institutional Arrangements for Corruption Prevention: Considerations for the Implementation of the United Nations Convention against Corruption Article 6," *U4 Issue 2009: 4*. Bergen, Norway: U4 Anti-Corruption Resource Centre.

Iarossi, G. (2009), *An Assessment of the Investment Climate in Kenya*. Washington, DC: World Bank.

IPAR (Institute of Policy Analysis and Research) (2006), "Public Procurement Reforms: Redressing the Governance Concerns," *Policy Review*, Issue 2, 1–7.

Ivanyna, M. and Shah, A. (2010), "Decentralization (Localization) and Corruption: New Cross-Country Evidence," *Policy Research Working Paper 5299*. Washington, DC: World Bank Institute.

Joaquin, E.T. (2004), "Decentralization and Corruption: The Bumpy Road to Public Sector Integrity in Developing Countries," *Public Integrity*, 6(3), 207–19.

KACC (Kenya Anti-Corruption Commission) (2005), *The Public Procurement Act, What You Need to Know*. Nairobi: KACC.

— (2010), *National Enterprise Survey on Corruption 2009*. Nairobi: KACC.

Kamau, M. (2009), "MPs Corrupt at Expense of Kenyans, Says Karua," *East African Standard*, December 4, p. 4. Available at: http://www.marsgroupkenya. org/multimedia/?StoryID=274443 [Accessed June 21, 2010].

Kar, D. and Cartwright-Smith, D. (2010), *Illicit Financial Flows from Africa: Hidden Resource for Development*. Washington, DC: Global Financial Integrity.

Kaufmann, D. (1997), "Corruption: The Facts," *Foreign Policy*, 107(Summer), 114–31.

— (2004), "Corruption Matters: Evidence-Based Challenge to Orthodoxy," *Journal of Development Policy and Practice*, 1(1), 1–24.

— (2006), "Human Rights, Governance and Development: An Empirical Perspective," *Development Outreach*, October, 15–20.

Kaufmann, D., Kraay, A., and Mastruzzi, M. (2009), "Governance Matters VIII: Aggregate and Individual Governance Indicators 1996-2008," *Policy Research Working Paper 4979*. Washington, DC: World Bank.

Khadiagala, G. (2009), "Transparency and Accountability in Kenya's Budget Process." In D. de Ferranti, J. Jacinto, A. Ody, and G. Ramshaw, *How to Improve Governance: A New Framework for Analysis and Action*. Washington, DC: Brookings Institution Press, pp. 127–41.

Khamisi, J. (2011), *The Politics of Betrayal: Diary of a Kenyan Legislator*. Bloomington, IN: Trafford Publishing.

Kiai, M. (2010), "The Crisis in Kenya." In L. Diamond and M. F. Plattner (eds), *Democratization in Africa: Progress and Retreat*. Baltimore, MD: Johns Hopkins University Press, pp. 212–18.

Leftie, P. and Mwaura, K. (2010), "House Fight Looms over MPs' Pay Rise," *Daily Nation*, July 6, 1–2.

Luh, J. (2003), "Public Officer Ethics Act Provisions for Declarations of Income, Assets, and Liabilities: Evaluation and Recommendations." Available at: http://www.tikenya.org/documents/assetdeclaration.pdf [Accessed June 30, 2010].

Lumumba, P. L. O. (2011), "Promoting Ethics and Integrity in the Workplace." Public Lecture at the Kenya College of Accountancy University (KCAU), Nairobi, February 24.

Mars Group Kenya Media (2004), "Bribery a Thriving Vice in Parliament," October 24, http://www.marsgroupkenya.org/multimedia/?StoryID=80726 &p=State+House&page=382 (Accessed June 21, 2010).

Mogeni, D. (2009), "Why Corruption Persists in Kenya," *Daily Nation*, February 5. Available at: http://www.nation.co.ke/oped/Opinion/-/440808/525272/-/42v0lp/-/index.html [Accessed May 12, 2010].

Moulid, H. (2010), "European Union Warns Kenyan Leaders Over Corruption," *All Headline News*, March 26. Available at: http://www.allheadlinenews. com/articles/7018224433?European%20Union%20Warns%20Kenyan%20 Leaders%20Over%20Corruption [Accessed June 23, 2010].

Mueller, S. (2008), "The Political Economy of Kenya's Crisis," *Journal of Eastern African Studies*, 2(2), 185–210.

Murage, G. (2011), "Speaker Says 70 Percent Projects Money Stolen," *The Star*, March 29, Online Edition. Available at: http://www.nairobistar.com/

national/national/18952-corruption-graft-linked-to-theft-of-70-state-cash [Accessed March 30, 2011].

Murungi, K. (2003), "Statement by Hon Kiraitu Murungi, MP, Minister for Justice and Constitutional Affairs and Head of Delegation at the High Level Political Signing Conference of the UN Convention Against Corruption in Merida, Mexico—December 9–11. Available at: http://www.un.org/webcast/merida/statements/keny031209en.htm [Accessed May 25, 2010].

Mutua, M. (2010), "How Kibaki, MPs Saved Face on Pay Standoff in Parliament," *The Standard*, July 23, 1 and 4.

Mwanzia, M. and Gichura, G. (2010), "Report: Council has 4,000 'Ghost' Workers," *The Standard*, June 18, 10.

NACCSC (National Anti-Corruption Campaign Steering Committee) (nd), "NACCSC Mandate." Available at: http://www.naccsc.go.ke/index2.php?option=com_co ntent&task=view&id=1&pop=1&page=0&Itemid=1 [Accessed July 7, 2010].

— (2010), *Progress Report: 1st July, 2008–31st December, 2009*. Nairobi: NACCSC.

NACP (National Anti-Corruption Plan) Secretariat (nd), *National Anti-Corruption Plan*. Available at: http://www.kacc.go.ke/Docs/Ntional%20Anti-%20 Corruption%20Plan.pdf [Accessed July 3, 2010].

NTA (National Taxpayers Association) (2011), "Launch of NTA Citizens' Audit of CDF and LATF Funds." Available at: http://www.nta.or.ke/events/277-nta-phase-iii-cdf-and-latf-ranking-2011 [Accessed March 31, 2011].

Ochami, D. and Njiraini, J. (2010), "Sh270b: That's What We Lose to Graft Yearly," *The Standard*, December 3, 1 and 4.

Odhiambo, W. and Kamau, P. (2003), "Public Procurement: Lessons from Kenya, Tanzania and Uganda," *Working Paper No. 208*. Paris: OECD Development Centre.

Odinga, R. (2010), "Foreword" to *Public Sector Transformation Strategy: From Reform to Transformation 2010-14*. Nairobi: Public Sector Transformation Department, Office of the Prime Minister.

Ogot, M., Nyandemo, S., Kenduiwo, J., Mokaya, J., and Iraki, W. (2009), "The Long Term Policy Framework for Public Procurement in Kenya." Available at: http://www.uneskenya.com/download/Draft_Zero_Long_Term_Public_ Procurement_Policy%20-%20Revision3.pdf [Accessed July 1, 2010].

Okanja, O. (2010), *Kenya at Forty-Five: 1963-2008: Economic Performance, Problems and Prospects*. London: Athena Press.

OP (Office of the President) (2010), *Report of the Workshop on Strategies to Fight/ Eliminate Corruption in the Public Service for Permanent Secretaries/Accounting Officers and Chief Executives of State Corporations*. Nairobi: Office of the President.

Opiyo, D. (2010), "Measures to Dismantle Corruption Cartels," *Daily Nation*, June 23, 11.

Orowe, L. (2004), "Corruption: The Role of Government in the Anti-Corruption Fight as Opposed to the Role of Individuals and Organizations." Available at: http://www.c4idea.com/presentations/Eradicating_Corruption.pdf [Accessed July 4, 2010].

Otieno, G. (2005), "The NARC's Anti-Corruption Drive in Kenya," *African Security Review*, 14(4), 69–79.

Otieno, J. (2009), "UK Withholds Kenya Grant Over Corruption," *Daily Nation*, December 11. Available at: http://www.nation.co.ke/News/-/1056/820998/-/view/printVersion/-/ulotlx/-/index.html [Accessed June 24, 2010].

PCSC (Public Complaints Standing Committee) (nda), *The First Quarterly Report for the Year 2009/2010 Covering the Period 1st July 2009 to 30th September 2009*. Nairobi: PCSC.

— (ndb), *The Second Quarterly Report for the Year 2009/2010 Covering the Period 1st October 2009 to 31st December 2009*. Nairobi: PCSC.

PricewaterhouseCoopers (2010), "Economic Crime in Kenya." Available at: http://www.pwc.com/en_KE/ke/pdf/gec-kenya.pdf [Accessed June 21, 2010].

Ranneberger, M. (2010), "Reform, Partnership, and the Future of Kenya: Speech to the American Chamber of Commerce, Nairobi," January 26. Available at: http://nairobi.usembassy.gov/speeches/2010-speeches/sp_20100126.html [Accessed June 22, 2010].

Republic of Kenya (nda), "Governance, Justice, Law and Order Sector (GJLOS)." Available at: http://www.justice.go.ke/index.php?option=com_content&task =view&id=35&Itemid=52 [Accessed July 5, 2010].

— (ndb), "Public Complaints Standing Committee (PCSC)." Available at: http://www.justice.go.ke/index.php?option=com_content&task=view&id=22&Itemi d=83 [Accessed July 7, 2010].

— (2003a), *The Anti-Corruption and Economic Crimes Act, 2003*. Nairobi: Republic of Kenya.

— (2003b), *The Public Officer Ethics Act, 2003*. Nairobi: Republic of Kenya.

— (2003c), *Kenya: Economic Recovery Strategy for Wealth and Employment Creation 2003-2007*. Nairobi: Ministry of Planning and National Development.

— (2004), *The Government Financial Management Act, 2004*. Nairobi: Republic of Kenya.

— (2005a), *Report of the Judicial Commission of Inquiry into the Goldenberg Affair*. Nairobi: Republic of Kenya.

— (2005b), "The Public Procurement and Disposal Act, 2005," *Kenya Gazette Supplement No. 77 (Acts No. 3)*. Nairobi: Government Printer.

— (2009a), *Quarterly Economic and Budgetary Review: Third Quarter 2008/2009*. Nairobi: Office of the Deputy Prime Minister and Ministry of Finance.

— (2009b), *The Proceeds of Crime and Anti-Money Laundering Act No., 9 of 2009*. Nairobi: Republic of Kenya.

— (2009c), "National Anti-Corruption Campaign Steering Committee," *The Kenya Gazette*, August 14. Nairobi: Republic of Kenya.

— (2010a), *The Constitution of Kenya, 2010*. Nairobi: Republic of Kenya.

— (2010b), *Review of Performance Contracting in the Public Sector: Report by the Panel of Experts*. Nairobi: Office of the Prime Minister.

Rugene, N. (2009), "Bribery in Kenya's Parliament," *Daily Nation*, May 16. Available at: http://www.nation.co.ke/News/-/1056/599016/-/u6adu9/-/index.html [Accessed May 12, 2010].

Rugene, N. and Shiundu, A. (2010), "Kibaki Reins in MPs Over Pay," *Daily Nation*, July 23, 2.

Shiundu, A. (2010), "US Suspends Kenya Education Cash," *Daily Nation*, January 26. Available at: http://www.nation.co.ke/News/-/1056/849984/-/vpg3t6/-/index.html [Accessed June 24, 2010].

Sichei, M. M. (2010), "Impact of Corruption on the National Economy." In J. Kivuva and M. Odhiambo (eds), *Integrity in Kenya's Public Service: Illustrations from the Goldenberg and Anglo-Leasing Scandals*. Nairobi: CLARION (Center for Law and Research International), pp. 123–51.

Stone, C. and Ward, H. (2000), "Democratic Policing: A Framework for Action," *Policing and Society*, 10(1), 11–45.

Thiankolu, M. (2006), "The Anti-Corruption and Economic Crimes Act, 2003: Has Kenya Discharged Her Obligations to Her Peoples and the World?." Available at: http://www.kenyalaw.org/Downloads_Other/Muthomi%20 Thiankolu%20-%20AntiCorruption%20And%20Economic%20Crimes%20 Act%202003.pdf [Accessed June 12, 2010].

TI (Transparency International) (2009), *Global Corruption Report 2009*. Cambridge, UK: Cambridge University Press.

— (2010a), *Global Corruption Report 2010*. Cambridge, UK: Cambridge University Press.

— (2010b), *The Anti-Corruption Catalyst: Realizing the MDGs by 2015*. Berlin: TI.

TI-Kenya (Transparency International—Kenya) (2008), *The Kenya Bribery Index 2008*. Nairobi: TI-Kenya.

— (2009), *Corruption Trends Analysis: Tracing Corruption Trends in Kenya's Public Sector*. Nairobi: TI-Kenya.

— (2010a), *The East African Bribery Index 2010*. Nairobi: TI-Kenya.

— (2010b), *A Report on Integrity: A Study of the Kenyan Parliament*. Nairobi: TI-Kenya.

— (2010c), *Corruption and the New Order: National Opinion Poll on Kenyans' Expectations of Corruption Trends Under the New Constitution*. Nairobi: TI-Kenya.

Tuta, J. K. (2005), "Legal Framework for Control of Corruption." In L. Chweya, J. K. Tuta, and S. K. Akivaga (eds), *Control of Corruption in Kenya: Legal-Political Dimensions 2001-2004*. Nairobi: Claripress Limited, pp. 144–242.

UNODC (United Nations Office on Drugs and Crime) (2010), "United Nations Convention against Corruption." Available at: http://www.unodc.org/unodc/en/treaties/CAC/signatories.html [Accessed July 6, 2010].

USAID (United States Agency for International Development) (2007), *USAID Program Brief: Anticorruption and Police Integrity: Security Sector Reform Program*. Washington, DC: USAID.

Wabukala, E. (2010), "Chairman's Message." In NACCSC (National Anti-Corruption Campaign Steering Committee), *Progress Report: 1st July, 2008—31st December, 2009*. Nairobi: NACCSC.

Waki Commission (Commission of Inquiry into Post-Election Violence) (2008), *Report of the Commission of Inquiry into Post-Election Violence* (Waki Report). Nairobi: Waki Commission.

Wamwere, K. (2010), "Top Leadership Must Be in the Forefront if the Battle on Corruption Is To Be Won." Available at: http://www.nation.co.ke/oped/Opinion/-/440808/1046170/-/nw15ccz/-/index.html [Accessed November 5, 2010].

Warren, M. E. (2004), "What Does Corruption Mean in a Democracy?," *American Journal of Political Science*, 48(2), 328–43.

Wikipedia (2010), "Corruption in Kenya." Available at: http://en.wikipedia.org/wiki/Corruption_in_Kenya#Corruption [Accessed June 17, 2010].

World Bank (2009a), *Kenya: Economic Development, Police Oversight, and Accountability: Linkages and Reforms*. Washington, DC: World Bank.

— (2009b), *Kenya Poverty and Inequality Assessment: Executive Summary and Synthesis Report*, Report No. 44190-KE. Washington, DC: World Bank.

— (2010), "Silent and Lethal: How Quiet Corruption Undermines Africa's Development Efforts." An Essay Drawn from Africa Development Indicators 2010. Washington, DC: World Bank.

World Economic Forum (2009), *The Global Competitiveness Report 2009-2010*. Geneva: World Economic Forum.

Wrong, M. (2009), *It's Our Turn to Eat: The Story of a Kenyan Whistle-Blower*. New York: Harper.

Zutt, J. (2010), "Corruption in Kenya." Available at: http://blogs.worldbank.org/africacan/corruption-in-kenya [Accessed November 17, 2010].

5

Decentralization and Local Governance

Since African countries achieved independence, more than four decades ago, the legal status and approach of their decentralization programs and policies have been stipulated in one of two ways: (1) by the enactment of lower-level laws and/or use of administrative regulations; or (2) explicitly in a constitution. Kenya has now opted for the latter as per the 2010 constitution. Prior to the passing of the 2010 constitution in Kenya, among African countries, only South Africa had relied on rigorous planning to implement decentralization policies. It is not surprising, therefore, that most African countries have no mechanisms in place to assess the conduct and impact of such policies (Letaief et al., 2008). In fact, as this book shows, prior to the enactment of the 2010 constitution, the autonomy of local governments in Kenya was restricted by the national government's oversight of the local authorities and their actions.

However, decentralization and local governance in Kenya got a positive boost, on August 04, 2010, when Kenyans voted affirmatively with a more than two-thirds majority (67%) in a referendum for a landmark 2010 constitution which, among other things, recognizes the sovereignty of the people and enshrines a Bill of Rights. One of the other laudable key elements contained in this 2010 constitution of Kenya is the creation of institutions to strengthen and sustain governance both nationally and locally. Prominent among the local institutional structures to be created are those related to devolved government. Devolved government or devolution (also referred to as democratic decentralization) represents the transfer of power and resources to lower (subnational) levels of government that are both (relatively) independent of national government and democratically elected. Beginning as early as Chapter Two in the 2010 constitution, "devolution and access to services" is delineated as the third of eight items defining the Republic of Kenya.

In addition, Chapter Eleven of the 2010 constitution also spells out, in meticulous detail, the objects and principles of devolved government; the nature of devolved governments (47 counties plus yet to be determined urban areas and cities); the functions and powers of these 47 county governments; the boundaries of the counties; the relationships between and among county governments and the national government; the rationale and manner of suspension of county governments; and general issues including county assembly powers and gender balance and diversity. Moreover, other chapters in the constitution cover such matters as fiscal decentralization, equitable sharing of national revenue between the national and county governments, the borrowing powers of the counties, and staffing of county governments. There are also Schedules on the timelines (18 months) for legislation to be enacted to give effect to devolved government as well as on the transitional and consequential provisions.

Below, the structure and benefits of decentralized government in Kenya are discussed and, against that background, advocates, provides justification for, and also recommends a program of actions to build the required institutions to underpin and support the ongoing implementation of decentralized government structures that the constitution proposes for improving local and, consequently, national governance in the country. Any future assessed success or failure of devolved government hinges critically on the nature and capacity of the institutional framework that is put in place, from the inception, to drive and sustain the process for deriving the intended benefits of decentralization and local governance that the citizenry have agitated for and also deserve.

Local Government Structure in Kenya

During the colonial era, local governments in Kenya were considered to be fairly autonomous and had significant sources of revenue. However, after the country attained independence in 1963, local authorities were weakened and simultaneously developed a bad reputation for incompetence (Oloo, 2008). After independence was achieved, the assumption of power by Kenyan political leaders triggered the consolidation of local governance that saw successful attempts to recentralize which, in turn, undermined both the link and the relationship between local authorities and their constituents (Oloo, 2008). The recentralization took form through measures that saw the emergence of an administrative structure consisting of local authorities and national government administrative units that make up what is termed provincial administration. This dual system remained the basic framework for local governance and public service delivery in Kenya (Menon et al., 2008), through to the 2010 constitution that was passed overwhelmingly by Kenyans on August 4, 2010.

Following the attainment of independence, local authorities continued to be supported by a robust revenue base and grants from the national government. Under the existing law, the local authorities were required to provide only a small number of services and any other programs they considered essential for improving services to their residents. The major services they had responsibility for were primary education, health care, road maintenance, and agricultural extension. However, in pursuit of its recentralization policy, the national government decided to keep the pre-independence structure of local government but transferred most of the key functions and powers back to the national government, thereby severely restricting the autonomy of the local governments (Oloo, 2008). This was formalized in 1969 following the enactment of the Transfer of Functions Act which provided the national government with the powers to take over the responsibilities for the provision of primary education, health care, and roads maintenance. At the same time, the national government also took over key revenue sources from the local governments ostensibly to fund the newly acquired services and, since then, local governments in Kenya have been systematically weakened (Menon et al., 2008).

A good chronology of measures that have been used to weaken and undermine local governance in Kenya from the 1960s to present can be found in Menon et al. (2008). The government of Kenya has also undertaken periodic reviews of the structure and functioning of local governments in the country. The end result of these measures and periodic reviews—in addition to maintaining a heavily centralized form of control—was the rapid proliferation of local authorities which, in turn, led to the creation of several decentralized funds to support the management of the institutional framework. Local service delivery in Kenya is currently implemented through the following: (1) local authorities; (2) regional development authorities; (3) sector ministries; (4) provincial administration; (5) district funds for rural development (DFRD); (6) decentralized funds; and (7) development partners and NGOs. Presently, there are 175 local authorities in Kenya comprising of 1 city council, 45 municipal councils, 62 town councils, and 67 county councils. There are 6 regional development authorities that were established between 1974 and 1990 to harness local resources for local benefit and rationalize equitable and balanced sustainable regional and national development.

The sector ministries of the national government have delegated their functions to institutions within local areas. These local institutions are usually Boards such as the land, roads, health, education, and water boards, respectively, which are also organized into regional or district units but the exercise of authority for that service remains with the relevant national ministry (Republic of Kenya, 2008). Provincial administration has been designated by the national government as the prefectural authority in the local areas, thus rendering decision-making a centralized practice (Muia, 2008;

Oloo, 2008). There are eight provinces in the country with each headed by a Provincial Commissioner who is assisted by District Commissioners, District Officers, Chiefs, and Assistant Chiefs. Provincial administration is a department in the Ministry of State for Provincial Administration and Internal Security in the Office of the President. Beginning with the first post-independence government of Jomo Kenyatta, the provincial administration amassed enormous powers. "The unlimited authority granted to the administration made them virtually lords in their own realms provided they administered their spheres efficiently on the regime's behalf" (Omolo, 2010: 28). However, according to the 2010 constitution, within five years after its effective date, the national government shall restructure the system of administration commonly known as the provincial administration to accord with and respect the system of devolved government established under the constitution (Republic of Kenya, 2010).

The DFRD is a strategy that is intended to bring about a complementary relationship between development approaches of ministries and the approach of districts in addressing local needs. The decentralized funds are resources transferred by the national government to the various decentralized ministries, departments, agencies, local authority boards, and regional development authorities. There are also numerous specific funds for public service delivery to local communities including the Local Authorities Transfer Fund (LATF), the Constituency Development Fund (CDF), the Road Maintenance Levy Fund (RMLF), the HIV/AIDS Community Support Initiative, the Constituency Bursary Fund (secondary education), the Community Development Trust Fund, the Poverty Reduction Fund, the Youth Development Fund, and the Women's Enterprise Development Fund. Development partners and NGOs are also actively involved in several initiatives supporting the local authorities or local communities directly (Republic of Kenya, 2008).

The Kenya 2010 constitution requires a two-tier government structure—national and county. Article 1 of that constitution establishes that sovereign power of the people is exercised at the national and county levels with the latter being the unit of devolution. The national government shall comprise the Executive (president, deputy president, and a cabinet of 14 but no more than 22 cabinet secretaries); the Bi-Cameral Legislature (National Assembly and the Senate); and the Judiciary and Tribunals. The 47 county governments shall each be composed of the Executive (governor, deputy governor, and county executive committee) and a county assembly. County governments established under this Constitution are to be based on: (1) democratic principles and the separation of powers; (2) have reliable sources of revenue to enable them to govern and deliver services effectively; and

(3) have no more than two-thirds of the members of representative bodies in each county government being of the same gender. Every county government is also required to decentralize its functions and the provision of its services to the extent that it is efficient and practicable to do so (Republic of Kenya, 2010).

For each county, the governor and deputy governor are the Chief Executive and Deputy Chief Executive, respectively. The county governor shall be elected directly by the voters registered in the county for a term of five years and can hold office for no more than two terms. Each candidate for election as county governor shall nominate a person who is qualified for nomination for election as county governor as a candidate for deputy governor. However, no separate election for deputy governor is required. The Independent Electoral and Boundaries Commission is simply required to declare the candidate nominated by the person who is elected county governor to have been elected as the deputy governor (Republic of Kenya, 2010). However, the likely practice is that the nominated candidate for deputy governor would be the running mate of the gubernatorial candidate.

Each county will also have a county assembly, elected for a five-year term, consisting of: (1) members elected by the registered voters of the wards, each ward constituting a single member constituency; (2) the number of special seat members necessary to ensure that no more than two-thirds of the membership of the assembly are of the same gender; (3) the number of members of marginalized groups, including persons with disabilities and the youth, prescribed by an Act of Parliament; and (4) the speaker, who is an *ex officio* member. Each county assembly will have a speaker elected by the county assembly from among persons who are not members of the assembly. The speaker of a county assembly shall preside over the sitting of the county assembly (Republic of Kenya, 2010). Each county assembly is vested with the legislative authority of a county and has the power to: (1) make any laws that are necessary for, or incidental to, the effective performance of the functions and exercise of the powers of the county government as stipulated in the constitution; (2) exercise oversight over the county executive and any other county executive organs, while respecting the principle of the separation of powers; and (3) receive and approve plans and policies for the management and exploitation of the county's resources and the development and management of its infrastructure and institutions (Republic of Kenya, 2010).

The executive authority of a county is vested in, and exercised by, a county executive committee. The county executive committee consists of: (1) the county governor and the deputy governor; and (2) members appointed by the county government, with the approval of the assembly, from among persons who are not members of the assembly. The number of members appointed shall not exceed: (1) one-third of the number of members of the county assembly, if the assembly has less than 30 members; or (2) ten, if the assembly has 30 or more members. Members of a county executive committee are accountable to the county governor for the performance of the functions and exercise of their powers (Republic of Kenya, 2010). The functions of a county executive committee are to: (1) implement county legislation; (2) implement, within the county, national legislation to the extent that the legislation requires; (3) manage and coordinate the functions of the county administration and its departments; and (4) perform any other functions conferred on it by the constitution or national legislation. A county executive committee may also prepare proposed legislation for consideration by the county assembly as well as provide the county assembly with full and regular reports on matters relating to the county (Republic of Kenya, 2010).

The 2010 constitution also provides for the equitable sharing of national revenue among the national government and county governments. The determination of the equitable shares is governed by a set of criteria that include: (1) the national interest; (2) the need to ensure that county governments are able to perform the functions allocated to them; (3) the fiscal capacity and efficiency of county governments; (4) developmental and other needs of counties; (5) economic disparities within and among counties and the need to remedy them; (6) the desirability of stable and predictable allocations of revenue; and (7) the need for economic optimization of each county and to provide incentives for each county to optimize its capacity to raise revenue. Moreover, the 2010 constitution also provides for the equitable share of the national revenue that is allocated to county governments to be not less than 15 percent of all revenue collected by the national government (Republic of Kenya, 2010). There is also a further 0.5 percent of all the revenue collected by the national government each year which is to be set aside in an equalization fund to be used to provide basic services including water, roads, health facilities, and electricity to marginalized areas to the extent necessary to bring the quality of those services in those areas to the level generally enjoyed by the rest of the nation, as far as possible (Republic of Kenya, 2010).

In addition, the 2010 constitution requires that a revenue fund be established for each county government into which shall be deposited all monies raised for or received on behalf of a county government, except money reasonably excluded by an Act of Parliament. Along with the fiscal transfers from the national government, a county government may also mobilize revenue by (1) levying taxes such as property, entertainment, and any other tax or licensing fees that it is authorized to impose by an Act of Parliament; and (2) by borrowing. However, a county government may borrow only with the approval of the county government's assembly and if the national government guarantees the loan (Republic of Kenya, 2010).

Kenya's Potential Benefits from Devolved Government

The process of devolution envisaged in the 2010 constitution will, at the outset, seem very complicated as well as a daunting task. However, the benefits of this exercise will, in the long-run, far outweigh any potential implementation problems. Devolved governments tend to improve governance at the local level with positive externalities for national governance. Decentralization/ devolution is therefore an unambiguously desirable phenomenon. Drawing on the vast lessons of experience of decentralization/devolution processes around the world it is possible to draw conclusions on the potential benefits of devolved government for Kenya as discussed below.

Greater Responsiveness to Local Needs

As observed by Omolo (2010), African states, such as Kenya, with centralized systems of government have suffered multiple symptoms associated with poor governance. Decentralization, whether through devolution or other approaches, is seen as a means of bringing government closer to the people. This is geared toward greater responsiveness to local needs through the transfer of power, authority, functions, responsibilities, and resources from the national government to local governments which are closer to the public to be served. In Kenya, one of the key factors that have been frequently cited as a contributing force to the postelection violence in 2008 is the centralization of power in the executive branch of the government and more specifically in the highly personalized Presidency (Mueller, 2008). "What evolved over time was an ineffectual, weak and corrupt judiciary, a provincial prefecture neither accountable nor transparent to citizens, and finally growing powers of the Presidency" (Menon et al., 2008: 5).

The extent of this Presidential power is a holdover from the colonial era and has changed little since independence in 1963 until the signing of the National Accord and Reconciliation Agreement (NARA), in February 2008, which stipulated a power-sharing arrangement between the President and Prime Minister. Now, the 2010 constitution provides for a legal foundation for entrenching distributive power. Consequently, by devolving government there will be a shift in some power, authority, functions, responsibilities, and resources from the center to the grassroots with, hopefully, a concomitant response to the needs and aspirations of Kenyans in the local areas.

Decentralization to officials responsible for the delivery of public services to the local communities makes it easier for claimants to gain access to goods and services to which they are entitled. Decentralization leads to more efficient delivery of public services by reducing costs, exposing problems in delivery mechanisms, and generating more sympathetic attitudes toward government programs. Decentralization also has the value of reducing red tape and bureaucratic formalism. It greatly facilitates the access of the people to policy and decision-makers by rendering them more visible and making the loci of power easier to identify. By so doing, more decisions are made at the local level, closer to the voters, resulting in more responsive and efficient local governance (Hope, 2000, 2002).

Enhanced Citizen Participation

Kenya's current model of citizen participation can be termed "democratic centralism"—not in the strict Leninist sense—in the context of citizens being able to participate in elections, for example, but with a centralism of decision-making that those citizens are expected to support whether or not decisions made are in their best interests. This democratic centralism has therefore constrained citizen participation and decision-making, and there is no doubt that, currently, Kenyans feel they are subjects not citizens and decisions are made remotely about their lives without consulting them.

Through devolution, decision-making will be local and local citizens will have opportunities to contribute to decision-making where their local affairs are concerned and thereby leading to enhanced citizen participation and decision-making. By promoting and realizing citizen participation and decision-making, decentralization/devolution would also positively contribute to political stability, improved governance, and improved citizens' welfare. Devolved governments will be much more knowledgeable about, and more responsible to, the needs of local populations, inclusive of the majority poor (Crawford and Hartmann, 2008).

Consequently, decentralization may create opportunities for a more accountable government. Residents participating in decision-making can easily and better monitor and evaluate the government's compliance with the decisions made, can demand speedier government operations, and push local institutions to enhance their capabilities in undertaking functions that have not been usually performed well by the national government on its own (Schiavo-Campo and Sundaram, 2001). Moreover, such participation in decision-making can also result in more flexible and effective administration since the decentralized government can tailor its services to the needs of the various groups it serves.

Better Service Delivery

Decentralization/devolution which is geared toward greater responsiveness to local needs, leads to better access to adequate and relevant services that are more efficiently provided by a local government structure that understands the needs of those to be served and effectively leverages local knowledge and resources. Decentralized service delivery is based on the conviction that the government at the local level has a better understanding of community needs, and is, therefore, better placed in delivering relevant and responsive services. Even when it is not explicit (as in the case of Kenya), improving service delivery is an implicit motivation behind most decentralization efforts.

Roughly speaking, decentralization/devolution improves service delivery outcomes to the extent that physical proximity increases citizen information, participation, as well as monitoring of performance, and to the extent that narrowing the scope of responsibilities of the two tiers of government (national and county) decision-makers reduces their ability to shirk on some responsibilities. All of this can then lead to a more transparent and egalitarian distribution of resources. In fact, the poor in Kenya may be empowered as opposed to feeling powerless to act as they are in the current situation of centralized power and State authority relations.

Moreover, as observed by Foster and Glennester (2009), decentralization improves public service delivery for the following main reasons:

- Decentralization allows for greater diversity in the type of public services delivered and how they are delivered so that services can more closely reflect the different priorities of different regions of the country.
- By reducing the distance (both geographically and bureaucratically) between governments and the citizenry, decentralization can reduce the cost of service delivery, and can increase the speed and efficiency with which local governments respond to the needs of the local community.
- Decentralization can also improve service delivery by reducing the distance that individual citizens must travel to complain about services and the number of bureaucratic layers that they have to go through to lodge their complaint.

Reduction of Regional Inequalities, Instability, and Poverty

Calls for devolution of economic and political power in Kenya have been particularly emotive and an important part of the political and constitutional debate. Regions, somewhat neglected in the socioeconomic development planning, have been, and continue to be, used by politicians as a proxy for ethnicity and calls to action for political competition. Moreover, the centralized state has greatly contributed to the skewed development of regions. Through decentralization/devolution, a much more equitable distribution of national resources is envisaged and, now consistent with the *Kenya Vision 2030*, county governments will have a much greater say on actions and programs to avoid gross economic disparities; reduce poverty; minimize the differences in income opportunities and access to social services, paying special attention to the most disadvantaged communities in the arid and semi-arid lands and urban slums; and reducing gender inequities in all areas as necessary.

As discussed in Chapter 1, the *Kenya Vision 2030* is the country's development blueprint covering the period from 2008 to 2030. It intends to adopt a democratic decentralization process with substantial devolution in policy making, public resource management, and revenue sharing through selected devolved funds (Republic of Kenya, 2007). Through the *MTP 2008-2012*, the *Kenya Vision 2030* defines devolution as a "shift in power resources, and responsibilities from the center to other lower levels of government" and decentralization is defined as "any change in the organization of government which involves the transfer of some powers from the national level to any sub-national levels, or from one sub-national level to another lower level" (Republic of Kenya, 2008: 135).

Decentralized forms of government tend to be much more responsive to the needs of the poor. Because decentralization brings government closer to the governed—both spatially and institutionally—government will be more knowledgeable about, and responsive to, the needs of the poor. Focused local development programs that are locally conceived will have a much greater impact on reducing rural poverty and improving human development than broader and more generalized national programs originating from the center. In fact, one major consequence of decentralization is that the local knowledge advantage of local governments can lead to a more equitable distribution of public resources within their jurisdiction and a better match of available resources with local demand and the needs of the poor.

Moreover, if done properly and with appropriate institutional capacities in place, decentralization can lead to improved local economic development and poverty reduction through the provision of services that serve as production and distribution inputs for local firms or entrepreneurs or potential investors, and by coordinating key local public, private, and community actors in creating partnerships that promote development with significant pro-poor elements.

Also, decentralization/devolution has the ability to contribute to national unity and political stability. This is a very important benefit since, in this author's view, devolution was the principal reason Kenyans overwhelmingly voted for the 2010 constitution. There is a persistent belief that local democracy is necessary for national unity. In countries with great social diversity and regional disparities, such as Kenya, it is indeed necessary to satisfy the legitimate political aspirations of subgroups. Decentralization can therefore be used to satisfy the demands for recognition of identity or to defuse civil strife/civil war of the type experienced by Kenya in 2008.

Controlling Corruption

As discussed in Chapter 4, by distributing authority over public goods and revenues, decentralization/devolution makes it difficult for individuals or groups of individuals to collude and engage in corrupt practices. Anti-corruption is part and parcel of the good governance agenda: an agenda, as this book argues, that is reinforced through the implementation of decentralization/devolved government. Moreover, decentralization/devolution can be a first step toward transparency in government. Such transparency can be one of the best deterrents in efforts to control corruption.

Decentralization/devolution can, therefore, be regarded as an important element of combating corruption in countering the lack of transparency and accountability in centralized systems of government such as Kenya's. Moreover, as corruption levels can vary depending on the presence and functioning of democratic institutions, adopting decentralization to institutionalize local democracy offers a tool to fight corruption and thereby disrupt Kenya's current trend toward becoming a predatory State. Decentralization/devolution has the potential to be a very powerful tool with a significant positive good governance effect on corruption.

Implementing Decentralization/Devolution

To derive the foregoing benefits, as well as the objectives and principles of devolved government as spelled out in the 2010 constitution, the program of actions discussed below needs to be implemented, and on an ongoing basis where applicable. The establishment of the 47 counties is the most significant and far-reaching element of the devolution process required by the 2010 constitution and also represents a major restructuring not only of local government in Kenya but also of governance institutions in the country. Devolution requires the building and sustainability of the requisite local institutional structures and capacity to, among other things, formulate and implement relevant policies, create and maintain financial viability, mobilize and manage resources, establish and maintain appropriate operational modalities, and remove potential implementation constraints.

In other words, and as Kanu (2009) found to be the case in Sierra Leone, and in addition to financial management, managing and sustaining decentralized governance for effective delivery of services require adequate capacity in institutions, networks, organizational structures, facilities and equipment, human resources, data, and information, as well as a supportive and conducive legal and policy environment. Thus, the effective functioning of the new local government structure in Kenya could only be guaranteed if they have the requisite capacity and environment to perform their functions and responsibilities.

Training/Re-training of Local and National Government Personnel and Capacity Development

To meet both immediate and longer-term needs, training and re-training of personnel will have to be undertaken and this should best be done in the context of capacity development at the institutional and individual levels. Most of this training needs to be directed at the potential local (county) government personnel level and there should be a bias toward training or re-training of those with the capability to become trainers: a training of trainers as it were—to help sustain capacity development. These trained trainers will be used to train other personnel. On the assumption that some, if not most, of the existing personnel in the pre-2010 constitution local government set up are likely to migrate to the county governments, then the training activities should target these individuals first.

The recommended training programs can be conducted quite successfully in Kenya. There are many institutions with the wherewithal and experience in conducting the needed training which would require both short-term (1–7 days) and medium-term (2–6 weeks) engagements. Longer-term training programs (toward certificates, diplomas, or degrees) can be considered in the future when staffing complements are settled and permanent (career) staff identified by the county governments themselves. Training will be required to cover the following areas:

- Understanding the Kenya 2010 Constitutional Mandate on Devolved Government. This must be designed to orient, sensitize, and educate personnel on the new local government system, roles and responsibilities, functional relationships, and accountabilities
- Local Government Principles and Practice
- Local Government Administration and Management
- Local Government Finance
- Local Government Budgeting and Accounting

- Project Implementation
- Procurement and Supplies Management

Indeed, the capacity development being advocated here should have two goals. The first is to provide the means to enable institutional stakeholders to effectively execute their roles and responsibilities within decentralized government. The second is to establish and sustain capacities to deliver services, promote development, and improve the welfare of the local people. The long-term objective of the capacity development effort should be to ensure that both the county governments and the national government have the capacity to respond to the institutional transformation and develop their policy implementation roles vis-à-vis decentralization/devolution. This approach to capacity development will not only contribute significantly to the establishment and functionality of the 47 counties but would also potentially lay the foundation for improved performance of local government under the framework of the 2010 constitution.

Building Physical Structures

Some new physical structures will definitely need to be built to accommodate county staff, elected officials, and local development program implementation. To accomplish this in a cost-effective and efficient manner, it is recommended that, as a first order of business, a physical structure needs assessment be conducted to be followed by very specific recommendations of what will be required to meet the immediate and future physical structure needs of the various envisaged county governments taking into consideration the existing stock of infrastructure in the current local government arrangements that may/can be converted to county use immediately and in the future.

Establishing Operational Modalities and
the Financial Viability of County Governments

The new structure of county governments will require new and innovative operational modalities to appropriately implement the devolved structure as the 2010 constitution mandates. These operational modalities must take into consideration internal processes and relationships between and among counties and the national government. The need for new guidelines, strategic plans, codes, and so on will also have to be factored into these operational modalities. The objectives are basically to provide a framework for the operations of county governments and their relationships with each other and the national government.

This program of action will also require the need to undertake studies to determine financial viability and make recommendations on how to improve the same including on revenue enhancement possibilities. The objectives are to assist county governments to better meet their fiscal obligations and provide a sound approach for good financial sustainability with reliable sources of revenue including financial governance, asset management, and potential sources of additional revenue for each county, and also providing for targeted support to counties for consideration by the national government and others.

Financial management capacity issues are critical to fiscal decentralization in any country and Kenya is no exception. Supporting the county governments to maximize their revenue mobilization must be a high priority since this is one way to ensure the sustainability of decentralized governance and make the county governments even more accountable to local taxpayers. If county governments are to be truly independent, the importance of own-revenue mobilization by them cannot be overemphasized. Undoubtedly, the county governments will probably have to rely on national government transfers for most of their funding for the foreseeable future. However, the more resources that Kenyan counties are able to generate internally, the more autonomy they will have and the more viable they will be. Complementary to revenue mobilization is the existence of staff with the requisite financial management qualifications and experience. The overall objective is to build and maintain strong financial management capacity so that the county governments can manage the resources that are transferred to them and cope with the financial reporting requirements as demanded by the 2010 constitution.

Funding and Technical Assistance

To accomplish the foregoing program of actions with the greatest possible sustainable efficiency will require extensive funding. However, the funds needed to undertake the recommended program of actions may not be available or may be insufficient. It is, therefore, recommended that the government seek additional funding, as well as technical assistance, from donors that promote and have active programs on decentralization and local governance. These donors include the EU, DfID, USAID, and the World Bank, for example.

Conclusions

The practice of decentralization raises questions not simply of local management but, in the wider sense, also of local governance. Decentralization, as an aspect of local governance, helps to shift thinking away from state-centered perspectives to include elements which are often considered to be outside the public policy process. They include, for example, privatization and cost recovery. Decentralization, therefore, allows for the reconsideration of local government as more than just a technical or administrative extension of the national government and/or a bureaucratic structure with new autonomous powers and functions (Hope, 2000). The notion of local governance can, accordingly, be regarded as an attempt to come to grips with the limitations of state-centered local management, and leads to a move away from statist perspectives.

Decentralization, whether through devolution or otherwise, is a necessity for countries such as Kenya with highly centralized government systems that have negative impacts on democratization. Devolution is, consequently, a critical strategy to improve governance and remedy institutional deficiencies that highly centralized governments have engendered. These include "bureaucratic inefficiencies, poor accountability and transparency, unequal distribution of resources and low levels of community participation in local development" (Omolo, 2010: 14). The benefits of decentralization, such as good governance and improved service delivery can, among other things, maintain political stability and a sense of pride and ownership in local affairs which, in turn, influences national development outcomes (Hope and Chikulo, 2000). Building and sustaining the framework in support of devolved government must, therefore, now be seen as imperative in Kenya. The 2010 constitution provides the national mechanism, identifies the legal framework, and defines some of the required administrative arrangements to enhance the smooth implementation of decentralization and good local governance in Kenya.

It may also be useful that the planning for implementation of the devolved government structure include the rapid development of sector devolution plans. Each relevant Ministry, Department, or Agency must continuously develop such plans to meet the requirements of the constitution and consistent with its (the constitution's) demand for provincial administration to be restructured to accord with and respect the system of devolved government within five years of the effective date of the constitution (Republic of Kenya, 2010). When effectively planned and implemented, decentralization and local governance will facilitate creating a culture and an environment that promote citizens' active engagement in governance. The ultimate product will be to improve voice and accountability, culminating in improved and satisfactory governance. As further noted by Wekwete (2007), when backed by adequate resources and capacities, decentralization has the potential to increase both productive and allocative efficiencies through increased participation, better prioritization of projects, and better utilization of local resources.

Finally, let me stress a word of both concern and caution. Now, or in the future, the national government must resist any attempt to impose or transfer systems or structures on the counties. Equally, the county governments, when operational, must be totally cognizant of their constitutional mandate and functions and reverse any structures or systems that they may have inherited from the national government, but which they deem to be inappropriate for their local needs and desires.

The 2010 Constitution very clearly defines the functions, powers, and responsibilities for each level of government. The national government cannot, therefore, dictate to the devolved governments what the latter should be doing and how they should be doing it. The establishment of devolved government, to be consistent with the constitution, is not about taking national government systems such as those related to staffing/human resources or financial management, for instance, and imposing them on the devolved governments (Hope, 2010). The constitution quite clearly states, with respect to staffing/human resources, for example, that: "A county government is responsible, within a framework of uniform norms and standards prescribed by an Act of Parliament, for –

(a) establishing and abolishing offices in its public service;
(b) appointing persons to hold or act in those offices, and confirming appointments;
    and
(c) exercising disciplinary control over and removing persons holding or acting in those offices." (Republic of Kenya, 2010: Article 235)

Similarly, it is for the counties to decide what type of financial management information system they want to put in place consistent with the constitutional requirements pertaining to financial control, accountability, and audits. The constitution mandates, for example, that "the accounts of all governments and State organs shall be audited by the Auditor-General" and that "the accounting officer of a county public entity is accountable to the county assembly for its financial management" (Republic of Kenya, 2010: Article 226).

Consequently, apart from facilitating the process of establishing the devolved governments, as per the constitution, the national government should stay aside and allow the devolved governments to exercise their own constitutional rights to put their own, and respective, administrative management and operational systems in place that are consistent with local community needs and standards as well as the principles of local governance and the 2010 Constitution.

References

Crawford, G. and Hartmann, C. (2008), "Introduction: Decentralization as a Pathway Out of Poverty and Conflict?" In G. Crawford and C. Hartmann (eds), *Decentralization in Africa: A Pathway Out of Poverty and Conflict?* Amsterdam: Amsterdam University Press, pp. 7–32.

Foster, E. and Glennester, R. (2009), "Impact of Decentralization on Public Services: Evidence to Date." In Y. Zhou (ed.), *Decentralization, Democracy, and Development: Recent Experience in Sierra Leone.* Washington, DC: World Bank, pp. 73–84.

Hope, K. R. (2000), "Decentralization and Local Governance Theory and the Practice in Botswana," *Development Southern Africa*, 17(4), 519–34.

— (2002), *From Crisis to Renewal: Development Policy and Management in Africa.* Leiden: Brill Publishers.

— (2010), "Toward Devolved Government in Kenya: A Foundation Approach", *Advisory Note 3*. Nairobi: Office of the Prime Minister.

Hope, K. R. and Chikulo, B. C. (2000), "Decentralization, the New Public Management, and the Changing Role of the Public Sector in Africa," *Public Management: An International Journal of Research and Theory*, 2(1), 25–42.

Kanu, A. (2009), "Administrative Decentralization: Building the Non-Financial Capacity of Local Communities." In Y. Zhou (ed.), *Decentralization, Democracy, and Development: Recent Experience in Sierra Leone.* Washington, DC: World Bank, pp. 28–59.

Letaief, M. B., Mback, C. N., Mbassi, J-P. E., and Ndiaye, B. O. (2008), "Africa." In *Decentralization and Local Democracy in the World.* Barcelona: United Cities and Local Governments and World Bank.

Menon, B., Mutero, J., and Macharia, S. (2008), "Decentralization and Local Governments in Kenya," *Working Paper 08-32*, International Studies Program, Andrew Young School of Policy Studies. Atlanta, GA: Georgia State University.

Mueller, S. (2008), "The Political Economy of Kenya's Crisis," *Journal of Eastern African Studies*, 2(2), 185–210.

Muia, D. M. (2008), "Devolution: Which Way for Local Authorities?" In T. N. Kibua and G. Mwabu (eds), *Decentralization and Devolution in Kenya: New Approaches.* Nairobi: University of Nairobi Press, pp. 137–68.

Oloo, A. (2008), "Devolution and Democratic Governance: Options for Kenya." In T. N. Kibua and G. Mwabu (eds), *Decentralization and Devolution in Kenya: New Approaches.* Nairobi: University of Nairobi Press, pp. 105–35.

Omolo, A. (2010), "Devolution in Kenya: A Critical Review of Past and Present Frameworks." In A. K. Mwenda (ed.), *Devolution in Kenya: Prospects, Challenges and the Future.* Nairobi: Institute of Economic Affairs, pp. 14–47.

Republic of Kenya (2007), *Kenya Vision 2030: A Globally Competitive and Prosperous Kenya.* Nairobi: Republic of Kenya.

— (2008), *Kenya Vision 2030: First Medium Term Plan (2008-2012).* Nairobi: Republic of Kenya.

— (2010), *The Constitution of Kenya*, 2010. Nairobi: Republic of Kenya.

Schiavo-Campo, S. and Sundaram, P. S. A. (2001), *To Serve and to Preserve: Improving Public Administration in a Competitive World.* Manila: Asian Development Bank.

Wekwete, K. H. (2007), "Decentralization to Promote Effective and Efficient Pro-Poor Infrastructure and Service Delivery in the Least-Developed Countries." In G. S. Cheema and D. A. Rondinelli (eds), *Decentralizing Governance: Emerging Concepts and Practices.* Washington, DC: Brookings Institution Press, pp. 242–65.

6

Public Sector Management and Reform

Effective public sector management is also a critical ingredient for sustainable development in Africa. Consequently, public sector reform remains a necessary and ongoing policy objective for such countries as Kenya. This is being done to overhaul their administrative systems to better serve the needs of both government and the citizenry with improved delivery of public services to reduce poverty, improve livelihoods, and sustain good governance. Although the first attempts at the reform and transformation of the public sector in Kenya began in 1965 (OPM/PSTD, 2010), it was not until the early 1990s that serious efforts were made toward the reform and transformation of the country's public sector management. Like other African countries, these efforts in Kenya have been driven primarily by the fact that the state bureaucracy in the country has been underperforming and public service delivery has not been serving the public interest within its most optimal capability. The reforms in Kenya evolved and culminated in the notion of reengineering of the public sector in the context of public sector transformation, drawing on elements of what came to be known in the literature and practice as the "New Public Management" (NPM). This NPM broad term symbolizes the aim of fostering a performance-oriented culture that seeks to revamp the process through which public organizations operate in order to increase efficiency, effectiveness, and encompassing client-oriented, mission-driven, and quality-enhanced management. It is intended to better serve the needs of both government and the citizenry with improved delivery of public services to reduce poverty, improve livelihoods, and sustain good governance (Hope, 2001).

The NPM movement is driven to maximize productive and allocative efficiencies that are hampered by public agencies unresponsive to the demands of citizens and led by bureaucrats with the power and incentives to expand their administrative empires (Hope, 2002). In addition, the NPM makes a rigid formal separation between policy-making and service delivery. It is used to describe a management culture that emphasizes the centrality of the citizen or customer, as well as accountability for results. Moreover, the concept is centered on the proposition that a distinct activity—management, as opposed to administration—can be applied to the public sector, as it has been applied to the private sector, and it includes a number of elements:

- An emphasis on efficiency in the services provided directly by the public sector;
- A movement away from input controls, rules, and procedures toward output measurement and performance targets;
- The devolution of management control with improved reporting and monitoring mechanisms;
- The flexibility to explore alternatives to direct public provision and regulation that might yield more cost-effective policy outcomes;
- The strengthening of strategic capacities to guide the transformation of the state and allow it to respond to external changes and diverse interests automatically, flexibly, and at least cost.

Public Sector Reform and Transformation

The government of Kenya currently "regards [its] public sector transformation strategy as a dynamic and focused process designed to fundamentally reshape the Public Service to accomplish its role in the achievement of Vision 2030" (Isahakia, 2010: 5). This transformation strategy is also seen as representing a transition for the public service and the beginning of a more cohesive, long-term approach to reform (Isahakia, 2010). The efforts to create an efficient government and engender a culture of performance and quality service delivery across the entire Kenyan public sector has a lengthy history, beginning as early as 1965 when the government set forth an institutional framework for reform through its *Sessional Paper No. 10* (OPM/PSTD, 2010).

However, although the Kenyan civil service operated effectively since that time, and was seen as one of the best in sub-Saharan Africa, it began declining around the end of the 1970s (World Bank, 2001). The "problems that developed in tandem with expansion included excessive employment with attendant overstaffing, and declining productivity, service levels, pay, morale, discipline and ethics" (World Bank, 2001: 2). Oyugi (2006: 41) has further observed that "by the late 1970s the situation had gone out of control" quoting the then Head of the Civil Service who lamented that "the problem of indiscipline in the Service was such that it posed a challenge to the future of the Service." This state of affairs was attributed to the fact that, over time, the powers and responsibilities of the statutory appointing and disciplinary institutions had been eroded and usurped by powerful forces with influential connections to the apex of power.

Several decades later, beginning in 1993, the government returned to a specific focus on public sector reform and transformation. Those efforts, since then to date, can be classified into four periods. The first period either covers the years 1993–7 according to World Bank (2001); 1993–8 according to Republic of Kenya (2008) and Marwa and Zairi (2009); or 1993–2000 according to Oyugi (2006). From this author's perspective it covered the years 1993–8. Nonetheless, this period evolved when the government launched the Civil Service Reform Program (CSRP) I in 1993 to enhance public service efficiency and productivity. The focus was on cost containment (OPM/PSTD, 2010), and the program was influenced largely by the fiscal need to reduce the size of the mainstream civil service (World Bank, 2001). Implementation was driven through a Steering Committee at the national, provincial, and district levels and in each Ministry with a national Secretariat as its operational arm (Marwa and Zairi, 2009).

There were five broad policy areas examined under the CSRP I:

- *Civil Service Organization*—The streamlining of organizational structure to reflect better defined ministerial and departmental functions, including clear definition and specification of the internal functions of ministries and departments, clear hierarchy of authority and span of control, and more accurate job descriptions.
- *Staffing Levels*—Including downsizing of the service; establishment of appropriate staffing levels for all cadres in the service; and improving staffing control mechanisms through computerization of the establishment and improvement of the payroll system.
- *Pay and Benefits*—The achievement of compensation levels that were geared toward attracting and retaining professional and managerial talent in a competitive market economy as well as monetization of allowances.
- *Personnel Management and Training*—Including the rationalization of personnel management policies; identification of inadequacies in the existing personnel planning and vacancy management; improvement of disciplinary systems; promotion; and capacity development.
- *Financial and Performance Management*—Including transparency and accountability in financial management; institutionalization of control systems including computerization; management of the national budget; clear standards against which performance can be accurately measured; perfection of performance evaluation instruments; and use of performance evaluation to impinge upon personnel replacement, training, discipline, and rewards for enhanced productivity. (Nzioka, 1998)

The Deputy Director of the CSRP Secretariat at the time (see Nzioka, 1998) noted that there were some achievements recorded under the CSRP

I. They included: (1) the success of the Voluntary Early Retirement Scheme (VERS) with the government attaining its target number of retirees; (2) the abolition of more than 26,000 posts in addition to the freezing of posts that fell vacant due to the VERS; (3) the development of an Integrated Payroll and Personnel Database (IPPD) system; (4) decompression of pay scales; (5) development of a training policy; and (6) design and introduction of unique identification numbers for civil servants to assist in the improvement of establishment control and maintenance of payroll integrity including elimination of ghost workers.

However, despite these achievements, many of the activities in the CSRP I did not contribute significantly to the improvement of wider public sector performance. This was so because they were not anchored in a coherent strategy for reforming the role of government writ large. For example, the World Bank (2001: 3) observed that:

> although the initial civil service retrenchment exercise proceeded quickly, its cost containment objectives were rapidly contradicted and frustrated by the awarding of a huge pay rise to the Teachers' Service and the politically motivated hiring of a large number of additional teachers in the run-up to the 1997 elections.

In addition, Oyugi (2006) noted that the CSRP I was, more or less, a stand-alone initiative that was not integrated with budgetary reforms and generally did not have the required impact of a downward push on the government wage bill while, at the same time, the quality of public service delivery deteriorated. Moreover, a number of lessons learned were identified by Nzioka (1998) with the key ones being the following:

- The need for adequate planning before implementation of any reform to, among other things, prioritize activities and allocate adequate time and resources for implementation;
- Training and capacity development are of vital importance for the success of any reform initiative. If civil servants are not prepared, for example, to respond to the demands of a rapidly changing socioeconomic environment, then the result can be a loss of momentum for reform activities;
- The need to adopt new technologies, especially information technologies, which are necessary for timely and accurate decision-making;
- The importance and need to build acceptance of reform initiatives particularly among top managers in the service.

Building on the experience gained and lessons learned under the CSRP I, the government reformulated and reconfigured the CSRP and outlined the strategies for a CSRP II. Toward the end of 1999, the government announced a comprehensive and integrated public sector reform program to tackle the challenges facing the entire public sector. The CSRP II was focused on performance improvement and there were plans for a CSRP III whose focus was to be on consolidating and sustaining the gains made (OP/PSRDS, 2005; OPM/PSTD, 2010). The CSRP II spanned the years 1999–2002 and was the second period of public sector reform and transformation.

The priority reform areas under the CSRP II were identified as:

- *Rationalization of Ministerial Functions and Structures*—The undertaking of a comprehensive assessment of ministerial functions including identifying overlapping and duplicating functions as well as functions that can be commercialized, contracted-out and privatized; reviewing of organizational structures; determination of optimal staffing levels; and the updating of job descriptions, regrading of posts and introduction of a new performance appraisal system.
- *Staff Rationalization and Management of the Wage Bill*—Improvement of the design and implementation of the VERS; developing an overall structure for establishment and payroll; developing and implementing a new IPPD system; and a ban on recruitment except in critical and essential services.
- *Pay and Benefits Reforms*—Including increasing the housing allowance for all civil servants and teachers; enhancement of salaries and allowances for civil servants and the security forces; undertaking a comprehensive job evaluation and regrading exercise; establishment of a Permanent Public Service Remuneration Review Board (PPSRRB) to address, among other things, salaries and benefits for all public servants in a holistic and rationalized manner; and implementing a pilot program on a performance-related pay system.
- *Performance Improvement Initiatives*—Including formulation of a strategy for performance improvement in the public service; introduction of results-based management (RBM) in the public service to shape organizations and work activities for the achievement of predetermined outputs/results and reorientate the goals and objectives of the workforce toward cost-effectiveness and responsiveness to customer demands and needs; and developing a modern performance appraisal system.
- *Training and Capacity Building*—Undertaking a training needs assessment to determine the existing performance gaps in terms of the skills requirements; addressing issues of succession management in the public service; retraining of civil servants to cope with the increased job demands and improve operational flexibility by extending the range of skills through

multiskilling; and strengthening the Kenya Institute of Administration (KIA) in providing high quality market-oriented training courses to current civil servants and retirees. (OP/PSRDS, 2005; Oyugi, 2006; World Bank, 2001)

The foregoing areas were established by the government to be the priority areas for CSRP II. However, there were a number of additional areas that were also pursued. They included development and implementation of a Medium-Term Expenditure Framework; strengthening of government finance and accounting functions; and legal and judicial reform (World Bank, 2001).

The CSRP II was deemed to have suffered the same fate as the CSRP I to the extent that it failed to arrest declining public confidence in public sector management standards and conduct or deteriorating public satisfaction with government services (OPM/PSTD, 2010). In fact, the World Bank rated the overall performance of both the CSRP I and CSRP II as unsatisfactory. This outcome rating was derived from the Bank's finding that both its own role and that of the government implementation performance were unsatisfactory (World Bank, 2001).

A number of exogenous and endogenous factors have been determined to have affected the implementation and outcome of the CSRP II. With respect to the exogenous factors (those outside the control of government), the main argument here seems to have been that the economy was weak due to bad weather which affected productivity and, hence, government revenues. That, in turn, influenced government spending decisions, or became an excuse for such, including not accessing already available World Bank credit for the CSRP. This was reflected in long delays in the processing of payments and a slow public procurement process. Processing time was 25 days longer than usual (World Bank, 2001).

In terms of the endogenous factors, the main ones were: (1) there was little indication of government's commitment to consistent and steady reform processes and this was reflected in the slow rate of implementation of reform activities; (2) the implementing agency, the Directorate of Personnel Management (DPM), under which the CSRP Secretariat fell, lacked the necessary clout and political backing to implement the reforms; (3) reform activities lacked proper sequencing and many were added, some at the behest of donors it must be noted, without proper planning; and (4) there was a lack of ownership (Oyugi, 2006; World Bank, 2001). This last point on ownership is of major significance for successful outcomes of programs geared toward public sector reform which also encompass capacity development. Hope (2011), for example, has pointed out that local ownership with control is a key principle for achieving results in reform programs. It must be a local endogenous process to better reflect local priorities and interests and avoid being donor-driven or imposed.

In December 2002, a new government was elected on a platform of reforms and, among other things, committed itself to do business differently. This was Kenya's first transfer of power through elections since independence, and this newly elected government wanted to quickly exhibit its reformist credentials and stamp them on the nation. With the country facing challenges that required urgent attention, the government announced its socioeconomic blueprint in 2003, entitled *Economic Recovery Strategy for Wealth and Employment Creation (ERS) 2003-2007* as discussed in Chapter 1. The *ERS 2003-2007* also kick-started the new government's public sector reform efforts which covered the years 2003–07 and was Kenya's third period of public sector reform and transformation.

The *ERS 2003-2007* had, as a fundamental pillar, the strengthening of institutions of governance. It noted that "the Government is convinced that good governance underpins sustainable development" (Republic of Kenya, 2003: ix). In that regard, the *ERS 2003-2007* outlined various reforms in, among others, public administration, further noting that:

> Improving public administration is essential to economic recovery. The sector is excessively large thereby absorbing inordinately large amount of national resources. The sector is also characterized by wastefulness and inefficiency. Consequently, the sector has become a bottleneck to the overall development of Kenya. (Republic of Kenya, 2003: 11)

Furthermore, the *ERS 2003-2007* announced that "the government is committed to accelerating the Public Service Reform to create a leaner, efficient, motivated and more productive Public Service that concentrates public finance and human resources on the delivery of core government services" (Republic of Kenya, 2003: 11). The reforms were to also focus on providing adequate incentives to attract and retain skilled personnel to achieve a pay structure and size of the civil service consistent with both macroeconomic objectives and a sustainable wage bill. The key elements of this civil service reform strategy and activities, and which were envisaged for implementation by June 2004, included the following:

- Accelerating the ongoing ministerial rationalization and developing strategic plans for ministries/departments in order to allow proper utilization of resources on clearly identified core functions, determination of appropriate staffing levels, objective appraisal of staff, and better and improved methods of supervising staff based on achievement of set targets, among others;

- Developing, introducing and institutionalizing performance-based management practices in the public service;
- Undertaking job evaluation to form a basis for determining a rational grading structure and terms of service for civil servants;
- Undertaking service delivery surveys in all ministries/departments and developing and installing service charters with clear service benchmarks and standards in order to enhance efficiency, transparency, and accountability in service delivery;
- Developing a clear recruitment and training policy aimed at ensuring proper supply and development of skills in the civil service and pegging promotion on both performance and training;
- Putting all Permanent Secretaries and Chief Executives of parastatals on performance contracts (PCs). (Republic of Kenya, 2003)

Concerned with the slow pace of implementation of its reform initiatives, the government took a Cabinet decision in September 2004 to formally prescribe results-based management (RBM) as its strategy for changing the culture and *modus operandi* of the public sector (OPM/PSTD, 2010). RBM is a program approach to management that integrates strategy, people, resources, processes, and measurements to improve decision-making, transparency, and accountability (CIDA, 2009). It focuses on achieving outcomes, implementing performance measurement, learning, adapting to change, as well as reporting performance. It is not a management tool, but rather a way of working that looks beyond activities, processes, and outputs to focus on actual results—the outcomes of RBM projects and programs.

To operationalize the RBM strategy, a rapid results approach was adapted by the government as a structured methodology for building and practicing RBM, This led to the introduction of a rapid results initiative (RRI). The RRI was introduced to cultivate a strong focus on results and was used to attempt to fast track improvements in service delivery and/or working conditions by several public sector institutions. According to OPM/PSTD (2010: 3), "many RRIs succeeded in delivering tangible results to citizens and helped consolidate support for reform." It was further deemed that some of the building blocks for institutionalizing and mainstreaming RBM had been put in place. They included strategic planning, performance contracting, annual work plans, and service delivery charters (OPM/PSTD, 2010).

The political negotiations that resulted from the violence in 2008, that followed the elections in December 2007, eventually led to the formation of a Grand Coalition Government (a government of national unity) and also the establishment of the Office of the Prime Minister (OPM). These political developments formed an important part of the context of reforms in the public sector in the fourth period of public sector reform and transformation covering the years 2008 to present. In 2008, the government released its *MTP 2008-2012* which, as discussed in Chapter 1, is the first of the successive medium-term plans being used to outline policies, reform measures, projects, and programs that the government is committed to implementing in support of the *Kenya Vision 2030*. The *MTP 2008-2012* recognizes that an effective and efficient public sector is essential to achieving the *Kenya Vision 2030* by creating an enabling environment for the private sector as the engine of growth for the country's economy. Transparency, accountability, participation, and the rule of law are to constitute an integral part of the reform agenda (Republic of Kenya, 2008).

With the establishment of the OPM, the Prime Minister, as per the *National Accord and Reconciliation Act, 2008*, was mandated to coordinate and supervise the execution of the affairs and functions of the government including Ministries. The OPM also published a Strategic Plan in 2009 covering the period 2009–12 (OPM, 2009). This Strategic Plan brought to life the constitutional mandate of the Prime Minister and set out the goals of the OPM. In it, the Prime Minister noted that:

Citizens expect the government to provide quality and timely services at all times. Demand for improved government performance has grown recently and we must listen and be responsive. Although the e-Government, Performance Contracting and Rapid Results Initiatives have led to significant improvements, more remains to be done. Therefore, this Plan will give priority to improving service delivery by accelerating existing initiatives and extending them across all public services. We will work with Ministries to identify the next wave of initiatives and we will coordinate implementation of service improvement initiatives by Ministries, Departments and Agencies of Government. (Odinga, 2009: vii)

The Prime Minister further said:

the strategic objectives for the plan period are to: improve service delivery; build strong capacity for policy development and coordination; create a new culture of setting priorities; focus government on effective delivery of policies and priorities; and steer Public Service Reform as an enabler of good policy and delivery. This plan is thus about working towards giving Kenyans the Kenya they want—a prosperous, democratic, equitable and modern nation. (Odinga, 2009: vii)

Consequently, there was a shift in emphasis from the narrow civil service to the broader public sector and, in order to drive the public sector reforms,

a Public Service (Sector) Transformation Department (PSTD) was cre-
ated by separating and absorbing the public sector reform functions of the
Department of Public Sector Reform and Performance Contracting. The
PSTD was charged with two principal responsibilities:

(1) To lead the transformation of the public service (including the revised
     strategy for public sector reform) so as to strengthen and build the
     capacity of the public service;
(2) To improve delivery of services to citizens. (OPM, 2009)

To engage the public sector reform agenda, as envisaged in the OPM Strategic
Plan, the PSTD embarked on the preparation of a public sector transformation strategy which it released in January 2010 with the title *Public Sector
Transformation Strategy: From Reform to Transformation 2010-14* (PSTS) (OPM/
PSTD, 2010). This PSTS established a broad policy framework to guide the
introduction and implementation of new policies and legislation aimed at
making the public sector work better (Isahakia, 2010). It defines transformation in the public service as "a fundamental and sustainable change that meets
citizen needs and aspirations" (OPM/PSTD, 2010: 8). It further regards the
public sector as having three attributes. First, engagement with and services to
the citizens of Kenya should engender trust and be based on respect. Second,
the machinery of government should function smoothly in a coordinated
and efficient manner to respond to the needs of Kenyans and to achieve
shared goals without organizational barriers and selfish interests compromis-
ing common purpose. Third, every ministry, department and agency in the
public sector is to be goal-driven and have the systems, tools, organizational
culture, and management practices in place to deliver demonstrable benefit
to the citizens of Kenya now and in the future (OPM/PSTD, 2010).

The PSTS comprises three components: (1) Service and Openness; (2)
Coordination and Cooperation; and (3) Effectiveness and Accountability.
The first component is intended to transform delivery of public sector services and engagement with citizens. This means that services are: (a) available
to those who need them; (b) easily accessible; (c) relatively affordable and of
acceptable quality; and (d) provide adequate information to assist in decision-
making. The intended outcomes are: (1) citizens' satisfaction with government
service delivery; (2) citizens' confidence in government communications; and
(3) mutually respectful and sustainable public sector stakeholder partnerships.
It is about the type of image the public sector presents to Kenyans. Moving
from being closed and secretive, insensitive and self-interested, risk-averse and
preoccupied with protecting of turf, to being open, respectful, and responsive
to the needs of the public (OPM/PSTD, 2010).

The second component seeks to strengthen capacity across the whole of government to coordinate and cooperate on policy development and program delivery. Its focus is on crossing institutional boundaries and working collectively to foster an enabling environment that supports public sector institutions to deliver. It also entails making a concerted effort to ensure that government institutions are not operating as islands disconnected from each other but rather that government is working as one joined-up or linked-up entity. The envisioned outcomes are: (1) institutionalized, sequenced, and systematic approach to government policy, planning, budgeting, and delivery that is directly linked to the *Kenya Vision 2030* and other national development priorities—a clear line of sight from national priorities to all government program policies and implementation; (2) synergy in government functions and operations—to increase both the perception and the reality that the government is working together in a cohesive manner by strengthening the frameworks, systems, and approaches of government that transcend organizational boundaries resulting in one government that speaks with one voice; and (3) fit for purpose government institutional arrangements and structures—enhancing effectiveness and efficiency of government sectors and institutions by strengthening coordination structures and mechanisms, mobilizing resources, building capacity, developing partnerships with public sector stakeholders, and developing mechanisms for joint reclassification of sectors (OPM/PSTD, 2010).

The third and final component focuses on enabling government institutions to conduct their ongoing program business in a goal-driven manner, which means to plan, allocate resources, deliver, monitor, and report on the contribution they make in the lives of Kenyans. This means developing government institutions and ensuring that each of them is efficiently, effectively and ethically able to fulfill its mandate, The sought after outcomes are: (1) programs and priorities of institutions are aligned to the *Kenya Vision 2030* and other national development goals; (2) improved capacity to manage for results by creating an enabling internal environment for RBM in each public sector institution, and the embedded practice of RBM in the normal business activities of each organization; and (3) achievement of high standards of public management by enabling public sector institutions to ensure that their standards of public management conform to established government-wide and generally accepted international standards (OPM/PSTD, 2010).

To implement the PSTS, a work plan, results framework, and governance framework have been developed. In addition, a number of cross-cutting issues with potentially significant impacts on outcomes have been identified. They include gender mainstreaming, youth mainstreaming, the challenge of

HIV/AIDS, environmental management, drug and alcohol abuse, and public sector governance. The OPM, through its PSTD, will oversee implementation of the PSTS and, particularly, the institutionalization of RBM which requires various and different initiatives from institutions. The PSTD will provide the leadership and coordination to the implementation and monitoring of the reform initiatives. Its primary mission will be to drive forward the implementation agenda for transforming the public service, improving the quality and responsiveness of public services, and promoting a strong and professionally well-managed public sector, that is capable of enabling and facilitating the achievement of the *Kenya Vision 2030* (OPM/PSTD, 2010).

Implementation of the PSTS therefore will rest with the public sector institutions. Transformation is neither regarded nor seen as the sole responsibility of one central agency but rather as the accountability of every public sector organization and to be undertaken directly by them, with the OPM, through the PSTD, providing technical support and partnership for realizing results. A monitoring and evaluation framework will be used to track progress. It will evaluate the extent to which the PSTS targets and outcomes are being accomplished and will also assist in the identification of corrective measures in a timely manner. The results framework—with its outcomes, indicators, and outcome measures—is to play a significant role in the monitoring and evaluation process (OPM/PSTD, 2010).

In August 2010, Kenyans also approved a new constitution, as referenced throughout this book. That constitution contains various principles and elements that will have both direct and indirect impacts on public sector performance, reform, and transformation *ad infinitum*. For example, Article 47 in Part 2 of the Bill of Rights states, among other things, that "Every person has the right to administrative action that is expeditious, efficient, lawful, reasonable and procedurally fair." In Chapter 6 of the 2010 constitution on "Leadership and Integrity," it sets out a framework of leadership and integrity as it pertains to officers of the State as discussed in Chapter 4 of this book. Furthermore, and as also discussed in Chapter 4 of this book, the 2010 constitution, in Article 232, lays out values and principles of public service which apply to public service in both levels of government and all State corporations as well (Republic of Kenya, 2010a).

All of these principles and elements in the 2010 constitution are also consistent with, and related to, the components of the PSTS and this foundation augurs well for a much more successful effort at public sector reform, this time around, compared to the past. There is now a supreme, lawful and legally binding basis for Kenyan public servants and their institutions to modify their behavior in delivering public services and interacting with their fellow Kenyans in that pursuit. Both the 2010 constitution and the PSTS are anchored in the view that public services are not a privilege in a democratic environment. In fact, they are a legitimate expectation of Kenyans.

Reforming and transforming the public sector for improved delivery of public services means redressing the imbalances of the past by focusing on meeting the needs of all Kenyans. Improving service delivery also calls for a shift away from inward-looking, over-centralized, hierarchical and rule-bound bureaucratic systems, processes, and attitudes, that currently permeate the Kenya public service, and a search for new ways of working which put the needs of the public first, is better, faster, and more responsive to the citizens' needs. It also means a complete change in the manner that services are delivered. The objectives of service delivery must, therefore, include not only equity but also efficiency as was recognized by the government of South Africa, for example, in its public sector transformation strategy (Republic of South Africa, 1997).

It must also be noted here that the introduction of a public sector reform and transformation program cannot be achieved in isolation from other fundamental management changes within the public sector. It must, therefore, be part of a fundamental shift of culture whereby public servants see themselves first and foremost as servants of the people of Kenya and where the public service is managed with service to the public as its primary goal. Public sector reform and transformation is also a dynamic process out of which a completely new relationship is developed between the public service and the public (Republic of South Africa, 1997). To implement a public sector reform and transformation program successfully requires the use of new management tools such as performance contracting, for example, which is discussed in greater detail below.

Performance Contracting as a Performance Management Tool

Performance management is a distinct element of public sector reforms and performance contracting is a key tool of performance management. The establishment of performance management systems is regarded as a means of getting results from individuals, teams, and the organization at large within a given framework of planned goals, objectives, and standards. It allows for the setting of targets and the development of indicators against which performance can be later measured. It is an integral part of the public service delivery mechanism and is a process by which an organization can assess whether or not it is delivering the appropriate services, according to its mission and objectives, in the appropriate quantity, at the appropriate cost, at the appropriate time, and to the appropriate people (Xavier, 2010).

Performance contracts or agreements specify standards of performance or quantifiable targets that a government requires public officials or the management of public/state-owned agencies or ministries/departments to meet over a stated period of time, and also provides incentives for achieving these targets (Hope, 2008). At the end of the stated period, performance can then be measured against these standards or targets. As part of the performance management orientation in government, the common purposes of performance contracting are to clarify the objectives of public service institutions and their relationship with government, and to facilitate performance evaluation based on results instead of conformity with bureaucratic rules and regulations. Performance contracting has been found to be quite successful in a large and diverse set of countries such as France, Pakistan, South Africa, Australia, Canada, Malaysia, South Korea, Ghana, Botswana, and India, for example (Hope, 2010; Xavier, 2010).

Performance Contracting in Kenya

The PC process in Kenya is currently administered by the Performance Contracting Department (PCD) in the OPM. The literature on performance contracting in the country suggests that the concept was first introduced in the country in the late 1980s (Kobia and Mohammed, 2006). In 1989, Kenya Railways was subjected to PCs and in 1990 the National Cereal and Produce Board also signed PCs. In 2003, the government reintroduced performance contracting—in its *ERS 2003-2007*—for adoption as a tool in the management of public resources and as a key element of the civil service reform strategy as discussed earlier. Consequently, a Performance Contracts Steering Committee (PCsSC) was also established by the government in August 2003 and in 2004 PCs were piloted in 16 state-owned commercial enterprises that were selected based on representation of a wide cross-section of sectors and the existence of their Strategic Plans (Obong'o, 2009).

Subsequently, and in a gradual manner, the implementation of performance contracting was expanded and by 2006 almost the entire Kenyan public service on the executive side was participating in PCs (Trivedi, nd). That meant that almost all Ministries, state corporations, and local authorities had become engaged in performance contracting. That group, by March 2010, included 46 ministries and departments, 151 state-owned enterprises (SOEs), 68 tertiary institutions, and 175 local authorities (municipalities, local, county, and urban councils) (OPM/PCD, 2010). For ministries and departments, the PC is signed between the Cabinet Secretary (principal) and the relevant Permanent Secretary (agent). For SOEs, the PC is signed between the Permanent Secretary of the administrative ministry responsible for supervising that SOE (principal) and the Board of Directors of the said

SOE (agent). For local authorities, the PC is signed between the Permanent Secretary of the Ministry of Local Government (principal) and the Council of the local authority (agent). Each PC is then also countersigned by the relevant Cabinet Minister to ensure that it receives full recognition and support from the political leadership and government (OPM/PCD, 2010).

Furthermore, there are two entities that have been put in place by the government to assist with the design, implementation, and evaluation of the PCs. The first is the previously mentioned PCsSC and the other is the Ad Hoc Negotiation/Evaluation Task Force, more commonly referred to as the Ad Hoc Task Force (AHTF). The PCsSC is responsible for the overall administration and coordination of PCs in the public service including developing policy frameworks, providing technical support to the performance contracting parties, and advising the government on the enabling legal and institutional framework for smooth implementation of the performance contracting process. The PCsSC is assisted by AHTFs in the process of implementing the PCs (OPM/PCD, 2010).

The AHTFs are composed of experts drawn from professional associations, academia, the business community, and the community of retired public servants. They are to be a completely neutral third party for ensuring the quality and integrity of the PCs. These AHTFs are responsible for negotiating the PCs and evaluating and moderating the performance of ministries/departments on behalf of Permanent Secretaries and the Cabinet Secretary and Head of the Public Service. The AHTFs also evaluate and moderate the performance of SOEs, local authorities, and tertiary institutions (OPM/PCD, 2010).

In Kenya, performance contracting is a part of the ongoing broader public sector reforms that are aimed at improving efficiency and effectiveness in the management of the public service. The country's public sector PCs are therefore seen and regarded as embracing the national management accountability framework "premised on the need to build the country's competitive advantage around the performance of the public service" (Odinga, 2010a: v). "The system redefined public sector 'performance' to mean focusing on outputs and outcomes, not on inputs, processes, or preoccupation with activities" (Odinga, 2010a: v).

PCs in Kenya are freely negotiated agreements between the government and the management of a public entity. Each PC quite clearly specifies the intentions, obligations, as well as responsibilities and powers of the contracting parties (OPM/PCD, 2010), and is anchored, essentially, on an institution's Strategic Plan (PCD, nd). It also addresses economic, social, and other tasks to be undertaken for economic or other desired gain. "It is therefore a [performance] management tool for ensuring accountability for results by public officials, because it measures the extent to which they achieve targeted results" (OPM/PSRPC, nda: 1) and, as the maxim says, "If you cannot measure, you cannot control, if you cannot control, you cannot manage, if you cannot manage, you cannot deliver."

One significant aspect of PCs in Kenya is the involvement of citizens in the process through the use of Citizen Service Delivery Charters (CSDCs). The CSDCs are key performance indicators in the PCs of the public institutions. These Charters are written statements that indicate the nature, quality, and quantity of service that citizens should expect from a respective institution. They provide information on (1) what services are provided; (2) the standard of the services to be provided; (3) the time frame within which services will be provided; (4) any user charges; and (5) the manner in which clients (users) may seek redress if they are not satisfied with services received or if they are of the view that an institution is not living up to the commitments in its Charter (OPM/PSRPC, ndb; Trivedi, nd).

Each PC is subjected to evaluation based on a set of indicators (measures by which the performance of an institution is assessed). These indicators and their associated weights are updated and published regularly by the PCD in the guidelines which it issues to provide guidance on the process of implementing performance contracts in the Public Service. Institutions are expected to select, as much as possible, indicators from the *Sector Performance Standards* (the composite set of sector performance benchmarks, including performance levels, based on international best practices) which have also been issued by the PCD. Also, institutions are to ensure that each performance target (the desired level of performance for a performance indicator) progressively approaches and/or exceed the levels set out in the *Sector Performance Standards* (PCD, nd). The assessment measurement of the extent to which public agencies achieve negotiated performance targets are to be established using the following equation (PCD, nd):

Managerial Performance = Agency Performance ± Exogenous Factors,

where exogenous factors refers to those events which cannot reasonably be planned for, controlled, or predicted by the manager.

Currently, the process for evaluating how Kenya's public entities have performed is undertaken in three stages (OPM/PCD, 2010). First, there is a self-evaluation by each institution, utilizing the evaluation methodology in the performance contracting guidelines. The second stage is the primary evaluation, also utilizing the evaluation methodology in the performance contracting guidelines, where a group of experts undertake what is supposed to be an exhaustive assessment of institutional performance in the PC year and then assign a composite score which then indicates the overall performance of the institution. This score is adjusted for factors beyond the control of the manager during the PC year to determine the performance of the manager. The final stage is the quality control or moderation stage wherein a team of independent experts attempt to ensure that the evaluations have been completed within the guidelines and that all relevant tools and instruments have been uniformly applied. Any contentious issues are also considered at this stage, the institutions are then ranked based on their performance, and the final evaluation report is prepared (OPM/PCD, 2010).

Performance Contracting as a Performance Management Tool for Good Governance in Kenya

Among the key elements of good governance is the existence of a public sector that is responsive to the needs of the citizenry (its clients); a public sector that creates an enabling environment for the private sector to sustainably be the engine of growth for the economy; a public sector that conducts its business with transparency and accountability as fundamental principles of its functioning in support of its delivery of public goods and services; a public sector that subscribes to the values of integrity and ethics; a public sector that demonstrates a total and complete intolerance for corruption and financial mismanagement; and a public sector that is goal-driven in support of the national vision and socioeconomic and political development priorities. In Kenya, many of these characteristics of the public sector are also envisaged in the PSTS as previously discussed (OPM/PSTD, 2010).

Performance contracting, as a tool of performance management for strengthening governance, is also crucial for achieving the objectives of the *Kenya Vision 2030* through the *MTP 2008-2012* and complemented by the PSTS. As discussed in Chapter 1, the *Kenya Vision 2030* is the country's development blueprint, covering the period 2008 to 2030. An efficient, motivated and well-trained public service is one of the major foundations of that Vision with public service reforms further enhancing, among other things, performance contracting (Republic of Kenya, 2007), to build capacity in governance and inculcate public service values and ethics for national transformation (Republic of Kenya, 2008, 2010b). The PSTS outcomes, and consequently those of the *Kenya Vision 2030*, are ultimately about improving economic and democratic governance and performance in Kenya. As Prime Minister Odinga (2010b: 4) has noted in his Foreword to the PSTS:

> The Public Sector exists to translate the priorities and directions of the Government into tangible benefits and results for Kenyans. Today it is more

important than ever that the Public Sector carry out its mandate as effectively as possible and adhere to the highest standards of public [performance] management so that it justifies the confidence of the Government and the trust of Kenyans. The Public Sector is the face of the Government and each citizen will judge how well the Government represents their interests by the manner in which the Public Sector serves them.

The Prime Minister further observed that "The overarching goal of transformation must be to create a Public Sector that is trusted, goal driven and responsive to the needs of Kenyans" (Odinga, 2010b: 4) and that "public sector transformation affords an exciting opportunity to make a dramatic leap forward toward our shared goal of a just, equitable, and prosperous Kenya" (Odinga, 2010b: 4).

Through performance contracting, the performance of public sector institutions can be better managed, monitored, and measured—the three M's of performance contracting—in a transparent manner for the benefit of the citizenry. PCs are tools of performance management that are intended to commit public officials to, and hold them accountable for, specified results. The desired outcome is to improve the efficiency of public service delivery while creating transparency in the management and use of public resources. In this regard, the use of CSDCs contributes to the strengthening of governance by involving and empowering the public to demand transparency and accountability from public servants and the holders of political office.

So, whether by accident previously, or now by design as espoused by Prime Minister Odinga, performance contracting in Kenya is a primary tool in the performance management arsenal for strengthening governance (both economic and democratic). With better economic and democratic governance, Kenya can then return to the path which had seen the country being regarded by international observers as a model of stability and future positive possibilities prior to the postelection crisis that erupted in 2008 (Mueller, 2008). The mood was therefore optimistic and many thought Kenya was capable of fulfilling its development promise by improving its low scores (below the mean for sub-Saharan Africa) on such governance indicators as political stability, control of corruption, and the rule of law, as well as improving economic performance.

Nonetheless, whether governance is seen from the perspective of improving public sector management and performance, or as strengthening government capacity to perform essential functions and deliver goods and services to the citizenry, the use of PCs as a performance management tool to get there can be summarized as having a number of benefits as discussed below.

Greater Transparency

Transparency is taken here to mean that reliable, relevant, and timely information about the activities of government is available to the public. Schiavo-Campo and Sundaram (2001) have argued that transparency is one of the four pillars of good governance with the other three being accountability, predictability, and participation. Transparent governance means that the citizens know what the public administration is doing, how it is doing it, and why it is doing it, including its planning for the future. According to Pardo (2007: 10):

> There is [also] a strong belief that a transparent administration and a transparent decision-making process strengthen the democratic nature of institutions and the public's confidence in the administration. It gives the administration democratic legitimacy.

Associated with transparency is the concept of openness whereby public participation in shaping and implementing government policy is encouraged and guaranteed. Openness of public information and universal access to it have become key mechanisms for obtaining good governance, since citizens can hold their government accountable by knowing what that government is doing and how (Pardo, 2007). Open governments are institutional structures where all public servants are held responsible for their decisions, where public actions can be closely monitored and where citizens can obtain all relevant information to accomplish both (Pardo, 2007). In other words, and as noted by OECD (2005: 29), an open government is one in which:

> citizens, businesses and civil society organizations have: firstly, the ability to request and receive relevant and understandable information; secondly, the capacity to obtain services and undertake transactions, and thirdly, the opportunity to participate in the decision-making process.

Where there is transparency, government officials will be prevented from exercising discretionary powers and will be taken to task, by the public in general and the press in particular, for violating the terms of their PCs—which are public documents, open to scrutiny, and readily available on websites. Transparency, therefore, complements and reinforces predictability, reduces uncertainty, and inhibits and reduces the scope for corruption and unethical behavior among public officials (Schiavo-Campo and Sundaram, 2001; Siegle et al., 2004). Greater transparency also exposes the shortcomings and any deliberate secrecy or misreporting of the operations of any given public institution.

Generally, countries characterized by a relatively high degree of transparency have exhibited greater political and economic discipline and, in many instances, have been able to achieve a more robust political and economic performance compared to countries with less transparent policies. PCs, to the extent that they enhance transparency in Kenya, will raise the domestic legitimacy of the government. On the other hand, transparency will also increase the political risk arising from the real or perceived nonperformance of public sector institutions. Transparency is a prerequisite for genuine accountability and reinforces predictability. Inefficiency and corruption thrive best in the dark, and the capacity to press for change from outside government requires a public with adequate information on the activities and standards by which to judge the performance of public services (Schiavo-Campo and Sundaram, 2001).

Improved Public Accountability

Transparency is also vital for accountability as noted above. In fact, a system of government that is open and transparent is also likely to be accountable. Accountability means that systems are in place and are facilitated by public institutions to hold public officials to account for their behavior, actions, and decisions. A system of public accountability is required so that public officials and governments act in ways that are broadly approved by society. Accountability is fundamental to any society with pretensions to achieving good governance. Public institutions are created by the public, for the public, and need to be accountable to it. The concern with public accountability expresses the continuing need for checks, oversight, surveillance, and institutional constraints on the exercise or potential abuse of power.

Related to public accountability is the notion of responsibility. Responsibility refers to those rules that influence the behavior of public officials in ways that encourage them to be responsive to public demands and act in the interest and welfare of citizens. PCs provide for all of these elements. The measurement and evaluation of performance in the context of the contents of the PCs will, therefore, expose any deficiencies in accountability by public officials and public institutions alike. In other words, the application of PCs will determine where public accountability is greatest, and where it is faulty and what should be done to improve it. Improved public accountability will also improve the performance of public institutions while the public scrutiny derived from PCs will provide the impetus for conscious efforts at improving public accountability and overall institutional performance.

Enhanced Policy Coherence

Coherent policy for socioeconomic development is derived from good governance. Those countries that have pursued policy reforms have made better development management choices and improved their socioeconomic performance. Developing and implementing coherent policies is a requirement of good governance. By being subjected to PCs, Kenya's public institutions will have their policy decisions and their application scrutinized. The result can be a substantial positive bearing on policy outcomes. PCs can therefore stimulate better policy choices and lead to future policy change. With better policy choices, society wins and the prospects for improving governance are thereby enhanced.

Strengthened Capacity

Improving governance requires a capable or performing State with the requisite capacity to consistently improve on policy and development outcomes as discussed in Chapter 7. Through performance measurement and evaluation, in the framework of PCs, any capacity constraints will be identified and recommendations offered on how to develop Kenya's required indigenous capacity to improve institutional performance and contribute to better governance. It has become recognized in the development literature that sustainable development can best be achieved in environments of developed human and institutional capacities (Hope, 2011).

Toward a More Credible Measurement and Evaluation of the Performance of Public Sector Institutions in Kenya

As the foregoing demonstrates, performance contracting can and should be used as a powerful tool for strengthening governance in Kenya. The country, now suffering from major governance deficits—as measured by such indices as corruption (real and perceived), public financial mismanagement, state weakness, and centralization of power, for example—needs to utilize performance contracting, as a performance management tool, in a much more robust way as part of its arsenal for improving institutional performance (particularly in the context of the *Kenya Vision 2030* and the PSTS) as well as for strengthening governance. A significant element of such an approach would, however, require a much more credible measurement and evaluation of public sector performance in relationship to the PCs.

It was generally agreed in the literature that performance contracting had been showing some success in Kenya (see, e.g., Kobia and Mohammed,

2006; LOG Associates, 2010; Obong'o, 2009; Republic of Kenya, 2010c; and Trivedi, nd). Indicators of that success included:

- Evidence on improved accountability;
- Some improvement in transparency;
- Positive changes in attitude toward work and work ethics by public employees;
- Significant growth in tax collections;
- Receipt by the Government of the 2007 United Nations Public Service Award in Category 1: Improving Transparency, Accountability, and Responsiveness in the Public Service.

However, recently there has been much debate and criticism, both inside and outside of government, on the measurement of performance in the public sector institutions and the consequent rankings of those institutions based on that performance in the context of their PCs. Public sentiment indicates that the rankings of some public sector institutions are not consistent with their performance as the public perceives it. That is to say, questions have been raised on how some public sector institutions got such high rankings when the public perception (and perhaps the reality) reveals that those entities have not performed to those standards. Similarly, for instance, Ministries that are perceived by the citizens to have performed well were lowly ranked (Hope, 2010).

The debate on the perception (both inside and outside of government) of performance in public sector institutions versus the official performance rankings of those institutions was aptly captured by Kimani (2010: 5) thus:

Over the past three weeks since the 2008/2009 performance evaluation results for Government agencies were released, tens of institutions have raised queries over the ranking . . . Several Government institutions . . . were questioning the results, as it emerged some of them were marked down during the final stage of the three-level evaluation process without explanation. . . . The development comes at a time when concerns are piling that the tool is far from achieving its main goal—perfecting management of public affairs.

The nature of this public perception must also be placed in the context of the 2008 violence that followed the December 2007 elections in Kenya. As previously noted in this book, that violence was the culmination of what has been referred to by Mueller (2008) as the political economy of Kenya's crisis. It brought to the fore issues related to inequality in the distribution of national resources; the inadequate role of public institutions in service delivery for meeting the needs of the public; the general environment of maladministration in public institutions with a culture of corruption and its attendant impunity; and the deliberate weakening of institutions outside of the executive branch in favor of personalized and centralized power.

In response to this state of affairs, Prime Minister Odinga appointed a Panel of Experts in May 2010 to review the performance contracting system, "amid rising disquiet among State institutions that the measurement tool is flawed" (Kimani, 2010: 5). The Prime Minister noted that "the performance contracting process is facing several challenges, prompting the need to refine the system" (Kimani, 2010: 5) and that "the urgent issue is to ensure that it captures and reports on results that affect the lives of ordinary Kenyans" (Kimani, 2010: 5). According to Republic of Kenya (2010c), the Terms of Reference of the Panel included:

- A Review of the design of the performance contracting system applied since 2004 and the design of the process and drawing lessons therefrom;
- A review of the performance contracting evaluation system and drawing learning points therefrom;
- A review of the performance evaluation results reported over the past three financial years, conducting a detailed analysis and drawing critical learning points therefrom;
- The generation, with justification, of critical recommendations for focused improvement of the performance contracting and evaluation in public service institutions in Kenya.

PCs generally have inherent difficulties. There is the classic principal–agent information asymmetry and moral hazard problem. Managers enjoy an information advantage over owners and can negotiate targets that are difficult for outsiders to evaluate and/or are very easy to achieve. Some managers tend to operate as opportunistic agents who exploit the inherent asymmetries in information—by knowing more about what they are doing, and what they may or may not be accomplishing, than their bosses—they put self-interest above the public interest (Schick, 2003). In fact, in the case of Kenya, one consultancy report notes that:

> some institutions have developed methods where they deliberately set low targets for themselves. Such institutions therefore are able to score highly without "stretching" so high. This has been one of the biggest challenges to the performance contracting system as currently implemented. (LOG Associates, 2010: vi)

In addition, in some PCs, the incentives and penalties may not be credible or sufficient. And, political owners may not always be committed to performance management or improved efficiencies in a consistent manner.

However, having said that, it is not to say that PCs in Kenya have now become useless. It is quite the contrary. We should not attempt to throw out the baby with the bath water. There is need to build on international experience and best practice in designing these contracts and then being able to evaluate performance more effectively. The Performance Contracting Department needs to deal purposefully with the challenges of information asymmetry, smart incentives, and credible commitments, for instance.

Below are some recommendations for putting the performance contracting system back on track in the country, bring credibility to the measurement and evaluation process, and win back public confidence in both the performance results and the public institutions themselves:

(1) The AHTF should no longer be regarded as *Ad Hoc* or treated as such. It should be renamed as the Assessment and Evaluation Task Force (AETF). These various AETFs should also be composed of a group of *bona fide* experts with a combination of expertise in monitoring and evaluation as well as in the subject matter relevant to the public institution to be negotiated with and evaluated. For example, if the Ministry of Finance is being engaged, then the AETF members should also have a combination of expertise in economics, finance, budgeting. This combination of expertise would also be very useful in the negotiation phase of the PCs—allowing for the right questions to be asked and for demanding appropriate and relevant information and data to counteract the information asymmetry problem.

(2) In addition to ensuring the right mix of expertise, the members of the AETF should also be without any conflict of interest. A conflict of interest occurs when an individual or organization is involved in multiple interests, one of which could possibly corrupt the motivation for an act in another. To the extent that the parties involved in evaluating performance are not at arm's length, they have weaker capacity to act independently, to follow the guidelines and to enforce its terms. Moreover, "a cosy relationship may encourage collusion and logrolling at the expense of the public interest; and by making [performance contracting] less transparent, it may open the door to corruption" (Schick, 2003: 91). Part of the employment terms for members of the AETF should therefore be the requirement for them to voluntarily recuse themselves in the event they recognize they may have a conflict of interest. If a conflict of interest is brought to light and the concerned member(s) has/have not

voluntarily recused, they should be summarily dismissed as a member(s) of the AETF.

(3) Similarly, the rules on conflict of interest outlined above must also apply to those involved in the moderation stage.

(4) A much greater focus and weight need to be put on the CSDCs and the results of benchmarking and customer surveys in the assessment and evaluation phase. Indeed, these surveys should also be released and published in the press with the same fanfare that now accompanies the release of the annual report on evaluation of performance of the public agencies. Citizen inclusion in measuring the performance of public institutions adds value to the process and better informs policy decisions. Furthermore, there is a considerable body of research—pointing to international best practice—that shows that there are tangible benefits to the inclusion of citizens in the performance of public agencies. Broad public participation and informed public judgment create opportunities for deliberation, debate, and informed decision-making for citizens, elected officials, and managers alike.

(5) Successful performance measurement systems adhere to the following principles and Kenya's should be no different: (1) measure only what is important and measure only those things that impact performance; (2) focus on customer (citizen) needs; and (3) involve employees (not just management) in the design and implementation of the measurement system. Give employees a sense of ownership, which can also lead to improvements in the quality of the measurement indicators. In that latter regard, this author strongly believes that adjustments should be made to the list of performance indicators and for the accompanying reasons. The performance indicator (PI)—Compliance with Strategic Plan—should be eliminated. If we assume that current Strategic Plans are now consistent and compliant with the *Kenya Vision 2030* and its applicable medium-term plan, then the Strategic Plan should no longer be an indicator of performance. Moreover, a Strategic Plan should be a dynamic rather than static document, covering current issues and priorities, so that it can comply with the directives of the government, which are being pursued through medium-term plans, to fulfill the objectives of the *Kenya Vision 2030*. In addition, when PCs were originally tied to Strategic Plans the latter provided the only road map on what individual public institutions were trying or hoping to get accomplished. Hence, those Strategic Plans became the source of performance targets. Now that road map can be derived from the national *Kenya Vision 2030*. Consequently, the PI should be Compliance with the *Kenya Vision 2030* and its current medium-term plan. Also, the two PIs on Compliance with

set Budget Levels and Utilization of Allocated Funds, respectively, taken together deal with fiscal responsibility and disbursement efficiency. It, therefore, makes sense to seek the follow-up on performance with respect to overall financial management by adding a PI on Compliance with Internal and External Audit Reports.

(6) The first stage of the measurement and evaluation process should be eliminated. If there is to be a truly credible assessment then it should all be done independently of what a given public institution thinks of its own performance. Consequently, there should be only two stages in the measurement and evaluation process. Stage I should be the primary evaluation by the AETF, and Stage II should be the quality control and moderation phase. However, this should not preclude public institutions from conducting their own self-evaluations as an additional input into their internal processes for managing and monitoring their performance.

(7) PCs should also be extended to all public institutions in all branches of government. That means that the legislative and judiciary branches should be encouraged to get on board. However, since they can claim to be independent of the executive branch (especially in light of the 2010 constitution), they may need to establish their own performance contracting administrative arrangements.

(8) Finally, very serious attempts should also be made by the Performance Contracting Department to reduce the lag time between the end of a PC year and the evaluation and eventual release of the performance results. By doing so, there would be a better understanding and judgment of the results by all parties in relationship to the perceived levels of performance during the PC year.

Conclusions

Kenya has been undertaking public sector reform and transformation since the mid-1960s. This suggests the country has taken cognizance of both the need for such ongoing reforms and transformation as necessary and essential to bring about governance improvements that are needed for sustainable poverty reduction and development, and the application of current best practice in public sector reform and transformation for a performance-oriented public service culture. Public sector reform and transformation are means to an end. It is a means toward achieving higher-order development goals—particularly growth, poverty reduction, peace and stability—through better public management and improved public service delivery. Consequently, developing countries, such as Kenya, must endeavor to undertake and implement public sector reform and transformation as necessary.

Among those reforms must be the permanent pursuit of performance-oriented initiatives, where performance measures are objectively deployed to tackle performance flaws. Currently, performance contracting is the principal method so deployed to tackle performance flaws in Kenya. PCs represent a state-of-the-art tool for improving public sector performance. In fact, they are now considered an important tool for enhancing good governance and accountability for results in the public sector. Kenya's public sector performance contracting process had been somewhat successful and provided some of the desired outcomes related to improved institutional performance. However, the recent results of the evaluation of the performance of public agencies were not consistent with the perception (both inside and outside of government) of the performance of those agencies and that brought to the surface that there are some flaws in the administration and evaluation of PCs. Nonetheless, performance contracting remains a viable and important tool not only for improving performance but also for strengthening governance as a key element of the *Kenya Vision 2030* goals. The chapter has also provided recommendations on the way forward toward a more credible measurement and evaluation of the performance of public sector institutions in the country. Recently, a Policy Steering Committee on Performance Management was established by the government and given overall responsibility for the management and coordination of performance management in the three arms of government, including oversight of the implementation of reforms in the performance contracting system. Those reforms will also entail implementation of the recommendations made by the Panel of Experts which encompass most of the recommendations advocated in this chapter and originally derived from Hope (2010).

Performance measurement can be the first step toward improving the performance of public sector institutions, and, when backed by an appropriate incentive system, it can also help shift organizational focus from inputs to outputs and outcomes and, consequently, improve efficiency and effectiveness (Schiavo-Campo and Sundaram, 2001). Introducing a stronger performance orientation in Kenya's public sector is very important for improving the performance of the country's public sector institutions. While performance can be regarded as complex because it also entails a subjective dimension, in terms of results, it is important for the Kenyan authorities not to neglect entirely the subjective effort but recognize it in appropriate ways. However, performance should be measured primarily in terms of results.

References

CIDA (Canadian International Development Agency) (2009), "Results-based Management." Available at: http://www.acdi-cida.gc.ca/acdi-cida/ACDI-CIDA.nsf/eng/NIC-31595014-KEF [Accessed December 12, 2010].

Hope, K. R. (2001), "The New Public Management: Context and Practice in Africa," *International Public Management Journal*, 4(2), 119–34.

— (2002), "The New Public Management: A Perspective from Africa." In K. McLaughlin, S. R. Osborne, and E. Ferlie (eds), *New Public Management: Current Trends and Prospects*. London: Routledge, pp. 210–26.

— (2008), *Poverty, Livelihoods, and Governance in Africa: Fulfilling the Development Promise*. New York: Palgrave Macmillan.

— (2010), "Performance Contracting as a Performance Management Tool for Strengthening Governance in Kenya," *Briefing Paper I*. Nairobi: Office of the Prime Minister.

— (2011). "Investing in Capacity Development: Towards an Implementation Framework," *Policy Studies*, 32(1), 59–72.

Isahakia, M. (2010), "Preface." In OPM/PSTD (Office of the Prime Minister/ Public Sector Transformation Department), *Public Sector Transformation Strategy: From Reform to Transformation 2010-14*. Nairobi: OPM/PSTD, pp. 5–6.

Kimani, M. (2010), "Team to Review Performance Contracts," *Business Daily*, Thursday May 20, 5.

Kobia, M. and Mohammed, N. (2006), "The Kenyan Experience with Performance Contracting." Paper Presented at the 28th African Association for Public Administration and Management Annual Roundtable Conference, Arusha, December 4–8. Available at: http://www.unpan.org [Accessed May 5, 2010].

LOG Associates (2010), *Evaluation of Performance Contracting*. Nairobi: Office of the Prime Minister, Performance Contracting Department.

Marwa, S. M. and Zairi, M. (2009), "In Pursuit of Performance-Oriented Civil Service Reforms (CSRs): A Kenyan Perspective," *Measuring Business Excellence*, 13(2), 34–43.

Mueller, S. D. (2008), "The Political Economy of Kenya's Crisis," *Journal of Eastern African Studies*, 2(2), 185–210.

Nzioka, G. (1998), "Kenya." In K. Kiragu (ed.), *Civil Service Reform in Southern & Eastern Africa: Lessons of Experience*, Report on Proceedings of a Consultative Workshop, Arusha, March 4–6. Available at: http://www.utumishi.go.tz/index2.php?option=com_docman&task=doc_view&gid=59&Itemid=57 [Accessed December 12, 2010].

Obong'o, S. O. (2009), "Implementation of Performance Contracting in Kenya," *International Public Management Review*, 10(2), 66–83.

Odinga, R. A. (2009), "Foreword" to *Strategic Plan 2009-2012*. Nairobi: OPM, pp. vii–viii.

— (2010a), "Foreword" to *Report on Evaluation of the Performance of Public Agencies for the Financial Year 2008/2009*. Nairobi: OPM/PCD (Office of the Prime Minister, Performance Contracting Department), pp. v–vii.

— (2010b), "Foreword" to *Public Sector Transformation Strategy: From Reform to Transformation 2010-14*. Nairobi: OPM/PSTD (Office of the Prime Minister, Public Sector Transformation Department), p. 4.

OECD (Organization for Economic Cooperation and Development) (2005), *Modernizing Government: The Way Forward*. Paris: OECD.

OP/PSRDS (Office of the President/Public Service Reform and Development Secretariat) (2005), "Donor/GOK Consultative Meeting: Report." Available at: http://siteresources.worldbank.org/INTKENYA/Resources/psrd_sec_rpt.pdf [Accessed December 11, 2010].

OPM (Office of the Prime Minister) (2009), *Strategic Plan 2009-2012*. Nairobi: OPM.

OPM/PCD (Office of the Prime Minister, Performance Contracting Department (nd), *Performance Contracting Guideline: 7th Edition*. Nairobi: OPM/PCD.

— (2010), *Report on Evaluation of the Performance of Public Agencies for the Financial Year 2008/2009*. Nairobi: OPM/PCD.

OPM/PSRPC (Office of the Prime Minister, Public Sector Reforms and Performance Contracting) (nda), "What is a Performance Contract." Available at: http://www.psrpc.go.ke [Accessed May 12, 2010].

— (ndb), "Citizen Service Delivery Charters." Available at: http://www.psrpc. go.ke [Accessed May 5, 2010].

OPM/PSTD (Office of the Prime Minister, Public Sector Transformation Department) (2010), *Public Sector Transformation Strategy: From Reform to Transformation 2010-14*. Nairobi: OPM/PSTD.

Oyugi, W. O. (2006), "Public Service Reform in Kenya: Lessons of Experience." In K. Kiragu and G. Mutahaba (eds), *Public Service Reform in Eastern and Southern Africa: Issues and Challenges*. Dar es Salaam: Mkuki na Nyota Publishers, pp. 3–65.

Pardo, M. (2007), "Preface." In M. Pardo (ed.), *Transparency for Better Governance*. Brussels: International Institute for Administrative Sciences, pp. 9–24.

Republic of Kenya (2003), *Kenya: Economic Recovery Strategy for Wealth and Employment Creation 2003-2007*. Nairobi: Ministry of Planning and National Development.

— (2007), *Kenya Vision 2030: A Globally Competitive and Prosperous Kenya*. Nairobi: Republic of Kenya.

— (2008), *Kenya Vision 2030: First Medium-term Plan (2008-2012)*. Nairobi: Republic of Kenya.

— (2010a), *The Constitution of Kenya, 2010*. Nairobi: Republic of Kenya.

— (2010b), *First Annual Progress Report on the Implementation of the First Medium-term Plan (2008-2012) of Kenya Vision 2030*. Nairobi: Republic of Kenya.

— (2010c), *Review of Performance Contracting in the Public Sector: Report by the Panel of Experts*. Nairobi: Office of the Prime Minister.

Republic of South Africa (1997), *Batho Pele—"People First": White Paper on Transforming Public Service Delivery*. Available at: http://www.dpsa.gov.za/documents/acts&regulations/frameworks/white-papers/transform.pdf [Accessed December 12, 2010).

Schiavo-Campo, S. and Sundaram, P. S. A. (2001), *To Serve and to Preserve: Improving Public Administration in a Competitive World*. Manila: Asian Development Bank.

Schick, A. (2003), "The Performing State: Reflection on an Idea Whose Time Has Come but Whose Implementation Has Not," *OECD Journal on Budgeting*, 3(2), 71–103.

Siegle, J. T., Weinstein, M. M., and Halperin, M. H. (2004), "Why Democracies Excel," *Foreign Affairs*, 83(5), 57–71.

Trivedi, P. (nd), "Performance Contracts in Kenya: Instruments for Operationalizing Good Governance." Available at: http://www.performance. gov.in/International-Experience.html [Accessed May 12, 2010].

World Bank (2001), *Implementation Completion Report on a Credit in the Amount of SDRs 17.2 Million to the Government of the Republic of Kenya for an Institutional Development and Civil Service Reform Project.* Washington, DC: World Bank.

Xavier, J. A. (2010), "Establishing Key Performance Indicators for the Upper Echelons of the Senior Public Service," *Commonwealth Innovations*, 16(1), 15–25.

7

Sustaining Growth and Development:
Some Aspects of Policy

This chapter broadens the discussion and analysis, thus far, by offering some aspects of policy for sustaining growth and development in Kenya. Sustaining growth and development in Kenya, and the rest of Africa for that matter, must remain the fundamental goal of development policy. Growth and development, in an environment of good governance, like a rising tide that lifts all boats, remains the only means and, indeed, the only path for improved economic performance, poverty reduction, low rates of unemployment, and generally better living standards and livelihoods.

Kenya now has a tremendous opportunity to get it right in terms of its development outcomes. The overwhelming support for the 2010 constitution demonstrated that Kenyans were signaling to the political leadership that they want an environment of good governance, peace, stability, and socioeconomic prosperity. The emergence of the Second Republic is essentially a rebirth of Kenya. It provides the basis for a "New Deal" in the country. If appropriately marshaled and managed, then the future of Kenya is very bright indeed. In fact, on a string of criteria, Kenya has reasserted itself as the leader of the Eastern African subregion with its position, vis-à-vis its neighbors, being stronger than ever. Nonetheless, as this book has demonstrated, there are a number of persistent and/or long-term development challenges that must be tackled if the country is to fulfill its development promise and provide the benefits that the citizens demanded when they voted overwhelmingly in favor of the 2010 constitution.

As Prime Minister Odinga (2010: 1) observed in his speech at the ceremony to promulgate the 2010 constitution and usher in the Second Republic:

The Fourth of August will go down in history as the date on which we, the people of Kenya, formed a more united nation, and established the groundwork for justice, unity and the full blessings of liberty for ourselves and for posterity. No one could have thought that out of the bitter harvest of the disputed election and the violence that pitted our people against each other just two years ago, we would be witnessing today the birth of a national unity that has eluded us for more than 40 years . . . We gather here now to ratify the pledge we made to ourselves and to the world, that Kenya shall redeem herself and extend the frontiers of democracy and freedom. This freedom has eluded us for more than forty years . . . The promise of this new beginning will be challenged by our traditional enemies; corruption and negative ethnicity. We must be vigilant and stop corruption from stealing our future and negative ethnicity from weakening our nationhood. To those in charge of public affairs, may public service be what it is; public service; not self-service.

Savings Mobilization

The basic starting point here is that Kenya's domestic savings rate is relatively low, averaging 14–15 percent of GDP during the period 2000–09. This is both inadequate to finance the growth target and considerably lower than the planned rate as expressed in the *Kenya Vision 2030* and the *MTP 2008-2012*. Moreover, to sustain the ongoing efforts to both reduce the public debt and rely more on domestic sources of finance also requires that the domestic savings rate be significantly increased. Kenya's ability to finance a greater share of its development needs from domestic sources would give it much-needed flexibility in the formulation and implementation of policies to address development challenges, direct resources into high priority areas, and strengthen state capacity. There are many reasons for Kenya's low savings rates, including inadequate availability of financial services, households' physical distance from banking institutions, high minimum deposit and balance requirements, and restrictive entry as well as access to balances.

In fact, barriers to accessing formal sector banking services are problematic not only for the poor but for all potential customers. This author experienced these problems firsthand in 2010 when attempting to open accounts at the two largest banks in Kenya. The process took several days and entailed meeting demands by the banks for letters of introduction, letters from my employer, more than one piece of identification, and other documentation. For the poor and others working in the informal sector obtaining all such documentation is a major challenge if not virtually impossible.

These reasons represent the factors that have resulted in the situation whereby much of the population still lacks access to banking services. As discussed in this book, although access to banking services in Kenya has increased over the years, there is still a considerable proportion of the population, especially in the rural areas, that are unbanked. Consequently, the country's large informal sector holds considerable financial resources that are not deposited in savings accounts or pass through other formal financial channels. In fact, as discussed in Chapter 3, informal savings mobilization is a significant method through which credit and expenditure planning are achieved by the poor.

The policy choices available to the Kenyan authorities for increasing domestic savings are neither new nor unknown. What is really required is concentration on efforts to implement these available policy options to be accompanied by more innovative financial sector products. Ideally, two approaches have to be pursued to target two different groups of Kenyans: one group being the unbanked, and the other the banked. The unbanked have been recently targeted, and successfully so, through innovative mobile phone financial services technology, as discussed in Chapter 1. However, greater financial inclusion is still required for this group. As also discussed in Chapter 1, to tap into the unbanked population, it is absolutely necessary that the financial institutions introduce (supply) new financial products or instruments that respond to the savings needs of the group. For the banked group (households and non-bank financial intermediaries such as insurance companies and pension firms), incentives need to be provided through high-yield savings products to encourage larger liquid savings volumes as opposed to savings being held in tangible assets such as livestock.

Basically, the Kenyan authorities need to provide the regulatory, supervisory, and guarantor frameworks for the financial institutions to roll out savings products that will appeal to the two groups of savers. For the unbanked, transaction savings accounts that permit easy accessibility and allow for small transactions at frequent intervals would encourage households to shift to the formal system, thereby making such assets available for productive investments also (Dovi, 2008). If households determine that there are barriers to entry for making savings deposits and also barriers to access those deposits, whenever needed, then said households would most likely conclude that the transaction costs of holding savings assets are too high. This rational behavior is observed in the informal financial sector where financial transactions are typically small and frequent, reflecting the low level of disposable income and the high liquidity preference of poor households and small businesses. Furthermore, the success of M-Pesa and similar mobile phone financial services technology, as discussed in Chapter 1, has demonstrated the importance of easy entry and easy access to household financial resources.

In addition, there is no shortage of willingness to save among the unbanked. The fact that poorer households save through ROSCAs, for example, where there is no return on their savings (negative interest), is testimony to both the importance of savings services for poor households and the willingness of such households to save (UNCTAD, 2007). Consequently, tapping into this group of savers in Kenya would be relatively straightforward if given the availability of easy entry and easy access to deposits, and particularly if accompanied by innovative entry and access mechanism such as the mobile phone financial services, like M-Pesa, that are now a standard part of the country's financial landscape, and catering to the unsecured and traditionally unbanked.

For the already banked, savings products with positive interest rates would be much more of a determinant for increasing savings volumes from this group. Positive savings interest rates would be a significant competing influence on the choice of assets held by households. This is so simply because we know that asset choice reflects returns on different assets. Households and individuals face a number of options as they consider whether or not to put wealth into particular assets, and the current dominance of nonfinancial assets in household portfolios reflects both the view and consequence of low expected returns to holding financial assets.

Undoubtedly, increasing savings and ensuring they are directed to productive investment are central to accelerating economic growth in Kenya and other African countries. Savings are a hugely important part of a country's growth and a county's financial development. In fact, domestic savings is the most important and predictable source of financing investment and thus boosting growth. Increasing domestic savings and generally strengthening domestic resource mobilization, combined with improvements in the efficiency and efficacy in the use of such resources, will not only reduce or eliminate the resource gap, it will also increase the policy space available to the authorities to enable them to define their development goals and the means to achieve them (UNCTAD, 2007).

Therefore, there must be ongoing efforts to reform and improve the formal financial sector to enhance savings mobilization from both the excluded Kenyans and those Kenyans already being served. Furthermore, despite the importance of, and necessity for, informal finance, particularly to serve the needs of the poor, informal finance institutions should become a complement, rather than a substitute, to formal finance in that they serve those members of society that are excluded by the other sector. This is also consistent with the argument advanced in Chapter 3 that the informal and formal economies are complementary to each other.

Private Enterprise-Led Growth and Industrialization

The point of departure here is that growth is stimulated by private sector economic activities, as opposed to public sector activities, and that governments are solely responsible for creating the environment for private enterprise-led growth. Moreover, it is only through private sector economic activities that there can be sustained employment and wealth creation which, in turn, is poverty-reducing. Other significant benefits of private sector economic activities are technology transfer, increases in capital stock, and contributions to balance of payments and GDP. Industrialization, obviously, is a function of private enterprise-led growth.

Any strategy for industrialization in Kenya must be aimed at attracting and encouraging investment from both formal and informal sector activities. Both large-scale and MSMEs' industrial activities must be targeted. Industrialization is taken here to mean the development of industry on an extensive scale. It is a process of social and economic change whereby a human society is transformed to a newly industrializing society or from a newly industrializing society to an industrial one. As stated in the *Kenya Vision 2030*, the country aims to transform itself to a "newly industrializing, middle income country providing a high quality of life to all its citizens in a clean and secure environment" (Republic of Kenya, 2007a: vii).

To accomplish that vision the government intends, among other things, to continue its economic reform programs to give the country an internationally competitive business environment. In that regard, the manufacturing sector looms large (Republic of Kenya, 2007a). As stated in the *MTP 2008-2012*, manufacturing activities in Kenya are to lead a "robust diversified and competitive manufacturing sector" (Republic of Kenya, 2008: 74). "The role of the manufacturing sector in the Vision 2030 is to support the country's social economic development agenda by creating jobs, generating wealth, and attracting Foreign Direct Investment (FDI)" (Republic of Kenya, 2008: 74).

The route to industrialization in countries like Kenya is, undoubtedly, through the growth of the manufacturing sector with the ultimate intention of boosting manufacturing exports. To grow the manufacturing sector requires the consideration and application of policies that go beyond those expounded in the *MTP 2008-2012* and as discussed in Chapter 1. Growing the manufacturing sector can only be accomplished through significant investment in both new economic activities and existing economic activities. In addition to current government policy for expanding manufacturing activities, this author advocates that consideration be given to reducing business taxes as an incentive for encouraging investment. Kenya has reduced corporate taxes in recent years by making them more comparable with those of its neighbors in East Africa. The country's general corporate income tax rate in 2010 was 30 percent, with a branch of a foreign company (nonresident) taxed at 37.5 percent (KRA, 2009). However, these rates are relatively high when compared with what obtains in most other African emerging market economies or newly industrializing countries with good economic management. In South Africa, for example, the most industrialized African country, the corporate tax rate ranges from 28 to 33 percent, in Botswana it ranges from 15 to 25 percent, while in Mauritius it is 15 percent (Tax Rates.cc, 2010).

There is a body of literature that indicates that corporate tax rates influence the magnitude of investment (see, e.g., Cerda and Larrain, 2010; de Mooij and Ederveen, 2003; Djankov et al., 2010; Klemm and Van Parys, 2009; Mintz, 2007; Norregard and Khan, 2007; Schwellnus and Arnold, 2008). All of the specific published studies, although showing some substantial variations in the quantitative results, show that there is a large adverse incentive effect of corporate taxation on investment. In other words, there is a negative relationship between private investment flows and corporate income tax rates. The literature analyses undertaken by de Mooij and Ederveen (2003) found that, on average (the mean value), the tax rate elasticity of FDI is approximately -3.3 percent. That means that a 1 percent reduction in the effective tax rate on capital can increase FDI in that country by 3.3 percent. The substantial variation among studies can be partly explained by the underlying study characteristics with the choice of tax data a major influence on the variation in elasticities. In particular, studies using effective tax rates or average tax rates yield larger elasticities than studies adopting country statutory tax rates. The effective tax rates based on tax codes—marginal and average—tend to yield relatively high elasticities when compared to average tax rates based on micro or macro data (de Mooij and Ederveen, 2003).

Privatization is also another area that needs to be rigorously revived in Kenya for the country to promote and benefit from private enterprise-led growth and industrialization. As discussed below, there are still too many SOEs in Kenya that can be privatized for the country to take advantage of the economic benefits of privatization. As observed by Pamacheche and Koma (2007: 3):

Through privatization, sub-Saharan African countries [including Kenya] can achieve an expanded and more dynamic private sector, more efficient and effective infrastructure provision and increased investment, both domestic and foreign. These positive developments emanating from privatization will subsequently lead to the achievement of poverty alleviation goals, given their direct impact on economic growth and, subsequently, job creation in these countries.

In this work, privatization is defined as the transfer of operational control and responsibilities, or of a substantial part thereof, of government functions and services to the private sector—private enterprises or private voluntary organizations (Hope, 1996, 2008). It entails a transaction or transactions utilizing one or more of the methods resulting in either the sale to private parties of a controlling interest in the share capital of a public enterprise or of a substantial part of its assets. From a wider perspective, privatization encompasses a wide range of policies to encourage private sector participation in public service provision and eliminate or modify the monopoly status of public enterprises. Privatization can be a complex process, frequently involving choices between the need to improve financial and economic efficiency; political opposition and varying degrees of unpopularity; and distinguishing between sectors and services that are essentially in the public interest and those which should be hived off to the private sector (Hentic and Bernier, 1999; Hope, 2008; Savas, 2000).

In Kenya, the privatization strategy and process are currently guided and implemented by a Privatization Commission. The Commission was established as a corporate body, within the Ministry of Finance, Under Part II of the Privatization Act, 2005, which came into force on January 01, 2008. The membership of the Commission comprises a Chairman appointed by the President; the Attorney General; the Permanent Secretary to the Treasury; seven members, not being public officers, appointed by the Minister of Finance and approved by the relevant committee of Parliament, by virtue of their expertise in such matters as will ensure that the Commission achieves its objectives; and the Executive Director. The Commission has been charged with responsibility to:

- Formulate, manage, and implement the privatization program;
- Make and implement specific proposals for privatization in accordance with the privatization program;
- Undertake such other functions as are provided for under the Act;
- Undertake such other functions as the Commission considers advisable to advance the privatization program. (Republic of Kenya, 2005a)

The enactment of the Privatization Act, 2005; the establishment of the Privatization Commission; and the recognition in the *MTP 2008-2012* of the importance of privatization for growth and development in Kenya seems to suggest that the hostility to privatization in Kenya has subsided. In the past, privatization was viewed with much skepticism across most of Africa. In particular, African officials and intellectuals, including those in Kenya, had the tendency to view the public sector as the promoter and defender of indigenous interests and to therefore believe that privatization would empower and enrich foreigners at the expense of indigenous people leading to vandalization of the continent (Obeng, 2007; Pamacheche and Koma, 2007).

However, the benefits of privatization for Kenya are now being publicly touted. According to the Privatization Commission, those benefits include:

- The improvement of infrastructure and delivery of public services by the involvement of private capital and expertise;
- The reduction of the demand for government resources;
- The generation of additional government revenues by receiving compensation for privatizations;
- The improvement of the regulation of the economy by reducing conflicts between the public sector's regulatory and commercial functions;
- The improvement of the efficiency of the Kenyan economy by making it more responsive to market forces;
- The broadening of the base of ownership in the Kenyan economy;
- The enhancement of the capital markets. (Privatization Commission, nda)

Nonetheless, data from the World Bank's privatization database indicate that the Kenya Treasury reaped US$1.3 billion from the privatization of SOEs during the period 2004–08, comprising only five transactions and all of which were in the infrastructure sector (World Bank, nda). According to information published on the website of the Privatization Commission, by April 2011, there were still at least 15 SOEs, that are in the approved privatization program, which are in various stages of privatization with only five of these having detailed proposals submitted to the government for approval pursuant to the Privatization Act, 2005 (Privatization Commission, ndb). However, there is no information available on when (how long ago) the proposals were sent to the government for the required approval. Clearly, the privatization process in Kenya needs to be scaled up.

As already been argued, through its economic benefits, privatization has a potentially high impact on poverty reduction also. Having gotten over the resistance to privatization, and keeping in mind that the aim of the *Kenya Vision 2030* is to transform the nation into a "newly industrializing, middle income country providing a high quality of life to all its citizens in a clean and secure environment" (Republic of Kenya, 2007a: vii), then the Kenyan authorities need to approach privatization with greater urgency. Privatization is also necessary for Kenya to counteract the economic inefficiencies and poor service delivery derived from government ownership of economic and productive resources.

Infrastructure Development

To achieve a credible level of industrialization also requires a credible level of infrastructure. Infrastructure (both economic and social)—roads, electricity supply, water supply, sanitation systems, irrigation, schools, hospitals, clinics, airports, telecommunications, and so on—plays a vital role in economic and social development. Increasingly interdependent, infrastructure systems are a means toward ensuring the delivery of goods and services that promote economic prosperity and growth, and contribute to quality of life. Infrastructure is, therefore, not an end itself. Rather, it is a means for ensuring the delivery of goods and services that promote prosperity and growth and contribute to quality of life, including the social well-being, poverty reduction, health and safety of citizens, and the quality of their environments (OECD, 2008; UN-HABITAT, 2011).

Undoubtedly, reliable, efficient infrastructure is crucial to economic and social development and the promotion of pro-poor growth. Poor infrastructure impedes a nation's economic growth and international competitiveness (Delmon, 2011). In fact, it has long been recognized that an adequate supply of infrastructure services is an essential ingredient for productivity and growth. For East African countries, depending on the scenario used, infrastructure development would increase growth in the range of 1.0–1.6 percent while their Gini coefficient would achieve a decline averaging just over 0.03 (Calderón and Servén, 2010).

The infrastructure requirements for sustainable development in Kenya are seriously lacking and that means that the country's infrastructure stock needs to be upgraded. The inadequate and poorly performing infrastructure is a major challenge to Kenya's economic development and growth, and constitutes a major impediment to the achievement of the country's Vision 2030 as well as the Millennium Development Goals (MDGs). The country's infrastructure needs are broad-based and current infrastructure investment levels are far below those required. Consequently, the necessary infrastructural conditions for sustained private investment are lacking.

One factor that is particularly often cited as a major constraint is electricity supply. The frequent and lengthy power outages in Kenya are now more than just annoying and businesses (formal and informal), government offices, private residences, and all others who can afford it have had to invest in generators as a fundamental necessity of daily functioning. This, in turn, has been a major obstacle to private investment. Own-generation therefore now constitutes a significant proportion of total available power capacity. This unreliable power supply situation in the country can be measured by the number of days of power outages per year which exceeded 50 in 2007 compared to 41 in other African low-income countries and 6 in African middle-income countries; the percentage of firms owning a generator (66 percent) in 2007 compared to 18 percent in South Africa and 16 percent in Botswana; the proportion of electricity coming from firms' generators (9.6 percent) compared 1.9 percent in South Africa and 0.8 percent in Mauritius; and the value lost due to power outages was 6.3 percent of sales in 2007 compared to 1.6 percent of sales in South Africa and 1.4 percent of sales in Botswana (AICD, 2010; World Bank, ndb). The major victims of unreliable power supply are in the informal sector where survey evidence suggests that generator ownership is an order of magnitude less prevalent than in the formal sector (Foster and Steinbuks, 2009).

During the last decade, infrastructure contributed almost 1 percent to Kenya's annual per capita GDP growth (AICD, 2010). Currently, the country's infrastructure indicators look relatively good when compared with other low-income countries in Africa. However, they are far below the levels found in Africa's middle-income countries. Simulations conducted by some analysts suggest that by raising the country's infrastructure endowment to that of the region's middle-income countries could increase annual per capita growth rates by more than 3 percentage points with a substantial share of that impact coming from improvements in the power sector alone (AICD, 2010).

Two areas where there is need for special focus are in the power and ports subsectors. With respect to the former, the AICD (2010) claims that the institutional reforms of recent years have led to efficiency gains of 1 percent of GDP. Among those reforms was the separation of the national power utility into a generation utility named Kenya Electricity Generating Company Limited (KenGen) in 1998 and a transmission and distribution utility named Kenya Power and Lighting Company Limited (KPLC). More recently, in 2008, the Kenya Electricity Transmission Company Limited (KETRACO) was incorporated by the government to accelerate transmission infrastructure development by planning, designing, constructing, owning, operating, and maintaining new high-voltage electricity transmission lines and fiber optic cables. KPLC retained and continues to operate all previously existing transmission systems (KETRACO, nd). Due to reforms and other measures, such as improved revenue collection, declining distribution losses, and pricing that rose with costs, the hidden costs (under-pricing, collection losses, and distribution losses) of the power subsector fell from 1.4 percent of GDP in 2001 to 0.4 percent of GDP by 2006 and were largely eliminated by 2008. This, in turn, has provided a dividend to Kenya of more than 1 percent of its entire GDP and also resulted in the sector being in a better financial position (AICD, 2010).

Undoubtedly, Kenya's greatest infrastructure challenge lies in the power sector. The country's power supply remains unreliable due to the fact that generation and transmission are overstretched. It has been estimated that the burden of power outages on the economy is as high as 2 percent of GDP

(AICD, 2010; Eberhard et al., 2008), and that the country needs a further 1,000 megawatts of generating capacity over the next decade (AICD, 2010). However, the *MTP 2008-2012* indicated that a National Electricity Supply Master Plan would identify new generation and supply sources to ensure that the national electricity supply dependable energy is tripled in the next ten years from the current 1,050 megawatts (2008) to 3,000 megawatts by 2018 (Republic of Kenya, 2008). The *MTP 2008-2012*, in its implementation matrices, also had, as an objective, the generation of an additional 505 megawatts of electricity during 2008–12 to meet the growing demand for electricity (Republic of Kenya, 2008). Yet, the progress report on the implementation of the *MTP 2008-2012* stated that one target in the power subsector for 2008–09 was to install 75 megawatts of additional power capacity, but that the target was surpassed as a total of 124 megawatts was installed and commissioned (Republic of Kenya, 2010a).

Meeting the electricity demand and needs of Kenya remains a major challenge for the country in the context of its socioeconomic development aspirations as espoused in the *Kenya Vision 2030*. In addition to generating additional in-country power capacity, Kenya will also need to develop or reinforce cross-border transmission links with its neighbors Tanzania, Ethiopia, and Uganda to obtain access to relatively inexpensive hydropower and improve overall system security (AICD, 2010). In the progress report on the implementation of the *MTP 2008-2012*, the government has highlighted several implementation challenges being experienced in the power subsector (see Republic of Kenya, 2010a: 33).

The power crisis in Kenya, like it is in the majority of African countries, is therefore well understood. Overcoming the challenges it presents must become an added priority of the government and careful assessment and use must be made of a variety of power generation technologies and that include both renewable energy technologies (RETs) as well as the conventional generation technologies. Although conventional power generation still holds the advantage for large-scale needs, it is off-grid and mini-grid generation that is necessary to meet the needs of a sparsely distributed population (such as found in Kenya's rural areas) and to enable businesses to expand their geographic spread, especially the smaller formal firms and informal businesses that are unable to absorb the costs of generator power as previously discussed.

In March 2011, the International Atomic Energy Agency (IAEA) approved Kenya's application for its first nuclear power station which is to be a 35,000 megawatt facility to be built at an estimated cost of the approximate equivalent of US$11.6 billion and completed by September 2012. Once complete, this nuclear power plant is expected to provide 90 percent of the country's electricity needs, making Kenya the world's biggest consumer of nuclear energy, by energy supply, ahead of France which derives 80 percent of its electricity from nuclear sources (Kusi, 2011).

In terms of the ports subsector, although there are ongoing attempts at establishing another port in Lamu, the Port of Mombasa remains, and probably will always be, the port of record for Kenya. The Port of Mombasa is one of the largest and busiest on the African continent. It is the largest in East Africa and the principal conduit for the movement of goods for Kenya and its neighbors including fellow members of the EAC (Burundi, Rwanda, Tanzania, and Uganda) and Eastern Democratic Republic of Congo, Southern Sudan, and Ethiopia. Mombasa is the second largest port, in sub-Saharan Africa, in terms of tonnage and containers handled after the Port of Durban (South Africa). Alongside Dar es Salaam, one of the key trading centers for the East Africa region, the Port of Mombasa is also a natural transshipment point for East Africa (Republic of Kenya, 2010b).

As seen in Figures 7.1 and 7.2, throughput at the Port of Mombasa has been increasing significantly. Cargo traffic handled at the port rose by 80 percent from 10.6 million tons to 19.12 million tons between 2002 and 2009 while containerized cargo more than doubled from 305,427 Twenty Foot Equivalent Units (TEUs) to 618,816 TEUs between 2002 and 2009 (KPA, nda, ndb). TEU is the standard measurement of port activity. The port's

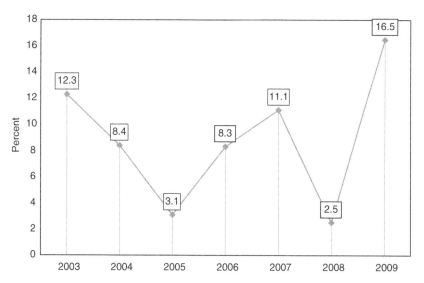

FIGURE 7.1 Port of Mombasa total throughput growth rate, 2003–09 (%)
Source: Author, based on data from KPA (nda, ndb).

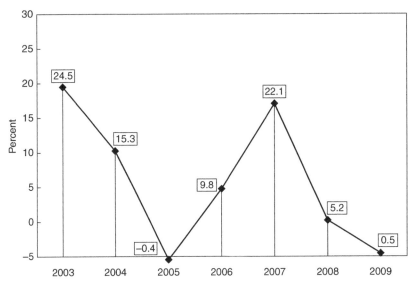

FIGURE 7.2 Port of Mombasa container throughput growth rate, 2003–09 (%)
Source: Author, based on data from KPA (nda, ndb).

traffic cargo is projected to reach about 25 million tons by 2025 (Republic of Kenya, 2010b). In order to cope with the expanded growth, it is the view of the government that the Kenya Ports Authority (KPA), which has responsibility for the management and administration of the port, will need to invest in improvement in the facilities of the current container terminal; construction of a second container terminal which would increase annual capacity of the port to about 1.8 million TEUs; and construction of other import facilities such as for bulk cargo, petroleum products, and a motor vehicle handling section (Republic of Kenya, 2010b).

The foregoing recommendations of the government are derived from the fact that the Port of Mombasa is already operating at full capacity but at low efficiency. In terms of performance indicators, the port compares relatively well with other ports in Eastern and Southern Africa but not by international standards (AICD, 2010; Republic of Kenya, 2010b; World Bank, 2010a). The KPA has embarked on some construction and upgrades. A new terminal, that will double the port's handling capacity, will have its first phase fully operational by 2013 and will handle 450,000 TEUs (KPA, 2010). The new facility will be operated by a private concessionaire thus bringing about competition and enhancing efficiency and effectiveness in service delivery at the port. In addition, to cope with the continuing container growth, before the second terminal enters into service several berths will be upgraded and converted to another container terminal which will also be offered on a concessionary basis to a private operator. It is expected that this additional capacity will attract further transshipment traffic and act as a feeder point for the Seychelles, Mauritius, Madagascar, and Zanzibar (KPA, 2010).

As noted by others, port infrastructure is also at the heart of regional integration and the Port of Mombasa is a critical link in the logistical chain and the major channel for the importation of raw materials for manufacturing in Kenya and its neighbors (KPA, ndc; Republic of Kenya, 2008; World Bank, 2010a). Consequently, the operational effectiveness of the port has a major influence on productive activities in Kenya and, hence, the cost of goods in the EAC. A port is a vital interface between land and sea transport. For the Port of Mombasa, there are three commodities flows in and out: imports, exports, and transshipments. Imports arriving in Kenya at the port generate jobs and income through the transportation of goods from the port to their next destination, further assembly or manufacture of raw or partially processed materials, and/or wholesale and retail selling of finished products in the country. Exports leaving Kenya through the port, similarly, generate jobs and income for the country from the growth, harvesting, and processing/packaging of in-state agricultural products, extraction of natural resources, assembling and manufacturing of products, and transportation of goods to the port. Transshipments include cargo arriving at the port and being moved on to another port in another country and they could have impacts similar to those of either imports or exports to the extent that their volume will determine the number of jobs created and the multiplier effects of incomes generated to both employees and the port.

Moving forward, in addition to investing in removing capacity constraints and congestion, the KPA also needs to embark on some institutional reforms to increase the efficiency of port operations. One key reform that this author recommends, and consistent with meeting the aim of the *Kenya Vision 2030*, is privatization through lease and/or concession arrangements where the government is able to maintain ownership and provide the port infrastructure, while the private sector provides port services. These arrangements should be applied to all port services. They have become standard practice across the globe including in many African countries. They take care of the economics and efficiency of port operations while maintaining country sovereignty over a vital national asset.

Addressing Kenya's infrastructure deficit will require sustained expenditure. It has been estimated that Kenya needs to spend almost US$4 billion per year through to 2015 as shown in Table 7.1. Capital investment would account for about 72 percent of that amount while operations and maintenance

TABLE 7.1: Estimated infrastructure investment needs, 2006–15 (US$ million per year)

Sector	Capital expenditure	Operations and maintenance	Total
ICT	485	44	529
Irrigation	13	2	15
Power	745	274	1,019
Transport	232	242	474
Water and sanitation	1,375	555	1,930
TOTAL	**2,850**	**1,118**	**3,968**

Source: AICD (2010).

would take up the other 28 percent. The relative sector distribution shows that the bulk of the spending needs would be for water supply/sanitation and power. These two sectors would account for almost 75 percent of the total spending requirement (AICD, 2010). Kenya's infrastructure spending requirements are very high. At just over 20 percent of the country's GDP, this would represent a little more than a doubling of the country's current infrastructure spending which is estimated at US$1.6 billion annually equivalent to 9 percent of its GDP (AICD, 2010; Foster and Brinceño-Garmendia, 2010). This, therefore, indicates that a substantial funding gap exists.

Kenya's infrastructure funding gap will need to be addressed primarily through efforts to raise additional financing. Some efforts in that regard are underway by the government including such methods as the issuance of infrastructure bonds which have proven to be very attractive investments and, consequently, successful in terms of their subscription. Nonetheless, given the order of magnitude of the annual infrastructure spending requirements, there is need to mobilize other sources of investment capital and more needs to be done to attract private investment and PPPs, in particular private participation in infrastructure (PPI).

There is no hard-and-fast definition of PPPs, P3s, or Ps[3] as they are sometimes referred to. It broadly refers to long-term, contractual partnerships between public and private sector agencies, especially targeted toward financing, designing, implementing, and operating infrastructure facilities services that are traditionally provided by the public sector. Recently, the Government of India proposed a definition of PPPs, which seems to best capture the essence of the concept, as follows:

> PPP means an arrangement between a government or statutory entity or government owned entity on one side and a private sector entity on the other, for the provision of public assets and/or related services for

public benefit, through investments being made by and/or management undertaken by the private sector entity for a specified time period, where there is substantial risk sharing with the private sector and the private sector receives performance linked payments that conform (or are benchmarked) to specified, pre-determined and measurable performance standards. (Government of India, 2010: 6)

The most industrialized country in Africa—the Republic of South Africa—defines PPP as a contract between a public sector institution/municipality and a private party, in which the private party assumes substantial financial, technical, and operational risk in the design, financing, building, and operation of a project (Republic of South Africa, nd). Two types of PPPs are specifically defined: (1) where the private party performs an institutional/municipal function; and (2) where the private party acquires the use of State/municipal property for its own commercial purposes. However, a PPP may also be a hybrid of these two types but payment in any scenario involves one of three mechanisms: (1) the institution/municipality paying the private party for the delivery of a service; or (2) the private party collecting fees or charges from users of a service; or (3) a combination of the two (Republic of South Africa, nd).

In 2009, the Kenya government, through the Minister of Finance, issued the official regulations on PPPs pursuant to the powers conferred by the Public Procurement and Disposal Act, 2005. Those regulations defined PPP as follows:

Public private partnership means an agreement between a procuring entity and a private party under which

(a) the private party undertakes to perform a public function or provide a service on behalf of the procuring entity;

(b) the private party receives a benefit for performing the function, either by way of: (1) compensation from a public fund; (2) charges or fees collected by the private party from users or customers of a service provided to them; or (3) combination of such compensation and such charges and fees;

(c) the private party is generally liable for risks arising from the performance depending on the terms of the agreement. (Republic of Kenya, 2009: 147–8)

Based on the foregoing the key features of PPI can be identified as:

- A private partner investing in public infrastructure, and providing related noncore services to the government or to the community on the government's behalf;

- The government retaining responsibility for the delivery of core services;
- The government and private entity working together under long-term arrangements, whereby the payments to the private sector partly depend upon its continuing to deliver the specified services to the agreed performance standards.

Expanding the private sector role allows public agencies to tap private sector technical, management, and financial resources in new ways to achieve certain public agency benefits (Ncube, 2010). The use of PPI, or PPPs in general, provides a number of benefits for both governments and taxpayers alike. Since they operate at the boundary of the public and private sectors (not being fully privatized assets and services), from a political standpoint, they represent a third way in which governments can deliver some key public services to the people. The principal benefits to governments and taxpayers are the following:

- *Increased Investment in Public Infrastructure*—Investments in public infrastructure have traditionally been funded by government and, in many cases, have added to levels of overall public debt. PPI can reduce a government's capital costs, helping to bridge the gap between the need for infrastructure and a government's financial capacity.
- *Value for Money*—By taking advantage of private sector innovation, experience and flexibility, PPI can often deliver services more cost-effectively than traditional approaches. The resulting savings can then be used to fund other needed services. The forms that value for money can take include lower construction costs, lower operating costs, and perhaps even more efficient maintenance in the long run than comparable public sector projects. Value for money is the ultimate test and underlying rationale for engaging PPI.
- *Reduced Public Sector Risk*—By transferring to the private partner those risks that can be better managed by that private partner. The ability to transfer certain risks to the private partner has a value because it eliminates risks for governments and taxpayers. For example, a company that specializes in building and/or operating hydro dams may be better positioned than a government to manage risks associated with the changing demands of hydro dam design and engineering. Risk can take many forms including those pertaining to design and construction, financing, operations and maintenance, market and revenue, political, legal, environmental, and *force majeure*.
- *Improved Budget Certainty*—Transferring risk to the private sector can reduce the potential for government cost overruns from unforeseen

circumstances during project development or service delivery. Services are provided at a predictable cost, as set out in contract agreements. The elimination of these quantifiable risks by a government therefore provides greater certainty in its future financial commitments.

- *Better Use of Assets*—Private sector partners are motivated to use facilities fully, and to make the most of commercial opportunities to maximize returns on their investments. This can result in higher levels of service, greater accessibility, and reduced occupancy and carrying costs for the public sector. In general, costs can be driven down through increased efficiency from the use of the private sector.
- *Quicker Project Delivery*—Making use of the private partner's increased flexibility and access to resources allows for quicker execution of investments after contracts are signed.
- *Improved Service Delivery*—By allowing both sectors (public and private) to do what they do best, expectations for access to more and better service can be met. The core business of government is to set policy and serve the public. It is better positioned to do that when the private sector is given responsibility for noncore functions such as operating and maintaining hydro dams. (Gerrard, 2001; Ncube, 2010; Partnerships British Columbia, 2003; Webb and Pulle, 2002)

PPI and PPPs can be formulated in many types and they differ by the extent of the risk that each party assumes. Below is a list of the more popular types of PPI/PPPs used globally. A good discussion of these can be found in Grimsey and Lewis (2007), NCPPP (nd), Savas (2000); Sluger and Satterfield (2010), and Webb and Pulle (2002):

- Lease-Develop-Operate (LDO)
- Build-Own-Maintain (BOM)
- Design Build (DB)
- Build-Own-Operate- Transfer (BOOT)
- Design-Build-Maintain (DBM)
- Build-Own-Operate (BOO)
- Design-Build-Operate (DBO)
- Operations and Maintenance (O&M)
- Design-Build-Finance-Operate-Maintain-Transfer (DBFOMT)
- Build-Operate-Transfer (BOT)
- Design-Build-Operate-Maintain (DBOM)
- Design-Build-Finance-Operate (DBFO)
- Design-Build-Finance-Operate-Maintain (DBFOM)
- Operations, Maintenance and Management (OMM)

For Kenya, although the country allows for many other types of PPP arrangements, but which would require Cabinet approval, its regulations on PPPs currently permit only PPP arrangements that are categorized as: (1) a management contract; (2) a lease; (3) a concession; (4) a BOOT; and (5) a BOO (Republic of Kenya, 2009).

As we are reminded by the World Bank (2008), Kenya has used PPI, in all of its major infrastructure subsectors, for leveraging public resources and donor funding, and improving the efficiency of these subsectors. Consequently, the country has some experience in that regard. From 1990 to 2007, for example, PPI in Kenya brought in a little more than US$3.6 billion in investment spending from a total of 17 projects (World Bank, 2008). During that period, the telecommunications sector accounted for the majority of the investment commitments with more than 70 percent. Since 2007, a number of PPI project contracts have been signed covering the power, roads, and port subsectors, for example.

Undoubtedly, Kenya needs to explore and exploit PPI much more aggressively. In fact, after several years of consideration and discussion on the establishment of a PPP Unit within the Ministry of Finance (see, e.g., Ong'olo, 2006; World Bank, 2008), the government established, in 2009, a Public Private Partnership Steering Committee whose Secretariat is in the Ministry of Finance. This PPP Steering Committee has been vested with the following functions:

(1) Spearhead the public private partnership process and promote understanding and awareness of PPPs among key stakeholder groups;
(2) Review challenges constraining the participation or realization of the full benefits expected from PPPs, and formulate time-bound solutions to address the challenges and to create an enabling environment;
(3) Establish PPP standards, guidelines and procedures including development of standard procedures for conceptualization, identification, prioritization, development, assessment of PPP projects and development of standardized bid documents;
(4) Review direct and indirect liabilities and assess contingent liability risk exposure of the Government and advice on the acceptable levels of direct and indirect liabilities;
(5) Ensure that all proposed PPP projects are consistent with the country's national priorities outlined in various policy documents;
(6) Coordinate with the PPOA established under the Act to ensure that all tender-phase activities of PPP projects conform to procurement best practices;
(7) Approve PPP projects submitted to the Committee in accordance with the provisions of the PPP regulations. (Republic of Kenya, 2009)

The PPP Steering Committee must continue to move forward to implement its mandate in the best interests of Kenya. Whether known as PPP units or PPP Steering Committees or some other variant, institutions for facilitating and managing PPI investments are necessary for developing country governments and have recently begun to proliferate in such countries. Many countries, like Zambia, for example, have simply added PPP functions to the responsibilities of their centralized privatization units. Other countries, like South Africa, have created new specialized units to focus only on PPPs. South Africa's PPP Unit is located in its National Treasury (Ministry of Finance).

Engaging the Youth: Empowerment, Education, and Employment

Youth bulges have become a global phenomenon and Kenya is no exception to this trend. A youth bulge occurs when more than 20 percent of a country's population is composed of youth. As discussed in Chapters 1, 2, and 3, the youth bulge in Kenya presents a number of challenges for both the youth and the country. Youth represent the most abundant asset Kenya has or will have over the near future. Nonetheless, there have been a considerable number of surveys conducted and reports and studies published that invariably conclude that there are persistent risks and challenges faced by Kenyan youth that include: unemployment, marginalization, harassment by the police, and impediments in accessing essential facilities and services such as education and health care (see, e.g., Mutuku, 2009; NPI-Africa, nd; Republic of Kenya, 2006; UNDP, 2010). An excellent analytical profile providing a coherent picture of the state of youth in Kenya can also be found in Njonjo (2010).

The youth are, and will remain, a significant share of Kenya's population for the foreseeable future. Developing and implementing appropriate strategies, policies, and programs to mitigate the risks and challenges they (the youth) face must be much more of a priority for the government than it currently is. Any failure to provide appropriate opportunities for this large segment of the population could have enormous economic, political, cultural, and social consequences. Engaging the youth population fully is therefore no longer a choice but an imperative in the development process. For sure, the government of Kenya has embarked on a number of efforts to address the youth challenges. Mutuku (2009: 4) claims that "youth marginalization in Kenya has persisted since independence in spite of various policies formulated and even implemented to assist them." However, this seems exaggerated given the country's demographic history. What is evident though is that, in the last several years, the government has taken steps to engage the youth. Prior to that, the government's most notable youth intervention was the establishment of the National Youth Service in 1964 (Republic of Kenya, 2006).

Among the recent efforts was the creation of the Ministry of State for Youth Affairs (MOYA) in December 2005 to address youth concerns in the country. This had been grounded in the realization that the government may not achieve the MDGs without adequately dealing with the many socioeconomic challenges facing the Kenyan youth (Republic of Kenya, nda). In 2006, the government developed its first Kenya National Youth Policy (KNYP). The KNYP, which defined the youth as persons resident in Kenya in the age bracket of 15 to 30 years, has as its Vision a society where youth have an equal opportunity as other citizens to realize their fullest potential, productively participating in economic, social, political, cultural, and religious life without fear or favor (Republic of Kenya, 2006). The five key principles underlying the policy are: (1) respect of cultural belief systems and ethical values; (2) equity and accessibility; (3) gender inclusiveness; (4) good governance; and (5) mainstreaming youth issues (see, for greater details, Republic of Kenya, 2006).

Although aimed at all the youth in Kenya, the KNYP targets some priority groups. These are (1) youth with disability; (2) street youth; (3) youth infected with HIV/AIDS; (4) female youth; (5) the unemployed youth; and (6) out-of-school youth. The priority strategic areas are (1) employment creation; (2) health; (3) education and training; (4) sport and recreation; (5) the environment; (6) art and culture; (7) youth and the media; and (8) youth empowerment and participation in national life. Among the institutions to be created, as part of the mechanisms for implementing the KNYP, are an interministerial committee on youth comprising representatives of relevant ministries dealing with youth issues and a National Youth Council (NYC) (Republic of Kenya, 2006).

Although conceived by the government in 2006 as one of the strategies for addressing youth unemployment, a Youth Enterprise Development Fund (YEDF) was officially launched in February 2007. It was then transformed into a state cooperation in May 2007. The fund was established to:

- Provide loans for on-lending to youth-owned enterprises;
- Attract and facilitate investment in micro, small and medium enterprises' commercial infrastructure, such as business or industrial parks, stalls, markets or business incubators that will be beneficial to youth-owned enterprises;
- Support youth-oriented micro, small and medium enterprises to develop linkages with large enterprises;

- Facilitate marketing of products and services of youth-owned enterprises in both the domestic and the international markets;
- Provide funding and business development services to youth-owned or youth-focused enterprises;
- Facilitate employment of youth in the international labor market. (YEDF, nda, ndb)

Treasury allocations to the YEDF through to FY 2009/10 made for an accumulated total of approximately US$34 million. The majority of these allocations were budgeted for loans which are disbursed by the YEDF using three methods:

(1) The Constituency Youth Enterprise Scheme (C-YES) which finances projects of registered youth groups. The loans are approved by community committees at the constituency level. The maximum amount lent through this component is the approximate equivalent of US$635.

(2) The Easy Youth Enterprise Scheme (E-YES) which component finances projects of individuals who belong to groups that have completed repayment of the C-YES loan. Individuals begin with loans of the approximate equivalent of US$318 and graduate upward up to the approximate equivalent of US$1,272 after which they can access loans through financial intermediaries.

(3) Financial intermediaries that are in partnership with the YEDF. These financial intermediaries, currently totaling 32, are provided with term loans by the YEDF at 1 percent interest and they on-lend to the youth at 8 percent interest. The 7 percent difference spread is used to cover administrative costs and to mitigate losses that may arise from lending to a clientele perceived as risky. All of the risk associated with the on-lending is shouldered by the intermediaries and they can on-lend up to the approximate equivalent of US$12,720. (YEDF, nda)

As of June 2010, the YEDF had disbursed loans totaling the cumulative approximate equivalent of US$36 million to 87,281 enterprises (YEDF, nda). Loans given through financial intermediaries have a very good repayment rate of 98 percent while, for the C-YES, loan performance is considered not as high but not quantitatively stated (YEDF, nda). Measures are being taken to mitigate against low repayment rates in the C-YES component including the opening of 25 regional offices and intensified entrepreneurship training. More than 150,000 youth have so far been trained (YEDF, nda).

In March 2007, the government released its Strategic Plan (2007–12) targeting the youth. The Plan set out a road map to direct the future course of the

MOYA by articulating the mission, vision, and strategic goals and objectives as well as the strategies that the Ministry intends to follow. The intent is to help develop a country where the youth grow up knowing that they have opportunities and can make a positive contribution to society (Republic of Kenya, 2007b). The Plan's strategic themes to guide the MOYA toward achieving its vision are: (1) youth and employment; (2) youth empowerment and participation; (3) youth education and training. (4) youth and ICT; (5) youth and health; (6) youth, crime, and drugs; (7) youth and environment; and (8) youth, leisure, recreation, and community service (Republic of Kenya, 2007b).

In May 2008, the government transferred the Department of Sports, in the Ministry of Gender, Sports, Culture and Social Services, to the MOYA creating the Ministry of Youth Affairs and Sports (MOYAS) with a mandate to:

- Promote youth development by designing policies and programs that build young people's capacity to resist risk factors and enhance protective factors;
- Develop a National Youth Policy to ensure Kenyan youth participation in the development of the country;
- Facilitate establishment of a National Youth Council (NYC) to popularize the youth agenda;
- Coordinate youth organizations in the country to ensure youth development through structured organizations, collaborations and networking;
- Facilitate training and preparation of the youth for nation-building. (Republic of Kenya, ndb)

In March 2009, the President and Prime Minister launched the *Kazi Kwa Vijana* (KKV) ("Jobs or Work for Youth") program. The KKV mandate was essentially to tackle poverty/hunger and unemployment among the youth by creating employment through government-related projects. As originally conceived, the KKV was intended to afford—during a period of the triple "F" crisis (food, fuel, and financial)—immediate relief to young people by way of providing them with income support through employment in public works. Its objective was to employ 200,000–300,000 young people who are at risk of hunger and starvation. Some of the projects, especially those providing irrigation and water supply, were also intended to enhance food production in the areas most affected by drought (Isahakia, 2010).

The KKV projects are being coordinated by the Office of the Prime Minister and implemented through line Ministries. The program is being financed by the government with support from development partners. Total funding from a supplementary budget in FY 2008/09 was US$43 million and the budget allocation for FY 2009/10 was approximately US$84 million (ILO, 2010; Republic of Kenya, 2010c). Depending on the source, by the end of 2010 between 195,458 and 296,000 youths, aged 18–35 years, were said to have benefited from employment in KKV projects (Isahakia, 2010; OPM/KKV, 2011).

In 2009, the government passed the NYS Act which was assented to on December 31 and commenced on January 6, 2010. The functions of the NYC are:

- Regulate and co-ordinate activities and initiatives, relating to the youth, being undertaken by youth groups, youth-focused community-based organizations, nongovernmental organizations, civil society movements, and other organizations;
- Promote and popularize the national youth policy and other policies that affect the youth;
- Lobby for legislation on issues affecting the youth;
- Promote relations between youth organizations and other bodies both nationally and internationally with similar objectives or interests;
- Formulate operational guidelines that protect the youth against any form of abuse or manipulation;
- Act as a voice and bridge to ensure that the Government and other policy-makers are kept informed of the views and aspirations of the youth;
- Promote research, collation, and analysis of data on youth issues;
- Promote the inclusion of youth agenda in the formulation of policy by public institutions and organizations;
- Promote the inclusion of youths in decision-making bodies, boards, agencies, and other public institutions and organizations;
- Inspire and promote the spirit of unity, patriotism, volunteerism, and service among the youth;
- Promote and popularize the Youth Enterprise Development Fund and such other devolved funds targeting the youth as may be established from time to time.

In January 2010, the government released a Kenya Youth Empowerment Project (KYEP) document. This document had been necessitated to meet the World Bank requirement for the development of an Environmental and Social Management Framework (ESMF) in pursuit of financial assistance from the Bank for the KKV program (Republic of Kenya, 2010c). The ESMF is a common framework for ensuring that possible risks and impacts are prevented, minimized, or compensated. It allows a government to examine project alternatives, identify ways of improving project design, siting, planning, and implementation of preventive or mitigation measures throughout project implementation.

In May 2010, in a World Bank project update, it was stated that the development objective of the KYEP is to support the government of Kenya's efforts to increase access to youth-targeted temporary employment programs and to improve youth employability. There are three components to the project. The first is labor-intensive works and social services. This is to support the government's efforts in reducing the vulnerability of unemployed youth by expanding and enhancing the effectiveness of the KKV program. This component finances labor-intensive projects that provide income opportunities to participating youth, and at the same time, enhance the communities' access to social and economic infrastructure. The target group here is unemployed youth in the 18–35 age bracket, the same age bracket as for the current KKV program (World Bank, 2010b).

The second component of the project is private sector internships and training. This component is to improve youth employability, by providing youth with work experience and skills through the creation of internships and relevant training in the formal and informal sector. This component is a pilot that addresses the lack of skills and work experience for unemployed young people. It will provide youth, who have been out of school for at least a year, and are not working, with an opportunity to acquire relevant work experience and skills through a private sector internship and training program. It will support three activities: (1) creation of internships in the private sector; (2) provision of training relevant to their work experience; and (3) monitoring and evaluation to capture lessons from the pilot (KEPSA, 2010; World Bank, 2010b).

The Kenya Private Sector Alliance (KEPSA) has been chosen to implement this second component. KEPSA is an apex body and single voice of the private sector in Kenya for engaging in public policy and influencing public policy formulation. It brings the private sector in the country under one umbrella, positioning the private sector as an equal partner with government in pursuit of an enabling business environment (KEPSA, nd). KEPSA will provide internships and training for 10,800 youth. The internships will last for periods of 4–6 months, with 50 percent of each internship being spent in the workplace and the remaining time being made up of training with a third party training provider. Internships will be provided in the six sectors of growth identified in the *Kenya Vision 2030*: (1) Energy; (2) Finance; (3) Tourism; (4) ICT; (5) Manufacturing; (6) MSMEs. For the first cohort of youth to be selected for Nairobi, there were more than 9,000 applications, of which 5,583 were found to be eligible for the 900 internships that were available to this first group (KEPSA, 2011).

The third component of the project is capacity and policy development. The primary objective here is to enhance the capacity of the MOYAS to implement the national youth policy and increase the institutional capacity for youth policy planning. This will be accomplished through activities in three areas: (1) training of MOYAS staff, particularly the district youth officers; (2) communication activities to increase awareness of the project; and (3) policy development, through the provision of technical assistance (KEPSA, 2010; World Bank, 2010b).

The foregoing clearly demonstrates that the Kenyan government has been advancing and implementing several policy frameworks and programs to tackle the challenges confronting the Kenyan youth. Nonetheless, the government itself has also recognized that some of its youth initiatives have encountered their own share of implementation problems. The Permanent Secretary in the OPM observed that the KKV program, for example, had experienced a lack of timely allocation of financial resources from the center to the project units on the ground, reporting by these units on project status and emerging issues back to the center as well as sensitization of various stakeholders (Isahakia, 2010).

Others have also weighed in with criticisms. In a letter to the press, Sindabi (2011: 16) was of the view that "The *Kazi Kwa Vijana* project initiated to create jobs for the youth seems like a political gimmick to hoodwink Kenyans the government is concerned about the plight of the youths." He further said that "it was alleged some officials demanded bribes, tribalism and nepotism was rife. Only road construction jobs were available and favored men." Muthee (2010: 1) was categorical that:

> Kenya's KKV and YEDF fall short. Their activities overlap, and their objectives are too broad, which makes them unachievable within a reasonable time-frame. They are also constrained by heavy government control . . . As a consequence, the programs are burdened by politics rather than professionalism.

Similar sentiments were echoed by the then US Ambassador to Kenya as he announced the establishment of a US government US$10 million Youth Innovate for Change Fund that will provide youth with an opportunity to access capital for economic development. The fund is youth-owned, led, and managed, and will expand economic opportunities for all Kenyan youth. This fund is in addition to the US$45 million "Yes Youth Can" youth empowerment program the US government is also funding in support of activities of the National Youth Forum—a controversial intervention that has been criticized by several politicians including President Kibaki. The Ambassador said:

> We have heard loud and clear from you [the youth] that government programs like *Kazi Kwa Vijana*, the Youth Enterprise Development Fund, and the Youth Employment Marshall Plan have not proved effective or sufficient to create real economic opportunities, because they are not owned by youth and are not transparent. (Ranneberger, 2010: 15)

The government is aware of these criticisms and concerns and has taken steps to revamp some of its initiatives. For example, in March 2011, the government announced that the stalled KKV program was being revived with an approximate US$60 million cash injection (PMPS, 2011). Prime Minister Odinga stated: "We have received the funds from the World Bank to re-launch the programme but this time we have re-organized and revamped the KKV" (PMPS, 2011: 10). He said further that "the revamped phase incorporated sustainable projects that create employment." To that end, the KKV program was relaunched in April 2011, as KKV II, with supposedly more stringent measures being put in place to prevent mismanagement, fraud, and corruption and ensure accountability. This second phase of the KKV is expected to entail 1,200 projects for empowering youth aged between 18 and 35 years, with lifelong skills, internships, and long-term employment. A total of 230,000 youths are slated to be employed under this revamped program (*The Standard*, 2011).

However, despite the various youth initiatives that have been embarked upon by the government, and for which much credit must be given, there is still room for a greater integration of the three key areas that are critical to the success of programs designed to provide opportunities for the youth. These key areas are the three E's of youth engagement and development—Empowerment, Education, and Employment. When fully integrated into youth policy frameworks, these three areas offer the best possibility for arriving at outcomes that give the youth a potentially good start for better long-term livelihoods. It is a losing proposition to empower the youth to access education and training, for example, and not provide sufficient and appropriate education and training facilities. Similarly, when those youth access and acquire education and training, they must thereafter be able to find appropriate employment.

Empowerment

Empowerment is both an end and a means. Just because all of the conditions of empowerment are not in place in Kenya, it does not mean the society cannot empower young people to help bring those conditions about. What should be obvious, however, is that the youth cannot be expected to accomplish the job on their own without assistance, nor should empowerment be considered a responsibility solely of government. Consequently, empowerment does not entail shifting of responsibilities onto the shoulders of the youth. And, some of those responsibilities must be shouldered by nonstate stakeholders such as NGOs, donors, and the private sector.

Empowerment means creating and supporting the enabling conditions under which young people can act on their own behalf, and on their own terms, rather than at the direction of others. It can be regarded as an attitudinal, structural, and cultural process whereby young people gain the ability, authority, and confidence to make decisions and implement change in their own lives and the lives of other people, including both youth and adults. In fact, the youth can be considered as empowered when they themselves acknowledge that they have created, or can create, choices in life, are aware of the implications of those choices, make informed decisions freely, take actions based on those decisions, and accept responsibility for the consequences of those actions (Commonwealth Secretariat, 2007).

Empowerment is, therefore, a process that strengthens and activates the capacity of the youth to satisfy their own needs, solve their own problems, and acquire the necessary resources to take control over their lives. Empowering the youth is important because empowerment leads to competence and confidence which, in turn, are linked to self-esteem and self-actualization. Based on a review of the literature and case studies, there are three factors which can be identified as influencing the accomplishment of empowerment by the youth that are applicable to the Kenyan situation.

These factors, which need to be given serious consideration in Kenya's policies, programs, and strategies for youth empowerment, are noted below. It is also important to indicate the interrelated and dynamic nature of these factors:

- *Experiencing an Environment of Safety, Closeness, and Appreciation*—A welcoming and safe social environment where youth feel valued, respected, encouraged, and supported is a key element of youth empowerment. Such an environment allows the youth opportunities to express their own creativity and be free to voice their opinions in decision-making. It also allows for the promotion of the positive potential and actual achievements of the youth (Cargo et al., 2003; DiBenedetto, 1992; Jennings et al., 2006).
- *Meaningful Participation and Engagement*—Participating in activities relevant to their own lives allow the youth to contribute to more sustained

and prolonged engagement, necessary for, among other things, analysis of issues critical to their well-being and for skill development and overall positive development of self-identity, an increased sense of self-worth, and enhanced self-efficacy (Cargo et al., 2003; Chinman and Linney, 1998; Flores, 2008; Jennings et al., 2006; Subramaniam and Moncloa, 2010).

● *Experiencing and Exercising Power*—The experiencing and exercising of power is at the root of empowerment and this can only take place through shared leadership (and power). The youth must be allowed to equitably share power with adults to result in youth-determined and youth-directed activities and decision-making. In practice, this is sometimes difficult to achieve. Enacting shared leadership with the youth therefore takes effort, commitment, and positive insight about the significance of shared power and the acceptance of the notion of non-authoritarian adult leadership (Cargo et al., 2003; Jennings et al., 2006; Lansdown, 2001).

When these three factors are fully integrated within youth planning and programs, youth empowerment tends to be much more of a realized objective and the benefits to the youth and the society at large are enormous (Anderson and Sandmann, 2009; Huebner, 1998; Jennings et al., 2006). Through empowerment, Kenyan youth can be provided with opportunities to develop some of the competencies they need to become successful adults. Youth are not truly empowered if they do not have the capacity to address the various structures, processes, social values, institutions, and practices that confront them daily. Successful youth empowerment leads to the youth gaining control and mastery of the social, economic, and political elements that influence and affect their lives, in order to improve equity and the quality of life through to adulthood (Anderson and Sandmann, 2009; Jennings et al., 2006). Societies that foster youth empowerment do, generally, exhibit positive youth development.

One other variable to consider here, in the quest for youth empowerment in Kenya, is the 2010 constitution. In the Kenya 2010 constitution, in the Bill of Rights, there is a specific application of rights for the youth. If applied as it reads, it provides not only the best policy guidance of what needs to be done to successfully accomplish youth engagement and development, but also a firm legal foundation for challenging the government if it fails to do so. The constitution states that:

The State shall take measures, including affirmative action programs, to ensure that the youth:

● Access relevant education and training;
● Have opportunities to associate, be represented and participate in political, social, economic and other spheres of life;

- Access employment;
- Are protected from harmful cultural practices and exploitation. (Republic of Kenya, 2010e: Article 55)

In addition, the 2010 constitution also stipulates youth representation in legislative bodies. For the Senate, there should be "two members, being one man and one woman, representing youth" (Republic of Kenya, 2010e: Article 98c). For the National Assembly, there shall be at least one member, nominated by parliamentary political parties, to represent the youth. The youth will also be represented in all 47 county assemblies as prescribed in the Act of Parliament pertaining to county assemblies.

Education

Education is the next important area for engaging the youth and for youth development. In fact, youth access to relevant education and training is also entrenched in the 2010 constitution. Beyond building human capital to raise worker productivity, another institutional function of education and training is to provide young people with what they need to become effective agents of change. In order to find a decent job, for example, Kenyan youth need to develop a range of skills and knowledge that are typically gained through education and training. Moreover, a reduction in youth inequality is determined, to a significant extent, by the quality of education and training that youth receive (UN-HABITAT, 2010). The association between the level of education and training, on the one hand, and opportunity and inclusion, on the other hand, is statistically significant and that corroborates the fact that better educated and trained people enjoy better access to opportunities than others.

Providing the relevant education and training is a critical factor for youth engagement and development. What the majority of the Kenyan youth need is access to skills training. In other words, what is relevant is not access to formal academic curricula (which is in abundance) but access to acquire appropriate skills to fit the educational background and demand of the majority of the youth as well as the Kenyan job market both now and in the future. Skills-based training is an area that must be scaled up by the government. It has been a neglected area of education and training policy. The *MTP 2008-2012*, for example, noted that the training being provided by the Technical, Industrial, Vocational, Entrepreneurship Training (TIVET) institutions "has been hindered by inadequate facilities and inappropriate curriculum, hence most graduates at this level lack appropriate skills" (Republic of Kenya, 2008: 90).

Furthermore, it has also been acknowledged that there is a mismatch between level and type of skills imparted by training institutions and the requirements of the labor market, which need to be realigned in order to meet the demands of the economy and improve youth opportunities to participate effectively in said economy (Republic of Kenya, 2008). Skills-based training is best pursued through the universally-tried and proven conduit of technical and vocational education and training (TVET) institutions. Globally, the TVET model remains an effective means of empowering the youth to engage in productive and sustainable livelihoods and is quite familiar to Kenyans. TVET is also an important element in support of capacity development activities that also have a strong consideration for the national labor market (Hope, 2011).

As recommended by two international organizations covering this field, TVET

> is used as a comprehensive term referring to those aspects of the educational process involving, in addition to general education, the study of technologies and related sciences, and the acquisition of practical skills, attitudes, understanding and knowledge relating to occupations in various sectors of economic and social life. (UNESCO and ILO, 2002: 7)

TVET is further understood to be:

- An integral part of general education;
- A means of preparing for occupational fields and for effective participation in the world of work;
- An aspect of lifelong learning and a preparation for responsible citizenship;
- An instrument for promoting sound sustainable development;
- A method of facilitating poverty alleviation. (UNESCO and ILO, 2002)

In its broadest definition, TVET includes technical education, vocational education, vocational training, on-the-job training, or apprenticeship training, delivered in a formal and non-formal way (NICHE, 2010). Technical education primarily refers to theoretical vocational preparation of students for jobs that are based in manual or practical activities, traditionally non-theoretical and totally related to a specific trade, occupation, or vocation (NICHE, 2010). TVET is therefore particularly focused on producing readily employable skilled personnel for the labor market. It provides students with the competencies, skills, and attitudes needed for the workplace and thereby facilitates access to employment.

In recent years, the terms "skills development," "skills-based training," or "skilling" have emerged in the development literature as concepts that are synonymous to TVET, as defined above, demonstrating the greater awareness and need for vocational education to provide general skills. Moreover, TVET is regarded as an instrument in creating new employment opportunities and income-generating activities in both the formal and informal sectors of an economy. These trends are likely to improve the transition of the youth to work and their participation in lifelong learning (Atchoarena, 2007).

As noted before, Kenya has experience with the TVET model of youth engagement and development. The country has made deliberate efforts to structure and deliver TVET education through establishment of TVET institutions either by the government or the private sector (Nyerere, 2009). As early as the 1950s, industrial depots were upgraded to vocational schools and, by the early 1960s, they were further converted to secondary vocational schools (Simiyu, 2009). By 1970, TVET in Kenya had expanded tremendously with many institutions across the country providing post-secondary school technical training through community managed *Harambee* (let us pull together) Institutes of Technology (Ngerechi, 2003). By 2007, TVET student enrolment exceeded 76,000 (Nyerere, 2009). In March 2011, there were some 408 fully validated and registered TVET institutions with a composition of 330 (81%) being private and 78 (19%) being public (Republic of Kenya, 2011a). There are also an additional 146 private TVET institutions that are provisionally registered by the government (Republic of Kenya, 2011b). This means that, in the first quarter of 2011, Kenya had a total of 554 TVET institutions that could legally offer training to the youth and others.

Kenya was also among the first countries in Africa to introduce aspects of entrepreneurship education in its education and training systems, and this has helped to increase awareness among TVET graduates about the current demands of the employment sector (Simiyu, 2010). The basic rationale was to create awareness among the youth of the potential options available in the work environment. Entrepreneurship is one of the guiding principles considered as a major driving force for TVET in Kenya (Simiyu, 2010). It is an important consideration given the fact that the government expects the majority of the youth to be employed in the informal sector as discussed in Chapter 3. By integrating entrepreneurship into the TVET curriculum, trainees are taught business techniques such as costing, pricing, preparing financial statements, keeping business records, marketing, preparing business plans, and so on (Simiyu, 2010).

The overall government policy on TVET is to enhance skills development and the critical stock of the country's human resource. The aim of public investment in this subsector is therefore to enhance skills development for increased productivity in order to stimulate economic growth and employment creation (Republic of Kenya, 2005b). The objectives of TVET in Kenya are to:

- Provide increased training opportunities for school leavers that will enable them to be self-supporting;
- Develop practical skills and attitudes which will lead to income-earning activities in the urban and rural areas;
- Provide technical knowledge, vocational skills and attitudes necessary for manpower development;
- Produce skilled Artisans, Craftsmen, Technicians and Technologies for both formal and informal sectors. (Republic of Kenya, 2005b)

Given the lessons of experience with TVET in Kenya, the way forward suggests the following four recommendations, applicable to both public and private institutions delivering TVET:

(1) *Targeted Funding/Investment*—Funding for, and investment in, TVET institutions need to be priority targeted at ensuring that the required facilities, tools, and equipment (infrastructure) are in place for an effective learning experience. Particular attention should be given therefore to the material resources required for TVET. Priorities should be established with respect to current needs and planning for future expansion and technological improvements. Adequate funding should also be sought, from all possible sources, for recurrent spending for supplies and maintenance and repair of equipment.

(2) *Curriculum Development*—Some refocusing of the TVET curricula is required to match current labor market demands. In fact, no TVET curriculum should be static. It must be a dynamic thing that can be occasionally revised to be relevant to the existing economic and market situation prevailing in the country. It should also conform to the principle that technical and vocational education, as preparation for an occupational field, should provide the foundation for productive and satisfying careers while designed as comprehensive and inclusive to accommodate the needs of all potential students with particular emphasis on motivating girls and women. In fact, for the female gender, their equal access and participation should be ensured.

(3) *Internships/Apprenticeships/On-the-Job Training (OJT)*—Internships, apprenticeships and OJT provide for hands-on proficiency skills being acquired that are applicable to a specific profession or job. An internship

is a system of OJT, similar to an apprenticeship, providing opportunities for experience to be gained in a given field. This approach to learning should be built into TVET curricula. In this regard, TVET institutions should develop a cooperative and collaborative relationship with the KEPSA and formalize programs for internships, apprenticeships, and OJT as integral elements of the learning experience that make learners more attractive to potential or current employers upon completion of their training programs. By providing internships and apprenticeships, employers are also able to identify future employees who can hit the ground running after their training is completed.

(4) *Instructional Staff*—To ensure the quality and the integrity of the instruction and learning process in TVET institutions, it is also necessary to pay attention to the recruitment and retention of the instructional staff. This requires, in the first instance, that sufficiently attractive—competitive in the Kenyan context—emoluments packages and conditions of service be offered. If facilities, materials, and equipment are of the adequate standard but the instructors are not, then students will be shortchanged and become disadvantaged in the job market. If, on the other hand, the instructors are of the adequate standard but the facilities, materials, and equipment are not, then the instructors may be inclined to become demoralized and either leave or stay on and perform with insufficient effort and enthusiasm. Either way the students will be shortchanged and then disadvantaged in the job market.

Employment

The final key area of youth engagement and development is employment. Having been sufficiently empowered or not, and having accessed education and training or not, the youth still need to find jobs to actualize their livelihood through to adulthood. In Kenya, as this book has shown, youth unemployment is a major development challenge. The government has attempted to tackle this challenge through several initiatives that include (1) the KKV, previously discussed; (2) participating in the consultative forum of the Youth Entrepreneurship and Sustainability (YES)-Kenya Network, which is a national youth multistakeholder network involved in promoting youth entrepreneurship and employment in Kenya; (3) entertaining the notion of a Youth Employment Marshall Plan in 2009 which was to incorporate KKV projects: (4) organizing and hosting a National Youth Employment Conference in 2009 whose objectives included the formulation of policy recommendations to provide an enabling environment for youth employment creation, and the identification of areas and measures to create large-scale employment opportunities for the youth in the short-term; and (5) actively supporting the March 2010 launch, and partnering thereafter, in the efforts of the Kenya Youth Empowerment and Employment Initiative (KYEEI), which is an initiative—under the leadership of Africa Nazarene University (ANU)—whose goals are to prepare youth for the world of work and to facilitate job creation in Kenya and the East Africa region, if possible.

Not surprisingly, in a recent survey of youth on their expectations and priorities, 45 percent of them ranked job opportunities as their top priority (Njonjo, 2010). Other surveys have similarly confirmed that the leading challenge faced by youth respondents was unemployment (see, e.g., NPI-Africa, nd). Employment creation therefore looms large in strategies for youth engagement and development. Essentially, there are two methods which need to be emphasized and pursued for job creation in Kenya. These are (1) economic growth and (2) the establishment of a conducive environment for entrepreneurship in the informal sector.

The first, economic growth, is a guaranteed method of employment creation despite a lag that necessarily accompanies such growth. Though growth is not youth specific, it can have a significant impact on youth by creating more and better jobs. In fact, economic growth and job creation benefit most participants in the labor market, youth included. "When labor demand is strong, youth employment and labor force participation for both males and females increases while the unemployment rate for youth tends to go down" (World Bank, 2009: 16). This will be of major benefit to the youth, therefore, given their considerable proportion among the unemployed as well as among new labor force entrants.

Economic growth generates job opportunities and, hence, stronger demand for labor, the main and often the sole asset of the youth. In turn, increasing employment has been crucial in delivering higher growth. This relationship between growth and employment remains robustly positive despite recent signs of "jobless growth" in Kenya and elsewhere. But even in circumstances of a weakening relationship between growth and employment, this may suggest a stronger rationale for a higher growth strategy in the future. Furthermore, such a trend may mask improvements in productivity that could provide the basis for the creation of even more job opportunities in the future (DfID, 2008). Consequently, the post-2008 economic recovery in Kenya constitutes a sound framework for expanding employment in the country.

However, generating and sustaining economic growth requires that certain conditions be present. First, despite the use of public employment programs, such as the KKV, to provide jobs for the youth, the public sector is not an engine of economic growth and, therefore, cannot create and sustain job growth over the long term. The role of the public sector is to provide an enabling environment for the private sector to expand both in size and economic activities undertaken. The importance and benefits of private enterprise-led growth were previously discussed. The role of the public sector, and the Kenyan government more specifically, is to create a climate which ensures, to the extent possible and within the rule of law, political stability and security; that needed infrastructure is in place as discussed above; and an operative sound macroeconomic policy framework encompassing elements, already discussed also, such as an improved regulatory and tax climate for business corporations, an increased pace of privatization, and an export and savings mobilization orientation. Growth is best sustained when there is predictability in both the policy and physical environment which, in turn, encourages private investors to make long-term commitments.

Finally, a similarly conducive environment for economic activities, through entrepreneurship, also needs to be created in the informal sector. As this book has shown, the informal economy is an unavoidable reality in Kenya, very much like the country's urbanization. Moreover, the government has embraced and earmarked this sector as the primary contributor to employment creation for the youth. And, indeed, this book has also provided evidence which suggests that informal sector employment should not be seen as the disadvantaged counterpart of the formal sector but as a legitimate alternative, one that fosters entrepreneurial ambition. In fact, the development of MSMEs, as the government also advocates, must be regarded as a credible springboard for local entrepreneurial activities and for encouraging the youth to shift from that of job seekers to job creators.

Encouraging and supporting youth entrepreneurship will require a full court press by both the government and donors. Beyond the initiatives already discussed above in this respect, more will need to be done. The youth bulge in Kenya, and the rest of Africa for that matter, has emerged as the single most important development challenge of this modern era. It must, therefore, be treated as such. Large numbers of idle youth creates a ticking time bomb for the country especially when considered in the context of the 2008 postelection violence. Idle youth, whether out of work or not in school, are vulnerable to exploitation and incitement. More funds need to be made available and more accessible to potential youth entrepreneurs. By encouraging informal sector enterprises to grow, without encouraging and encountering illegal activities and tax evasion, several productive jobs can be created for the youth (World Bank, 2009).

One often-cited success story, which can be a good example for Kenya, is Brazil during the Presidency of Lula da Silva. Through a combination of sound macroeconomic policy that included the three commitments of the control of inflation (even with high interest rates if necessary), a free exchange rate mechanism, and fiscal responsibility (in a politically stable and secure environment), Brazil was able to create more than 1.3 million jobs annually during 2004–10 and 19 million people made it out of poverty during 2002–10 (Ituassu, 2010; Luna, 2010). There is no reason why Kenya cannot achieve some closely similar results.

State Capability, Good Governance, and the Rule of Law

Prior to the postelection violence in 2008, the international community had seen Kenya as an island of stability in an unstable region, though its record on corruption was poor. Since a power-sharing government was put in place in 2008, the country was pulled back from the brink, more or less, and there were concerted efforts at peacebuilding and consolidation of economic progress. A new 2010 constitution was hammered out and overwhelmingly approved by the citizenry. Since the constitution was promulgated, however, the outcomes from two factors, that have emerged, can potentially influence and possibly threaten Kenya's future stability and development promise in the run-up to the 2012 elections and beyond.

The first is the constitutional requirement for elections in 2012, and every five years thereafter. These constitutionally mandated elections are now required for a number of existing and newly created (under the 2010 constitution) national and subnational politico-executive-legislative positions including President and Deputy President, Members of the National Assembly, Members of the Senate, County Governors and Deputy Governors, and Members of County Assemblies. Not surprisingly, there has been much jockeying for these positions and this has led to somewhat unprincipled and divisive competition for political power by members of the political class who, invariably, claim to speak for unified ethnic communities—a state of affairs defined as political tribalism (Klopp, 2002; Lonsdale, 1994, 2008)—in justification of their words and deeds.

Unfortunately, in many African countries, including Kenya, the main criteria by which sociopolitical groups define and identify themselves is rooted in ethnicity rather than class. It is through ethnic identification that competition for influence in the State and in the allocation of resources takes place, instead of it being a contest between the "haves" and "have nots" (Rawlinson, 2003). Although it is not the case that all Kenyan politicians, and other elites too, are unprincipled profiteers who exploit ethnic appeals for personal advantage without regard to the wider consequences, it is enough that some are. This represents a challenge created by those whose only appeal is to ethnicity through which they attempt to demonstrate their popularity, rivalry, and/or competition stemming from their own self-importance.

Every election since the multi-party system was allowed in 1991 has witnessed widespread violence. Such violence has been linked to the long-standing grievances about the highly unsatisfactory fulfillment of economic and social rights and failures of governance that are exploited during election campaigns and organized along the lines of ethnicity (HRW, 2008; KNCHR, 2008; Le Bas, 2010; UNHCHR, 2008). Underlying this state of affairs is the fact that Kenya has a history of widespread corruption and systemic abuse of office by public officials that has resulted in a situation in which political contests became all the more impassioned because of what is at stake. "Those who [are able to grab] political power can benefit from widespread abuses including impunity for political manipulation of violence, criminal theft of land, and the corrupt misuse of public resources—indulgences which occur at the expense of groups who are out of power" (HRW, 2008: 11).

Political violence—which relates to acts of violence that are undertaken primarily as a means of achieving political influence or power—in Kenya has been used to reinforce and/or activate ethnic cleavages. Elections tend to trigger heightened group insecurity and concerns about the intentions of other groups, thus leading to a fuelling of violent behavior connected to the political manipulation of identity (Hansen, 2009; Le Bas, 2010). Over time, it has resulted in the emergence of what Le Bas (2010: 8) refers to as "an opportunistic and well-institutionalized economy of political violence." However, it must also be noted that although the political manipulation of ethnicity is almost a tradition in Kenyan politics that is more visible during election campaigns, its violent element is also known to exist as an everyday phenomenon usually perpetrated through criminal groups (Hansen, 2009).

The second factor pertains to the summonses for criminal responsibility that were handed down by Prosecutor Luis Moreno-Ocampo of the International Criminal Court (ICC) in March 2011 against six Kenyans in relationship to their alleged role in the postelection violence of 2007–08 (ICC, nd). Dubbed as the "Ocampo Six," three of these Kenyans are prominent politicians. At the date of their summonses, one (Uhuru Kenyatta) was the leader of the Kenya African National Union (KANU), one of the large established political parties in Kenya, son of the first post-independence leader and President of Kenya (Jomo Kenyatta), and a Deputy Prime Minister and Minister of Finance; two others (William Ruto and Henry Kosgey) were deputy leader and chairman, respectively, of the Orange Democratic Movement (ODM), another major political party—of which Prime Minister Raila Odinga is the leader—and former government Ministers who had, prior, been suspended from their Cabinet positions pursuant to alleged corruption charges against them. Of the other three, one (Hussein Ali) was Postmaster General and a former Commissioner of Police; another (Francis Muthaura) was Head of the Civil Service and Secretary to the Cabinet; and the other (Joshua Sang) was a radio personality.

It should be noted here that KANU is also a member of the Party of National Unity (PNU) which was originally founded as a political coalition of parties by President Kibaki in September 2007 to contest the December 2007 elections. The PNU has since become a political party in its own right headed by President Kibaki. The grand coalition government that emerged after the postelection violence in 2008 is, therefore, composed of the PNU and the ODM. The PNU was severely trounced by the ODM in the December 2007 elections. The ODM won more than twice as many parliamentary seats than the PNU (99 versus 43 for the PNU).

The issuance of the ICC summonses has stirred some raw emotions. The government and Parliament, within and among them, became split on how to respond. Having foregone an opportunity to establish a local tribunal to investigate and prosecute those who were criminally responsible for the postelection violence, in favor of the ICC taking that role—with slogans such as "Don't be vague, let's go to the Hague" or "Don't be vague, we want the Hague"—three years later, after the ICC had indeed taken over the cases and summonses were handed down against very prominent individuals, some members of both the executive and parliament became a bit less enthusiastic and the new slogan became "Let's not be vague, avoid the Hague."

The result was the surfacing of attempts by one group of members in the coalition government—led by President Kibaki—to have the cases deferred until such time that Kenya had demonstrated its capacity to handle the cases in Kenya. What became termed as "shuttle diplomacy" took off with representations being made to, and support being sought from, the AU and the UN, among others. In fact, an application was filed by the government before the ICC seeking to challenge the ICC's jurisdiction over the cases as well as the admissibility of the cases before the ICC; a mission that, ultimately, failed. So what began as "shuttle diplomacy" was soon dubbed by the media as "shattered diplomacy." Not seemingly considered was the view of the ordinary Kenyans, 61 percent of whom in April 2011 wanted the "Ocampo Six" tried by the ICC up slightly from 60 percent in December 2010 (see, e.g., Njagih, 2011), and, even more importantly, the more than 1,000 Kenyans estimated to have lost their lives and the more than 300,000 who were displaced (Waki Commission, 2008).

The other partner in the government—led by Prime Minister Odinga—opposed the deferral excursions and eventually settled on a position of referral. That is, to have the cases referred back to Kenya subject to an independent investigative and trial process with investigations being conducted by such bodies as the Federal Bureau of Investigation (FBI) of the United States or Scotland Yard of the United Kingdom. In that latter regard, Prime Minister Odinga told Parliament that: "As for now the Kenya Police cannot investigate because they also stand accused of perpetrating the criminality through shootings and killings" (Mayoyo and Namunane, 2011: 4). In other words, the Prime Minister's counter-argument was for an ICC-led process in Kenya as provided for in the ICC Statute.

It would seem that the row over the ICC cases erupted shortly after it was revealed who the six people to be summoned were. Some quarters were, apparently, shocked upon learning some of the names among the six, at least two of whom (Uhuru Kenyatta and Francis Muthaura) are close confidants of President Kibaki, and Mr Kenyatta is also considered to be a potential Presidential candidate in 2012. A drawn out prosecution and trial process would detract from, or prevent altogether, Mr Kenyatta's candidacy for President and some of his supporters find such a notion abhorrent.

However, in this author's view, the case for justice and the need to establish accountability for the postelection violence crimes, as supported by the wider Kenyan public, CSOs, and many members of the UN Security Council, suggest that these ICC trials will not necessarily ignite further violence. In fact, as observed by Alai and Mue (2010: 5):

The ICC's role is perceived as particularly crucial in regard to balancing peace and justice, since many hope that accountability for those responsible for past violence will deter future violence during the next election, scheduled for 2012. It is widely hoped that criminal accountability will end this cycle of violence—keeping politicians from establishing and using militias for their own political gain and manipulating ethnic divides, which creates long-term grievances for short-term political gains.

Nonetheless, given the vitriolic and insulting language (in many instances bordering on hate speech and for which warnings were issued by the National Cohesion and Integration Commission) that has been hurled by members of the "Ocampo Six"—particularly Mr Kenyatta and Mr Ruto—prior to the commencement of their first appearance at the ICC, and notwithstanding their being subsequently constrained by the ICC from engaging in hateful or inciting speech, there is indeed some possibility that if these two men are found guilty of serious crimes against humanity, whether by the ICC or in Kenya, then their followers may be moved to violence. Mr Kenyatta is the principal leader (political) of the Kikuyu tribal group and Mr Ruto perceives himself as a major leader of the Kalenjin tribal group. These two men are supported by Vice President Kalonzo Musyoka who is from the Kamba tribal group. This political marriage of these three politicians has been referred to as the "KKK" alliance—an acronym for Kikuyu, Kalenjin, and Kamba—with these tribal groups comprising more than one-third of Kenya's population. However, apart from Mr Kenyatta, it is not clear how influential these gentlemen really are with their respective tribal groups or whether they are simply strange bedfellows uniting against others with whom they are in political competition, in particular Prime Minister Odinga (a Luo), whose tribe they are apparently seeking to prevent from grasping political power (Kabukuru, 2011). The KKK Alliance was later reconstituted, expanded, and renamed as the G7 comprising four additional members from other tribal groups and regions. The KKK tag had become a liability. Nonetheless, the inner core remains the KKK. Of course, we shall see how all of this plays out in the next general elections. Incidentally, both Mr Ruto and Mr Musyoka are former stalwarts of Mr Kenyatta's KANU party.

Basically, there are now three areas, in Kenya's overall political and economic development that require extensive focus by all stakeholders. These three areas are interrelated and are fundamental to the achievement of sustainable development with peace, stability, and steady economic gains. They are: (1) state capability (building a capable state); (2) good governance (good enough or an improved governance environment); and (3) rule of law (respect for and promotion of the rule of law).

State Capability

Development progress will elude any country that lacks state capability. On the other hand, a capable state creates the environment which allows development progress to occur. In a capable state, the public sector is empowered to provide an enabling environment for economic growth, poverty reduction, peace, stability, and good governance. The capable state represents the means through which a government meets its basic obligations to its citizens and provides essential services. It is a crucial foundation for effective programs to tackle poverty, improve livelihoods, and sustain good governance (Hope, 2008). A capable state, therefore, possesses the appropriate capabilities to respond effectively, efficiently, and timely to domestic needs and demands as well as to meet global challenges.

A capable state, as opposed to a "weak or failed state," is also a precondition for effective engagement in enhanced partnerships with international partners. State transformation in Kenya, as part of the country's overall public sector reforms, must be aimed at, among other things, sustaining a capable state. Capable states demonstrate governance at all levels. They are at war with corruption, for example (Benn, 2004). When states are not capable they become weak states. When states are weak for long periods, they run the risk of becoming failed states with all the attendant negative outcomes of such a nature of being.

Weak states are countries that lack the essential capacity and/or will to fulfil four sets of critical government responsibilities: (1) fostering an environment conducive to sustainable and equitable growth; (2) establishing and maintaining legitimate, transparent, and accountable political institutions; (3) securing their populations from violent conflict and controlling their territory; and (4) meeting the basic human needs of their population (Rice and Patrick, 2008). Weak states tend to contain ethnic, religious, linguistic, or other tensions that limit or decrease their ability to deliver political goods. The rule of law is also weakly applied (Kirwin and Cho, 2009; Patrick, 2006; Robb, 2004).

Failed states are countries that can no longer deliver positive political goods to their people. Their governments lose legitimacy and, in the eyes and hearts of a growing plurality of its citizens, the nation-state itself becomes illegitimate. They forfeit the distribution of political goods to warlords or nonstate actors, their economic infrastructure is virtually nonexistent, and corruption flourishes. Failure of a nation-state looms when violence cascades into all-out internal war, when standards of living massively deteriorate, when the infrastructure of ordinary life decays, and when the greed of rulers overwhelm their responsibilities to improve the lot of their people and surroundings (Di John, 2008; Robb, 2004; Rotberg, 2002). In the 2011 *Failed States Index*, 10 of the top 15 failed states are African, the top 4 are all African, and Kenya is ranked at number 16—an improvement from the ranking of number 13 in 2010 (FfP, 2010, 2011). They have failed because they lack the wherewithal to discharge their constitutional responsibilities and they disintegrate and lose their political and economic viability and legitimacy. Somalia remains the best African example of a failed state and tops the list of failed states globally.

From the foregoing, we can conclude that the capable state encapsulates the following critical dimensions: (1) society and people; (2) governance; and (3) economic orientation (Republic of Mauritius, 2007). Society and people are the basic welfare targets for directed government actions; governance provides the political leadership, administrative processes, and legal rules and framework toward those targets and with a philosophy of equality and fairness; and economic orientation creates the productive and trade framework to acquire and distribute resources, goods and services cost-effectively, and employment and other opportunities equitably.

Building state capability in Kenya, and most other African States, is, therefore, about laying the very foundations of an orderly society. When state capability is in place, such a state would be able to guarantee peace and security; create the enabling environment for equitably distributed economic growth coupled with the promotion of education, health, and social services; encourage freedom of expression and vigorous exchange of views; pursue sound macroeconomic management and institutional reform; deal swiftly and effectively with corruption; and build the enabling environment for the private sector to generate economic growth and employment (UNECA, 2004). Fundamentally, at the core of the capable state is good governance and a fair and consistent application of the rule of law. We move on to good governance next before discussing the rule of law.

Good Governance

Governance has to do with the manner in which responsibility is discharged. Such a responsibility may be acquired through election, appointment, or delegation in the public domain, or in the area of commerce (i.e., corporate governance) (Hope, 2005, 2008). Governance represents the overall quality of the relationship between citizens and government, which includes responsiveness, efficiency, honesty, and equity. Therefore, good governance is taken here to mean a condition whereby such responsibility is discharged in an effective, transparent, and accountable manner whereas bad governance is associated with maladministration in the discharge of responsibility (Hope, 2008). Good governance entails the existence of efficient and accountable institutions—political, judicial, administrative, economic, corporate—and entrenched rules that promote development, protect human rights, respect the rule of law, and ensure that people are free to participate in, and be heard on, decisions that affect their lives.

There are three conceptualizations of good governance of relevance to Kenya and the rest of Africa: (1) political (democratic), (2) economic, and (3) corporate. These three conceptualizations of governance refer to something broader than government. It is about stewardship and the rules of the game and they are also interdependent. For example, political governance (or democratic governance as it is more popularly termed) is regarded as a prerequisite for good economic and corporate governance. Where there exists bad economic and corporate governance, there will also generally be bad political governance. Indeed, it is good political governance that will influence all other facets of governance in society (Hope and Hamdok, 2002).

Following from Hope and Hamdok (2002), good political governance is defined as a societal state epitomized by the following principal characteristics: predictable, open, and enlightened policy-making; a bureaucracy imbued with a professional ethos; a strong civil society participating in public affairs; adherence to the rule of law, respect for basic human rights and freedoms, and judicial independence; consistent traditions and predictable institutions that determine how authority is exercised in a given nation-state including (1) the process by which governments are selected, held accountable, monitored, and replaced; (2) the capacity of governments to manage resources efficiently and formulate, implement, and enforce sound policies and regulations; and (3) the respect of citizens and the state for the institutions that govern economic and social interactions among them; and the establishment and protection of a political order and systems that are (a) legitimate and enjoy the support and loyalty of the people; (b) strong enough to defend and advance the sovereign interests of the people; (c) able to address the fundamental development interests of the people; (d) able to engage effectively with the various global processes that characterize the world economy; and (e) respectful of the need to prevent, minimize, and mitigate internal and cross-border conflicts.

Economic governance is about setting rules that induce economic actors to cooperate more effectively with each other, and that support the implementation of economic policy. It is about setting an economic constitution; that is, the rules, constraints, and norms which economic agents accept as binding upon them. Economic governance is not limited to a particular setting because there are many stakeholders that participate in it. Nonetheless, the State or government has an important role in coordinating the various institutional arrangements in economic policy-making (Gamble, 2000; Kjaer, 2004).

Good economic governance exists in those economies where the institutions of government have the capacity to manage resources efficiently; formulate, implement, and enforce sound policies and regulations; can be monitored and be held accountable; in which there is respect for the rules and norms of economic interaction; and in which economic activity is unimpeded by corruption and other activities inconsistent with the public trust. The key elements contributing to an environment of good economic governance are transparency, accountability, an enabling environment for private sector development and growth, and institutional development and effectiveness (Hope and Hamdok, 2002).

Good economic governance is necessary in order to enhance the capacity of the State to deliver on its economic mandate. That mandate includes eradicating poverty and improving economic growth. Good economic governance would attempt to evolve well-defined structures; harmonious and complementary fiscal, monetary, and trade policies; and establishment of monitoring and regulatory authorities for promotion and coordination of different economic activities. It consists of the entire institutional framework of a government engaged in the evolution and implementation of general economic policy affecting its internal and international economic relations. That institutional framework must be competent to undertake the implementation of economic policy and capable of making the necessary adjustments as necessitated by government policy.

Corporate governance refers to the mechanisms through which corporations (whether private, publicly traded, or state-owned) and their management are governed. It involves a set of relationships between a company's management, its board, its shareholders, and its other stakeholders, and also provides the structure through which the objectives and the monitoring of performance are determined. By its very nature, corporate governance structures are, therefore, less complicated than economic governance as conceptualized above.

Good corporate governance entails the pursuit of objectives by the board and management that represent the interests of a company and its shareholders including effective monitoring and efficient use of resources. Good corporate governance is influenced by a number of factors, primary among which is the nature of the overall institutional and legal framework that has been established by governments to effect such good governance (Hope and Hamdok, 2002). In attempting to effect good corporate governance structures, Kenya would therefore be primarily concerned with creating an enabling environment for all types of commercial entities to flourish within well-defined and predictable applications of rules. This again raises the question of the institutional framework.

Good governance is good for Kenya, and Africa in general. Countries attract more investment and achieve higher rates of per capita growth when the state improves certain basic aspects of its performance. A State that applies rules and policies predictably and fairly, ensures order and the rule of law, and protects property will generate confidence and attract more domestic and foreign investment. That, in turn, generates trade and faster economic growth as well as provide the wherewithal for sustainable development (Hope, 2008). George Saitoti, a former Kenya Vice President, and a Cabinet Minister at the time of my writing this book, was no doubt drawing on the poor Kenyan and other African country development performance when he observed that "good political and economic governance underpins sustainable development" (Saitoti, 2002: 257).

Good governance matters, therefore, primarily because it is a means to other ends. The principal benefit of good governance is the contribution it makes to improving a society's well-being, broadly defined but definitely including economic and social development (de Ferranti et al., 2009). In the pursuit of the good governance agenda, institutions, therefore, loom large. The existence of weak institutions of governance in Kenya, as a constraint on sustainable development, had become clear and convincing. Transparency and accountability were not considered norms to be upheld and corruption became a normal everyday activity (Anassi, 2004; Okanja, 2010). This has, accordingly, limited the public sector in the fulfillment of its economic functions and, in particular, demonstrating a strong, positive, and enabling role for the government. Those economic functions can be broadly classified into three distinct categories: (1) making and implementing economic policy; (2) delivering services; and (3) ensuring accountability for the use of public resources and public regulatory power (World Bank, 2000, 2008).

Institutions are needed to maintain fiscal and monetary discipline, mobilize resources, and set priorities among the competing demands for those resources as integral aspects of the making and implementation of good economic policy which, in turn, is critical to the success of the growth strategy. Similarly, institutional arrangements are required for the efficient delivery of public services that are also pro-poor. In addition, there must be good enough institutional mechanisms that ensure accountability through the capacity to monitor and enforce rules and to regulate economic activities in the public interest. However, regulatory frameworks should be minimal, simple, and easy to implement (Saitoti, 2002). They should also begin their existence after the regulatory hurdles and administrative processes faced by the private sector have been identified and streamlined.

Public institutions function at three levels to enhance state capability to achieve good governance in all its facets. The first pertains to rules and restraints within the public sector. These include the constitutional separation of powers; decentralization (divisions of responsibility among various levels of government); budgeting rules across public organizations; and formal rules and oversight arrangements within public organizations. The second relates to mechanisms that provide citizens voice and participation. These include various forms of representative decision-making and political oversight; direct involvement by users, nongovernmental organizations and other groups of citizens in the design, implementation, and monitoring of public policies; and the transparent production and dissemination of information. The third level is what can be referred to as mechanisms that promote competition. These include political competition; market competition among public agencies, or between public and private providers of information, goods, and services; and internal competition within public bureaucracies.

Moreover, governance is worth pursuing in its own right in Kenya. For instance, human rights and democratic principles, honest and good quality administration, and protecting the rights and freedoms under the rule of law are concerned with values that apply equally to every state and citizen. Democracy, for example, is a universally recognized ideal, based on values common to people everywhere regardless of cultural, political, social, or economic differences. These transcend the functional importance of aspects of good governance, such as for sustainable development. Good governance allows for the improvement of relations with donors and it has been demonstrated to improve, or end altogether, political and economic mismanagement and the consequential violent conflicts, instability, denial of democracy and human rights, and deepening poverty (Hope, 2008).

The Rule of Law

The rule of law concept is an ancient ideal in some societies. However, Kenya is not included among those societies. Nonetheless, current thinking in international development governance has elevated the rule of law concept to an ideal that all societies must respect and promote. While neither scholars nor practitioners have settled on an accepted definition, there are some fundamental elements that are common to the usage and application of the concept. The term rule of law refers to a principle of governance in which all persons, institutions and entities, public and private, including the State itself, are accountable to laws that are publicly promulgated, equally enforced and independently adjudicated, and which are consistent with international human rights norms and standards (UNSC, 2004).

The rule of law, therefore, not only transcends the authority of the individual, but is also inextricably linked to the good of a society as whole. As applied equally to everyone, the rule of law is perceived to benefit society as a whole. The definition of rule of law outlined here points to a universality of the principle. The rule of law is, consequently, not Western, European, or American. It is available and applicable to all societies. Given its universal applicability, the challenge is to find ways in which a society like Kenya may govern itself under the rule of law. By its definition also, the rule of law governs the relationship between institutions in a State, and between those institutions and the citizens. It enables individuals to hold their State to account for respecting their human rights, helps to manage disputes between individuals, and restrains the government by promoting certain liberties and creating order and predictability with respect to how a country functions. In its most basic sense, the rule of law represents a system that attempts to protect the rights of citizens from arbitrary and abusive use of government power (Bica-Huiu et al., nd; Kleinfeld, 2006; Yu and Guernsey, nd).

The rule of law requires, as well, measures to ensure adherence to the principles of supremacy of law, equality before the law, accountability to the law, fairness in the application of the law, separation of powers, participation in decision-making, legal certainty, avoidance of arbitrariness, and procedural and legal transparency (UNSC, 2004). Some experts (see, e.g, Fuller, 1977; Yu and Guernsey, nd), have identified eight elements of law which have been recognized as necessary for a society aspiring to institute the rule of law:

(1) Laws must exist and those laws should be obeyed by all, including government officials.
(2) Laws must be published.
(3) Laws must be prospective in nature so that the effect of the law may only take place after the law has been passed.
(4) Laws should be written with reasonable clarity.
(5) Laws must avoid contradictions.
(6) Laws must not command the impossible.
(7) Laws must stay constant through time to allow the formalization of rules. However, laws must also allow for timely revision when the underlying social and political circumstances have changed.
(8) Official action should be consistent with the declared rule.

The rule of law is also shaped by the institutional constraints on government. One such institutional constraint is the existence of an independent judiciary while another is developing ways of promoting good governance (Yu and Guernsey, nd). In addition, there have been five factors identified that, essentially, comprise the rule of law. Each must also be present for the rule of law to prevail and Kenya must therefore strive to ensure that they are indeed present and remain so:

- *Order and Security*—Public order and personal security are necessary for citizens to have faith in their government and institutions. Where public order breaks down, citizens may take the law into their own hands and vigilantism emerges as has been observed in some slums in Nairobi. This type of self-help conduct further undermines public order, safety, and security and runs contrary to the rule of law framework.
- *Legitimacy*—The existence of laws must represent the collective will. In societies where the rule of law is followed, almost all citizens obey the laws, even when doing so contravenes their personal interests. This perception of law, therefore, being legitimate and requiring adherence is necessary as a foundation for the principle of the rule of law.

- **Checks and Balances**—Checks and balances among the different levels of government act as a constraint on the arbitrary exercise of power. Excessive concentration of power in any one branch, institution, or level of government often leads to such arbitrariness and abuse as has been the case in Kenya. Separation of powers provides the checks and balances needed to keep government contained.
- **Fairness**—Fairness encompasses four sub-elements of: equal application of the law, procedural fairness, protection of human rights and civil liberties, and access to justice. The underlying idea here is that everyone is treated similarly and equally and that there be no discrimination whatsoever.
- **Effective Application**—The rule of law cannot prevail without application and enforcement of laws. This must also occur in a consistent manner to guarantee equality under the law. (Bica-Huiu et al., nd; USAID, 2008)

The foregoing factors, elements, and principles guiding the respect for, promotion, and implementation of the rule of law are, undoubtedly, well known to the key payers in the three branches of Kenya's government. The fundamental problem has been, as it is with other aspects of governance, such as anti-corruption efforts, the unwillingness to risk acting in a manner not consistent with the prevailing norms. The resulting consequence has been a perpetuation of the culture of impunity leading to the exhibition of bad governance.

Conclusions

Kenya has an unprecedented opportunity for transformation to sustained growth and development. The policy frameworks discussed above complement some of what the government has put forward in its socioeconomic plans in the quest for achieving the *Kenya Vision 2030* outcomes. As noted by the World Bank (2011), Kenya is among a handful of African countries that would not only be locomotives of their subregions but also promote regional solutions that help Africa overcome the constraints of size and markets.

However, much attention and effort must be particularly given to infrastructure development to allow the public and private sectors to implement policies successfully and deliver goods and services for poverty reduction and sustainable development. Infrastructure serves as a strategic foundation for economic transformation in general and the application of technology to development in particular. It is an essential element of the long-term development efforts envisioned by the *Kenya Vision 2030*. Infrastructure development in Kenya must include aspects that promote and allow for the pooling of resources with other countries where that could lead to the development of infrastructure serving common needs; that create and implement policies for the engagement of PPI; and that acquire and train human resources with the skills to improve the effective delivery and performance of infrastructure.

Also of critical importance is the need to maintain a focus on mitigating the challenges faced by the youth and that the youth bulge represents. The youth are a vital resource that must be tapped to promote Kenya's development. In fact, the realization of the *Kenya Vision 2030* and the attainment of sustainable growth and development depend on the degree of inclusion of youth in the development agenda and the outcomes of the steps taken to reduce unemployment among the youth and address their other multiple and diverse needs.

Finally, pursuing sustainable growth and development is best achieved where there is a capable state in a good enough governance environment, with respect for, and promotion of the rule of law, leading to a dynamic Kenyan State that is citizen-oriented as a precondition for the constitution of a legitimate economic, social, and political order. Good governance entails an orderly process for arriving at and implementing decisions regarding public goods and that is interdependent on a State that is capable of fulfilling a range of international and domestic responsibilities through institutions which, in turn, function to enhance state capability. Such institutions must have the capacity and the will to sustain democratic, responsive, transparent, and accountable government.

References

AICD (Africa Infrastructure Country Diagnostic) (2010), *Kenya's Infrastructure: A Continental Perspective*. Washington, DC: World Bank.

Alai, C. and Mue, N. (2010), "Kenya: Impact of the Rome Statute and the International Criminal Court," *ICTJ Briefing*, The Rome Statute Review Conference, Kampala, June. New York: ICTJ (International Centre for Transitional Justice).

Anassi, P. (2004), *Corruption in Africa: The Kenyan Experience*. Victoria, BC: Trafford Publishing.

Anderson, K. S. and Sandmann, L. (2009), "Toward a Model of Empowering Practices in Youth-Adult Partnerships," *Journal of Extension*, 47(2), Online Edition. Available at: www.joe.org/joe/2009april/pdf/JOE_v47_2a5.pdf [Accessed November 11, 2010].

Atchoarena, D. (2007), "Strategies for the Transition of Youth from School to Work," *IIEP (International Institute for Educational Planning) Newsletter*, 25(4), 7.

Benn, H. (2004), "Speech," Conference on Building Capable States in Africa—Policy Priorities for the G8, London, December 06. Available at: http://www.sarpn.org.za/documents/d0001032/P1144-benn_Dec2004.pdf [Accessed November 12, 2010].

Bica-Huiu, A., Aresty, J., Hudes, K., and Irish, L. (nd), "White Paper: Building a Culture of Respect for the Rule of Law." Available at: http://meetings.abanet.org/webupload/commupload/IC928000/sitesofinterest_files/Building.a.Culture.of.Respect.for.the.Rule.of.Law.Paper.Complete.Draft.pdf [Accessed December 20, 2010].

Calderón, C. and Servén, L. (2010), "Infrastructure and Economic Development in Sub-Saharan Africa," *Journal of African Economies*, 19(Supplement 1), i13–87.

Cargo, M., Grams, G. D., Ottoson, J. M., Ward, P., and Green, L. W. (2003), "Empowerment as Fostering Positive Youth Development and Citizenship," *American Journal of Health Behaviour*, 27(Supplement 1), S66–79.

Cerda, R. A. and Larrain, F. (2010), "Corporate Taxes and the Demand for Labor and Capital in Developing Countries," *Small Business Economics*, 34(2), 187–201.

Chinman, M. J. and Linney, J. A. (1998), "Toward a Model of Adolescent Empowerment: Theoretical and Empirical Evidence," *Journal of Primary Prevention*, 18(4), 393–413.

Commonwealth Secretariat (2007), *The Commonwealth Plan of Action for Youth Empowerment: 2007-2015*. London: Commonwealth Youth Programme, Commonwealth Secretariat.

de Ferranti, D., Jacinto, J., Ody, A. J., and Ramshaw, G. (2009), *How to Improve Governance: A New Framework for Analysis and Action*. Washington, DC: Brookings Institution Press.

Delmon, J. (2011), *Public-Private Partnership Projects in Infrastructure: An Essential Guide for Policy Makers*. New York: Cambridge University Press.

De Mooij, R. A. and Ederveen, S. (2003), "Taxation and Foreign Direct Investment: A Synthesis of Empirical Research," *International Tax and Public Finance*, 10(6), 673–93.

DfID (Department for International Development) (2008), *Growth: Building Jobs and Prosperity in Developing Countries*. London: DfID.

DiBenedetto, A. (1992), "Youth Groups: A Model for Empowerment," *Networking Bulletin*, 2(3), 19–24.

Di John, J. (2008), "Conceptualizing the Causes and Consequences of Failed States: A Critical Review of the Literature," *Working Paper No. 25*. London: Crisis States Research Centre, London School of Economics.

Djankov, S., Ganser, T., McLeish, C., Ramalho, R., and Shleifer, A. (2010), "The Effect of Corporate Taxes on Investment and Entrepreneurship," *American Economic Journal: Macroeconomics*, 2(3), 31–64.

Dovi, E. (2008), "Boosting Domestic Savings in Africa," *Africa Renewal*, 22(3), 12–14, 20.

Eberhard, A., Foster, V., Briceño-Garmendia, C., Ouedraogo, F., Camos, D., and Shkaratan, M. (2008), "Underpowered: The State of the Power Sector in Sub-Saharan Africa," *Background Paper 6*. Washington, DC: World Bank.

FfP (Fund for Peace) (2010), "The Failed States Index 2010." Available at: http://www.fundforpeace.org/web/index.php?option=com_content&task=v iew&id=452&Itemid=900 [Accessed January 12, 2011].

— (2011), "The Failed States Index 2011". Available at: http://www.fundfor-peace.org/global/?q=fsi [Accessed June 23, 2011].

Flores, K. S. (2008), *Youth Participatory Evaluation: Strategies for Engaging Young People*. San Francisco, CA: Jossey-Bass Publishers.

Foster, V. and Briceño-Garmendia, C. (2010), *Africa's Infrastructure: A Time for Transformation*. Washington, DC: World Bank.

Foster, V. and Steinbuks, J. (2009), "Paying the Price for Unreliable Power Supplies: In-House Generation of Electricity by Firms in Africa," *Policy Research Working Paper 4913*. Washington, DC: World Bank.

Fuller, L. L. (1977), *The Morality of Law*. New Haven, CT: Yale University Press.

Gamble, A. (2000), "Economic Governance." In J. Pierre (ed.), *Debating Governance: Authority, Steering, and Democracy*. Oxford: Oxford University Press, pp. 110–37.

Gerrard, M. B. (2001), "Public-Private Partnerships," *Finance & Development*, 38(3), Online Edition. Available at: http://www.imf.org/external/pubs/ft/fandd/2001/09/gerrard.htm [Accessed December 13, 2010].

Government of India (2010), "Approach Paper on Defining Public Private Partnerships: Discussion Note." New Delhi: Ministry of Finance. Available at: http://www.pppinindia.com/pdf/ppp_definition_approach_paper.pdf [Accessed December 10, 2010].

Grimsey, D. and Lewis, M. K. (2007), *Public-Private Partnerships: The Worldwide Revolution in Infrastructure Provision and Project Finance*. Cheltenham, UK: Edward Elgar.

Hansen, T. O. (2009), "Political Violence in Kenya: A Study of Causes, Responses, and a Framework for Discussing Preventive Action," *ISS Paper 205*. Pretoria: ISS (Institute for Security Studies).

Hentic, I. and Bernier, G. (1999),"Rationalization, Decentralization and Participation in the Public Sector Management of Developing Countries," *International Review of Administrative Sciences*, 65(2), 108–21.

Hope, K. R. (1996), "Privatization, Debt Management and Exchange Rates in Developing Countries: An Overview of Policy Reforms," *Bank of Valetta Review*, No. 14(Autumn), 1–20.

— (2002), *From Crisis to Renewal: Development Policy and Management in Africa*. Leiden: Brill Publishers.

— (2005), "Toward Good Governance and Sustainable Development: The African Peer Review Mechanism," *Governance: An International Journal of Policy, Administration, and Institutions*, 18(2), 283–311.

— (2006), "Prospects and Challenges for the New Partnership for Africa's Development: Addressing Capacity Deficits," *Journal of Contemporary African Studies*, 24(2), 203–28.

— (2008), *Poverty, Livelihoods, and Governance in Africa: Fulfilling the Development Promise*. New York: Palgrave Macmillan.

— (2011), "Investing in Capacity Development: Towards an Implementation Framework," *Policy Studies*, 32(1), 59–72.

Hope, K. R. and Hamdok, A. (2002), *Guidelines for Enhancing Good Economic and Corporate Governance in Africa*. Addis Ababa: UNECA (United Nations Economic Commission for Africa).

HRW (Human Rights Watch) (2008), *Ballots to Bullets: Organized Political Violence and Kenya's Crisis of Governance*. New York: HRW.

Huebner, A. J. (1998), "Examining 'Empowerment': A How-To Guide for the Youth Development Professional," *Journal of Extension*, 36(6), Online Edition. Available at: http://www.joe.org/joe/1998december/a1.php [Accessed December 12, 2010].

ICC (International Criminal Court) (nd), "Situation in the Republic of Kenya." Available at: http://www.icccpi.int/Menus/ICC/Situations+and+Cases/Situations/Situation+ICC+0109/Situation+Index.htm [Accessed March 16, 2011].

ILO (International Labor Office) (2010), "Innovations in Public Employment Programmes," *Global Jobs Pact Policy Brief No. 2*. Geneva: ILO.

Isahakia, M. (2010), "Foreword" to *Kazi Kwa Vijana Operations Manual: Volume I*. Nairobi: Office of the Prime Minister.

Ituassu, A. (2010), "Big Challenge for Brazil's New President is Going Beyond Lula." Available at: http://www.brazzil.com/articles/226-november-2010/10452-big-challenge-for-brazils-new-president-is-going-beyond-lula.html [Accessed December 20, 2010].

Jennings, L. B., Parra-Medina, D. M., Messias, D. K. H., and McLoughlin, K. (2006), "Toward a Critical Social Theory of Youth Empowerment," *Journal of Community Practice*, 14(1/2), 31–55.

Kabukuru, W. (2011), "Is Raila Odinga Losing Friends Fast?," *New African*, No. 504, March, 26–7.

KEPSA (Kenya Private Sector Alliance) (nd), "Message from the Chairman." Available at: http://www.kepsa.or.ke/?p=about-us&title=message-from-the-chairman [Accessed February 28, 2011].

— (2010), "Briefing on the Kenya Youth Empowerment Project: Background/Objectives of the Kenya Youth Empowerment Project (KYEP)." Available at: http://www.kepsa.or.ke/?p=strategic-partners&title=kyempowerment [Accessed December 21, 2010].

— (2011), "Update on the Kenya Youth Empowerment Project (KYEP)—January 2011." Available at: http://www.kepsa.or.ke/?p=kyempowerment&title=updateonkyep [Accessed February 28, 2011].

KETRACO (Kenya Electricity Transmission Company Limited) (nd), "Our History." Available at: http://www.ketraco.co.ke/about/history.html [Accessed January 12, 2011].

Kirwin, M. F. and Cho, W. (2009), "Weak States and Political Violence in Sub-Saharan Africa," *Afrobarometer Working Paper No. 111*. Available at: http://www.afrobarometer.org/index.php?option=com_docman&Itemid=39 [Accessed December 12, 2010].

Kjaer, A. M. (2004), *Governance*. Cambridge, UK: Polity Press.

Kleinfeld, R. (2006), "Competing Definitions of the Rule of Law." In T. Carothers (ed.), *Promoting the Rule of Law Abroad: In Search of Knowledge*. Washington, DC: Carnegie Endowment for International Peace, pp. 31–74.

Klemm, A. and Van Parys, S. (2009), "Empirical Evidence on the Effects of Tax Incentives," *IMF Working Paper WP/09/136*. Washington, DC: IMF.

Klopp, J. M. (2002), "Can Moral Ethnicity Trump Political Tribalism? The Struggle for Land and Nation in Kenya," *African Studies*, 61(2), 269–94.

KNCHR (Kenya National Commission on Human Rights) (2008), *On the Brink of the Precipice: A Human Rights Account of Kenya's Post 2007 Election Violence: Final Report*. Nairobi: KNCHR.

KPA (Kenya Ports Authority) (nda), "Port Throughput 2002-2006." Available at: http://www.kpa.co.ke/security/ISPS%20CODE/Documents/THROUGHPUT .pdf [Accessed December 12, 2010].

— (ndb), "Port Throughput 2005-2009." Available at: http://www.kpa.co.ke/ InfoCenter/Performance/Annual/Pages/TotalThroughput.aspxsed [Accessed December 12, 2010].

— (ndc), "Ports Vital in Improving Regional Trade." Available at: http:// www.kpa.co.ke/InfoCenter/News/Pages/PORTSVITALINIMPROVING-REGIONALTRADE.aspx [Accessed December 12, 2010].

— (2010), "New Second Terminal to Double Port Capacity." Available at: http:// www.kpa.co.ke/InfoCenter/News/Pages/NEWSECONDTERMINALTO-DOUBLEPORTCAPACITY.aspx [Accessed December 12, 2010].

KRA (Kenya Revenue Authority) (2009), "Income Tax Overview: 2009/2010." Available at: http://www.kra.go.ke/pdf/Income_Tax_Overview.pdf [Accessed December 4, 2010].

Kusi, A. A. (2011), "History Made as UN Clears Kenya's Sh950bn Nuclear Energy Project," *Daily Nation*, April 1, 1–2.

Lansdown, G. (2001), *Promoting Children's Participation in Democratic Decision-Making*. Florence, Italy: UNICEF Innocenti Research Centre.

Le Bas, A. (2010), "Ethnicity and the Willingness to Sanction Violent Politicians: Evidence from Kenya," *Afrobarometer Working Paper No. 125*. Available at: http:// www.afrobarometer.org/index.php?option=com_docman&Itemid=39 [Accessed March 10, 2011].

Lonsdale, J. (1994), "Moral Ethnicity and Political Tribalism." In P. Kaarsholm and J. Hultin (eds), *Inventions and Boundaries: Historical and Anthropological Approaches to the Study of Ethnicity and Nationalism*. Roskilde, Denmark: Institute of Development Studies, Roskilde University, pp. 131–50.

— (2008), "Moral Ethnicity and Political Tribalism." Available at: http://www. kenyaimagine.com/index.php?option=com_content&view=article&id=1338 &catid=266:international&Itemid=224 [Accessed December 20, 2010].

Luna, H. P. (2010), "The Legacy of Brazil's Lula da Silva: A News Analysis." Available at: http://latindispatch.com/2010/09/27/lula-da-silva-forever-news-analysis/ [Accessed December 20, 2010].

Mayoyo, P. and Namunane, B. (2011), "ODM Pushes for ICC-led Local Trials," *Daily Nation*, March 24, 1 and 4.

Mintz, J. M. (2007), "2007 Tax Competitiveness Report: A Call for Comprehensive Tax Reform," *C. D. Howe Institute Commentary No. 254*. Toronto: C. D. Howe Institute.

Muthee, M. W. (2010), "Tackling Youth Unemployment in Kenya." Available at: http://www.wilsoncenter.org/index.cfm?fuseaction=news.item&news_id =634085 [Accessed December 21, 2010].

Mutuku, C. M. (2009), "Youth Perspectives on their Empowerment in Sub-Saharan Africa: The Case of Kenya," Paper presented at the Annual Meeting of the Midwest Political Science Association 67th Annual National Conference, Chicago, April 2. Available at: http://www.allacademic.com/meta/p360666_ index.html [Accessed December 20, 2010].

NCPPP (National Council for Public-Private Partnerships) (nd), "Types of Public-Private Partnerships." Available at: http://www.ncppp.org/howpart/ppptypes.shtml [Accessed December 12, 2010].

Ncube, M. (2010), "Financing and Managing Infrastructure in Africa," *Journal of African Economies*, 19(Supplement 1), pp. i114–64.

Ngerechi, J. B. (2003), "Technical and Vocational Education and Training in Kenya." Paper Presented at the Conference on the Reform of Technical and Vocational Education and Training (TVET), Gaborone, Botswana, August 4–6. Available at: http://www.bota.org.bw/docs/TVET_in_kenya.pdf [Accessed December 20, 2010].

NICHE (Netherlands Initiative for Capacity Development in Higher Education) (2010), *NICHE Strategy on Technical and Vocational Education and Training (TVET)*. Available at: http://www.nuffic.nl/international-organizations/docs/niche/themes/labour-market/niche-tvet.pdf [Accessed December 20, 2010].

Njagih, M. (2011), "Kenyans Still Support Hague Trials," *The Standard*, April 6, 4.

Njonjo, K. S. (2010), *Youth Fact Book: Infinite Possibility or Definite Disaster?* Nairobi: Institute of Economic Affairs-Kenya.

Norregard, J. and Khan, T. S. (2007), "Tax Policy: Recent Trends and Coming Challenges," *IMF Working Paper WP/07/274*. Washington, DC: IMF.

NPI (Nairobi Peace Initiative) Africa (nd), *A Review of Challenges Faced by Kenyan Youth: Peace Agenda in Youth Development*. Nairobi: NPI-Africa.

Nyerere, J. (2009), "Technical & Vocational Education and Training (TVET) Sector Mapping in Kenya." Available at: http://schoklandtvet.pbworks.com/f/Microsoft+Word+-+Mapping+report+final-Nyerere+mrt+09+hp+2.pdf [Accessed December 20, 2010].

Obeng, A. V. (2007), "Vassal States, Development Options and African Development." In J. C. Senghor and N. K. Poku (eds), *Towards Africa's Renewal*. Aldershot: Ashgate Publishing, pp. 179–207.

Odinga, R. (2010), "Speech during Enactment of a New Constitution for Kenya," August 7. Available at: http://www.primeminister.go.ke/index.cfm [Accessed November 11, 2010].

OECD (Organization for Economic Cooperation and Development) (2008), "Infrastructure to 2030," *Policy Brief*. Paris: OECD.

Okanja, O. (2010), *Kenya at Forty-Five: Economic Performance, Problems and Prospects*. London: Athena Press.

Ong'olo, D. O. (2006), "Public Private Partnerships (PPP): Practice and Regulatory Policy in Kenya." Paper Prepared for the Institute of Economic Affairs. Available at: http://www.ieakenya.or.ke/documents/Public%20Private%20Parternerships.pdf [Accessed December 12, 2010].

OPM/KKV (Office of Prime Minister, *Kazi Kwa Vijana* Initiative) (2011), "*Kazi Kwa Vijana* Programmes Summary." Available at: http://www.kkv.go.ke/

index.php?option=com_content&view=section&id=9&Itemid=90 [Accessed February 28, 2011].

Pamacheche, F. and Koma, B. (2007), "Privatization in Sub-Saharan Africa—An Essential Route to Poverty Alleviation," *African Integration Review*, 1(2), 1–22.

Partnerships British Columbia (2003), "An Introduction to Public Private Partnerships." Available at: http://www.partnershipsbc.ca/pdf/An%20 Introduction%20to%20P3%20-June03.pdf [Accessed December 13, 2010].

Patrick, S. (2006), "Weak States and Global Threats: Fact or Fiction?," *The Washington Quarterly*, 29(2), 27–53.

PMPS (Prime Minister Press Service) (2011), "Sh4bn Injection Set to Revive *Kazi Kwa Vijana*," *Daily Nation*, March 17, 10.

Privatization Commission (nda), "Benefits of Privatization: Moving the Economy." Available at: http://privatisation.mackphilisa.net/pages/Benefits_of_ Privatization.vrt [Accessed December 12, 2010].

— (ndb), "Privatization Status." Available at: http://privatisation.mackphilisa. net/pages/Status.vrt [Accessed April 5, 2011].

Ranneberger, M. (2010), "Youth Can be Engine to Drive Fundamental Change," Abridged Version of Remarks at the National Youth Forum Conference, *The Standard*, November 12, 15.

Rawlinson, A. (2003), "The Political Manipulation of Ethnicity in Africa." Available at: http://home.sandiego.edu/~baber/globalethics/rawlinson-ethnicity.pdf [Accessed December 18, 2010].

Republic of Kenya (nda), "The Ministry." Nairobi: Ministry of Youth Affairs. Available at: http://www.youthaffairs.go.ke/index.php?option=com_cont ent&view=category&layout=blog&id=3&Itemid=7 [Accessed November 10, 2010].

— (ndb), "Mandate." Nairobi: Ministry of Youth Affairs and Sports. Available at: http://www.youthaffairs.go.ke/index.php?option=com_content&view=categ ory&layout=blog&id=6&Itemid=10 [Accessed November 10, 2010].

— (2005a), *The Privatization Act, 2005*. Nairobi: Republic of Kenya.

— (2005b), *Kenya Education Sector Support Programme 2005-2010: Delivering Quality Education and Training to all Kenyans*. Nairobi: Ministry of Education, Science and Technology.

— (2006), *Kenya National Youth Policy*. Nairobi: Ministry of Youth Affairs and Sports.

— (2007a), *Kenya Vision 2030: A Globally Competitive and Prosperous Kenya*. Nairobi: Republic of Kenya.

— (2007b), *Ministry of State for Youth Affairs—Strategic Plan 2007-2012*. Nairobi: Office of the Vice President and Ministry of State for Youth Affairs.

— (2008), *Kenya Vision 2030: First Medium Term Plan (2008-2012)*. Nairobi: Republic of Kenya.

— (2009), "The Public Procurement and Disposal (Public Private Partnerships) Regulations, 2009," *Kenya Gazette Supplement No. 17, Legislative Supplement No. 13*. Nairobi: Republic of Kenya.

— (2010a), *First Annual Progress Report on the Implementation of the First Medium Term Plan (2008-2012) of Kenya Vision 2030*. Nairobi: Republic of Kenya.

— (2010b), *Public Expenditure Review: Policy for Prosperity 2010*. Nairobi: Ministry of State for Planning, National Development and Vision 2030.

— (2010c), "Youth Empowerment Project: Environmental and Social Management Policy Framework (ESMF)." Available at: http://www.primeminister.go.ke/DOCS/ESMF.pdf [Accessed December 20, 2010].

— (2010d), *The National Youth Council Act, 2009*. Nairobi: Republic of Kenya.

— (2010e), *The Constitution of Kenya, 2010*. Nairobi: Republic of Kenya.

— (2011a), "List of 408 Fully Registered TIVET Institutions as at 07/03/2011 10:15AM." Nairobi: Ministry of Higher Education, Science and Technology. Available at: http://www.scienceandtechnology.go.ke/index. php?option=com_docman&task=cat_view&gid=47&Itemid=42 [Accessed March 21, 2011].

— (2011b), "List of 146 Provisionally Registered TIVET Institutions as at 07/03/2011 10:15AM." Nairobi: Ministry of Higher Education, Science and Technology. Available at: http://www.scienceandtechnology.go.ke/index. php?option=com_docman&task=cat_view&gid=47&Itemid=42 [Accessed March 21, 2011].

Republic of Mauritius (2007), "Mauritius Response Paper." Prepared for the Seventh Africa Governance Forum (AGF VII), Ouagadougou, Burkina Faso, October 24–26. Available at: http://www.sarpn.org.za/documents/ d0002885/index.php [Accessed November 20, 2010].

Republic of South Africa (nd), "What is PPP." Pretoria: PPP Unit, National Treasury. Available at: http://www.ppp.gov.za/ [Accessed December 11, 2010].

Rice, S. and Patrick, S. (2008), *Index of State Weakness in the Developing World*. Washington, DC: The Brookings Institution.

Robb, J. (2004), "Weak, Failed, and Collapsed States." Available at: http:// globalguerrillas.typepad.com/globalguerrillas/2004/05/failed_states.html [Accessed December 10, 2010].

Rotberg, R. I. (2002), "The New Nature of Nation-State Failure," *The Washington Quarterly*, 25(3), 85–96.

Saitoti, G. (2002), *The Challenges of Economic and Institutional Reforms in Africa*. Aldershot: Ashgate Publishing.

Savas, E. S. (2000), *Privatization and Public Private Partnerships*. New York: Chatham House Publishers, Seven Bridges Press.

Schwellnus, C. and Arnold, J. (2008), "Do Corporate Taxes Produce Productivity and Investment at the Firm Level?," *Economics Department Working Papers No. 641*. Paris: OECD.

Simiyu, J. W. (2009), *Revitalizing a Technical Training Institute in Kenya: A Case Study of Kaiboi Technical Training Institute*. Bonn: UNESCO-UNEVOC International Centre for Technical and Vocational Education and Training.

— (2010), "Entrepreneurship Education as a Tool to Support Self-Employment in Kenya," *TVET Best Practice Clearinghouse*, Issue 2. Bonn: UNESCO-UNEVOC International Centre for Technical and Vocational Education and Training.

Sindabi, E. (2011), "What Happened to *Kazi Kwa Vijana*?," *The Standard*, March 15, 16.

Sluger, L. and Satterfield, S. (2010), *How Do You Like Your Infrastructure: Public or Private?* Alexandria, VA: Society for Marketing Professional Services Foundation.

Subramaniam, A. and Moncloa, F. (2010), "Young People's Perspectives on Creating a 'Participation Friendly' Culture," *Children, Youth and Environments*, 20(2), 25–45.

Tax Rates.cc (2010), "Tax Rates for 2010-2011." Available at: http://www.taxrates.cc/html/tax-rates.html [Accessed February 20, 2011].

The Standard (2011), "Raila Announces Phase II of *Kazi Kwa Vijana*," April 7, 17.

UNCTAD (United Nations Conference on Trade and Development) (2007), *Economic Development in Africa: Reclaiming Policy Space: Domestic Resource Mobilization and Developmental States*. Geneva: United Nations.

UNDP (United Nations Development Programme) (2010), *Kenya National Human Development Report (KNHDR) 2009: Youth and Human Development: Tapping the Untapped Resource*. Nairobi: UNDP Kenya.

UNECA (United Nations Economic Commission for Africa) (2004), "African Development Forum (ADF) IV Consensus Statement," Addis Ababa, October 11–15. Available at: http://www.uneca.org/adfiv/adfiv_consensus_statement.htm [Accessed November 20, 2010].

UNESCO (United Nations Educational, Scientific and Cultural Organization) and ILO (International Labor Organization) (2002), *Technical and Vocational Education and Training for the Twenty-first Century: UNESCO and ILO Recommendations*. Paris: UNESCO.

UN-HABITAT (United Nations Human Settlements Programme) (2010), *State of the Urban Youth 2010/11: Leveling the Playing Field: Inequality of Youth Opportunity*. London: Earthscan Publications.

— (2011), *Infrastructure for Economic Development and Poverty Reduction in Africa*. Nairobi: UN-HABITAT.

UNHCHR (United Nations High Commission for Human Rights) (2008), *Report from OHCHR Fact-Finding Mission to Kenya, February 6-28*. Geneva: UNHCHR.

UNSC (United Nations Security Council) (2004), *The Rule of Law and Transitional Justice in Conflict and Post-Conflict Societies: Report of the Secretary-General*. New York: United Nations.

USAID (United States Agency for International Development) (2008), *Guide to Rule of Law Country Analysis: The Rule of Law Strategic Framework*. Washington, DC: USAID.

Waki Commission (Commission of Inquiry into Post-Election Violence) (2008), *Report of the Commission of Inquiry into Post-Election Violence* (Waki Report), Nairobi: Waki Commission.

Webb, R. and Pulle, B. (2002), "Public Private Partnerships: An Introduction," *Research Paper No. 1 2002-03*. Canberra: Parliamentary Library, Parliament of Australia.

World Bank (nda), "Privatization Database: Kenya." Available at: http://rru.worldbank.org/Privatization/QueryDetails.aspx [Accessed December 11, 2010].

— (ndb), "Enterprise Survey Database." Available at: http://www.enterprisesurveys.org/ExploreTopics/?topicid=8 [Accessed December 11, 2010].

— (2000), *Reforming Public Institutions and Strengthening Governance.* Washington, DC: World Bank.

— (2008), *Kenya: Accelerating and Sustaining Inclusive Growth.* Washington, DC: World Bank.

— (2009), *Africa Development Indicators 2008/09: Youth and Employment in Africa.* Washington, DC: World Bank.

— (2010a), *Kenya Economic Update: Running on One Engine: Kenya's Uneven Economic Performance with a Special Focus on the Port of Mombasa.* Nairobi: World Bank.

— (2010b), "Kenya Youth Empowerment Project." Available at: http://web.worldbank.org/external/projects/main?pagePK=64312881&piPK=64302848&theSitePK=40941&Projectid=P111546 [Accessed January 11, 2011].

— (2011), *Africa's Future and the World Bank's Support to It.* Washington, DC: World Bank.

YEDF (Youth Enterprise Development Fund) (nda), "Brief on the Youth Enterprise Development Fund: Fund Status Report as of 30 June 2010." Available at: http://www.youthfund.go.ke/index.php/component/docman/cat_view/50-fund-status-report-as-30th-june-2010.html [Accessed February 20, 2011].

— (ndb), "Fund Objectives." Available at: http://www.youthfund.go.ke/index.php/about-us/fund-objectives-mainmenu-28.html [Accessed February 20, 2011].

Yu, H. and Guernsey, A. (nd), "What is the Rule of Law?" Available at: http://www.uiowa.edu/ifdebook/faq/Rule_of_Law.shtml [Accessed February 20, 2011].

8

Bringing in the Future: Beyond 2012

Despite the potential obstacles in the way, Kenya needs to continue to build on the peace that has prevailed since the creation of the coalition government in 2008. The country cannot afford to descend into further chaos and violence. This is certainly not what the majority of Kenyans want and it is therefore incumbent upon the political leaders to demonstrate leadership by appealing to, and promoting, national values rather than whipping up tribal incitement. The challenge before Kenya is, therefore, one of balancing groups and national interests through the building of state capability; striving for good governance through, among other things, respecting and championing the rule of law, accountability, and transparency, for example; and supporting real devolution of power and power sharing. As also argued by Modi and Shekhawat (nd: 28), Kenya's "leaders need to rise above short-sighted, exclusionary, tribal, and power-grabbing politics." Accountability, for instance, which is the antithesis of impunity, is now demanded and expected by Kenyans. For the political leadership to act otherwise would lead to an unraveling of the compact Kenyans agreed to when they voted overwhelmingly in support of the 2010 constitution.

Kenya remains an important State—economically and politically—both in the East African region and beyond. As observed by Kagwanja and Southall (2009: 260), "although Kenya, East Africa's economic powerhouse, had not become a 'failed state', the [postelection violence] crisis had pushed it to the brink of collapse and failure." It is a frontline State and ally to the international community, in particular, in the struggle to weed out and contain terrorism and other security threats posed by having borders with weak and/or failed states such as Somalia and Sudan, for example. This geopolitical and economic importance is what drives donor engagement in the country; accompanied by the necessary scolding, nudging, and sanctions at times, to embarrass and encourage the political leadership into condemning and confronting their corrupt activities, impunity, and other aspects of their bad governance behavior. Nonetheless, as Chege (2008) rightly notes, the country is still at risk.

Kenya's future is, therefore, inexorably tied to the implementation of the 2010 constitution. Returning to a familiar theme running through this book, the 2010 constitution offers the best opportunity to the country in the quest for building a capable state with good governance and sustained economic progress. Whether the elections are held in August 2012 (which in this author's view is what the constitution mandates) or sometime after, as may be deemed necessary as per rulings of the Supreme Court or by other circumstances and agreed to by all stakeholders, the fate of the country will be determined by how well and consistently the 2010 constitution is implemented. In fact, sustained socioeconomic progress and political development in Kenya hinges critically on the country's approach to implementation of the 2010 constitution that has been so enthusiastically endorsed by Kenyans. The successful implementation of the 2010 constitution will enhance the chances of achieving the aspirations outlined in the *Kenya Vision 2030* of substantial improvements in the economic, social, and political fronts (Hope, 2011; IMF, 2011).

This 2010 constitution is therefore considered to be the most important political development in Kenya since independence was achieved in 1963. Since the introduction of the Independence Constitution and the proclamation of the First Republic one year later in 1964, no comprehensive constitutional reform had taken place until the people endorsed the 2010 constitution and thereby bringing to a close a several decades old quest for a new constitution. Glinz (nd: 1), noted that:

> As the Independence Constitution was drafted through negotiations with the colonial power this is the first reform which detaches the Constitution from its colonial origin and puts it on a new basis. Therefore, the new document is a genuine Constitution of the Kenyan people.

The 2010 constitution has also been hailed as a very modern document which compares favorably to the South African constitution, for example, as one of the most progressive constitutions in Africa (Akech, 2010; Glinz, nd). Also, as Akech (2010: 36) observes:

> In addition, the Constitution addresses issues of inequality and seeks to ensure inclusive citizenship. In doing so, it gives the country much-needed mechanisms for resolving perennial problems. But while it establishes a governance framework that can ensure the realization of a just society, much will depend on the extent to which its rules, values, and principles are realized day to day.

Since independence, Kenya has experienced periods that have included human rights violations, land clashes, massacres, arbitrary arrest, extrajudicial killings, detention without trial, torture, electoral violence, grand corruption, economic crimes, and tribal conflicts. "Most of these are directly or indirectly attributable to a constitutional order that concentrated power in the presidency and emasculated other arms of government and civil society" (Mue, 2010: 3). In fact, the independence constitutional order has been identified as being responsible for the postelection violence in 2008. The successive amendments of that constitution were deemed to have increased the powers of the President exponentially, and thereby vesting in him control over government institutions and leading to the emasculation of institutions with some degree of countervailing power such as the legislature and judiciary (Akech, 2010; Waki Commission, 2008). Consequently, Kenyans felt they had to resort to violence due to lack of their confidence in such institutions as the Electoral Commission and the Kenya Police, for example (Akech, 2010; ICTJ, 2010; Waki Commission, 2008).

On the other hand, the 2010 constitution, if implemented as intended, will address, among other things, the issues and root causes that led to the postelection violence in 2008. This has raised expectations in the country that a permanent solution to long-standing social and political challenges may be achievable. With this supreme legal foundation supporting them, public institutions will now be able to act in the public interest, uphold the rule of law, and more effectively deliver public services. This new approach should be fairly straightforward to accomplish given that, in the new legal framework of the 2010 constitution, among other things, Presidential power has been curtailed; an enforceable Bill of Rights is in place that includes social, economic, and political rights, among others; government power, functions, and resources have been devolved to regions (counties); land ownership is reformed; the judiciary and security sector have been overhauled; significant improvements have been made in the public expenditure and budgeting processes; and there will be increased participation and representation of the people at the subnational level through county assemblies and at the national level through a bicameral legislature (national assembly and senate) that will allow for greater scrutiny of the national government thereby providing the necessary checks and balances as required in a democratic environment within the new democratic dispensation that the constitution presents.

However, despite the importance of all institutions, the key here hinges critically on the performance of a few institutions. The promulgation of a constitution that holds great promise for the country is a necessary but not a sufficient condition for there to be meaningful socioeconomic and political outcomes. In this author's view, the following institutions will have to play pivotal roles to ensure that the benefits of the 2010 constitutional reforms are derived for all Kenyans: (1) the Independent Electoral and Boundaries

Commission (IEBC); (2) the justice system (Kenya Police, DPP, Attorney General, and the judiciary); (3) devolved governments; and (4) Parliament. These are the principal institutions for ensuring transparency, accountability, and enhancing checks and balances for a better governance environment with respect for the rule of law.

The Independent Electoral and Boundaries Commission

The IEBC begins life by restricting membership to preclude individuals—who are active in politics or attempted to become Members of Parliament, a county assembly, or the governing body of a political party in the five years preceding, or are holders of any State or public office—from becoming a member of the IEBC. By restricting membership this way, the IEBC is likely to achieve its independent status and not be subject to influence and manipulation by members with partisan political motives. It would also, therefore, be able to fulfill its mandate that includes, in addition to conducting and supervising referenda and elections to any elective body or office as per the constitution and any Act of Parliament:

- The delimitation of constituencies and wards;
- The continuous registration of voters and the regular revision of the voters' roll;
- The regulation and monitoring of compliance of the process and legislation relating to the manner by which parties nominate candidates for elections;
- The registration of candidates for elections;
- The regulation of the amount of money that may be spent on behalf of a candidate or a political party with respect to any election;
- The development and enforcement of a code of conduct for candidates and political parties contesting elections;
- The facilitation of the observation, monitoring and evaluation of elections;
- The settlement of electoral disputes, including disputes relating to or arising from nominations but excluding election petitions and disputes subsequent to the declaration of election results;
- Voter education. (Republic of Kenya, 2010)

The IEBC can be considered as—what is regarded in the democracy literature—an electoral management body (EMB) within the electoral governance field. An EMB is an organization or body which has the sole purpose, and is legally responsible for, managing some or all of the elements that are essential for the conduct of elections and of direct democracy instruments—such as referenda, citizens' initiatives and recall votes—if those are part of the legal framework. These essential or core elements include: (1) determining who is eligible to vote; (2) receiving and validating the nominations of electoral participants (for elections, political parties, and/or candidates); (3) conducting polling; (4) counting the votes; and (5) tabulating the votes (Wall et al., 2006).

Although there has been a trend toward the establishment of independent/autonomous EMBs, like the IEBC, there are also two other models of electoral management resulting in the existence of three such broad models: (1) the independent model; (2) the governmental model; and (3) the mixed model. The independent model exists in those countries where elections are organized and managed by an EMB which is institutionally independent and autonomous from the executive branch of government, and which has and manages its own budget. They are composed of members who are outside the executive while in EMB office. Most African countries have chosen this independent model of electoral management. The governmental model exists in those countries where elections are organized and managed by the executive branch through a ministry and/or through local authorities. The mixed model usually has two component EMBs with dual structures—a policy, monitoring, or supervisory EMB that is independent of the executive branch of government and an implementation EMB located within a department of a national government and/or local government. This mixed model is used in France and its former colonies, especially in West Africa, such as Togo, Senegal, and Mali, for example (Wall et al., 2006).

Irrespective of the model used, every EMB must ensure the legitimacy and credibility of the process for which it has been given a mandate. In that regard, there are some guiding principles to be observed that are essential to both the actual and the perceived integrity of the electoral process, which also need to be adhered to by the IEBC:

- *Independence*—No bending to the pressure or influence peddling from the government, politicians, political parties, or others.
- *Impartiality*—Treating all election participants and the entire process equally, fairly, and even-handedly, without giving advantage to any political tendency or interest group or political party.
- *Integrity*—Ensuring and guaranteeing the purity of the electoral process.
- *Transparency and Accountability*—Allowing for all necessary public scrutiny of the decisions and processes of the EMB to arrest any suspicion that fraudulent activities are taking place.

- *Efficiency*—EMBs must deliver their services as well use their funding efficiently ensuring that their programs serve electoral efficiency and are administratively efficient.
- *Professionalism*—Both the manner in which EMBs implement electoral procedures and the conduct of their staff must be done to the highest professional standards.
- *Service-Mindedness*—Establishing service standards and delivering services to meet those standards in the best interests of stakeholders and the fulfillment of the mandate. (Kerr, 2009; Wall et al., 2006)

The Justice System

The justice system has been considerably revamped under the 2010 constitution and this augurs well for justice to be sought and delivered and the rule of law to be observed. Under the old order, presidential control of the justice system meant that the institutions of the police, the Attorney General, and the judiciary lacked independence and were subject to the influence and interference from the Presidency. Consequently, impunity reigned supreme for the politically well-connected as the rule of law was not observed.

In the 2010 constitution, as discussed in Chapter 4, the Kenya Police has been restructured and reformed. Ongoing police reforms are being implemented under the auspices of the PRIC and this ought to, and must result, for the sake of Kenyans, in the evolution of democratic and equitable policing free from the influence of the well-connected. The 2010 constitution established a Kenya National Police Service consisting of the Kenya Police Service and the Administration Police Service headed by an Inspector-General of the National Police Service who has to be vetted by Parliament and can only serve a single four-year term. The objects and functions of the National Police Service have also been spelled out and they oblige the National Police Service to:

- Strive for the highest standards of professionalism and discipline among its members;
- Prevent corruption and promote and practice transparency and accountability;
- Comply with constitutional standards of human rights and fundamental freedoms;
- Train staff to the highest possible standards of competence and integrity and to respect human rights and fundamental freedoms and dignity;
- Foster and promote relationships with the broader society. (Republic of Kenya, 2010)

The National Police Service, whose composition, the 2010 constitution demands, shall reflect the regional and ethnic diversity of the people of Kenya, will also be subject to civilian oversight that is also a part of the package of ongoing police reform. Such civilian oversight is consistent with modern-day policing, which regards the use of such oversight mechanisms as necessary for ensuring police accountability. This may also result in bringing to justice those police officers and their handlers who are responsible for extrajudicial killings.

Civilian oversight of the police is a governance measure designed to improve police accountability. It refers to the ongoing monitoring of police activities with a view toward holding a police service accountable for the services it provides, the policies under which it operates, and the conduct of its members. It involves people from outside the police taking a role in calling the police to account for their actions, policies, and organization covering broad areas of police practice. It is an essential component of a democratic society. Effective civilian oversight and governance of the police is necessary to ensure that the police service uses its powers and authority in a manner reflecting respect for law and individual rights and freedoms (Miller, 2002; Sen, 2010; Walker, 2001). Ultimately, the task is one of striking a balance between police independence to conduct investigations and maintain order—without undue political or other influence—with the need for accountability to the public.

Community policing and better police training are also being publicized as key elements of the police reforms in Kenya. With respect to the latter, an elaborate launch ceremony in March 2011 rolled out a new training curriculum which requires police recruits to now undergo 15 months of training including three months of internship. Previously, police recruits were only required to have a grade of "D" at the Kenya Certificate of Secondary Examination (KCSE) and undergo nine months of training before becoming police officers. Under the newly launched training program police recruits have to be thoroughly vetted for suitability and must have a minimum grade of "C" at the KCSE. The new training curriculum also includes courses and lessons on respect for human rights, community policing, public relations, and customer care, for example, on which police recruits will be examined and certified (Momanyi, 2011; Ndirangu and Omune, 2011).

The Kenya Police view community policing as an approach to policing that recognizes the independence and shared responsibility of the Police and the community in ensuring a safe and secure environment for all citizens (Kenya Police, nda). It aims at establishing an active and equal partnership between the police and the public through which crime and community safety issues can jointly be discussed and solutions determined and implemented. It is founded on close, mutually beneficial ties between police and community members (Gitau, 2010; Kenya Police, nda). The implementation of community policing, within the context of Kenya's police reforms, holds the promise of aiding in the emancipation of the Police Service that will operate in conformity with democratic transformation from the current practice of regime policing to democratic (community) policing (Kenya Police, ndb). Nonetheless, as also recognized by the Kenya Police (nda: 4), "the greatest handicap in community policing is transcending the shift in paradigm necessary for attitudinal transformation from the current adversarial posture characterized by the mistrust and mutual blame to one of partnership and cooperation." However, this is where leadership and training, especially the former, will have to come into play.

The 2010 constitution has also separated out the powers of prosecution from the Office of the Attorney General and thus making them independent of each other. In the 2010 constitution, the task of exercising the power of prosecution on behalf of the State will be handled solely by the DPP. The primary functions of the Attorney General will be to give legal advice to the government and represent it in legal proceedings. Although both the Attorney General and the DPP have to be vetted and confirmed by the National Assembly, the DPP can only hold office for a single term of eight years. The DPP can only discontinue a prosecution with the permission of the court. Moreover, to prevent any abuse of prosecutorial powers, the 2010 constitution requires that, in exercising constitutional powers, the DPP shall have regard to the public interest, the interests of the administration of justice as well as the need to prevent and avoid abuse of the legal process (Republic of Kenya, 2010).

With respect to the judiciary, the 2010 constitution contains a number of elements that enhance the independence and accountability of the judiciary. First, the President can only appoint the Chief Justice and Deputy Chief Justice in accordance with the recommendation of the Judicial Service Commission and subject to the approval of the National Assembly. An attempt by President Kibaki—backed by his cronies (including Mr Ruto and Mr Kenyatta)—to appoint a Chief Justice, Attorney General, and a DPP in early 2011 without following the 2010 constitution was immediately deemed and ruled unconstitutional by the courts, the Speaker of the National Assembly, and many NGOs. President Kibaki was, therefore, forced to abort this brazen attempt to contravene the constitution which many saw as a move to put justice system personnel in place to benefit his cronies. It turns out that President Kibaki's pick for DPP was the Attorney representing Mr Ruto (one of the "Ocampo Six") in his corruption case.

All other judges are appointed by the President in accordance with the recommendations of the Judicial Service Commission. This, therefore, provides the judiciary with autonomy from the executive branch. The Judicial Service Commission has a designated membership of which only two members (a male and a female) are appointed by the President but must be approved by the National Assembly. Consequently, the executive branch no longer has power over the judiciary (Republic of Kenya, 2010).

Moreover, judicial authority has also been dispersed such that the Chief Justice no longer commands wide-ranging and unregulated powers. Although the Chief Justice is still the head of the judiciary and will preside over the Supreme Court, in addition to the subordinate courts, there are now two other superior courts plus the Supreme Court for a total of three superior courts. The other two superior courts (the High Court and the Court of Appeal) will be presided over by judges elected by the judges of each of those respective courts. In addition, judges have been provided with greater security of tenure as their dismissal or removal from Office will now have to follow a transparent, fair, and impartial process. The initiation of that process is the sole responsibility of the Judicial Service Commission acting on its own motion or on the petition of any individual. If the Commission is satisfied that the petition warrants a ground for removal, it shall send the petition to the President who shall, within 14 days of receipt of said petition, suspend the judge and appoint a tribunal to inquire into the matter and make binding recommendations to the President (Republic of Kenya, 2010).

Devolution

Based on discussions and interviews with Kenyans during the 2010 constitution referendum campaign, it is this author's view that the 2010 constitution was given overwhelming support by Kenyans primarily because of its strong focus on devolution. This was hardly surprising for as Ghai (2008: 215) informed:

> Wherever the CKRC [Constitution of Kenya Review Commission] went, it noted widespread feeling among the people of alienation from central government because of the concentration of power in the national government, and to a remarkable extent, in the president. They felt marginalized and neglected, deprived of their resources; and victimized for their political or ethnic affiliations. They considered that their problems arose from government policies over which they had no control. Decisions were made at places away from them. These decisions did not reflect the reality

under which they lived, the constraints and privations under which they suffered.

The potential benefits of devolution to Kenya have been discussed in Chapter 5. When elected and fully functioning beyond 2012, the devolved governments will represent another critical input to the attempts to rebuild Kenya, after the postelection violence in 2008, and move the country toward a more democratic path. Devolution, if implemented as per the spirit of the 2010 constitution, will provide for Kenyans greater responsiveness to their local needs; enhanced citizen participation and decision-making; better service delivery; a reduction of regional inequalities, instability and poverty; and some control over corruption. Devolution in Kenya can also be seen as a way to break out of the vicious circle of the ethnicization of the State by disposing State powers throughout the country and away from an executive presidency with enormous powers that has led to a lack of accountability, patronage politics, and arbitrariness and exercised for the benefit of certain ethnic communities at the expense of national unity (Ghai, 2008).

The issue of local autonomy—the ability of the devolved governments to initiate policies and act independently from the national government—is an important one for Kenya as it is in all States with established, or aspiring to, democratic traditions. The 2010 constitution attempts to guarantee this local autonomy by including provisions to preclude the national government from undermining county governments. For example, there are very specific mechanisms and processes for the sharing of revenue with the counties; the respective functions and powers of national and county governments have been carefully delineated; the rationale that can be used and the manner in which functions and powers can be transferred between levels of government have been spelled out; and the provisions on county government are shielded from being easily amended, requiring a referendum preceded by a process of parliamentary debate and public discussion (Akech, 2010; Republic of Kenya, 2010).

Devolution for Kenya therefore means the opening up of possibilities and opportunities. It disperses power; alters the structures of that power; takes decision-making closer to the people to better reflect local preferences; demands democratic accountability; and promises to intensify perceptions of national—as opposed to ethnic—values and citizenship and thereby empowering rather than marginalizing communities (Akech, 2010; Ghai, 2010). Devolution for Kenya also offers a more efficient system of government that guarantees better service delivery tailored to local community needs and standards. To ensure that all of these benefits are indeed derived, local autonomy is maintained, and that they are not undermined by the national government, county governments must eliminate any structures, processes, or administrative arrangements inherited from, or imposed by, the national government that are deemed by the county government leaders not to be in the interest of their county and replace them with those that are, if necessary.

Parliament

One key institution in Kenya's pursuit to build a capable state with good governance that respects and upholds the rule of law is Parliament. This institution, as per the 2010 constitution, has a major role to play beyond 2012 as a coequal branch of government. Various provisions in the 2010 constitution have beefed up the accountability of the legislature as well as its oversight role. Parliament is now required, for example, to determine the allocation of national revenue between the levels of government as per the process provided in the relevant articles, and to approve key appointments to State offices of the executive and judiciary branches. Beyond 2012, Parliamentarians will be just that. They are no longer eligible to be in Cabinet under the separation of powers or to hold any other State or public office and it is perhaps this fact also that has emboldened some of them to be in open dissension with their party leadership beginning with the 2010 constitution referendum campaign.

One critical component of Parliament's role—that will require capacity development—is that of oversight. Parliamentary oversight, or legislative oversight as it is more commonly known, refers to the parliament's review and evaluation of selected activities of the executive branch of government. The legislative branch conducts oversight activities because it not only enacts new laws and programs for a nation, but also has a duty to ensure that existing laws and programs are implemented and administered efficiently, effectively, and in a manner consistent with legislative intent. Although oversight is the specific focus of some legislative activities, it is also an integral part of the legislative process that is often difficult to separate from the lawmaking process. Oversight tends to be the focus of select committees and special oversight committees and can also be part of the hearings and work of standing committees.

Pursuant to the demands and requirements of the 2010 constitution, Kenya's Parliament needs to build further oversight capacity. Some assistance has been provided by USAID in this regard through its Parliamentary Strengthening Program (PSP) (2005–10) which was designed to strengthen the effectiveness of the Kenyan Parliament and increase the capacity of

MPs and staff in drafting and reviewing legislation and scrutinizing budget estimates and making concrete changes (USAID Kenya, nd). However, oversight is an ongoing significant tool in the parliamentary arsenal for monitoring government activities but, since independence, such oversight in the Kenya Parliament, particularly on budget matters, has been weak (Njuguna and Makau, 2009). Consequently, capacity development of Kenya's MPs is a necessity to which the Parliamentarians should be amenable. This takes on added significance given that Parliament is the only institution that is constitutionally mandated to debate budgets taking into account the interests and views of all stakeholders (Njuguna and Makau, 2009). One capacity development effort that has resonated with experts, donors, civil society, and MPs alike is the scaling up of the Parliamentary Budget Office (see, e.g., Straussman and Renoni, 2009). This is an initiative that needs to be pursued by Kenya's Parliament.

Conclusions

The 2010 constitution is Kenya's emancipation proclamation. Among other things, it has liberated the country from misrule, dictatorship, kleptocracy, and the primitive antics of election rigging. At least, short of further ethnic clashes, it has the potential to do so. As the country attempts to put its antidemocratic past behind, and move along a peaceful path to fulfill its development promise, all stakeholders must continually be aware that Kenya's economic prospects are tied to its political stability. One only needs to look back at the recent past (2008–09) to see what consequences the postelection violence wrought on economic performance. And, at the same time, without positive and sustainable economic progress, unemployment will be unmanageable and poverty and marginalization will soar. This, in turn, is a recipe for disaster particularly since the youth will be the most affected group.

By making institutions more accountable, transparent, and removed from control by an imperial presidency, democracy dawns in Kenya. Accountability is a reciprocal relationship between those who have been entrusted with certain functions and those who expect those functions to be performed. Accountability ensures that there will be trust and confidence in those assigned with the responsibilities. Transparency provides the public with access to information and knowledge to enable them to appropriately scrutinize government policies. It is about openness in the conduct of government which hinders the practice of corruption and promotes trust in, and legitimacy of, State institutions (Hope, 2008; UNECA, 2009). All of this augurs well for Kenya beyond 2012 but only in a peaceful environment. The country's political leadership would, therefore, do well to heed the advice of

Kofi Annan, a former UN Secretary-General who is also the Chief Mediator for Kenya, who remarked:

> Words can soothe, as well as inflame. I urge all Kenyans, particularly leaders, to be wise in their use of language . . . A Kenya free of hate and fighting impunity will be a united and secure Kenya—a country that will prosper and ensure the welfare of all its people. (See, Agina, 2011: 4)

Surely, the political leadership can agree with that and promote nationalism rather than incite hatred and violence in the run up to 2012 and beyond.

Should Kenya return to ethnic conflict and violence, the consequences would be severe not only for the country but for the whole of East Africa and beyond. As the International Crisis Group (ICG) has observed:

> More is at stake than the collapse of Kenya itself. Kenya is the platform for relief operations in Somalia and Sudan, a haven for refugees from throughout the region, a regional entrepôt, and a key anchor for long-term stabilization of Rwanda, Uganda and Burundi. (ICG, 2008: 29)

Consequently, any "paralysis of its infrastructure would deprive those countries of access to basic commodities, reduce trade opportunities, hamper foreign investment and see economic growth crippled" (ICG, 2008: 29). As stated at the top of this chapter, this is certainly not what most Kenyans, as well as the international community, want.

References

Agina, B. (2011), "Annan: Kenya is not on Trial at ICC," *The Standard*, April 6, 4.

Akech, M. (2010), *Institutional Reform in the New Constitution of Kenya*. Nairobi: ICTJ (International Center for Transitional Justice).

Chege, M. (2008), "Kenya: Back from the Brink," *Journal of Democracy*, 19(4), 125–39.

Ghai, Y. (2008), "Devolution: Restructuring the Kenyan State," *Journal of Eastern African Studies*, 2(2), 211–26.

Gitau, R. (2010), "Reforming the Police in a Fractured Society: Are the Police Reforms Mistaken: Social Responsibility of Containing Crime and Improving Security in Kenya," *Policy: Journal of the Institute of Economic Affairs*, No. 1 (October), 10–14, 23–8.

Glinz, C. (nd), "Kenya's New Constitution." Available at: www.kas.de/wf/doc/kas_22103-1522-2-30.pdf?110303092653 [Accessed March 20, 2011].

Hope, K. R. (2008), *Poverty, Livelihoods, and Governance in Africa: Fulfilling the Development Promise*. New York: Palgrave Macmillan.

— (2011), 'Toward Sustained Economic Progress and Socio-Economic Development in Kenya: Implementing the 2010 Constitution." Unpublished Manuscript.

ICG (International Crisis Group) (2008), "Kenya in Crisis." *Africa Report No. 137*, February 21. Available at: http://www.crisisgroup.org/en/regions/africa/ horn-of-africa/kenya/137-kenya-in-crisis.aspx [Accessed August 12, 2010].

ICTJ (International Center for Transitional Justice) Kenya (2010), "Security Sector Reform and Transitional Justice in Kenya," *ICTJ Briefing*. Nairobi: ICTJ Nairobi.

IMF (International Monetary Fund) (2011), *Kenya: Letter of Intent, Memorandum of Economic and Financial Policies, and Technical Memorandum of Understanding*. Washington, DC: IMF.

Kagwanja, P. and Southall, R. (2009), "Introduction: Kenya—A Democracy in Retreat?," *Journal of Contemporary African Studies*, 27(3), 259–77.

Kenya Police (nda), "Community Policing—Making Our Communities Safer." Available at: http://www.kenyapolice.go.ke/community%20policing. asp [Accessed December 12, 2010].

— (ndb), "Police Reforms." Available at: http://www.kenyapolice.go.ke/ police%20reforms.asp [Accessed December 12, 2010].

Kerr, N. N. (2009), *Electoral Governance in sub-Saharan Africa: Assessing the Impact of Electoral Management Bodies' Autonomy and Capacity on Citizens: Perceptions of Election Quality*. Washington, DC: IFES (International Foundation for Electoral Studies).

Miller, J. (2002), "Civilian Oversight of Policing: Lessons from the Literature." Paper Presented to the Global Meeting on Civilian Oversight of Police, Los Angeles, May 5–8. Available at: www.vera.org/download?file=93/ Civilian%2Boversight.pdf [Accessed November 23, 2010].

Modi, R. and Shekhawat, S. (nd), "The Kenyan Crisis: Post December 2007 Elections," *Working Paper No. 1*. Mumbai: Centre for African Studies, University of Mumbai.

Momanyi, B. (2011), "Kenya Police gets New Syllabus," *Capital News*, March 28, Online Edition. Available at: http://www.capitalfm.co.ke/news/Kenyanews/ Kenya-police-gets-new-syllabus.html [Accessed April 1, 2011].

Mue, N. (2010), "Foreword" to *Institutional Reform in the New Constitution of Kenya*. Nairobi: ICTJ.

Ndirangu, W. and Omune, P. (2011), "Move to Transform Police Force to Police Service Gets Underway," *Kenya Today* (Inside Government), April 04–10, 1 and 6.

Njuguna, S. N. and Makau, P. (2009), "The Parliamentary Budget Oversight in Kenya: Analysis of the Framework and Practices since 1963 to Date," *IEA Research Paper Series No. 19*. Nairobi: IEA-Kenya.

Republic of Kenya (2010), *The Constitution of Kenya, 2010*. Nairobi: Republic of Kenya.

Sen, S. (2010), *Enforcing Police Accountability through Civilian Oversight*. New Delhi: Sage Publications.

Straussman, J. D. and Renoni, A. (2009), "Establishing a Parliamentary Budget Office as an Element of Good Governance," *Comparative Assessment of*

Parliament (CAP) Note Series. Albany, NY: Center for International Development, Rockefeller College of Public Affairs and Policy, State University of New York.

UNECA (United Nations Economic Commission for Africa) (2009), *African Governance Report II: 2009.* Oxford: Oxford University Press.

USAID (United States Agency for International Development) Kenya (nd), "Parliamentary Strengthening Program." Available at: http://kenya.usaid.gov/programs/democracy-and-governance/570 [Accessed December 12, 2010].

Waki Commission (Commission of Inquiry into Post-Election Violence) (2008), *Report of the Commission of Inquiry into Post-Election Violence* (Waki Report). Nairobi: Waki Commission.

Walker, S. (2001), *Police Accountability: The Role of the Citizen Oversight.* Belmont, CA: Wadsworth.

Wall, A., Ellis, A., Ayoub, A., Dundas, C. W., Rukambe, J., and Staino, S. (2006), *Electoral Management Design: The International IDEA Handbook.* Stockholm: International IDEA (Institute for Democracy and Electoral Assistance).

Index